Disproportionate
Minority Contact

Disproportionate Minority Contact

Current Issues and Policies

Second Edition

Edited by

Nicolle Parsons-Pollard

CAROLINA ACADEMIC PRESS

Durham, North Carolina

Library of Congress Cataloging-in-Publication Data

Names: Parsons-Pollard, Nicolle Y., 1967- editor.
Title: Disproportionate minority contact : current issues and policies /
    [edited by] Nicolle Parsons-Pollard.
Description: Second Edition. | Durham : Carolina Academic Press, [2016] |
    Revised edition of Disproportionate minority contact, c2011. | Includes
    bibliographical references and index.
Identifiers: LCCN 2016045362 | ISBN 9781531002633 (alk. paper)
Subjects: LCSH: Discrimination in juvenile justice administration--United
    States. | Juvenile justice, Administration of--United States--Case
    studies. | Minority youth--United States.
Classification: LCC HV9104 .D57 2016 | DDC 364.973089--dc23
LC record available at https://lccn.loc.gov/2016045362

eISBN 978-1-53100-295-4

Carolina Academic Press, LLC
700 Kent Street
Durham, North Carolina 27701
Telephone (919) 489-7486
Fax (919) 493-5668
www.cap-press.com

Printed in the United States of America

*To those who continue to fight for justice in America
and across the globe—stay woke.*

NPP

Contents

Preface

People keep saying how timely this book is and even more so with the second edition. Nine of the original chapters were revised and three chapters were added. All of the revisions and writing took place after the Michael Brown shooting in Ferguson, Missouri; however, I am revising this section of the Preface after the shootings of Alton Sterling in Louisiana, Philando Castile in Minnesota, and the five police officers in Dallas, Texas. So this second edition is timely indeed. And while there are plenty of hashtags and demonstrations, the other work related to issues of disparity is complex and requires data. As I have listened to the news almost non-stop since this July 4th week of 2016, I realize that Aldous Huxley's quote is so true — "Facts do not cease to exist because they are ignored." My hope is that this book provides some clarity for those who are looking for empirical data to solve the multifaceted issues that face our nation.

Disproportionate Minority Contact: Current Issues and Policies focuses on a variety of topics related to minority overrepresentation and disparity in the criminal and juvenile justice systems. While there is a plethora of areas in which to focus related to this topic, I decided that this volume should provide a summary of the literature as well as examples of what various states are doing to address disparity and satisfy the federal mandate. Likewise, I wanted this volume to be appropriate for the classroom as well as practitioners in the field of criminal justice.

In the first chapter, Ashley Nellis provides an overview of policies and practices that impact overrepresentation. She notes that some of these policies, while designed with "good intentions," do not take into account their disparate impact on particular racial and ethnic groups. More specifically, Nellis focuses on school push-out policies, the presence of police in schools, unequal access to justice, and the use of detention to provide social services for youth.

The next chapter focuses on a historical and contemporary look at the disproportionate minority contact (DMC) mandate as prescribed in the Juvenile Justice and Delinquency Prevention Act of 1974, as amended. The chapter explores the evolution of the mandate, the relationship between the four requirements and the impact of new legislation. In addition, it focuses on why most jurisdictions have not been successful in reducing DMC and provides a summary of the Office of Juvenile Justice and Delinquency Prevention's initiatives to assist in DMC reduction.

In chapter 3, William Feyerherm examines the relative rate index (RRI) as a measurement of disproportionate contact. He discusses the development of the RRI, how it was influenced by legislative policy, provides an overview of the measurement and its utilization. Feyerherm points out the advantages of the RRI, the deficiencies, as well as how State and County data collection processes impact its usability.

In chapter 4, Michael Leiber, Jennifer H. Peck, and Myra Fields examine the effects of race on intake decisions. They utilize data from four different localities in Iowa to investigate the influence race, legal and extralegal factors have on intake decision-making over two different periods of time, before and after the DMC mandate. They also emphasize the consensus and conflict theories to frame the issues of legal and extra legal criteria as well as racial stereotyping.

To further explore what states are doing to address overrepresentation of minorities in the juvenile justice system, Mary Poulin, Stan Orchowsky, and Janice Iwama's chapter 5 focuses on Iowa and Virginia's efforts to deal with the DMC mandate. The chapter provides an overview on what each state has done in regards to DMC, issues faced while carrying out DMC initiatives, how and if the initiatives have been measured for success, and the lessons that have been learned along the way. The authors also offer a 2016 update on recommendations to improve the implementation of initiatives, data collection, and evaluation.

All too often the linkage between the justice systems and the child welfare systems are ignored in the discussion of DMC. Marian Harris reminds us that these linkages exist. She explores the extent of disproportionality and disparities for children of color in the child welfare system. Likewise, she discusses the steps Washington State has taken to address disproportionality through its Racial Disproportionality Advisory Committee.

Chapter 7 is new and focuses on the role school disciplinary actions have on disproportionality in the juvenile justice system. Cherie Dawson-Edwards, Nadia Nelson and Katie Nuss analyze zero tolerance policies and practices while also delving into theoretical explanations.

The next two chapters deal with issues that have been seen as possible reasons for increased overrepresentation of minorities in the criminal justice system — the War on Drugs and differential law enforcement practices. In chapter 8 Ojmarrh Mitchell and Michael Lynch examine the War on Drugs from 1986 to present and its impact on racial and ethnic minorities. The authors provide a historical backdrop for the War on Drugs and examine arrests, incarceration rates and explanations for disparity. John Reitzel's updated chapter 9 echoes their arguments of disparity, as he also examines arrests and incarceration rates from the 1990s and 2012. He focuses his investigation on what led to such race-differentiated crime and arrests by focusing on law enforcement practices that impact racial and ethnic minorities disproportionately.

Chapter 10 is a new addition to the second edition and Amy Kyle Cook, Shana Mell, and William V. Pelfrey Jr. introduce the concept of police legitimacy while exploring it through the use of body cameras. This chapter gets to the heart of public trust and policing and describes it in the context of the aftermath of the much-publicized shootings of unarmed black people.

No edited volume on DMC would be complete without mention of Hispanic overrepresentation. As Hispanics have become one of the fastest growing minorities in the United States, the issue of disparity must be addressed. George Wilson, Bryan Lagae, and Alex Piquero focus on the Mexican population in particular. The authors utilize National Election Survey data to investigate the differences in crime control ideology while taking into account class and immigrant status.

Chapters 12 and 13 both focus on the collateral consequences of DMC and its impact on communities. Isis Walton and Shanieka Jones examine the prison industrial complex and focus on how it has become a contributing mechanism for DMC. They lay out the perspective that incarceration has become big business and has been used to not just punish offenders but to turn a profit, which not only impacts the inmate but families and communities. Likewise, Cherie Dawson-Edwards focuses on another collateral consequence of mass incarceration—political disempowerment. Dawson-Edwards argues that as felon voting laws disenfranchise minorities the impact is felt in the community as well. She explores what happens when already socially disorganized communities are also politically weakened.

The last chapter is especially for practitioners who work in the field of criminal and juvenile justice. This chapter outlines how practitioners can work closely with universities and their faculty to fulfill the DMC mandate requirements. The chapter reviews the mandate and builds the case for partnering with local institutions of higher education to do some of the hard work necessary to address the five phases: identification, assessment, intervention, evaluation, and monitoring.

The goal of this edited volume is to provide an assortment of information related to overrepresentation and disparity in one collection. This volume is capable of serving as a standalone text or works well as a supplement to a traditional textbook on race and crime. Likewise, this volume is written in such a way that it is also practical enough for those working in the justice system to use it as a tool for exploring and implementing change in their jurisdiction. It was a pleasure collaborating with the contributing authors and we hope that you enjoy reading this second edition of *Disproportionate Minority Contact: Current Issues and Policies.*

Acknowledgments

I am truly grateful to all of the individuals who have supported me through the process of completing the second edition of this edited volume. First, I'd like to thank all of the contributing authors. This would not have been possible without your enthusiasm and commitment to this topic. I'd also like to especially thank those who contributed new chapters as it helps to not only update the book but to put into context what has occurred since the first publication. Second, I'd like to acknowledge the support of Virginia State University (VSU) and Monmouth University (MU). I began working on the new edition while still working at VSU and my new MU family is equally supportive of this endeavor. The first edition of this book was dedicated to Laura J. Moriarty for her friendship and support. I now have the pleasure of working with her each day and her support is unwavering. Third, I'd like to give a giant thank you to Daniel A. Goodall, Sr.—my friend and colleague. Danny and I have had many conversations about many issues and he always gives me a reason to see things slightly different and always clearer. Fourth, I'd like to recognize the wonderful people at Carolina Academic Press especially Beth Hall. Beth is a patient soul and a wonderful person. Fifth, I'd like to thank my family and friends for the support they provided to me and the prayers they had for me even when I did not know it. A special thank you to my husband, Donald, and my children, Donnie and Ally. Everyone needs a cheerleader and Donald has always been mine. Donnie and Ally were teenagers when the first edition was published and they were very vocal about the fact that they didn't understand what I was talking about and they were not very interested either. But today they are adults and they see the issues of disparity so clearly and I am proud that they are the next generation to support this movement and to change the world. Lastly, I'd like to thank the practitioners in the field who work everyday to ameliorate disparity in the criminal and juvenile justice systems. To every police officer, correctional officer, attorney, judge, counselor, social worker, educator and all of the people that work 'inside' the system—thank you for committing your professional life to justice. I hope that this book provides a foundation for continuing the fight against DMC.

Disproportionate Minority Contact

Chapter 1

The Worsening Problem of Racial Disparity in U.S. Juvenile Justice Systems

Ashley Nellis

Introduction

On February 26, 2012, an African American teenager named Trayvon Martin was shot to death by a member of the community acting as a volunteer neighborhood watchperson. At the time, Martin was walking down the street wearing a black hoodie and holding nothing more than a bottle of iced tea and a bag of candy, but his shooter, George Zimmerman, saw a predator. Martin's case, which made sustained national media attention, epitomizes the assumed associations between young black males and violence. The outrage following the failure to indict his shooter demonstrates the enduring damage caused by these associations. Since Martin's death, the media's focus on cases of unarmed black citizens being harassed, assaulted, or killed by white members of law enforcement has sparked a renewed concern about American race relations, particularly as they intersect with the justice system.

The rate at which African American youth enter and stay in the juvenile justice system far exceeds the rate at which this occurs among white youth. This difference is often unexplained by different patterns in delinquency: black and white youth both engage in offending at roughly similar rates for most crimes, but black youth more frequently find their misbehaviors handled by the juvenile justice system whereas white youth are diverted. Involvement in the juvenile justice system disrupts school, family, and community life, putting youth at high risk of lifelong collateral consequences. Most would agree that its use should be reserved for those who truly need to be removed from society temporarily, yet for African American youth, especially, this is not always the case.

Out of the one million cases that enter juvenile courts, a disproportionate share feature African Americans despite the fact that black youth comprise 16.2% of the general population of individuals age 10–18 (Puzzancherra, Sladky & Kang, 2015). Black youth account for 62.8% of juvenile arrests (Puzzancherra, Chamberlin & Kang, 2015), 42% of detentions, 35.9% of adjudications, and 40% of secure placements (Sickmund, Sladky & Kang, 2015). Official data from the Office of Juvenile Justice and Delinquency Prevention reveal that black youth are more than four times as likely to be committed as white youth, and Hispanic youth are 61% more likely. Additionally, black youth comprise 45% of waivers to adult court (Sickmund, Sladky & Kang, 2015). More than half of those serving life sentences for crimes committed as youth are black (Nellis, 2013.)

Most distressing about the racial disparities in the juvenile justice system is that they have actually increased over the past decade despite significant overall declines in the juvenile justice population. The population of young people who are confined as result of an adjudication of delinquency has been cut in half since 1999 (Sickmund, Sladky, and Kang, 2015). Though fragments of the harsh justice policies of the 1990s still exist, many states have enacted substantial juvenile justice reforms over the past fifteen years. For instance, there has been a considerable scaling back of juvenile transfer laws, many large prison-like youth facilities are being replaced by smaller, age-appropriate centers that are closer to home, and many more youth are diverted from detention altogether as systems begin to narrow their focus to more serious cases (Nellis, 2015).

At the same time, racial disparities in the juvenile justice system have increased. While the overall number of black youth has declined, the rate of the decline is slower for African American youth than for white youth, producing more disparity. This chapter describes the location and severity of racial disparities in the juvenile justice system, chronicling the stages where disparities mount. Following this is a discussion of the various contributors to racial disparity and the obstacles to reform that remain. The final section explores solutions that could remedy racial disparities in juvenile justice.

Arrest

Communities of color are patrolled more frequently by law enforcement, police-citizen encounters are more aggressive, and citizens report they feel over-policed (Brunson & Miller, 2006; Solis, Portillos & Brunson, 2009). Citizens who do not trust the police are less likely to cooperate with law enforcement to keep their communities safe, and evidence shows that residents in communities of color have less confidence in the police because of the difference in their experiences with police from those in white communities (Barnum & Perfetti, 2010; Meares, 2009).

Police encounters with black citizens may have intergenerational effects as well. Research in this area finds that black youth as young as 5th grade express more negative attributes toward police, and other research finds that black youth are especially more prone than white or Hispanic youth to view police as discriminatory despite lack of interaction with them (Unnever, Barnes, and Cullen, 2016).

Black and white youth both engage in delinquency for which they could be arrested. Estimates of involvement in crime are derived from three sources: official law enforcement data, self-report data, and victimization data (Lauritsen, 2005). For serious crimes that involve a victim, victimization data can be used to compare to official data and self-report data. For serious crimes, results from all three of sources tend to find that African American youth are more likely to be involved (Huizinga, Loeber & Thornberry, 1994; Lauritsen, 2005; McCord, Widom & Crowell, 2001). For less serious crimes, however, there is less certainty. In particular, self-report data show that there are few differences by race when it comes to property crimes (Snyder & Sickmund, 1999). When viewing the 2014 arrest rate for property crimes by race, black youth are arrested at nearly three times the rate for property crimes as white youth, and the black/white disparity has actually been increasing since 1990 (Puzzanchera & Hockenberry, 2015).

Potential overrepresentation of African American youth in drug arrests as well. Recent results from the Youth Risk Behavior Survey, which measures a variety of activities using self-report data from high school students nationwide, reports that while black youth are significantly more likely to engage in physical fights and use marijuana, white youth are considerably more likely to carry a weapon, drink alcohol, drive a car after drinking, and use hard drugs (Youth Risk Behavior Survey, 2015). This comports with research on drug offenses elsewhere that finds that blacks comprise a greater proportion of arrests for drug crimes than can be explained by self-reported involvement (Lauritsen, 2005).

Overall, the majority of scholarly research concludes that black/white disparities in serious crime can be largely explained by greater involvement by African American youth but the level of involvement in less serious crimes is less explained by racial differences (Lauritsen, 2005; Piquero & Brame, 2008).

Community-Based Arrests

Police make over one million arrests each year of individuals under 17 years old. Black youth are arrested at more than twice the rate of white youth, and this rate has worsened over time, despite a 50% decline in the number of youth arrested overall between 2005 and 2014 (Puzzanchera & Kang 2014). The rate of arrest for black youth is 6443.5 per 100,000 while the rate of arrest for white youth is 2537.8, creating a black/white ratio of 2.54:1.

Figure 1. Declines in Arrest, Rise in Disparity, 1995–2014

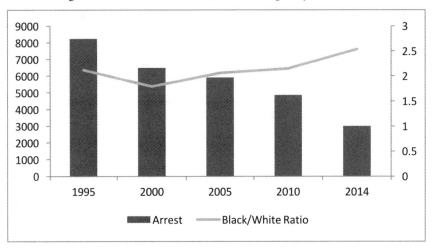

Source: Office of Juvenile Justice and Delinquency Prevention (2015). Statistical Briefing Book. Washington, DC: OJJDP.

School-Based Arrest

Historically, the first point of contact with the juvenile justice system occurred with a police encounter with youth on the street, but police have now come to play a central role in handling such matters that previously were dealt with by school personnel. Today, 42% of schools have a full- or part-time security guard, school resource officer or sworn law enforcement officer on staff and 28% of schools report that their security guard carries a firearm (Robers, Kemp and Truman, 2013). Over the past two decades, there has also been a transfer of disciplinary discretion from teachers and school administrators to disciplinary codes, such as zero-tolerance codes, that require exclusionary punishments (Hirschfield, 2008). These policies and practices push youth out of school and funnel them directly into the justice system. Since 1970, the rate of suspensions has doubled, and this is largely due to the expansion of policies that remove students from the learning environment as a disciplinary sanction (Perry & Morris, 2014).

More and more, black youth first experience the justice system through an encounter at school that results in a referral to law enforcement. Recent figures estimate that while black youth represent 16% of student enrollment they account for 27% of referrals to police from school and 31% of school-based arrests. By comparison, white students represent 51% of enrolled students, 41% of suspensions, and 39% of expulsions (U.S. Department of Education Office for Civil Rights, 2013). The black/white ratio of arrests from school is as high as 4:1 in states like Vermont and Minnesota, while the national average is 2:1 (U.S. Department of Education Office for Civil Rights, 2013).

The consequences associated with removal of students, regardless of race, from the learning environment as a form of punishment are long-lasting. But the important point is that the large-scale removal of students is happening more frequently to students of color, making them more vulnerable to involvement in crime and the justice system because of the high correlation between dropout and crime. A study in Florida of 180,000 students concluded that a single suspension in the 9th grade could drastically reduce the student's chance of graduating in a four-year time period (Balfanz, Byrnes, and Fox, 2012).

The negative impacts go beyond individual students who are subjected to unreasonable disciplinary practices. A large research study in Kentucky's school system between 2008 and 2011 found that high rates of suspension not only diminish the educational gains of suspended students, but create a ripple effect similar to David Garland's description of the American justice system as fostering a "culture of control" (2001). This phenomenon can be observed in the education system as well. The authors of the study describe a "diffusion of control, signaling how the threat and constancy of punishment permeates highly punitive environments, hindering academic performance of otherwise well-behaved students" (Perry & Morris, 2013). This, they observe, directly contradicts the purported goal of suspension, which is to restore order and safety to the school environment. Findings elsewhere that show that students feel less safe in schools where harsh disciplinary practices are in place (McNeeley, Nonnemaker & Blum, 2002). Mass incarceration expert and criminologist Todd Clear notes that school environments dominated with constantly fluctuating classrooms because of suspensions and arrest "create a volatile and socially disorganized environment similar to the effects of mass incarceration" (Perry & Morris, 2014, p. 1071).

Court Referrals, Detention, and Outcomes

Discrepancies are evident at the point of court referral as well. In 2013, 94 black youth per 100,000 were referred to court after arrest while 80 white youth per 100,000 were referred to court. As in the adult criminal justice system, juveniles can be held in confinement while awaiting their adjudication hearing, an option typically restricted to those perceived to be a flight risk or danger. Yet detention is used for other reasons also. A view held by some practitioners is that detention is actually good for some youth because it provides an opportunity for services they would not otherwise receive. Empirically, we know that detention is in fact highly detrimental to youth as it is associated with higher recidivism, vulnerability to physical and sexual abuse by staff, school dropout, and breaks with supportive family and peers. Nonetheless, some suggest that detention is the only place for poor, typically African American, youth to receive social services. Contortions like this allow disparities to continue.

Racial disparities are evident at the point of pre-adjudicatory detention, also. While overall trends in detention use show that the rate of detention for black youth is close to the rate for white youth, the black/white disparity for detention of young people accused of property crimes remains high: black youth who have been arrested for a property crime are 50% more likely to be detained awaiting their court hearing than white youth. This reflects a 20% increase in likelihood compared to 2005. The likelihood of detention for a violent crime has remained about 10% higher for black youth than white youth over this period (Puzzanchera and Hockenberry, 2015).

Black youth and white youth are formally charged with offenses at disparate rates as well. Black youth are approximately 20% more likely to be charged with a crime than white youth, and this discrepancy is mostly the result of disparate charging by race for property crimes. The adjudication of delinquency, the equivalent of being found guilty in the adult system is one stage in the system that reveals few differences by race. Unlike the disparities found at earlier points, national data show that black youth are slightly less likely to be adjudicated delinquent (Puzzanchera and Hockenberry, 2015).

Secure Placement, Transfer, and Sentencing

Though slightly less likely to be adjudicated delinquent, black youth are more likely to be sentenced to secure placement upon adjudication than white youth: national data show a 20% greater likelihood for black youth to be sent to a secure facility. Disparities in some states are extreme: in states with sizable African American youth populations, such as New Jersey and Wisconsin, commitment to secure facilities at rates 15 to 25 times higher than the rates for white youth (Rovner, 2016). And, unlike the adult system, placement in a secure facility in juvenile justice can translate to youth residence in a range of punitive settings. A large study in Philadelphia youth that tracked cases over a ten-year period found that, among youth adjudicated delinquent, black youth were significantly more likely to be given residential placement dispositions that emphasized some kind of physical regimen, such as boot camps or wilderness programs, while similar white youth were more likely to be sent to substance abuse or mental health facilities (Fader, Kurlychek and Morgan, 2014).

For both white and black youth, the number of cases transferred to adult court has declined considerably since the high point in the early 1990s. For black youth, the likelihood of transfer to the adult system has actually declined from its high point in 1992 to the most recent data reported in 2013, though it experienced a temporary rise between 2003 and 2008, which did not occur for white youth. Among youth transferred to the adult system, black youth represent 45% and white youth represent 52% among youth transferred to adult court.

Contributors to Disparity

That the system is unbalanced in terms of race and ethnic composition of those who become involved in it is not a matter of debate, and most would agree that a mix of factors creates and sustains this imbalance. The interaction of differences in offending patterns and enforcement patterns is complex. In a commentary on the relationship between race and crime, Piquero and Brame (2008) note, "for many criminologists, the relevant question is not whether race group differences can be attributed solely to differential involvement or selection. Rather, the key analytic task is to document the contribution of both mechanisms to the patterns observed in different populations at different time points" (p. 4).

Structural Disadvantage

Differential offending can explain some of the overrepresentation of youth of color in the system, particularly for violent crimes, when viewed in the context of risk factors that precede delinquency: youth of color encounter more risk factors than white children and these factors correlate with offending. It is not simply that youth of color have a greater tendency to engage in delinquency, but that structural disadvantages, a part of larger American society, have created massive inequalities which are related to who commits crime and who is equipped to desist from crime (Moffitt 1994; Piquero, Moffitt, and Lawton, 2005). More specifically, as a result of structural differences by race and class, youth of color are likely to experience unstable family systems, exposure to family and/or community violence, high elevated rates of unemployment, and more school dropout (Hawkins, Laub, Lauritsen & Cothern, 2000; Hsia, Bridges & McHale, 2004; Pope and Snyder, 2003). All of these factors are more likely to exist in communities of color and play a role in one's proclivity toward crime.

Criminologist Terrie Moffitt (1994) summarizes the experiences of a group of young persistent offenders in this way: "Among poor black families, prenatal care is less available, infant nutrition is poorer, and the incidence of exposure to toxic and infectious agents is greater, placing infants at risk for the nervous system problems that research has shown to interfere with prosocial child development. To the extent that family bonds have been loosened and poor black parents are under stress … and to the extent that poor black children attend disadvantaged schools … for poor black children the snowball of cumulative continuity may being rolling earlier, and it may roll downhill faster" (p. 39).

Parental Incarceration

One factor that has received little attention in the public discourse about race and juvenile justice involvement is the role of parental incarceration. The negative impact that parental incarceration has had on black communities is extraordinary and is an additional contributor to the persistent racial disparity observed in the juvenile justice system. Absence of a parent due to imprisonment is such a common experience now that the topic of mass incarceration was covered in a 2013 episode of *Sesame Street* (Public Broadcasting Service, 2013). Parental incarceration affects approximately 2.2 million children who have a parent in prison or jail, a 529% increase from 350,000 in 1980 (Roetger and Swisher, 2011). By age fourteen, one in twenty-five white children and one in seven African American children born in 1990 had an incarcerated parent (Wildeman, 2009). Fully half of black boys whose fathers who did not complete high school has experienced paternal imprisonment (Wildeman, 2009).

America's experiment with mass incarceration has set in motion severe ripple effects in its consequences on families and communities. Donald Braman notes that the sharp rise in the use of imprisonment in the last twenty years has "in many ways missed the mark, injuring the families of prisoners often as much as and sometimes more than the criminal offenders themselves" (Braman, 2002). The extent of mass incarceration on children is only beginning to gather national attention as a source of trauma for children and an explanation for problem behavior, including delinquency. In his ethnographic research on parental incarceration, Braman (2002) offers an especially vivid account by a young boy who witnessed his father's arrest:

> [The police] chased him in the house, and I was sitting there scream-ing, like "Daddy! Daddy!" ... The police came, and they pushed him down on the floor. He got up and pushed them off and ran through the front door, so I ran behind him ... [T]hey came and pulled my father from under the car and started beating him. And I was stand-ing there looking at them beating my father with night sticks, and they dragged him through the alley and put him in the paddy wagon (p. 70).

The documented effects on children of having a parent in prison are mani-fold; research documents both internalizing outcomes (e.g., depression, anxi-ety, social exclusion) and externalizing problems (e.g., fighting at school, drug use, school dropout) as a direct result of parental incarceration (Roettger & Swisher, 2011).

Race does not alter the strength of the relationship between parental incar-ceration and juvenile delinquency: black, white, and Hispanic boys are all sim-ilarly likely to engage in delinquency and be arrested if they have had an incar-cerated father. Of importance here is the fact that, though these findings persist regardless of race, the burdens of a family member's incarceration fall dispro-portionately on black and Latino youth because parents in these two catego-ries are much more likely to experience incarceration.

Selective Enforcement

Selective enforcement is another contributor to racial disparity (Feld, 1991; Huizinga, Thornberry, Knight, Lovegrove, Loeber, Hill & Farrington, 2007). From one's interaction with law enforcement to the probation stage of the sys-tem and the decision to sentence a young person to secure placement, bias can guide decisions about youth who break the law, and empirical evidence sug-gests that it does (see Fader, Kurleychek & Morgan, 2013). The role of individ-ual perceptions about people of different races or ethnicities appears to be an influential component in justice outcomes. An abundance of research finds that beliefs about dangerousness and threats to public safety overlap with individ-ual perceptions about people of color. Majd and Puritz (2009) note that the same behaviors that may be interpreted as "pranks" when committed by well-off white youth can easily be labeled as juvenile crime when engaged in by lower-income youth of color.

Implicit Bias

Some research finds that white Americans are more punitive than African Americans because of racial prejudice that exerts a large, negative impact on punishment preferences (Bobo & Johnson, 2004; Unnever & Cullen, 2010). Assumptions about youth based on skin color by key decision makers in the justice system can influence outcomes in a biased manner. In research on pre-sentence reports in the adult system, for example, scholars have found that people of color are frequently given harsher sanctions because they are perceived as imposing a greater threat to public safety and are therefore deserving of greater social control and punishment (Bridges & Steen, 1988). And survey data has found that, regardless of respondents' race, Americans associate African Americans with terms such as "dangerous," "aggressive," "violent," and "criminal" (Eberhardt, Goff, Purdie & Davies, 2004).

Media

Media portrayals about crime have a tendency to distort juvenile crime by selective news reporting that focuses on serious crimes and crimes committed by young people of color. The criminalization of African Americans, combined with negative media coverage fuels implicit bias (Cobbina et al., 2016). Reinforcing stereotypes and misrepresenting the true incidence of crime continues in a positive escalating loop. In the words of one observer, "Media messages are potent tools in the construction of 'otherness' and an 'us vs. them' discourse, common in crime stories, where 'us'—the good guys—need to be wary of 'them'—the predatory criminal, who is often portrayed as animalistic, vengeful, violent, and a member of a racial/ethnic minority group" (Barak, 1994; Cobbina et al., 2016). Since three-quarters of the public say that they form their opinions about crime from the news (Dorfman & Schiraldi, 2001), this misrepresentation contributes directly to the public's policy preferences and feelings about youth of color more broadly. And since policymakers are obligated to listen to and consult with their constituents—even if their constituents have been misguided—the media's role in policymaking is quite significant.

Research in this area that tests for policy preferences finds that more conservative opinions about the role of punishment are reinforced through media coverage. For instance, viewers who hold negative views about African Americans are more likely to correctly misidentify and recall an African American subject in a news story than a white subject, which sustains stereotypes (Garland, 2001).

"Race-Neutral" Policies

A variety of "race-neutral" policies and practices contribute to overrepresentation of youth of color in the juvenile justice system as well. Among these are administrative practices that draw minority youth into the system because of a failure to assess their differential racial impact (Bridges & Steen, 1998). Objective risk assessments, for instance, can have the negative consequence of drawing more minorities into the system (Bridges & Steen, 1998; Moore & Padavic, 2011). This is because questions about family life, school, employment, area of residence, and family structure are frequently related to neighborhood context. For example, young people of color may be less likely to be employed because they are more likely to live in economically distressed communities with fewer legitimate employment (Moore & Padavic, 2011).

Mandatory expulsion measures to enforce school discipline have also had a dramatically different impact on students of color. The collection of mandatory suspension and expulsion policies, together with law enforcement presence in schools has affected the school achievement and the juvenile justice involvement of youth of color especially. This is partly because these policies are more commonplace in urban low-income school districts, which already overuse suspension and expulsion to handle discipline and attendance problems (Skiba & Rausch, 2006; Verdugo, 2002).

Other Systems

The examination of the drivers of disparity must also consider forces outside the juvenile justice system that unfairly channel certain youth into the juvenile justice system. Juvenile justice does not operate in a vacuum. The youth who enter the juvenile justice system are often the same youth who are involved in child welfare and foster care systems, and other systems for at-risk youth. Reviews of other systems for youth reveals markedly different experiences for youth of color that reduce their chances for success. Disparate experiences by race are part of the school environment, housing access, healthcare, and community-based programming and services. Some have commented that the juvenile justice system has become the dumping ground for youth of color after a series of earlier systems has failed them (Bell, 2011). The failure of other systems to address and reduce racial disparities propels youth of color toward the juvenile justice system more frequently.

Unequal Access to Justice

Policies and practices that address delinquency must reflect the fact that not everyone has the same access to justice, and these differences often depend on the level of justice one can afford. A good example of this type of unequal justice is access to counsel. The 1967 U.S. Supreme Court decision, *In re Gault,* established that youth have a constitutional right to counsel. Unfortunately, the lack of regulations on how counsel is to be provided has created a patchwork of indigent defense systems that create inequalities more frequently affecting youth of color. This is because youth of color are more likely to fall into lower income brackets and are thus less able to secure private counsel for their defense, thus relying more on court-appointed attorneys who frequently carry heavy caseloads and are less likely to specialize in juvenile justice matters. A body of research finds that youth represented by a private attorney are more likely to have their cases dismissed or receive less serious punishments than youth represented by assigned counsel or having no counsel at all (Burrus & Kempf-Leonard, 2004).

Regulations and requirements for providing legal counsel differ widely across states and even across counties within a state. Thus the quality of counsel available depends on where one lives, which is intertwined with income and race. Without competent counsel, youth may "... suffer the consequences of false confessions, unconstitutional guilty pleas, wrongful convictions, pretrial detention, and incarceration in secure facilities" (Majd & Puritz 2009, p. 545).

Using the Justice System to Provide Social Services

Some explanation for the persistence of minority overrepresentation has recently been attributed to well-intentioned but misuse of the juvenile justice system to meet the needs of those who would otherwise not receive services such as mental health treatment (Bell et al., 2009; Cahn, 2006; Kempf-Leonard, 2007). To this point, Cahn (2006) notes, that sometimes it is not so much the delinquency that brings disadvantaged young people into the juvenile justice system, but the unavailability of alternatives and social services to provide for youth in the ways they need to be helped.

Youth of color are less likely to have access to community-based mental health services; one study in California found that they were half as likely as similar white youth (Janku & Yan, 2009). And, lack of services in some communities is associated with disparate rates of delinquency. One way this occurs is when assessment of current needs is based on past use of mental health services, as sometimes is the case, since African American youth are less likely to report mental health services in the past simply because of lack of access to them (Janku & Yan, 2009). Yet, detaining youth for the purpose of accessing services is not the intended purpose of the juvenile justice system and leads to many long-lasting collateral consequences for youth, including associations with high-risk individuals (Lowencamp & Latessa, 2004) and deviant labeling (Thio, 1972).

Recommendations for Reform

Repeal Disparity-Causing Policies

Policies discussed in this chapter include over-policing of schools, zero-tolerance school policies, indigent defense policies, and the use of assessments that are blind to contextual differences among youth experiences and behaviors. Efforts to provide youth, especially youth of color, with necessary programs and services will not show the desired results until disparity-causing policies are reversed. While some minority overrepresentation can be explained by differential offending patterns, and perhaps another portion can be explained by unequal services and opportunities available for youth of color, minority overrepresentation is also driven by policies and practices that disparately impact youth of color. At times these policies are called "race-neutral" but often these are the very policies that worsen racial disparity. Consider this comment from the American Sociological Association on the matter: "Those who favor ignoring race as an explicit administrative matter, in the hope that it will cease to exist as a social concept, ignore the weight of a vast body of sociological research that shows that racial hierarchies are embedded in the routine practices of social groups and institution" (quoted in Moore & Padavic, 2011, p. 6). On their own, efforts to provide youth of color with programs and services will not improve racial overrepresentation. These must be implemented along with the reversal of policies that cause the disparity in the first place.

Encourage Community-Based, Data-Driven Efforts to Reduce Disparity

Eliminating racial and ethnic disparities in the juvenile justice system is indeed a daunting task, but modest successes have been achieved and documented. The sharing of these successes is a critical component of overrepresentation of youth of color work so that effective strategies can be replicated in similarly situated environments.

A large-scale study in Pennsylvania, for example, found empirical evidence that racial disparities had been reduced due to the joint efforts associated with coming into compliance with the federal "DMC" mandate[1] and the investment by the MacArthur Foundation in its Models for Change initiative in the state (Donnelly, 2011). Her research tracked outcomes at multiple stages of the system between 1997 and 2011, and multivariate analysis allowed her to conclude that declines in contact with the system for youth of color were significant. In particular, the DMC intervention was associated with 315 fewer petitions and 10,254 fewer adjudications of delinquency among youth of color. In addition, DMC reduction interventions were associated with more than 6,000 youth of color to stay in the community-based options and over 350 to be diverted from secure placements to non-secure residential facilities. She concludes, "these figures translate into reductions in the state's processed minority youth population of .05% at petitioning, 31.44% at adjudication, 54.21% at placement, and 41.5% at secure confinement" (Donnelly, 2011, p. 14).

Promising strategies to reduce racial and ethnic disparity share a number of traits. First, they have community support, typically originating from local community concerns about mistreatment of minority youth. A successful campaign also includes stakeholders from the community who have been affected by minority overrepresentation (Bell, Ridolfi, Lacey, and Finley, 2009; Soler & Garry, 2009).

Second, the strategies consistently rely on data from a variety of sources to identify where efforts should be undertaken and whether these need to be modified over time (Bell & Ridolfi, 2008; Bell et al., 2009). For example, if it is determined that referrals to the police from school-based incidents are racially disproportionate, this could mean that school-based law enforcement strategies are contributing to racial and ethnic disparity. Third, effective strategies are transparent about their focus, their successes and their failures, and acknowledge that important lessons can be learned from both. And finally, they are committed to a long-term investment in reducing disparities that relies on evidence-based practices and follow-through with sustainable initiatives.

Systematic data collection is widely accepted as a key component of successful efforts to reduce racial and ethnic disparities. Most states now have systems in place that reliably capture race data, and some have begun to disaggregate race by ethnicity as well. This is in large part due to the federal mandate that is

---

1. Enacted by Congress in 1988 as part of the Juvenile Justice and Delinquency Prevention Act, and modified in 2002 to require states to address racial disparities at multiple points in the juvenile justice system or risk losing 20% of their federal juvenile justice funds.

part of the Juvenile Justice and Delinquency Prevention Act, which requires states to address racial disparities in order to receive federal support for juvenile justice programs and services at the state level. Yet, states continue to be beset with problems associated with tracking individual youth through the system due to an inability of data systems to communicate with each other. Police data are often disconnected from court data, which are also disconnected from placement data. This makes it difficult to follow individual youth through the system; instead, individual systems provide a snapshot of the youth population in a particular domain. Ideally, one should be able to follow each youth through the system via datasets that are linked together.

Community-level data collection is equally important to individual-level data for a complete understanding of disparities in the system. Analysis of community-level information allows jurisdictional differences to emerge. Juvenile justice expert Kimberly Kempf-Leonard (2007) notes that jurisdictional differences in the treatment of youth, the availability of alternatives to detention, and "... the culture of the system" can serve to explain overrepresentation of youth of color in one part of a state that does not exist in other parts of the state, despite other similarities (p. 81). The nuances of a particular area in terms of service availability, administrative or legal policies, and day-to-day practices could account for some minority overrepresentation, but need to be operationalized and measured in order to know whether this is the case. This was recently accomplished in a study of 1,195 youth in Michigan. Examination of differences in the pretrial detention decision showed that black youth were three times more likely than white youth to be detained, and that suburban white youth were significantly less likely to be detained than urban white youth or black youth from the suburbs or the city (Shook & Goodkind, 2009).

Finally, multilevel analyses that take macro-level factors (i.e., residential mobility, school enrollment, child welfare and foster care patterns, poverty, and unemployment) into account allows a fuller understanding of the contextual issues that accompany disparity in a particular jurisdiction. For the reasons described above, a single lens focus on juvenile justice involvement without incorporation of contextual factors limits understanding.

Enact Racial Impact Statements

Some policies and interventions have been designed with good intentions but nevertheless lack a mechanism to consider their disparate impact on various groups. A promising policy to respond to this reality is a racial impact statement, a tool for policymakers to use in assessing the potential of a policy to have disparate effects on youth of color *prior* to enactment or implementation of the policy. Similar to fiscal impact statements, these tools help lawmakers to identify unintended consequences while still able to modify their legislation or policy. Racial impact statements consider the reality that it is much more difficult to undo problematic legislation than it is to address unwarranted effects before they are adopted. Once enacted, the work of creating fair justice policies through racial impact statements can be guided by a number of agencies, including sentencing commissions, budget and fiscal agencies, and departments of corrections.

A 2007 study noted that Iowa topped the nation in racial disparity within its incarcerated population, and the state moved quickly to address this dubious distinction by requiring policymakers to prepare racial impact statements for proposed legislation that affects sentencing (Mauer & King, 2007). In 2008, Governor Chet Culver signed into law the Minority Impact Statement Bill (HF 2393), which requires legislators to have pending legislation reviewed to anticipate any disparate impact on race or ethnicity that might occur as a result of the legislation. Similar to environmental impact statements which require the inclusion of a social impact assessment, enacting laws requiring racial impact statements for pending legislation, as Mauer suggests (2008; 2009), is a legislative solution considered or adopted in a growing number of states.

Change Punitive School Policies

Leaving school is highly correlated with delinquency. Young people who drop out of school or are pushed out through suspensions and expulsions are more involved in all forms of delinquency and have greater involvement in the justice system compared to those who graduate. Keeping youth in school and engaged in the academic environment is good for public safety. Schools can revisit their zero tolerance policies and narrow them to apply only to truly dangerous behaviors so that they do not arbitrarily draw students to the system who are not a clear public safety risk.

There is some evidence of impressive reforms in this regard. Broward County, Florida is home to the nation's seventh-largest school district; significant racial disparities in school discipline policies have been documented for a number of years. During the 2011–2012 school year, black students comprised more than two-thirds of all suspensions despite the fact that they represented only 40% of the student population. In addition, 85% of the district's 82,000 suspensions during the year were for minor infractions.

In 2013, the Broward County Public Schools announced a comprehensive plan, the Cooperative Agreement on School Discipline, which was agreed to by a broad group of interested parties including the local NAACP chapter, a school board member, a public defender, the local sheriff, and a state prosecutor, among others. Together they outlined a new set of non-arrest procedures for handling low-level misdemeanors at school such as trespassing, harassment, and alcohol and marijuana-related incidents. Instead of the traditional law enforcement response, officials are urged to encourage counseling, mentoring, and relying on graduated sanctions that could result in an arrest only after the fifth incident. It is too early to see meaningful changes in disciplinary reports, but the collaboration across important allies is a critical first step in dismantling the school-to-prison pipeline.

Meaningful reforms have been observed as a result of changed policies in school discipline. In 2012, the Colorado state legislature passed House Bill 1345, the Smart School Discipline Law, after years of tireless advocacy for school discipline reform by state and national organizations. Written into the law is a formal acknowledgment of the existence of the school-to-prison pipeline, "the use of inflexible 'zero tolerance' policies as a means of addressing disciplinary practices in schools has resulted in unnecessary expulsions, out-of-school suspensions, and referrals to law enforcement agencies," and a call for an end to the inappropriate use of criminal and juvenile justice systems to handle "minor misbehavior that is typical for a student based on his or her developmental stage."

To improve troubling discipline practices through the state's schools, the law requires that all 178 public school districts implement "proportionate discipline" or graduated sanctions to reduce school suspensions, expulsions, and referrals to the police from school. Second, it requires implementation of evidence-based prevention strategies, restorative justice practices, peer mediation, and mental health counseling to divert youth from the school-to-prison pipeline and keep them in school. Third, the law requires systematic data collection and data reporting on school-based arrests, tickets, and referrals to juvenile court. And finally, the law mandates that school-based law enforcement officers are properly trained on appropriate disciplinary practices for vulnerable populations such as students of color, LGBT students, and those with disabilities. In addition to passing the Smart School Discipline Law, the Denver school district entered into an intergovernmental agreement with the Denver Police Department to revise and limit the role of police in schools. Likewise, a Code of Conduct was adopted in all 187 districts, which restricts the use of out-of-school suspensions, expulsions, and arrests. Following implementation of these reforms, there have been significant changes. In just the first year there were declines in out-of-school suspensions by 10%, expulsions by 25%, and referrals to law enforcement by 9% (Padres & Jovenes Unidos, "The Colorado School Discipline Report Card," March 2014).

Respond to Community Violence

It is well documented that youth who commit crimes—especially violent and serious crimes—have frequently been victims of abuse and neglect themselves (Nellis, 2012; Widom & Maxfield, 2001). A well-known longitudinal study identified a 59% greater likelihood of arrest among juveniles who were abused or neglected (Widom & Maxfield, 2001). The Department of Justice's *Defending Childhood* series, too, documents the cyclical effect of violence on families and communities (Listenbee, 2012). Cathy Spatz-Widom, one of the nation's preeminent scholars on handling youth involved in multiple systems, warns that children with abuse and neglect histories who exhibit behavior problems have the greatest risk of receiving a juvenile and adult arrest record as well as engaging in violent criminal behavior (Widom & Maxfield, 2001). As discussed already, the likelihood of family and community violence impacting the lives of youth of color is significantly greater than for white youth. Widom's suggestion is to intervene in the lives of these children as soon as possible with trauma-informed care so that their odds of involvement in the juvenile justice system are minimized. Juvenile justice systems can embrace a more holistic treatment model that appreciates the troubling experiences of youth before they encountered the juvenile justice system.

Conclusion

At the individual level, contact with the justice system reduces options for education, housing, and employment. At the jurisdictional level, it weakens the stability of communities of color. On a broader scale, the overuse of the justice system for youth of color results in a deepening of the divide between whites and nonwhites (Cahn, 2006; Clear, Rose & Ryder, 2001). Policies and practices that have a disparate impact on youth of color, even though they may be unintentional, have long-standing and far-reaching consequences.

When one segment of the youth population is provided with substantially worse educational opportunities, lives in low-income and sometimes violent neighborhoods with unsafe parks and limited after-school options, and is exposed to trauma of violence, its youth are already at a significant disadvantage compared to youth who receive high-quality education, live in communities with ample guardianship and safe outdoor spaces with wholesome after-school activities. There can be no denial that the differences between these groups fall on racial lines.

Though tremendous reforms to juvenile justice have been made—including the decline of commitments by 50% over the past fifteen years, racial disparities remain substantial. The core goal of juvenile justice reform efforts going forward should be to eliminate unwarranted racial disparities throughout the system.

References

Anderson, T. S. (2015). Race, ethnicity, and structural variations in youth risk of arrest: Evidence from a national longitudinal sample. Criminal Justice and Behavior, 42, 900–916.

Balfanz, R., Byrnes, V. & Fox, J. (2012). Sent home and put off-track: The antecedents, disproportionalities, and consequences of being suspended in the ninth grade. Prepared for the Center for Civil Rights Remedies and Research-to-Practice Collaborative, National Conference on Race and Gender Differences in Discipline.

Barak, G. (1994). Between the Waves: Mass Mediated Themes of Crime and Justice. Social Justice 21 (3): 133–147.

Barnum, C. & Perfetti, R. L. (2010) Race-sensitive choices by police officers in traffic stop encounters. Police Quarterly 13(2), 180–208.

Braman, D., (2002) Families and Incarceration, in Invisible Punishment: The Collateral Consequences of Mass Imprisonment, eds. Marc Mauer and Meda Chesney-Lind, New York: The New Press, p.118.

Bell, J. (2011). Prepared opening remarks. Northwestern Journal of Law and Social Policy 6(2): 279–284.

Bell, J. & Ridolfi, L. (2008). Adoration of the question: Reflections on the failure to reduce racial and ethnic disparities in the juvenile justice system. San Francisco: W. Haywood Burns Institute.

Bell, J., Ridolfi, L., Lacey, C. & Finley, M. (2009). The keeper and the kept: Reflections on local obstacles to juvenile justice systems and a path to change. San Francisco: W. Haywood Burns Institute.

Bishop, D. & Frazier, C. E. (1988). The influence of race in juvenile justice processing. Journal of Research in Crime and Delinquency 25(3): 242–263.

Blumstein, A. (1995). Youth violence, guns, and the illicit drug industry. Journal of Criminal Law and Criminology 86(1), 10–36.

Bobo, L. and Johnson, D. (2004). A Taste for Punishment: Black and White Americans' Views on the Death Penalty and the War on Drugs. DuBois Review: Social Science Research on Race 1(1): 151–180.

Bridges, G. & Steen, S. (1998). Racial disparities in official assessments of juvenile offenders: Attributional stereotypes as mediating mechanisms. American Sociological Review 63, 554–570.

Brunson, R. K. & Miller, J. (2006). Young black men and urban policing in the United States. British Journal of Criminology 46, 613–640.

Burruss, G. & Kempf-Leonard, K. (2004). The questionable advantage of defense counsel in juvenile court. Justice Quarterly 19, 37–67.

Cahn, E. (2006). How the juvenile justice system reduces life options for minority youth. Washington, D.C.: The Joint Center Health Policy Institute.

Centers for Disease Control and Prevention (2015). 1991–2013 High School Youth Risk Behavior Survey Data. Available online: http://nccd.gov/youth online.

Chapman, J. F., Desai, R. A., Falzer, P. R. & Borum, R. (2006). Violence risk and race in a sample of youth in juvenile detention: The potential to reduce disproportionate minority confinement. Youth Violence and Juvenile Justice 4(2), 170–184.

Clear, T. R., Rose, D. R. & Ryder, J. A. (2001) Incarceration and the community: The problem of removing and returning offenders. Crime and Delinquency 47(3), 335–351.

Cobbina, J. E., Owuso-Bempah, A. & Bender, K. (2016). Perceptions of Race, Crime, and Policing among Ferguson Protestors. Journal of Crime and Justice 39(1): 210–229.

Dorfman, L., & Schiraldi, V., Off Balance: Youth, Race, and Crime in the News, Building Blocks for Youth Initiative, http://www.hawaii.edu/hivandaids /Off_Balance__Youth,_Race_and_Crime_in_the_News.pdf.

Eberhardt, J.L., Goff, P.A., Purdie, V.J., and Davies, P.G. (2004). Seeing black: Race, crime, and visual processing. Journal of Personality and Social Psychology 87 (6): 876–893.

Fader, J., Kurleychek, M. & Morgan, K. (2014). The color of juvenile justice: Racial disparities in dispositional decisions. Social Science Research 44, 126–140.

Fagan, J., Geller, A., Davies, G. & West, V. (2009). Street stops and broken windows revisited: The demography and logic of proactive policing in a safe and changing city. In Race, Ethnicity and Policing (Steven Rice and Michael White, eds.). New York City: New York University Press.

Feld, B. (1995). Violent Youth and Public Policy: A Case Study of Juvenile Justice. Minnesota Law Review, 79: 965–1128.

Feld, B. (1991). Justice by geography: urban, suburban and rural variations in juvenile administration. The Journal of Criminal Law and Criminology, 82(1), 156–210.

Garland, D. (2001). The culture of control: Crime and social order in contemporary society. Chicago: University of Chicago Press.

Greene, J., Pranis, K. & Ziedenberg, J. (2006). Disparity by design: How drug-free zone laws impact racial disparity—and fail to protect youth. Washington, D.C.: Justice Policy Institute.

Guevara, L., Spohn, C., and Herz, D. (2004). Race, legal representation, and juvenile justice: Issues and concerns. Crime and Delinquency 50, 344–371.

Guevara, L., Herz, D., and Spohn, C. (2008). Race, gender, and legal counsel: Differential outcomes in two juvenile courts. Youth Violence and Juvenile Justice 6(1), 83–104.

Hawkins, D., Laub, J., Lauritsen, J. L. & Cothern (2000). Race, ethnicity, and serious and violent offending. Washington, D.C.: Office of Juvenile Justice and Delinquency Prevention.

Hirschfield, P. J. (2008). Preparing for prison? The criminalization of school discipline in the USA. Theoretical Criminology 12(1): 79–101.

Hsia, H., Bridges, G. & McHale, R. (2004). Disproportionate minority confinement: 2002 update. Washington, D.C.: Office of Juvenile Justice and Delinquency Prevention.

Huizinga, D., Loeber, R., amd Thornberry, T. (1994). Urban Delinquency and Substance Abuse: Initial Findings. Washington, DC: Office of Juvenile Justice and Delinquency Prevention.

Huizinga, D., Thornberry, T., Knight, K., Lovegrove, P., Loeber, R., Hill, K & Farrington, D. (2007). Disproportionate minority contact in the juvenile justice system: A study of differential minority arrest/referral to court in three cities. Washington, D.C.: Office of Juvenile Justice and Delinquency Prevention.

Janku, A. D. & Yan, J. (2009). Exploring patterns of court-ordered mental health services for juvenile offenders: Is there evidence of systematic bias? Criminal Justice and Behavior 36 (4): 402–419.

Jordan, K. L. & Freiburger, T. L. (2010). Examining the impact of race and ethnicity on the sentencing of juveniles in adult court. Criminal Justice Policy Review 21(2): 185–201.

Kempf-Leonard, K. (2007). Minority youths and juvenile justice: Disproportionate minority contact after nearly 20 years of reform efforts. Youth Violence and Juvenile Justice 5(1), 71–87.

Kim, C. Y. & Geronimo, I. I. (2009). Policing in Schools: Developing a governance document for school resource officers in K–12 schools. New York: American Civil Liberties Union.

Knoll, C. & Sickmund, M. (2010). Delinquency cases in juvenile court, 2007. Washington, D.C.: Office of Juvenile Justice and Delinquency Prevention.

Lauritsen, J. (2005). The Role of Race and Ethnicity in Juvenile Justice Processing. In (Hawkins, D. and Kempf-Leonard, K, eds.) Our Children, Their Children. Chicago: University of Chicago Press.

Listenbee, R., Report of the Attorney General's Task Force on Children Exposed to Violence (Washington, DC: U.S. Department of Justice, 2012).

Leiber, M. (2002). Disproportionate minority confinement (DMC) of youth: An analysis of efforts to address the issue. Crime and Delinquency, 48(1), 3–45.

Lowencamp, C. & Latessa, E. (2004). Understanding the risk principle: How and why correctional interventions can harm low-risk offenders. Washington, D.C.: National Institute of Corrections.

Lundman, R. J. (2003). The Newsworthiness and Selection Bias in News about Murder: Comparative and Relative Effects of Novelty and Race and Gender Typifications on Newspaper Coverage about Homicide. Sociological Forces

Majd, K. & Puritz, P. (2009). The cost of justice: How low-income youth continue to pay the price of failing indigent defense systems. Georgetown Journal on Poverty Law and Policy 21, 543–582.

Mauer, M. (2008). Racial impact statements as a means of reducing unwarranted sentencing disparities. Ohio State Journal of Criminal Law, 5(1), 19–46.

Mauer, M. (2009). Racial impact statements: Changing policies to address disparities. Criminal Justice, 23(4), 16–21.

Mauer, M. & King, R. (2007). Uneven justice: State rates of incarceration by race and ethnicity. Washington, D.C.: The Sentencing Project.

McCord, J., Widom, C.S. & Crowell, N.A., eds. 2001. Juvenile Crime, Juvenile Justice. Panel on Juvenile Crime: Prevention, Treatment, and Control. Washington, DC: National Academy Press.

McNeeley, C.A., Nonnemaker, J. M. & Blum, R. W. (2002). Promoting school connectedness: Evidence from the National Longitudinal Study on Adolescent Health. Journal of School Health 72(4): 138–146.

Meares, T. (2009). The legitimacy of the police among young African-American men. Marquette Law Review 92(4), 651–666.

Moffitt, T. E. (1994). Natural histories in delinquency. In E. Weitkamp and H.J. Kerner (eds.), Cross-national longitudinal research on human development and criminal behavior (pp. 3–61). Dordrecht: Kluwer Academic Press.

Morris, E. & Perry, B. (2014). The Punishment Gap: School Suspensions and Racial Disparity in Achievement. Social Problems 63(1): 68–86.

National Council on Crime and Delinquency (2007). And justice for some: Differential treatment of youth of color in the justice system. Oakland: National Council on Crime and Delinquency.

Nellis, A. (2015). A return to justice: Rethinking our approach to juveniles in the system. Lanham: Rowman and Littlefield.

Nellis, A. (2013). Life goes on: The Historic Rise in Life Sentences in America. Washington, D.C.: The Sentencing Project.

Nellis, A. (2005). Seven steps to develop and evaluate strategies to reduce disproportionate minority contact (DMC). Washington, D.C.: Justice Research and Statistics Association.

OJJDP Statistical Briefing Book. Online. Available: http://www.ojjdp.gov/ojstatbb /crime/qa05101.asp?qaDate=2014. Released on December 13, 2015).

Perry, B. L. & Morris, E. W. (2014). Suspending progress: Collateral consequences of exclusionary punishment in public schools. American Sociological Review 79(6): 1067–1087.

Piquero, A. (2008). Disproportionate minority contact. The Future of Children, 18(2), 59–80.

Piquero, A., Moffit, T. & Lawton, B. (2005). Race and Crime: The contribution of individual, family, and neighborhood risk facts to life course persistent offending. In D. F. Hawkins & K. Kempf-Leonard (Eds.), Our Children, Their Children (pp. 300–345). Chicago: University of Chicago Press.

Piquero, A. & Brame, R. W. (2008). Assessing the race-crime and ethnicity-crime relationship of a sample of serious adolescent delinquents. Crime and Delinquency 54(3), 390–422.

Pope, C. & Snyder, H. (2003) Race as a factor in juvenile arrests. Washington, D.C.: Office of Juvenile Justice and Delinquency Prevention.

Public Broadcasting Service (2013). Little children, big challenges. Sesame Street: PBS.

Puzzanchera, C., Sladky, A. & Kang, W. (2015). "Easy Access to Juvenile Populations: 1990–2014." Online. Available: http://www.ojjdp.gov/ojstatbb /ezapop/.

Puzzanchera, C., Chamberlin, G. & Kang, W. (2015). Easy access to the FBI's supplementary homicide reports: 1980–2013. Online. Available: http://www .ojjdp.gov/ojstatbb/ezashr/.

Puzzanchera, C. & Hockenberry, S. (2015). National Disproportionate Minority Contact Databook. Developed by the National Center for Juvenile Justice for the Office of Juvenile Justice & Delinquency Prevention. Online. Available: http://www.ojjdp.gov/ojstatbb/dmcdb/

Puzzancherra, C. & Kang, W. (2014). Easy access to FBI arrest statistics: 1994–2012. Washington: DC: Available Online.

Robers, S., Kemp, J. & Truman, J. (2013). Indicators of School Crime and Safety: 2012. Washington, DC: National Center for Education Statistics.

Roettger, M. E. & Swisher, R. R. (2011). Association of fathers' history of incarceration with sons' delinquency and arrest among black, white, and Hispanic males in the United States. Criminology 49 (4): 1109–1147.

Rovner, J. (2016). Racial Disparities in Youth Commitments and Arrests. Washington, DC: The Sentencing Project.

Shook, J. J. & Goodkind, S. A. (2009). Racial disproportionality in juvenile justice: The interaction of race and geography in pretrial detention for violent and serious offenses. Race and Social Problems 1: 257–266.

Sickmund, M., Sladky, A., and Kang, W. (2015). Easy Access to Juvenile Court Statistics: 1985–2013. Washington, DC: Office of Juvenile Justice and Delinquency Prevention.

Skiba, R. & Rausch, M. K. (2006). Zero Tolerance, Suspensions, and Expulsion: Questions of Equity and Effectiveness. In Everston & Weinstein (Eds.), Handbook of Classroom Management Research Practice and Contemporary Issues. Mahwah: Erlbaum Press.

Snyder, H. & Sickmund, M. (2007). Juvenile offenders and victims: 2006 national report. Washington, D.C.: Office of Juvenile Justice and Delinquency Prevention.

Soler, M. & Garry, L. (2009). Reducing Disproportionate minority contact: Preparation at the local level. Office of Juvenile Justice and Delinquency Prevention: Washington, D.C.

Solis, C., Portillos, E. L., and Brunson, R. K. (2009). Latino youths' experiences and perceptions of encounters. The Annals of the American Academy of Political and Social Science 623, 39–49.

Sweeten, G., Bushway, S. D. & Paternoster, R. (2009). Does dropping out of school mean dropping into delinquency? Criminology 47(1), 47–92.

Thio, A. (1972). The poverty of the sociology of deviance: Nuts, sluts and perverts. Social Problems, 20(1), 103–120.

Tracy, P. E. (2005). Race, ethnicity, and juvenile justice. In D. F. Hawkins & K. Kempf-Leonard (Eds.), Our Children, Their Children (pp. 300–345). Chicago: University of Chicago Press.

Unnever, J., Barnes, J., and Cullen, F. (2016). Racial invariance theory revisited: Testing an African American theory of offending. Journal of Contemporary Criminal Justice 32(1): 7–26.

Unnever, J. & Cullen, F (2010). The social sources of American punitiveness: A test of three competing models. Criminology 48(1): 99–129. and Cullen,

U.S. Department of Education Office of Civil Rights (2014). Civil Rights Data Collection: Data Snapshot (School Discipline) March 21, 2014. Available online: http://ocrdata.ed.gov/Downloads/CRDC-School-Discipline-Snap shot.pdf.

U.S. Department of Health and Human Services (2001). Youth violence: A report of the Surgeon General. Rockville: U.S. Department of Health and Human Services.

Verdugo, R. R. (2002). Race-ethnicity, social class, and zero-tolerance policies: The cultural and structural wars. Education and Urban Society 35(1): 50–75.

Widom, C. & Maxfield, M. (2001). An update on the 'cycle of violence.' Washington, DC: National Institute of Justice: Research in Brief.

Wildeman, C. (2009). Parental imprisonment, the prison boom, and the concentration of childhood disadvantage. Demography 46(2): 265–280.

Chapter 2

Disproportionate Minority Contact (DMC): A Historical and Contemporary Perspective

Nicolle Parsons-Pollard

Background

Disproportionate Minority Contact (DMC) in the juvenile justice system has long been a phenomenon that has plagued States and localities. Due to the advocacy of various groups, particularly the Coalition for Juvenile Justice (CJJ), Congress responded in 1988 by mandating States participating in Part B of the Title II Formula Grant Program to address disproportionality in secure detention and correctional facilities and adult jails and lockups. This mandate was strengthened in 1992 becoming the fourth core requirement of the Juvenile Justice and Delinquency Prevention (JJDP) Act of 1974, as amended, behind Deinstitutionalization of Status Offenders (DSO), [Sight and Sound] Separation, and Jail Removal tying 25% of a State's Title II Formula Grant funds to compliance. When the JJDP Act was reauthorized in 2002, the scope was broadened requiring States to provide direct services to prevent minority youth from coming into contact with the juvenile justice system, to examine how State and local juvenile justice systems operate to determine why disproportionality is occurring,

The first edition of this chapter was authored by Andrea R. Coleman in 2011. *(The ideas expressed are attributed to the author, and do not reflect the positions of the U.S. Department of Justice).*

reducing compliance to 20% of the Title II Formula Grant allocation for each of the four requirements, and for participating in the Grant Program. The changes were critical because they allowed States to address disproportionality and minority overrepresentation throughout the juvenile justice continuum not just in secure juvenile detention and correctional facilities and adult jails and lockups.

Although the 2002 amendment of the JJDP Act required States to provide direct services to prevent minority youth from having contact with the juvenile justice system and to examine how State and local systems operate, it did not address the relationship between DMC, DSO, [Sight and Sound] Separation, and Jail Removal. For example, this relationship is evident because many jurisdictions that have high rates of DSO (i.e. youth ordered to secure detention on a status offense) also have high rates of minority youth securely detained due to these offenses. This is problematic for various reasons as inconsistent or inappropriate decision-making criteria can cause disproportionality. This is also true for [Sight and Sound] Separation (i.e., requires youth to be physically separated by sight and sound from adult offenders) and Jail Removal (i.e., juveniles cannot be securely detained in any adult jail or lockup); however, when there are violations, minority youth are adversely affected as they tend to have higher rates of secure detention and confinement relative to white non-Hispanic youth. While the 2002 amendment of the JJDP Act does not address the relationship between all four core requirements, potential to begin this work rests in the reauthorization of the legislation. Introduced in the 111th Congress, Senate Bill (SB) 678 and House Resolution (HR) 6029 provide stronger language of how States, localities, and tribal jurisdictions should address racial, ethnic, and gender disparities as result of DMC throughout the juvenile justice system, and as an unintended additional benefit, could positively impact the high rates of all four-core requirements. The stronger language is needed as States and localities, except for a few jurisdictions, have not reduced DMC for a plethora reasons that include but are not limited to: lack of access to data and/or inconsistent data collection and analysis, funding universal delinquency prevention programs that are not DMC focused, and lack of understanding of DMC versus racial and ethnic disparities. Thus, this chapter will discuss the relationship between the four requirements and the potential impact of the provisions in SB 678 and HR 6029, why most States and local jurisdictions have not been able to reduce DMC, and finally, provide a summary of the U.S. Department of Justice Office of Juvenile Justice and Delinquency Prevention's (OJJDP) current initiatives and how they can assist States and local jurisdictions with reducing DMC.

Making the Connection: DSO, [Sight and Sound] Separation, Jail Removal, and DMC

Though the 2002 amendment of the JJDP Act instructs States how to process juveniles in secure detention and correctional facilities and adult jails and lockups, it does not compel them to identify whether DMC is occurring, and if so, to what extent. For example, when minority youth come into contact with law enforcement for a status offense (i.e., offenses that would not be criminal if committed by an adult such as truancy, incorrigible behavior, minors in possession of alcohol, curfew violations, some traffic offenses, etc.) there is no formal examination of the racial and ethnic breakdown. This is especially prevalent in communities that have a constant police presence, which are generally poor and/or have a high volume of minorities. Per Section 223(a)(11) of the JJDP Act of 1974, as amended, once juveniles are charged with a status offense they cannot be detained in a secure detention facility for more than 24 hours pending an initial court appearance (excluding holidays and weekends), thus a citation is often issued as an Alternative to Detention (ATD) or being held non-securely in an adult jail or lockup pending transport to the juvenile facility or awaiting to be picked up by a parent or guardian. Though juvenile justice systems operate differently, once the citation is issued a youth is usually referred to court. This has a significant impact on DMC because, according to OJJDP's national *Databook*,[1] the Relative Rate Index (RRI) for referrals to court in 2007 is 1.1 for all minorities meaning they are referred more than 1 time compared to White non-Hispanic youth; the rate is slightly higher for Black youth at 1.2. After the referral to court youth can be placed in diversion[2] (which occurs more frequently for youth charged with a delinquent act) to give them an opportunity to participate in various activities such as volunteer work, trainings, workshops, or other community alternatives to prevent formal charges from being filed. Although the empirical research and literature (Shelton, 2007;

---

1. The RRI provides a single index number that indicates the volume of the form of contact or activity differs for minority youth compared to white youth. See Chapter 1 of OJJDP's DMC *Technical Assistance Manual, 4th Edition* for a detailed discussion (http://www.ncjrs.gov/html/ojjdp/dmc_ta_manual/dmcch1.pdfl).

2. OJJDP defines diversion as "all youth referred for legal processing but handled without the filing of formal charges. Youth referred to juvenile court for delinquent acts are often screened by an intake department (either within or outside the court). The intake department may decide to dismiss the case for lack of legal sufficiency, resolve the matter informally (without the filing of charges), or resolve it formally (with the filing of charges)" (2009; Chapter 1; 7).

Cahn, et al., 2006; Bynum and Thompson, 1996:4; Lundman, 1993; Davidson et al., 1990) shows all youth benefit from diversion, particularly African-American males who are not serious, violent, and/or chronic offenders, the RRI at diversion for all minority youth is 0.7 and is slightly higher for American Indian/Alaska Native, and 0.9 Asian, Hawaiian/Pacific Islander youth which means they are referred less than 1 time compared to White non-Hispanic youth.

Similarly, disproportionality can also occur in adult jails and lockups as minority youth are more likely to be placed there versus being issued a citation for a court referral or immediately released in the field to a parent or guardian. Section 223(a)(13) of the JJDP Act of 1974, as amended, says that juveniles who are accused of non-status offenses can be held non-securely in an adult jail or lockup no longer than 6 hours for the purposes of processing, transfer to a juvenile facility, or waiting for a court appearance. The only exceptions are if the initial court appearance occurs 48 hours (excluding weekends and holidays) after the youth is taken into custody, the facility is outside a metropolitan statistical area (i.e., Rural Exception), there is inclement weather, or "a lack of highway, roads, or transportation" (2002; 21). Though the national *Databook* provide data of minority youth in secure detention, there is no way to distinguish how many of these youth were processed in an adult jail or lockup pending transfer to the facility which is an enormous gap in the 2002 amendment of the JJDP Act of 1974. If States were provided a framework so they could disaggregate their secure detention data to determine *how* (i.e., were they detained non-securely at an adult jail or lockup pending transfer to the facility or ordered by traditional means) youth were placed, they could implement effective system improvement strategies thus potentially mitigating disproportionality in secure detention.

Though race and ethnicity data are not collected and analyzed at adult jails and lockups, or when youth are referred to secure detention for status and delinquent offenses, over 20 States have implemented various Alternatives to Detention (ATD) models with the goals of protecting public safety and providing viable community options for youth and reducing DMC. For example, the Annie E. Casey's Juvenile Detention Alternatives Initiative (JDAI) has been successful with reducing the overall volume and rates of secure detention; however, DMC rates have not decreased and in some jurisdictions they have worsened. According to the JDAI's *Pathway* series there are various reasons why RRIs have not decreased such as the "first to benefit from the reforms were white youth" and some local DMC coalitions became entrenched in discussing the larger contextual issues of poverty and racism (Hoytt et al., 2001; 31 and 32). Other national models have shown some reductions in percentages of minority youth in secure detention but not at other juvenile justice contact points. Though no formal outcome or impact evaluations have been conducted of the latter model, it has been theorized that the replacement effect is occurring (i.e., the percentages for minority youth have increased dramatically at other juvenile justice system contact points due to the reform efforts at secure detention) (Coleman, 2010). On the surface, the national *Databook* somewhat validates this theory; for example, the RRI in 1990 was 1.6 for all minorities, it increased to 1.8 in 1991, decreased slightly to 1.7 in 1992 and began to drop steadily to 1.4 starting in 1998. Over the next fifteen years it remained steady between 1.4 and 1.3 with a few years at 1.2. Conversely, the RRIs at arrest for minority youth have remained at 1.7 or above, as evidenced in 1992 when it was 1.8 and increased to 1.9 in 1993. African-American youth have consistently had the highest RRIs of all minorities increasing from 2.0 in 1990 to 2.3 in 2013 despite all of the reform efforts. Similarly, the RRIs for American Indian/Alaska Native youth at arrest have remained constant at 1.0 in 1990, increasing to 1.1 from 1995–1997, decreasing slightly to 0.9. Again, the trend for these youth is alarming due to their small volume of the total youth population ages 10–17 meaning the magnitude of the disproportionality is equal or greater for this group than African-American youth.

As with all of the four requirements, youth must not have any contact with adult inmates per Section 223(a)(12) of the JJDP Act of 1974, as amended, even if the secure facilities are colocated (i.e. both the juvenile and adult facilities are physically located on the same grounds) 2002; 17–18; 21; (Formula Grants Consolidated Regulation 28 CFR Part 31 Section § 31.303(d)). Keeping youth physically sight and sound separated from adult inmates is a difficult task within itself, however if there is disproportionality in the numbers it compounds the issue because not only is there the potential for immediate harm due to physical contact, there is the possibility of Civil Rights of Institutionalized Persons Act (CRIPA) of 1984, as amended,[3] violations if there is overwhelming evidence that disparate treatment has occurred as a result of DMC; this could also occur with DSO and Jail Removal. Again, because the 2002 amendment of the JJDP

---

3. CRIPA authorizes the U.S. Attorney General to investigate conditions of confinement at State and local government institutions such as prisons, jails, pretrial detention centers, juvenile correctional facilities, publicly operated nursing homes, and institutions for people with psychiatric or developmental disabilities. Its purpose is to allow the Attorney General to uncover and correct widespread deficiencies that seriously jeopardize the health and safety of residents of institutions.

Act of 1974 does not require States to collect and analyze data by race and ethnicity for DSO, Jail Removal, and Separation there are no definitive data to show whether minority youth are disproportionately securely detained or confined with adult inmates.[4]

JJDP Act Reauthorization: Senate Bill (SB) 678 and House Resolution (HR) 6029

The JJDP Act of 1974, as amended, has been on a continuing resolution since 2007 because legislation was not passed during the 111th Congress, the 2002 amendments are still in effect. However, this may soon change as both chambers did introduce their respective Bills to reauthorize the Act: Senate Bill (SB) 678 and House Resolution (HR) 6029. Both were very similar in that they greatly expanded the 2002 amendment to DMC requiring States, tribal jurisdictions, and localities to implement policy, practices, and systems improvement strategies to identify and reduce racial and ethnic disparities. HR 6029 went even further by requiring jurisdictions to also identify gender disparities for youth who come into contact with the juvenile justice system. Other similarities between SB 678 and HR 6029 included but were not limited to: requiring States and tribal jurisdictions to establish coordinating bodies composed of juvenile justice stakeholders to oversee and monitor their efforts, identify specific juvenile justice contact points where racial and ethnic disparities are occurring, and again, HR 6029 was more specific as it named these points (arrest, referrals to court, informal resolution (e.g., diversion), detention, petitions (e.g., charges filed), adjudication (e.g., finding of delinquency),[5] probation, placement [in a secure correctional facility], and transfer to the criminal adult system. This language is radically different from the 2002 amendment in that it assumed there are racial and ethnic disparities in the juvenile justice system versus disproportionality. The difference between the two is that with racial and ethnic disparities there may be an assumption of dissimilar or inequitable

---

4. According to Section 103 (26) an adult inmate is defined "reaching full criminal responsibility under applicable state law" or is charged with a serious offense (i.e. murder, robbery, manslaughter, etc.). However in several States the age of majority is 16 or 17. This poses a problem because most States will not transfer them to secure adult facilities until they turn 18. If this is the policy or regulation, they must be kept sight and sound separated from all youth under the age or 16 or 17.

5. Adjudication/finding of delinquency is the same as a finding of guilt in a criminal court.

treatment and that juvenile justice stakeholders are solely making decisions based on intentional or unintentional biases. Whereas disproportionality means there is a difference in the total volume of activity for minority youth compared to White non-Hispanic youth or the majority population and further examination is needed to determine whether it is due to racial and ethnic disparities and/or other contributing mechanisms[6] (Coleman, 2010).

Race and Ethnicity Categories Required by OJJDP for Data Collection and Analyses

White (non-Hispanic): A person having origins in any of the original people of Europe, the Middle East, or North Africa.

American Indian or Alaska Native (non-Hispanic): A person having origins in any of the original peoples of North and South America (including Central America) and who maintains tribal affiliation or community attachment.

Asian (non-Hispanic): A person having origins in any of the original peoples of the Far East, Southeast Asia, or the Indian subcontinent including, for example, Cambodia, China, India, Japan, Korea, Malaysia, Pakistan, the Philippine Islands, Thailand, and Vietnam.

Black or African-American (non-Hispanic): A person having origins in any of the black racial groups of Africa.

Hispanic or Latino: A person of Cuban, Mexican, Puerto Rican, South or Central American, or other Spanish culture or origin, regardless of race.

Native Hawaiian or other Pacific Islander (non-Hispanic): A person having origins in any of the original peoples of Hawaii, Guam, Samoa, or other Pacific islands.

Source: U.S. Office of Management and Budget (1997)

To determine the contact points where racial and ethnic disparities are occurring jurisdictions may also have to develop and implement data collection and analyses systems to track and analyze the disparities, develop and implement plans with measurable goals and objectives, and to report annually to the public on these efforts. The only vestiges remaining in HB 678 and HR 6029 from the 2002 amendment is that jurisdictions may have to implement systems improvement strategies and that there will be no required numerical standards or quotas as a benchmark for reduction.

---

6. Contributing mechanisms are factors based on empirical research that are highly associated with creating DMC. For a detailed description see Chapter 2 of OJJDP's *DMC Technical Assistance Manual, 4th Edition* (http://www.ncjrs.gov/html/ojjdp/dmc_ta_manual/dmcch2.pdf).

Since both Bills are so similar no matter which version becomes law the impact on States and localities will be enormous. One huge impact would be developing and implementing data collection and analyses systems to track and analyze racial and ethnic disparities. Currently States are required to submit data for all nine contact points statewide and for at least three local jurisdictions, typically those with the highest minority populations. Once these data are entered into OJJDP's DMC Web-Based System they are computed into the RRI for all youth ages 10–17 for all major race and ethnicity categories. Data collection is the most difficult component of the Identification Phase of OJJDP's DMC Reduction Model because States and localities must gather data from various sources which include schools that have School Resource Officers (SROs) that arrest youth and/or make referrals to court. Although the mandate of developing and implementing a data collection system may give States more leverage in obtaining data from the various sources, the language in SB 678 and HR 6029 was vague leaving more questions than answers to include:

- Will these systems be computerized and if so who will manage them?
- If they are computerized which agencies will fund them?
- Further, what type of data will be entered into the system? Will it include any cross-system (i.e. child welfare, education, etc.) data and information, and if so, who will execute any Memorandum of Understanding (MOU) for all pertinent agencies to share these data?
- Will States have to use Title II Formula Block Grant or other Federal block grant funding to develop and implement a system and if so, will it affect existing programs and services?
- For States that are unable to develop and implement a computerized system, how will they be able to comply with this mandate?

Currently, there are a number of States that have some form of a computerized system that enables them to collect data from within and across systems. The remaining States collect data from various sources and are often tasked with mining and/or aggregating them in a way that can be interpreted and analyzed. Not only is the requirement to implement a data collection system vague, requiring States to publicly report their results is also ambiguous leaving more questions such as: how would the results be reported and in what form (i.e., an annual report detailing the extent of racial and ethnic disparities with recommendations)? Additionally States could be required to have coordinating bodies to facilitate their initiatives. Based on the Fiscal Year 2011 DMC Compliance Plans, 41 States have statewide committees however some of them have not been able to effectively address and reduce DMC do to various contextual issues (i.e., they only focus on funding universal delinquency prevention programs, do not follow their DMC Compliance Plans, etc.).

Another potential impact of SB 678 and HR 6029 or other proposed legislation to reauthorize the JJDP Act of 1974, as amended, is how they could influence DSO, [Sight and Sound] Separation, and Jail Removal. First, HR 6029 specifically named the juvenile justice contact points where States must identify racial and ethnic disparities are occurring. This would enable States to not only collect data by race and ethnicity at the secure juvenile detention contact point as it combines the language from the new legislation with the 1992 amendment to the JJDP Act of 1974, as amended, which focused on addressing disproportionality in juvenile detention and secure correctional facilities and adult jails and lockups. As stated in the previous section, if States were provided a framework to disaggregate their secure detention data to determine how youth were placed, they could implement, based on the language in SB 678 and HR 6029, policies, practices, and systems improvement strategies to reduce racial and ethnic disparities. If HR 6029 is reintroduced in its current form, jurisdictions will also have to address gender disparities, which would require implementing gender specific policies, practices, and systems improvement strategies. This definitely will have an impact on DSO [Sight and Sound] Separation, and Jail Removal because there is no empirical research and little data on how girls are processed, particularly when held non-securely in adult jails and lockups and how they are separated from adult inmates. In most jurisdictions when juveniles are taken to adult jails and lockups they go through separate entrances from adult arrestees and inmates. There is emerging research on how girls are processed in the juvenile justice system and the causes and correlates that contribute to their delinquency. For example, Zahn, Agnew, and Fishbein et al. (2010) asserts that although girls' offenses are less serious and chronic than boys' offenses they often hide more serious problems: "... Studies of girls who are chronic runaways document significant levels of sexual and physical victimization" (3). They also discuss other contributing mechanisms that include but are not limited to biological and individual factors, stressors, mental health, trauma, early onset of puberty, and family influences. Though SB 678 and HR 6029 would have expanded how States and jurisdictions would have to address DMC, more specifically racial, ethnic, and gender disparities if the legislation had been passed and signed into law. OJJDP would have to provide intensive technical assistance to ensure the new mandates are carried out according to the intent of the law.

Why Most States and Local Jurisdictions Have Not Been Able to Reduce DMC

Although States and localities have made tremendous progress with addressing DMC which includes enhanced data collection and analyses by race and ethnicity, establishing coordinating bodies, designating staff to facilitate efforts, and implementing a wide array of delinquency prevention and systems improvement activities, there has not been widespread reductions of DMC since Congress issued the mandate in 1988 and elevated it to a core requirement of the JJDP Act of 1974, as amended, in 1992. In fact, many RRIs have remained the same or worsened despite State and local efforts. As many juvenile justice system stakeholders and practitioners search for "model programs" and best practices to reduce DMC, questions have now arisen as to whether any measurable reductions can occur. There are promising results in some States and local jurisdictions; however, there are various reasons why DMC reduction is not widespread. One reason is that many jurisdictions engage in a haphazard approach instead of implementing OJJDP's DMC Reduction Model to fidelity. For example, once the extent of DMC has been determined via the RRI, most States and localities go to the Intervention Phase and bypass the Assessment/Diagnosis Phase of the Model. The Assessment/Diagnosis Phase is critical because it assists with determining *why* DMC is occurring. Many jurisdictions think funding should be used for direct services instead of conducting a formal study; so as a result, most interventions do not reduce DMC because they are not directly related to the contributing mechanisms. Additionally, most of the strategies and programs are general delinquency prevention programs, some in minority communities, and are not aimed specifically at reducing DMC. This occurs frequently because the thought is that since minority youth are receiving services it will reduce the likelihood they will have contact with the juvenile justice system. Though the empirical literature supports that delinquency prevention programs that address specific risk factors (i.e., individual, family, and social) can greatly reduce the probability of juvenile justice system involvement, it will do so for all youth and not impact DMC. This is because most programs do not formally evaluate whether their interventions prevent minority youth from engaging in delinquent behavior and/or having negative contact with law enforcement, which is typically the entry point into the juvenile justice system.

DMC is not reduced when States and localities propose to improve how their juvenile justice systems operate overall as illustrated by the Annie E. Casey's JDAI, which significantly reduces the rate of secure detention for White non-Hispanic youth but does not for minority youth. To remedy this problem and ensure DMC is reduced and/or mitigated, States and localities must implement specific delinquency prevention and systems improvement strategies that are aimed at minority youth. This includes conducting formal outcome and impact evaluations that are directly tied to whether the strategies reduce the probability of minority youth engaging in delinquent behavior and ensuring that those already in the system are processed equitably based on various factors that include but are not limited to: static risk predictors (i.e., factors or characteristics that do not change) such as the number of prior arrests, age at first arrest, number of times incarcerated, and dynamic risk predictors (i.e., factors or characteristics that contribute to their risk but can change) such as peers, Alcohol, Tobacco, and Other Drug (ATOD) use, "criminal" thinking, lack of school attachment, etc. (Latessa and Allen, 2003; 295; Hawkins and Catalano, 1992). Another reason why States and localities cannot reduce DMC is because they do not follow their strategic plans or they do not have a plan with measurable goals and objectives. For example, some jurisdictions say they will eliminate DMC, though honorable the probability is highly unlikely so anything less is viewed as failure. Also, it is very easy when groups convene to discuss larger societal issues that will not directly impact DMC, such as structural racism, or to play the "blame game" strictly attributing DMC to intentional bias when the empirical research says that bias and disparate treatment are two of many contributing factors. When an assessment study is not conducted and/or strategic plans are not followed or are not realistic, many groups become stagnate or disband because they are unable to move forward. Tangentially, many jurisdictions are also slow to embrace the empiricism of DMC reduction due to the fact that race is at the core of this phenomenon as result of structural racism and historical trauma most minorities have withstood since the inception of the United States as a sovereign nation. Though keeping these issues in mind is vital to any successful DMC initiative, many groups make decisions solely based on these factors. Again, racial and ethnic disparities can be a result of disproportionality, empirically speaking, because there is no way to establish why it is occurring once it has been identified and the extent has been determined based on the RRI; further assessment and examination are needed to detect the *why*.

Conclusion

This chapter provided a past and current perspective of DMC which includes the 1988 congressional mandate, its elevation to a core requirement in 1992 which tied 25% of Title II Formula Grant funds to compliance with the JJDP Act of 1974, as amended, and the expansion to addressing disproportionality throughout the juvenile justice system in the 2002 amendment reducing compliance to 20% of the Title II funds. Information was also provided on the relationship between DMC and the remaining core requirements of the JJDP Act of 1974, as amended, (Deinstitutionalization of Status Offenders, [Sight and Sound] Separation, and Jail Removal) which primarily examines how the extent of contact in secure juvenile detention and secure correctional facilities, adult jails and lockups, can negatively impact DMC and how the 2002 amendment does not explicitly address the association. As a result, the chapter discussed the impact of the JJDP Act's potential reauthorization, particularly SB 678 and HR 6029 introduced in the 111th Congress which further expanded the DMC core requirement mandating that participating States address racial and ethnic disparities, implement coordinating bodies to facilitate initiatives, implement data collection systems, and publicly report on the progress of DMC. HR 6029 went even further by requiring States to also address gender disparities.

Though the expanded language as primarily positive, there could have been unintended consequences, particularly the difficulty with implementing data collection systems, whether they will be computerized and who will manage them. As jurisdictions and practitioners await reauthorization of the JJDP Act of 1974, as amended, many questions have been raised as to why there are few cases where DMC has been reduced. One reason is that once the extent of DMC is determined via the RRI States and local jurisdictions do not conduct a formal methodological assessment but will fund and implement universal delinquency prevention programs and systems improvement activities that are not DMC focused which has been evident with national models such as the Annie E. Casey's JDAI that reduced the overall utilization of secure detention for White non-Hispanic youth but not for minorities. Most jurisdictions, with a few exceptions, have not conducted formal outcome and impact evaluations based on static and dynamic risk predictors to determine whether their strategies have reduced and/or mitigated DMC. Other reasons include engaging in discussions on larger societal issues such as structural racism only attributing DMC to overt bias and disparate treatment, which are only two of the many contributing mechanisms, based on the empirical research. In the midst of these looming issues, OJJDP current initiatives, include providing training and technical assistance for new DMC Coordinators, States, and localities on the DMC Reduction Model, data collection and analyses strategies, and assessment plan development, and are aimed to assist States and local jurisdictions with reducing DMC. In addition, starting in 2009 OJJDP implemented various initiatives and demonstration projects that include:

- *Native American/Alaska Native Interagency Initiative*[7]—OJJDP has partnered with the Bureau of Justice Statistics (BJS), the Bureau of Indian Affairs (BIA) and the Justice Research and Statistics Association (JRSA) to determine the extent of DMC for this population via the RRI and revision of the Title II Formula Grant Pass-Through allocations for States that have significant Native populations and tribal law enforcement functions, and identifying promising delinquency prevention and systems improvement strategies.
- *OJJDP Field Initiated Research and Evaluation's (FIRE) DMC Data Analysis and Patterns Project*[8] — The overall goals of this research project are to conduct a national analysis of RRI data to identify jurisdictions that have shown a consistent positive movement in the values over 3 consecutive years, to obtain detailed information on the approaches used by these jurisdictions, and to produce detailed case studies that can be replicated by other jurisdictions.
- *DMC Community and Strategic Planning (CASP) Demonstration Project*[9]—The purpose of the CASP Project is to provide effective strategies to facilitate state and local DMC initiatives to reduce and/or mitigate disproportionality throughout the juvenile justice system. These strategies include: hiring and/or designating staff as DMC Coordinators; facilitating the DMC Reduction Model; tracking expenditures of the DMC portion of the Title II Formula Grant and/or other funds; providing training to local jurisdictions and stakeholder agencies; and assisting with conducting a process evaluation. Targeted DMC reduction sites will engage in community capacity building activities that include: implementing a community collaborative; conducting a local assessment; and assisting the State DMC Coordinator with monitoring delinquency prevention and systems improvement activities.
- *Relative Rate Index Modification (RRI) Project*—The purpose is to assist the U.S. Territories, the District of Columbia, and some States, where minority youth comprise the majority of the total youth population ages 10–17. The preliminary revisions to the RRI include but are not limited to: designating "minority youth" that comprise the majority of the total youth population as the denominator in the RRI, making in between race

---

7. From the pending OJJDP publication *Disproportionate Minority Contact: American Indian and Alaska Native Youth* (2010).

8. This is the project summary in the 1st Quarterly Progress Report submitted to OJJDP for review and approval.

9. This is the project overview in the FY 2010 Request for Applications.

comparisons (i.e. comparing the rate of contact of African American youth to Hispanic/Latino youth) and enhancing the current formula to more accurately reflect DMC for minority youth that comprise the majority of the total youth population.

Although reauthorization of the JJDP Act of 1974, as amended, has not occurred and States and localities still have a long way to go in implementing initiatives to reduce and/or mitigate DMC, there are some promising data and the hope is that there are more to come. In the end, no matter when reauthorization happens and what challenges lay ahead, it is clear there is a deep commitment by States, localities, practitioners, and communities to ensure that all youth regardless of race and ethnicity who come into contact with the juvenile justice system are treated fairly and equitably and that the processing and dispositions are in proportion to static and dynamic risk predictors. If this occurs, then there truly will be justice for all.[10]

References

Bynum, J.E. and Thompson, W.E. (1996). *Juvenile delinquency: A Sociological Approach 3rd Edition.* Needham Heights, MA: Allyn and Bacon. P.

Cahn, E.S. (2006). *How the Juvenile Justice System Reduces Life Options for Minority Youth.* Washington, DC: Joint Center for Political and Economic Studies Health Policy Institute.

Coalition for Juvenile Justice. *A Delicate Balance.* (1988). Washington DC: Coalition for Juvenile Justice.

Coleman, A.R. and Rosen, L. (2010). *Disproportionate Minority Contact: American Indian and Alaska Native Youth.* Washington DC: U.S. Department of Justice, Office of Justice Programs, Office of Juvenile Justice and Delinquency Prevention.

Davidson II, W.S., Redner, R. Amdur, R.L., and Mitchell, C.M. (1990). *Alternative Treatments for Troubled Youth: The Case of Diversion from the Justice System.* New York, NY: Plenum Press.

Hawkins, D.J. and Catalano, R.F. (1992). *Communities That Care.* South Deerfield, MA: Channing Bete Company.

---

10. As of May 2016, neither Senate Bill 678 nor House Resolution 6029 has passed as legislation. SB 678 was never voted on and HR 6029 was sent to the House Education and Labor Subcommittee on Healthy Families and Communities.

Hoytt, E.H., Schiraldi, V., Smith, B.V., and Ziedenburg, J. (2001). *Pathways to Juvenile Detention Reform: Reducing Racial Disparities in Juvenile Detention*. Baltimore MD: Annie E. Casey Foundation.

Latessa, E.J. and Allen, H.E. (2003). *Corrections in the Community, 3rd Edition*. Cincinnati, OH: Anderson Publishing Company.

Lundman, R. J. *Prevention and Control of Delinquency*. (1993). New York: Oxford University Press.

Office of Management and Budget. (1997). *Revisions to the Standards for the Classification of Federal Data on Race and Ethnicity Federal Register Notice*. Washington, DC: United State Government Printing Office.

Shelton, D. (2007). *An Evaluation of the Status Offense Diversion Program in the Juvenile Court of Washtenaw County, Michigan*. Eastern Michigan University; University of Nevada, Reno: The Grant Sawyer Center for Justice Studies.

United States Congress. Juvenile Justice and Delinquency Prevention as amended, Pub. L. No. 93-415 (1974). Washington, DC: U.S. Government Printing Office.

United States. Department of Justice, Office of Justice Programs, Office of Juvenile Justice and Delinquency Prevention. *Disproportionate Minority Contact Community and Strategic Planning (CASP) Demonstration Project Request for Application*. (2010). Washington DC: U.S. Department of Justice, Office of Justice Programs, Office of Juvenile Justice and Delinquency Prevention.

United States. Department of Justice, Office of Justice Programs, Office of Juvenile Justice and Delinquency Prevention. *Disproportionate Minority Contact Technical Assistance Manual*, 4th Edition. (2009). Washington DC: U.S. Department of Justice, Office of Justice Programs, Office of Juvenile Justice and Delinquency Prevention.

United States. Department of Justice, Office of Justice Programs, Office of Juvenile Justice and Delinquency Prevention. *Field Initiated Research and Evaluation's (FIRE) DMC Data Analysis and Patterns Project*. (2010). Washington DC: U.S. Department of Justice, Office of Justice Programs, Office of Juvenile Justice and Delinquency Prevention; Bethesda, MD: Development Services Group.

Zahn, M.A., Agnew, R., Fishbein, D., Miller, S., Winn, D.M., Dakoff, G., Kruttschnitt, C., Giordano, P., Gottfredson, D., Payne, A.A., Feld, B.C., and Lind, M.C. (2010). *Causes and Correlates of Girls' Delinquency*. Washington DC: U.S. Department of Justice, Office of Justice Programs, Office of Juvenile Justice and Delinquency Prevention.

Chapter 3

Measuring DMC: The Origins and Use of the Relative Rate Index

William Feyerherm

Although research on racial and ethnic disparities in juvenile justice reaches back nearly to the beginnings of the juvenile court, the formal recognition of the issue at the federal level first appeared in 1988. The purpose of this chapter is to examine the measurement of disproportionate contact, showing how it was influenced by the policy requirements in the legislation, how it is measured today and to provide a brief view of the picture those measurements paint of the different experiences that minority groups have with the U.S. juvenile justice systems.

Legislative Background

In 1988 the annual report to Congress by the Coalition of Juvenile Justice in a report entitled "A Delicate Balance" called on Congress to address the growing racial disparities found in the juvenile justice system (Gardell et al., 1989). Following that report, Congress amended the Juvenile Justice and Delinquency Prevention Act (JJDPA) to include what has become known as the DMC initiative. The wording of that initiative in 1988 contained language which clearly prescribed the way in which racial disparities in the experience with the juvenile justice system would be measured and assessed. That language required States receiving funds under JJDPA authorizations "to address efforts to reduce the proportion of juveniles detained or confinement in secure detention facilities, secure correctional facilities, jails, and lockups who are members of minority groups if such proportion exceeds the proportion such groups represent in the general population" (Hsia, 2008).

That language clearly prescribed two characteristics of the DMC initiative, which governed for the next 14 years. First was that the initiative was focused on detention or confinement and therefore the focus of measurement was on juveniles placed in such secure facilities. Second is that the measurement was to be defined for comparing proportions of the confined group with proportions that such groups representing the general population. Following 14 years of experience with the DMC initiative, a growing body of research literature, and increasing awareness of racial disparities throughout the justice system, Congress revised the DMC initiative in 2002 with language that changed it from a focus on confinement to focus on justice system contact. The 2002 Amendments to the Juvenile Justice and Delinquency Prevention Act (JJDPA) also moved away from language which explicitly required comparing proportions of youth in the various stages of the system with proportions in the general population.

The relevant portion of the Amendment requires states receiving JJDPA funds to "Address juvenile delinquency prevention efforts and system improvement efforts designed to reduce, without establishing or requiring numerical standards or quotas, the disproportionate number of juvenile members of minority groups who come into contact with the juvenile justice system."

In that revised description of DMC there are changes to two fundamental characteristics of the DMC initiative. First, it broadened the scope away from simply confinement to recognize that any contact with the juvenile justice system has potentially harmful consequences for juveniles and should be viewed as a last resort in controlling and correcting their behavior. Second, it moved away from the strict comparison with proportions in the general population and instead focused on the question of numbers of youth in contact with the juvenile justice system, which OJJDP (the agency responsible for administering the JJDPA) has interpreted to mean disproportionate rates of contact with the juvenile justice system (Hsia, 2009).

Developing the Current Measurement System

Following the passage of the 2002 amendments, OJJDP convened a workgroup to develop a new system of measurement for the revised DMC initiative (Butts et al., 2003). That working group developed a new system based on four principles:

1. Use existing juvenile justice system data and information systems. A new metric should not require the development of new methods of data collection.
2. Focus and accelerate efforts at juvenile delinquency prevention and system improvement. Rather than simply identify that there is an over-representation of many minority groups in the juvenile justice system, the new metric should help to identify the parts of the system in which that disproportionate contact was most accentuated.
3. Reduce the dependence on data collected by the U.S. Census. Although census data is invaluable in examining any social phenomena such as juvenile delinquency, it was becoming widely known that census data suffered from issues of accuracy and undercount in assessing particular minority groups.
4. Finally, the metric should be mathematically independent of the demographics of the jurisdiction being studied. That is to say the measure should be comparable across multiple jurisdictions, multiple demographic groups, and across time.

The metric, which was developed by that working group, was termed the "Relative Rate Index" or RRI for short. At its simplest, the RRI consists of three components, a system map describing the major contact points or stages at which a juvenile may have additional contact or penetration into the justice system, a method for computing rates of activity (by race and ethnicity) at each of the stages, and a method to compare the rates of contact for different demographic groups at each of those stages (Feyerherm, Snyder & Villarruel, 2009).

In the case of the RRI for juvenile justice, the system map, which was developed, is depicted in Figure 1. That map consists of the general youth population and nine stages or decision points through which a juvenile may pass. The idea of the map is that these are major decision areas in the juvenile justice system, not that they are all of the decisions, but that by mapping the flow of juveniles past these nine points a fairly comprehensive view may be formed of any juvenile justice system in the U.S. (Figure 1.)

Once the system map is in place, the method of computing rates comes next. Figure 2 provides the computational methods used for each rate calculation. With the exception of the first rate (arrest) which is calculated using the base of the number of youth of each major race/ethnicity grouping in the general population, each of the rates is calculated on the basis of the volume of activity for that race/ethnicity group in a preceding stage in the juvenile justice system.

Figure 1. Basic Juvenile Justice System Flow Model for Constructing the Relative Rate

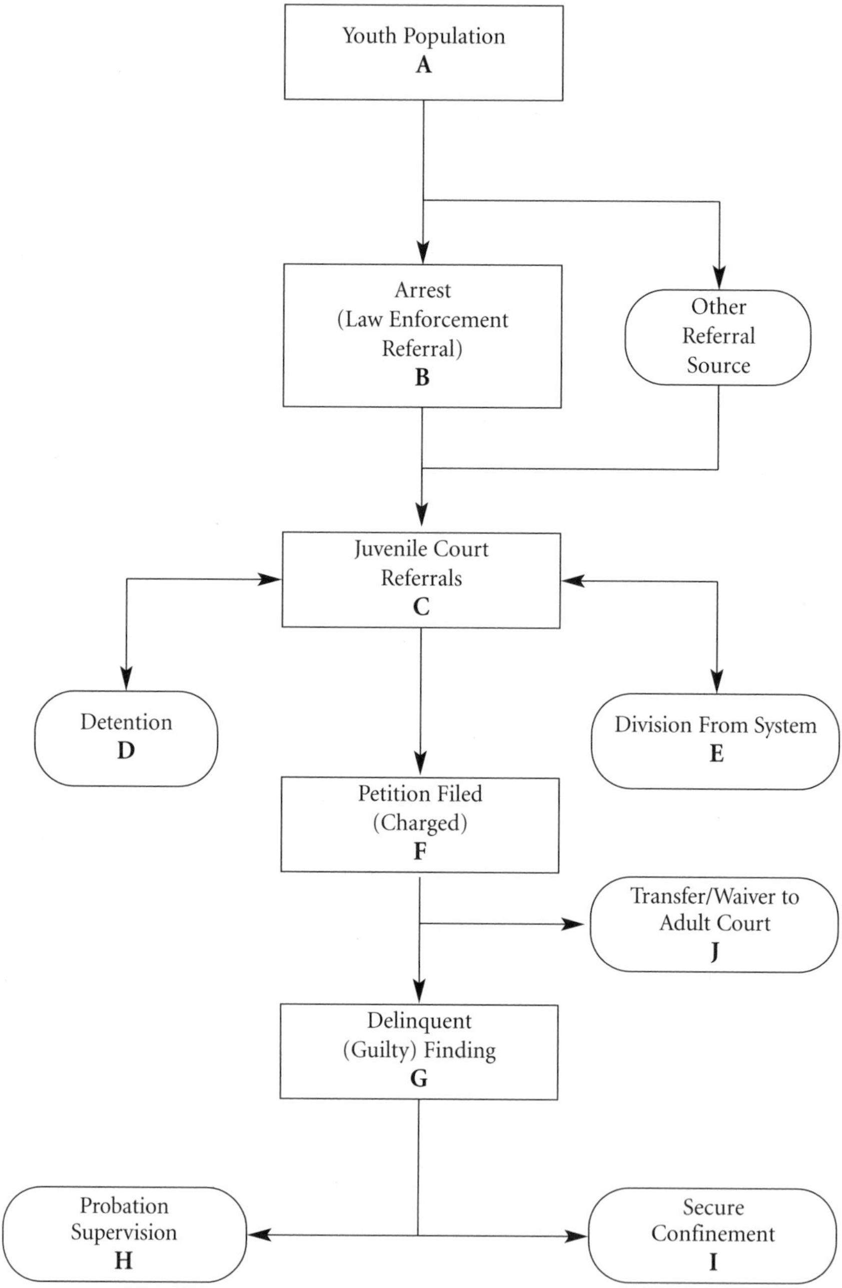

Figure 2. Base for Calculation of Rates at each
Stage of the Juvenile Justice System

- Juveniles arrested—rate per 1,000 population
- Referrals to juvenile court—rate per 100 arrests
- Juveniles diverted before adjudication—rate per 100 referrals
- Juveniles detained—rate per 100 referrals
- Juveniles petitioned—rate per 100 referrals
- Juveniles found to be delinquent—rate per 100 youth petitioned (charged)
- Juveniles placed on probation—rate per 100 youth found delinquent
- Juveniles placed in secure correctional facilities—rate per 100 youth found delinquent
- Juveniles transferred to adult court—rate per 100 youth petitioned

Finally, the comparison to create the metric to assess DMC is a fairly straightforward one:

$$\text{Relative Rate Index (RRI)} = \text{minority rate} / \text{white rate}$$

That ratio provides a number ranging (theoretically) from zero to infinity. An index of one would represent statistical equality. An index of 2.00 reflects a volume of justice contact for minority youth that is double the volume for white youth, while an index of .50 (the inverse) would reflect a volume of contact for minority youth that is only half the volume of contact experienced by white youth. Since there are nine rates calculated (shown in Figure 2) there are nine index values which can be calculated for each race/ethnicity group.

Modifications to that basic formula are needed when the dominant group is not white, or when white youth are such a small segment of the population that the rates of systems contact for white youth are not statistically reliable. Additional nuances in the calculation of the index are covered in the *Disproportionate Minority Contact Technical Assistance Manual*, available on the OJJDP website (OJJDP, 2009).

Returning to the four governing principles for creating this measure, it is useful to examine how those objectives are met by the RRI process.

1. *Use existing juvenile justice system data and information systems.* The RRI process is designed to use counts of information, essentially the simplest form of calculation. It does not require that the same youth be traced through the system, rather simply looks at the volume of activity

at specific points in the system. This also means that it does not really reflect the odds of a particular outcome occurring to any juvenile. The RRI information can be collected and calculated in a jurisdiction that does not have a sophisticated juvenile information system, but simply reports numbers of youth (or cases). Moreover, by not tracking cases, the index reports on the behavior of the system, not the youth. And that report on system behavior can be compiled relatively quickly—it does not need to wait until all cases initiated within a given year are resolved.

2. *Focus and accelerate efforts at juvenile delinquency prevention and system improvement.* The intent of the RRI model is to be able to identify those stages in which the greatest differences occur in contact between white and minority youth. By examining rates that are calculated on the basis of preceding stages in the justice system rather than on the basis of the proportion of the population, it is feasible to examine the incremental amount of disparity in contact that is introduced in each of these nine stages. From that vantage point, the objective of the method is to provide guidance for a jurisdiction in determining what parts of its justice system to focus on first. It is critical to realize that the RRI values were intended as a first step in the process of addressing DMC—they can serve to focus attention on a few stages of the juvenile justice system and can be used over time to monitor the general levels of DMC in a community. The RRI values, in themselves, are not sufficiently specific to fully inform the choice of an intervention strategy for a community to address DMC, nor are they specific enough to be used as the only evaluation tool in assessing whether a strategy is working. More specific assessment and evaluation strategies are needed for those tasks, but they are guided by the overall RRI findings. Additional details on these elements in the overall OJJDP strategy can be found in the Technical Assistance Manual, particularly chapters 2 and 5.

3. *Reduce the dependence on data collected by the U.S. Census.* The enumeration process used by the Census in 1990 and 2000 provides an undercount of numerous groups, but particularly with children and minority groups, both critical areas for juvenile justice issues (West & Robinson, 1999). Census technical documents provide this estimate of those impacts:

> "The data indicate that populations were undercounted at different rates. In general, Blacks, American Indians and Alaskan Natives, Asians and Pacific Islanders, and Hispanics were missed at higher rates than Whites. To cite an actual example, in the United States overall, we estimate a net undercount

of about 4.0 million people in 1990, giving us an undercount rate of approximately 1.6%. The estimate for Whites is about 1.8 million, for a rate of 0.9%. However, although fewer Blacks (1.4 million) than Whites were missed, they were missed at a higher rate, approximately 4.4%. Children were also disproportionately missed in the last census. The net undercount for children — about 3.2% — is twice the overall rate" (http://www.census.gov/dmd/www/ techdoc1.html).

The results of such undercounts generate the possibility that estimates of DMC may be based on erroneous information. By basing only the arrest rate (and index value) on Census information, the calculations for the remaining eight decision stages are based on counts of youth **within** the juvenile justice system, rather than being based on continuing comparisons to potentially undercounted Census information.

4. *Finally, the metric should be mathematically independent of the demographics of the jurisdiction being studied.* If the comparison is to the proportion of the population (DMC version 1.0) then the range of values for the index are limited by the proportion of the population that falls into the minority group. For example, a jurisdiction in which 10% of the population are minority youth will have a possible upper limit of 10 times the proportion (in a situation in which 100% of the youth in secure confinement were minority youth.) On the other hand, for a jurisdiction in which minority youth comprise 50% of the population, the most that can be measured is for the youth in secure confinement to be double (100%) the proportion of the general population. Thus, the numerical values of these two situations cannot be directly compared, meaning that it is not feasible to compare jurisdictions to one another, to compare different racial and ethnic groups to one another or to examine changes in the experiences of a group as it experiences rapid demographic changes. On the other hand, by examining rates, we avoid these problems — the range of possible values is always the same and the index is not "artificially" inflated or deflated as the demographic composition changes.

The Implementation of the RRI

Initially developed as a set of Excel spreadsheets, the RRI method has become a web-based data entry and analysis tool which is required for all states receiving JJDPA funding. The minimal requirement for participating States is that they complete the information for the State as a whole and for three jurisdictions (usually counties) that have the highest proportion of minority youth. That information is required to be provided every three years, although many States provide annual information. Moreover, many States provide information on many more than three counties, with a few States providing information on all counties within the State. As a result, the RRI data base does not give a fully representative picture of the national portrait of DMC, but rather gives a good picture of those jurisdictions that are actively engaged with the issue, as well as those jurisdictions in each State that have the highest proportion of minority youth. In that sense the data base is extremely useful to show the variations in DMC across communities. The combined national picture is better portrayed on the national DMC data book website, http://www.ojjdp. gov /ojstatbb/dmcdb/index.html (Puzzanchera & Adams, 2010).

The RRI Data

A snapshot of the DMC website data was taken on August 15, 2010. That snapshot was filtered to examine only the most recent entry from each county or State which had data entered into the system. A total of 1043 jurisdictions had data entered, 47 States (or State equivalent entities such as territories and the District of Columbia) and 996 sub-State jurisdictions, predominantly counties.

Although the intention of developing the RRI method was that jurisdictions would be able to use existing data collection systems rather than develop new ones, not all data systems contained the nine elements that were suggested in the RRI process. Table 1 contains the data element availability for each of the nine stages in the juvenile justice system. Separate calculations are presented for the set of States (N=47) and for the represented Counties (N=996).

As may be seen, none of the elements is universally available. Arrest data is the most frequently available data element for both counties and States. It is also interesting to note that some items (Referral, Detention, and Petition) are more likely available at the local level, while others Probation, Confinement, Transfer) are more available at a State level. These differences may reflect the level of government which is primarily responsible for each function, with the earlier set usually being a local function, and confinement and transfer frequently being State level responsibilities.

It is also the case that the availability of data elements varies depending on which racial or ethnic group is being examined. In Table 2 we can see that all of the States have data on African American (Black) youth, while Hawaiian/Pacific Islander youth are only represented in on quarter of the States. Of significant

Table 1. Data Element Availability

	Stage	County	State
1	Arrest	84%	81%
2	Referral	67%	53%
3	Diversion	64%	66%
4	Detention	70%	66%
5	Petition	73%	64%
6	Delinquent	72%	70%
7	Probation	72%	77%
8	Confinement	46%	79%
9	Transfer	19%	60%
	N	996	47

impact in the design and use of the RRI is the relatively high occurrence of "Other/Mixed" youth, which may represent a statistical challenge as these youth are represented in some data systems within a State but not others.

Table 2. Data Availability by Race / Ethnicity

		County	State
1	Black	89%	100%
2	Hispanic	86%	85%
3	Asian	75%	96%
4	Native	35%	83%
5	Hawaiian	5%	26%
6	Other / Mixed	41%	83%
7	N	996	47

The range of data scores for the Relative Rate Index is presented starting in Figure 3. In that figure we examine the decision points from arrest (#1) through transfer (# 9) within the set of 996 counties. For each decision point, three data points are presented, the 25th, 50th and 75th percentiles, with the 50th percentile being of course, the median value. The spread of values between the 25th and 75th percentiles (otherwise known as the inter-quartile range) gives us a good view of the amount of variability in the RRI values at each decision point. If we view the median as representing the "typical" jurisdiction, we can begin to describe the issues of disproportionate contact as follows. The highest level of disparity occurs at entry into the juvenile justice system, the arrest decision. Not only is the median value high, but there is substantial variability in the degree of disproportionate contact at this point, with nearly a quarter of the reporting counties having scores at the 4.00 level or higher. Next, the median value for referrals is near 1.0, with some indication that the distribution is skewed toward higher values. The value for diversion indicates that Black youth are less likely to receive diversionary options, with a quarter of the counties falling nearly at the .5 level or lower. The detention index indicates a higher use of detention for Black youth, and the portion of the bar above the median is clearly longer than below—in other words there is a tendency for some fairly high values (above 2.00) in extreme cases. In comparison, the stages involving judicial activity, filing a petition, finding of delinquency and placement on probation, all have very tight distributions centered near the line of 1.00, indicating statistically equivalent handling. When we examine more restrictive options, confinement and transfer to adult courts, we return to a pattern of higher median values and a distribution that shows a skewed set of values—the 75th percentile is substantially higher than the median and suggests that the full distribution has counties with quite high levels of disproportionate use of these options for Black youth.

Figure 3. Range of RRI Values for Black Youth, All Reporting Counties

	1	2	3	4	5	6	7	8	9
−75th percentile	3.9	1.5	1.0	2.0	1.3	1.3	1.1	2.5	4.6
◆ Median	2.7	1.0	0.8	1.3	1.1	1.0	1.0	1.4	2.1
−25th percentile	1.8	0.9	0.6	1.0	0.9	0.8	0.9	1.0	1.0

Decision Stage

Figure 4 presents the same information, compiled at the State level rather than the county level. Although the two figures are quite similar (as one might expect), what is notable about the differences in the figures is that the range of variation tends to be much smaller for the State level data. There are at least two ways of interpreting this. First is that when the results are aggregated from the community to the State level, the extreme scores in some communities tend to be attenuated or muted by the combination with other results in the State. The second possibility is that at the smaller numeric (population) level, it is possible to have random events (noise) that create larger perturbations in the index values. These two explanations have fairly different implications for the development of policies related to DMC. While it is not possible in this data to select between the explanations, it will be feasible to test the random noise hypothesis by examining whether the same communities are consistently in the high or low categories over multiple years. That examination is starting and will become easier as additional years of data are entered into the OJJDP web site.

Figure 4. Range of RRI Values for Black Youth, All Reporting States

	1	2	3	4	5	6	7	8	9
— 75th percentile	3.6	1.1	0.9	1.8	1.2	1.1	1.1	2.4	4.2
◆ Median	2.9	1.0	0.8	1.4	1.1	1.0	1.0	1.7	2.1
— 25th percentile	2.3	0.9	0.7	1.2	1.0	0.9	0.9	1.0	1.2

Decision Stage

While Figures 3 and 4 examined patterns for Black youth, other groups also experience issues with Disproportionate Contact. Figures 5 and 6 present similar data for Hispanic youth at the county and then State levels. Comparing Figures 3 and 5 gives us a sense of the areas in which the two groups have different experiences. First, with respect to arrest, the median RRI value is lower (1.2 for Hispanic youth, 2.7 for Black youth). Beyond that, the experiences of the two groups are quite similar until we get to the transfer stage, where again the value of the RRI for Black youth is quite a bit higher than for Hispanic youth.

It is also notable that in both arrest and transfer then 75th percentile values are also substantially higher for Black youth. In other words, there are counties in which the relative experience of Black and Hispanic youth in the juvenile justice system is markedly different from the experiences of white youth, and the extremes of those differences are more striking for Black youth than for Hispanic youth.

Figure 5. Range of RRI Values for Hispanic Youth, Counties

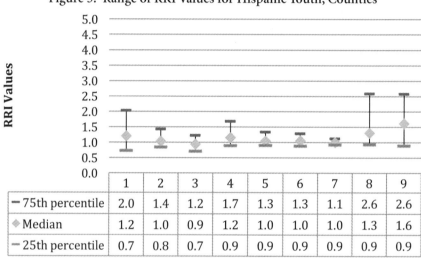

	1	2	3	4	5	6	7	8	9
─ 75th percentile	2.0	1.4	1.2	1.7	1.3	1.3	1.1	2.6	2.6
◆ Median	1.2	1.0	0.9	1.2	1.0	1.0	1.0	1.3	1.6
─ 25th percentile	0.7	0.8	0.7	0.9	0.9	0.9	0.9	0.9	0.9

Decision Stage

When our attention shifts to Figure 6, State level indices for Hispanic youth, familiar patterns emerge. Again, the medians are very similar to the county values, while the range of scores, the variability represented by the spread from the 25th to the 75th percentile, is smaller for the State data than for the county data. And again, although there are patterns which suggest that Hispanic youth experience greater contact with the juvenile justice system than do white youth, the extent of those differences (disparities) are not so large as those experience in general by Black youth.

Observations on the Implementation of the RRI

After roughly seven years of use, it is possible to draw some conclusions about the Relative Rate Index as a measuring tool for DMC. First, it is worth revisiting the principles used to establish the RRI. As noted, one objective was to be

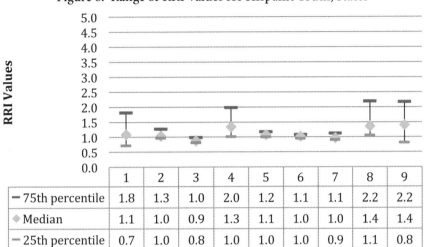

Figure 6. Range of RRI Values for Hispanic Youth, States

	1	2	3	4	5	6	7	8	9
— 75th percentile	1.8	1.3	1.0	2.0	1.2	1.1	1.1	2.2	2.2
◆ Median	1.1	1.0	0.9	1.3	1.1	1.0	1.0	1.4	1.4
— 25th percentile	0.7	1.0	0.8	1.0	1.0	1.0	0.9	1.1	0.8

Decision Stage

able to use existing data, not to require the collection of new sets of information. The major problem in that approach has been the difficulty in obtaining arrest information separately for Hispanic groups. Slightly less than two thirds of the jurisdictions reporting on the OJJDP web site were able to obtain that specific data element, primarily because the Uniform Crime Reports data collection system treats race and ethnicity as two distinct characteristics and does not provide means for identifying non-Hispanic and Hispanic members of different racial groups. On the other hand, most juvenile court information systems blend the two characteristics and count, for example, non-Hispanic whites as white youth, non-Hispanic Blacks as Black, etc. Both schemes have their merits, but the net result is that arrest numbers cannot easily be traced into the juvenile justice system to follow the cumulative impacts of arrest, referral, detention, etc.

A second objective of the RRI system was to focus reform efforts onto those areas having the greatest impact on the overall experience of DMC. Arguably, by presenting information on nine different stages of the justice system it has been feasible to identify those stages in which the greatest differentials occur. While the figures presented here suggest that in general the arrest, detention, confinement and transfer stages have higher median values for the RRI, it is the case that in some communities the balance of DMC has occurred at other stages, or may be best addressed at other stages. Thus, the method has served that purpose.

A third objective was to minimize dependence on general Census numbers. By basing the rates (and then the RRI calculations) on numbers generated within the justice system, that objective has been accomplished. Related to it was a fourth objective of generating a measure whose values are not dependent on or limited by the population demographics. In order to assess that, we may examine the correlation of the index values with the percent of the population that belongs to the two most populous minority groups, Black and Hispanic. Those correlations are provided in Table 3. What is fairly clear is that until we get to the later stages of the juvenile justice system there is at most a very weak negative correlation of the demographic composition of the community with the RRI values. In other words, the method seems to provide useable results that are statistically independent from the demographics of the community. At the confinement and transfer stages the correlations are somewhat stronger and indicate that those communities with lower proportions of minority youth are more likely to experience DMC issues with respect to confinement and transfer.

Table 3. Correlation of RRI Values with Percentage of County Population in Corresponding Groups

RRI Stage	Black	Hispanic
Arrest	−0.06	0.04
Referral	−0.04	0.03
Diversion	−0.05	−0.10
Detention	−0.10	−0.11
Petition	−0.08	−0.04
Delinquent	0.02	−0.07
Probation	−0.07	−0.10
Confinement	−0.15	−0.09
Transfer	−0.30	−0.31

Despite generally meeting those four objectives, there are other concerns which need to be raised about the current implementation and use of the RRI measure. Chief among them is that by segmenting the contributions to disparate experiences across nine decision points, the metric tends to diminish what is (at the national level) a large issue of disproportionate experiences with the justice system. The cumulative impact of multiple decisions, compounded with other social factors and the performance of other support systems such as education, public health, mental health and similar systems designed to support youth, means that as a generalization, minority youth do not have the same opportunities to attain success as white youth. While the RRI method helps to pinpoint segments of the justice system for attention, by segmenting the issues, it also downplays the cumulative impacts.

Related to that concern is that the RRI as a measure is simply a starting point for the analysis that leads to successful DMC programming. While the measure may identify a particular stage or stages as the most reasonable focal point for understanding and addressing DMC, that is not the same as understanding the policies, practices and procedures at work in that stage to generate DMC. The RRI is but one step in what OJJDP describes as a five stage iterative process.

Finally, there are some technical issues which are likely to bedevil any measurement of DMC. For example, there are limitations of any statistically based technique in examining the experiences of small groups of individuals. As a result, the RRI loses its value when the number of juveniles in a community is small, or when only a handful of juveniles are considered for some of the later stages in the system. Those concerns apply whether the small numbers are in a minority group or among white youth. Since the technique involves comparison of rates, if there are not sufficient white youth to generate a reliable estimate of a rate, then the technique loses its applicability. In some communities that are well past a "majority-minority" status, the reliability of the rates for white youth may be questioned. Also in the domain of technical issues are the problems of missing information (arrest rates for Hispanic youth), differing definitions and methods for defining racial and ethnic identity and the over simplification of race and ethnicity as reflecting a unitary or single identity for a juvenile, when many youth are celebrating the diversity of their backgrounds.

Conclusion

As a means of measuring Disproportionate Minority Contact, the Relative Rate Index was designed to provide a "lowest common denominator" approach to finding whether a jurisdiction has an issue related to DMC and if so, what part of the juvenile justice system seems to provide the largest contributions to that issue. Results from nearly 1,000 jurisdictions (both State and county level) have been initially examined. It is clear that the extent of DMC is something which varies fairly substantially across localities, with the variation across counties being greater than the variation across States. In that sense, it is clearly the case that DMC, although the subject of national policy concerns, is indeed a local issue, with local origins, local nuances and needing local solutions. Despite limitations and caveats, the RRI method gives us a clearer picture of the experiences of thousands of youth in this country. That is useful (but not sufficient) in the efforts to provide equal opportunity and equal justice to all youth.

References

Butts, J., Bynum, T., Chaiken, J., Feyerherm, W., Laws, M. B., Leiber, M., et al. (2003). *Report from The Disproportionate Minority Contact (DMC) Peer Review Meeting*. Unpublished manuscript, Washington, DC.

Feyerherm, W., Snyder, H. N. & Villarruel, F. (2009). Chapter 1: Identification and Monitoring. In OJJDP (Ed.), *Disproportionate Minority Contact Technical Assistance Manual*, 4th Edition.

Gardell, R., Button, A., Stansell, K., Forbes, D., Carlisle, A. L., Fedullo, R., et al. (1989). *Report on the Delicate Balance to the President, the Congress, and the Administrator of the Office of Juvenile Justice and Delinquency Prevention*. Bethesda, MD: National Coalition of State Juvenile Justice Advisory Groups.

Hsia, H. (2008). *A Disproportionate Minority Contact (DMC) Chronology: 1988 to Date*. Retrieved from www.ojjdp.gov/dmc/chronology.html.

Hsia, H. (2009). Introduction. In OJJDP (Ed.), *Disproportionate Minority Contact Technical Assistance Manual*, 4th Edition.

OJJDP. (2009). Disproportionate Minority Contact Technical Assistance Manual Available from http://www.ojjdp.gov/compliance/dmc_ta_manual.pdf.

Puzzanchera, C. & Adams, B. (2010, May 17, 2010). National Disproportionate Minority Contact Databook. from http://ojjdp.ncjrs.gov/ojstatbb/ dmcdb/.

West, K. & Robinson, J. G. (1999). *What Do We Know About The Undercount of Children?* Retrieved from www.census.gov/population/www/documentation/twps0039/twps0039.html.

Chapter 4

An Examination of the Effects of Race on Intake Decision-Making in Four Jurisdictions at Two Different Points in Time

Michael Leiber, Jennifer H. Peck, and Myra Fields

In 1989, the disproportionate minority confinement (DMC) mandate was passed with five states, including Iowa, to serve as models to other states and localities as to how to implement its base principles (Federal Register, 1991). DMC was included as a core requirement of the Juvenile Justice and Delinquency Prevention (JJDP) Act of 1974. Between 1992 and 1994, states participating in the Federal Formula Grants Program were required to determine whether disproportionate minority confinement exists, identify the causes, and develop and implement corrective strategies to reduce minority presence in the juvenile justice system (Haynes, 2012; Hsia, 1999). States failing to make progress or at least show a good-faith effort toward this endeavor risked losing one fourth of their formula grant funds for that year (now twenty percent) and having to direct the remaining amount toward achieving compliance. The JJDP Act was modified in 2002, changing the emphasis from "disproportionate minority confinement" to "disproportionate minority contact," requiring an examination of possible disproportionate representation of minority youth at all decision points in the juvenile justice system (Nellis, 2005). For all intents and purposes, this revision was a change in name only as the intent of the requirement from the start was a focus on decision-making at all stages in the system leading to confinement (Feyerherm, 1995). An underlying goal of the DMC mandate was and continues to be the equitable treatment of all youth within the juvenile justice system (Coalition for Juvenile Justice, 1993; Hsia, 2009).

The relative rate index or RRI, which is often used by states and localities to capture overrepresentation, is a practical indicator (easily calculated from data that are ordinarily available), yet nonetheless is crude and only provides descriptive accounts of DMC. Importantly, it cannot distinguish between overrepresentation that is attributable to differential offending by white and minority youth and which is due to disparities in the handling of racial groups by justice officials. Thus, RRIs are of limited value as a guide to juvenile justice planners and policy makers. Racial variations in offending demand solutions that are beyond those the juvenile justice system can provide; they call for efforts to alter the social and structural conditions that are the root causes of delinquency. However, inequalities in the handling of white and minority youth by justice officials may be ameliorated through strategic changes in juvenile justice policy, programming, and practice. Overall, twenty-five years after passage of the DMC mandate, views vary as to its effectiveness (e.g., Bell & Ridolfi, 2008; Davis & Sorensen, 2013; Donnelly, 2015; Jones, 2015; Kempf-Leonard, 2007; Leiber, 2002; Leiber, Bishop & Chamlin, 2011; Leiber & Rodriguez, 2011; Maggard, 2015; Nellis & Richardson, 2010; Piquero, 2008; Tracy, 2005).

Based on this historical context of the DMC mandate, the purpose of this study is to assess to what extent changes, if any, occurred in reducing racial disparities in juvenile justice processing in four juvenile court jurisdictions in the state of Iowa. While the research does not specifically examine the extent specific programs and strategies have been implemented in each of the four jurisdictions, we do examine the extent to which race and legal and extralegal criteria influenced intake decision-making at two different time periods, one before and another after the DMC mandate, to provide some indication as to whether greater parity in delinquency proceedings is evident. Insights from consensus and conflict models of social control are drawn upon to frame the study.

Theoretical Background

According to the consensus tradition, law, punishment, and treatment derive from a broad consensus of societal norms and values (Durkheim, 1964). State intervention into individual liberty and the incarceration of an individual results primarily from the occurrence, distribution and severity of criminal behavior. Due to the *parens patriae* foundation of the juvenile court, extralegal factors such as age (younger youth may be viewed differently than older youth), school (conduct problems or not attending) and the family (assessments about the ability of the youths' family to effectively supervise and socialize their child), also enter into decision-making outcomes (Rodriguez, Smith &

Zatz, 2009). Differences between whites and minorities in case processing and outcomes are attributed to differential involvement in crime (Tracy, 2005) and/or problematic school or family situations (Feld, 1999).

Derived from the conflict position of law and social control, the symbolic threat thesis is one example of a perspective that attempts to identify the contingencies of juvenile justice decision-making by focusing on the characteristics of youth, especially minorities, and the social psychological emotions of juvenile court officers (Tittle & Curran, 1988). These emotions include identification (or the lack of identification) with the youth and his/her behavior and subsequent feelings of fear and jealousy by the decision-maker. Emotions such as these are thought to manifest in beliefs that minority youth pose symbolic threats to middle-class standards and public safety.

Others have further refined the symbolic threat thesis with an emphasis on racial stereotyping and the perceptions of juvenile court personnel by focusing on the imagery of minority youth as "drug offenders" and "dangerous." Sampson and Laub (1993), for example, treated these perceptions as representative of symbolic threats to the middle-class and their standards and values. Bridges and colleagues examined the interplay between racial stereotypic images to causal attributions and concerns for the public and moral order of a community (Bridges, Conley, Engen & Price-Spratten, 1995; Bridges & Steen 1998; Graham & Lowery, 2004).

A common theme running through these theoretical revisions and empirical examinations is the identification of the variable effects of race on decision-making and the factors that foster these effects. Although the source of the contextual findings may vary, one emphasis is the racial stereotyping by decision-makers of African American youth. These stereotypes include African Americans as undisciplined, as living in dysfunctional families that are primarily headed by young mothers, and as sexually promiscuous, dangerous, delinquent, and prone to drug offenses (Feld, 1999; Leiber, 2003; Leiber & Mack, 2003; Sampson & Laub, 1993) or in need of more protection than whites (Bridges et al., 1995; Rodriguez, 2013). Thus, differences in case outcomes for whites and African Americans are due in part to racial stereotypes (Bishop, Leiber & Johnson, 2010; Pope & Feyerherm, 1993; Leiber & Johnson, 2008; Leiber, Brubaker & Fox, 2009; Rodriguez et al., 2009; Rodriguez, 2007).

Both consensus theory and the symbolic threat thesis with the emphasis on racial stereotyping serve as the backdrop for the present research and as a basis for evaluating the effect of race on intake decision-making in four juvenile courts at two different points in time. Next, a review of the literature is provided that covers the relative effects of race, and legal and extralegal factors on juvenile court outcomes.

Literature Review

While legal criteria have been reported to influence decision-making, race has been found to also have direct effects on juvenile court outcomes even after consideration of legal and extralegal factors (Bishop, 2005). Furthermore, race interaction effects or combination relationships with a number of legal and extralegal considerations have also been found (Bishop, 2005; Leiber et al., 2009; Peck, Leiber, Beaudry-Cyr & Toman, 2016; Rodriguez, 2013; Stevens & Morash, 2015). Research has shown race relationships with crime type in particular for person offenses, drug offenses, prior referrals, school problems, family structure, gender, and age (e.g., Bishop & Leiber, 2012; Cochran & Mears, 2015; Leiber & Johnson, 2008; Rodriguez et al., 2009). For example, traditionally, age has been seen not only as a legitimate extralegal criterion but a mitigating consideration by the juvenile court because of beliefs that younger offenders lack *mens rea* (or intent) due to immaturity, inexperience, and lack of education to evaluate the consequences of their conduct and to resist peer pressure (Mears et al., 2014; Steinberg & Scott, 2003).

There has also been the assumption that the younger the youth, the less culpable because of his/her malleability for rehabilitation (Roper v. Simmons, 2005). Accordingly, older youth are generally believed to be more responsible for their behavior and as a result handled more formally than younger youth (e.g., Champion, 2001; Leiber, Peck & Beaudry-Cyr, 2016). Leiber and Johnson (2008) discovered that this age relationship or "youth discount" extended to whites but not African Americans at intake proceedings. Younger white youths received more lenient intake outcomes while no such conditional effect was found to exist for African American youths. These findings involving race and age were interpreted as supporting the symbolic threat thesis and the emphasis on racial stereotyping of African American youth as threatening. Morrow and colleagues (2015) also examined the presence of the "youth discount" on court outcomes, and found that African American and Latino preteens were less likely than White pre-teens, mid-teens, and late-teens to receive diversion. Furthermore, African American mid-teens had a greater likelihood of being detained than their white counterparts.

Race and gender have also been found to act in combination to impact juvenile justice decision-making. Leiber and colleagues (2009) reported that as expected and consistent with prior research (e.g., Bishop & Frazier, 1996; Gaarder, Rodriguez & Zatz, 2004; Guevara, Herz & Spohn, 2006), relative to males, females were discovered to be the recipients of differential treatment as evidenced by the leniency given at detention, intake and petition. Gender and race were also found to impact these findings but not always as anticipated. The most significant findings are that white females did not receive differential treatment and African American females, for the most part, were not responded to as her male African American counterpart. Rather than being the recipients of more severe outcomes, as anticipated, African American females were discovered to receive lenient outcomes. Evidence for this leniency was found at intake and petition. African American males were found to receive more severe outcomes at detention and intake.

In regards to the DMC mandate, a review of the literature addressing race and juvenile court decision-making produced less than a handful of studies that compared the effects of race on case proceedings before and after the implementation of the federal legislation (Davis & Sorensen, 2013; Donnelly, 2015; Leiber et al., 2011; Maggard, 2015). In 2005, in a review of assessment studies that involved the examination of decision-making with data either before or after the implementation of the DMC mandate, Pope and Leiber discovered that despite variability in the research, most (n=32) studies reported evidence of race differences in juvenile justice outcomes not completely accounted for by differential involvement in crime (i.e., crime severity). In only twelve states, minority overrepresentation was the result of solely legal factors. These findings parallel those reported by four comprehensive reviews of the general literature on juvenile justice decision-making and demonstrate that legal and extralegal factors alone are unable to explain race differentials in involvement in the system (Bishop & Leiber, 2012; Engen, Steen & Bridges, 2002; Leiber, 2002; Pope & Feyerherm, 1993; Pope, Lovell & Hsia, 2002).

More recent, Leiber and colleagues (2011) examined the effectiveness of the DMC mandate in a single county in Iowa from 1980–2000 (approximately 10 years before and 10 years after the implementation of the mandate). Results indicated no substantial changes in race effects were found across both time periods; however unanticipated direct race findings emerged after the mandate at judicial disposition. While African American youth were more likely than whites to receive a referral at intake before and after the mandate, white youth were more likely to receive out-of-home placement instead of community sanctions compared to African Americans. Race also interacted with legal factors to produce varying degrees of social control. After the DMC mandate, race effects became more covert where African American youth from single parent families were treated more severe at intake, while prior to the mandate; race had a direct effect on intake decisions to the disadvantage of African Americans. White youth charged with property offenses were also more likely to receive an intake referral after the mandate compared to similarly situated African Americans. While this last finding may show a movement towards equality, the race of the youth should not be predictive of court outcomes. The finding that white youth received greater social control is more so evidence of overcorrection, not equality.

Davis and Sorensen (2013) investigated the extent to which the U.S. has been successful in the disproportionate sentencing of youth to residential placement since the implementation of the mandate (1997–2006). On average, results suggest a reduction of nearly twenty percent in the disproportionate African American/White ratio of incarcerations, controlling for each groups' rate of arrests. However, even after the mandate, African Americans are overrepresented relative to whites in placements and at every other stage in the process except for probation. As a group, African Americans are underrepresented in this category (Puzzanchera, Sladky & Kang 2015).

The results from Donnelly's (forthcoming) evaluation study of Pennsylvania's efforts to address DMC also show an optimistic pattern in the processing of youth (regardless of race/ethnicity) in the juvenile justice system. Using delinquency charges throughout the state from 1997–2011, results indicate a decrease within DMC intervention counties in the number of African American and Hispanic youth processed at adjudication, disposition to placement, and commitment to secure confinement. While the findings show a substantial decline in minority processing, more research is needed surrounding race differences in the treatment of youth who reach each stage and their subsequent outcomes.

Maggard (2015) assessed the effectiveness of the Juvenile Detention Alternatives Initiative (JDAI) in one Virginia court from 2002–2009. The main components of the JDAI is to decrease the use of secure detention, reduce racial disparities in juvenile justice processing that may stem from overuse of detention incidents and length of stays, and increase public safety. Findings from pre-JDAI and post-JDAI implementation suggest that greater emphasis was placed on legal factors in detention decisions post-JDAI. However, legal factors such as offense severity and prior record affected non-whites more than whites. For example, non-whites charged with felony offenses were nearly 18 times more likely to be detained, compared to similarly situated Whites (12 times). Therefore, while legal factors may influence detention decision-making post-JDAI implementation, race continues to interact or indirectly result in harsh outcomes through being charged with a serious offense and having a prior record.

In summary, the results from DMC evaluation studies, and overall research on juvenile justice processing lend support for consensus theory and the emphasis on the relative importance of legal factors in explaining race differentials in case proceedings (Tracy, 2005). Likewise, perspectives that emphasize the role of selection bias with racial stereotyping influencing decision-makers are also supported (Bishop et al., 2010). That is, of the studies conducted in response to the mandate using data either before or after 1989, results point to both legal criteria and race individually or interaction with other independent variables predictive of decision-making outcomes (e.g., Davis & Sorensen, 2013; Donnelly, forthcoming; Leiber & Rodriguez, 2011; Leiber et al., 2011; Maggard, 2015).

Study Sites

Iowa

Minority youths comprised 4.8 percent of the total population of Iowa, and up to 10 percent or more of some cities (Census Bureau, 1990). In the late 1980s and early 1990s, youth minority overrepresentation existed in Iowa's secure facilities (Moore & Kuker, 1993). Minority youth comprised 37 percent of juveniles held in jail/lockups, 32 percent in detention, and 28 percent of the admissions to the State Training School (Moore & Kuker, 1993). African Americans were the most overrepresented minority group in the system. For example, they accounted for 21 percent of the State Training School population (Moore & Kuker, 1993). Minority youth and especially African Americans also spent on average longer lengths of stay in both jail/lockup and detention than whites (Moore & Kuker, 1993). In 2000 and in 2008, minority youth were disproportionately arrested and once again in secure detention and secure correctional facilities and adult jails and lockups (Leiber & Fields, 2010). Overall, the extent of the disproportionate overrepresentation of minority youth parallels nationwide findings (Hartney & Vuong, 2009). Next, a brief overview of minority youth presence in each of the four jurisdictions to be studied—Black Hawk, Woodbury, Polk and Scott—is presented.

Jurisdictions

Population characteristics as well as the extent of minority overrepresentation in the juvenile justice system in each jurisdiction are discussed. For the purpose of this research, the discussion of minority overrepresentation will be for the year 2008. It is important to note that in the late 1980s and early 1990s minority youth overrepresentation was reported in all four jurisdictions (Moore & Kuker, 1993).

Polk has the largest population of the four counties (n=374,601), followed by Scott (n=158,668), Black Hawk (n=128,012) and Woodbury (n=103,877).

All four jurisdictions are predominately white or Caucasian. The largest minority presence is in Black Hawk (17%), followed by Scott (13.4%). African Americans comprise the largest percentage of minorities in all four jurisdictions.

Like paralleling state-wide trends, African American overrepresentation is evident in each of the four jurisdictions (National Resource Center for Family Centered Practice, 2009). In Black Hawk, relative to white youth, African American youth are disproportionately arrested (relative rate = 5.66), held in secure detention (relative rate = 1.40), and petitioned (relative rate = 1.58). In Woodbury, African Americans, Latinos and American Indians are overrepresented at arrest, court referral, and secure detention. Native Americans are also overrepresented in cases petitioned (relative rate = 1.49). In Polk, African Americans but not Hispanic or Asian youth are overrepresented in arrests (relative rate = 4.55). Both African Americans and Hispanics are overrepresented in secure detention and cases petitioned. Relative to white youth, African American youth are overrepresented in cases resulting in confinement in secure correctional facilities (relative rate = 1.89). Last, in Scott, African American youth are overrepresented at arrest (relative rate = 4.84), secure detention (relative rate = 2.34), and cases petitioned (relative rate = 1.42).

Implications for the Present Research

The DMC mandate has generated much discussion in terms of the attainment of greater equality in the treatment of all youth (Bell & Ridolfi, 2008; Kempf-Leonard, 2007; Leiber & Rodriguez, 2011). The most common indicator has been the reduction of minority representation in the juvenile justice system since the first enactment of the mandate in 1989 (e.g., Bell & Ridolfi, 2008). Recall that greater equality for minority youth is typically measured by the relative rate index involving comparisons of minorities to whites from arrest to secure confinement (Feyerherm, Snyder, H. & Villarruel, 2006). In addition to the relative rates, numerous studies have been conducted to assesses the extent race predicts decision-making. The goal of these assessment studies is to examine if any prior race effects disappear once legal and extralegal factors are considered (e.g., Bishop, 2005; Leiber, 2002; Leiber et al., 2011; Pope et al., 2002). If the race of the youth no longer predicts decision-making, differences in case outcomes can then be explained by differential offending and/or a need for intervention based on family and school problems.

A review of these studies has shown that differential offending as well direct and combination effects of race with extralegal considerations still predict decision-making. These results, along with those from the RRI's, suggest that the DMC mandate has failed to achieve the goal of equality for all youth (Bell & Ridolfi, 2008; Jones, 2015). A detailed discussion of the validity of such a conclusion is beyond the scope of this research. However, we believe further inquiry is needed that assesses the effectiveness of the DMC mandate to bring about equality for all youth. Recall less than a handful of studies have examined changes in race effects with case outcomes before and after the implementation of the mandate (e.g., Davis & Sorensen, 2013; Donnelly, forthcoming; Leiber et al., 2011; Maggard, 2015). The lack of research within this context serves as the impetus for the present research.

DMC strategies and interventions have been implemented in each of the four jurisdictions in the current study. Still, minority youth are overrepresented in all four jurisdictions. An important component for understanding DMC, however, can be derived from the examination of the determinants of decision-making and the extent these determinants impact case outcomes for minority youth compared to white youth before and after the DMC mandate. We attempt to do this by comparing the predictors, including race, of intake decision-making for two different time periods that represent pre- and post-implementation of the DMC mandate.

The Present Research

Data and Sampling

Data were collected at two different time frames and reflect different techniques. Time 1 data was collected from juvenile court case files for each of the four jurisdictions from 1980 to 1990. The second time frame used data gathered from Iowa's Justice Data Warehouse (JDW). JDW is a central repository of key criminal and juvenile justice information. Information for the warehouse is taken from the Iowa Court Information System (ICIS). ICIS is operated on 100 local data bases and is comprised of subsystems: juvenile court services, consolidated case processing, financial reporting, jury selection, appellate records management, scheduling, etc. Concerns with the validity of the information collected for JDW impacted the years examined for the jurisdictions included in the research. Earlier on, data was more complete in terms of the legal and extralegal information for Black Hawk and Scott than for Polk and Woodbury. Thus, delinquent cases were sampled for Black Hawk and Scott starting in 1998 to 2008. For Woodbury and Polk the sampling came from delinquent cases referred starting in 2004 to 2008. Data that has come from the state-wide computer system will represent Time 2.

Each of the jurisdictions differs in their racial composition and in the number of referrals. Different sampling techniques were used to create racial comparison groups in each jurisdiction and in each time frame. Random sampling was used for whites and minorities were over-sampled. All cases have been weighted to reflect the racial distribution of cases handled in each court. The sample size for Time 1 is 7,207 weighted cases while for Time 2, there are 12,553 weighted cases.

Variables

Table 1 presents the coding and distribution of the independent and dependent variables in this study. Selection and operationalization of the variables were based on theory and prior research (Bishop & Frazier, 1988; Rodriguez, 2007).

Race is defined as white, African American, Native American, and Hispanic. African American youth represent the largest minority group referred in both time frames in all four jurisdictions. Other social traits are gender (male vs. female), age (continuous), family status (two parent household vs. one parent household), and school status (attending, attending but problems, and drop out). Information on family status and school status is not reported in the state-wide system and therefore is not included as variables in Time 2.

Two measures of legal history are included. Prior record is measured in terms of the number of prior referrals each youth had with the juvenile justice system (continuous). The second measure (court authority) is an indicator of whether the individual was under formal court authority/supervision at the time of the current offense (the latter is not reported for Time 2, see above text).

Several measures of characteristics of the current offense are included in the analysis. The first is a simple count of the number of charges (continuous) included in the current referral. We assume that the greater the number of charges, the more serious the offense. Crime severity distinguishes between misdemeanors and felonies. We also capture a measure of offense type. Due to the theoretical importance of crime type in juvenile justice decision making (e.g., Sampson and Laub, 1993), dummy variables were created to differentiate between crimes against persons, property offenses, drug offenses, and offenses against public order (the reference category). In both time frames, most cases were classified as misdemeanors and most involved property crimes. The distribution for the samples in terms of offense type and severity comports with national aggregate juvenile arrest data (Snyder, 2005).

Intake decision making has three outcomes: release, diversion, and court referral. The intake stage will be the dependent variable. For the purpose of this

Table 1. Case-Level Characteristics, Codes, and Distributions by Jurisdiction and Time Period

	Code	Time 1 (N=7,207)								Time 2 (N=12,553)							
		BlackHawk		Woodbury		Polk		Scott		BlackHawk		Woodbury		Polk		Scott	
		N	%	N	%	N	%	N	%	N	%	N	%	N	%	N	%
Independent Variable																	
Social Traits																	
Race[a]	0=White	1818	90	1593	81	1476	82	996	70	1872	60	1397	53	2659	70	1378	46
	1=African American	202	10	98	5	322	18	427	30	1272	41	287	11	877	23	1612	54
	2=Native American			275	14							723	28				
	3=Hispanic											213	8	263	7		
Gender	0=Male	1644	81	1455	74	1405	78	1148	81	2139	68	1790	68	2614	69	2099	70
	1=Female	376	19	511	26	393	22	275	19	1005	32	830	32	1185	31	890	30
Age	Years Mean =	15.5		14.3		15.3		14.3		15.31		15.15		15.15		15.52	
Family status	0=Two parents present	1193	59	1211	62	871	49	774	54								
	1=One parent present	827	41	756	38	927	51	649	46								
School status[b]	0=Attend-no problems	1436	71	1439	74	1489	83	1083	76								
	1=Attend-problems	394	20	362	18	117	6	261	18								
	2=Not attending	190	9	166	8	192	11	78	6								
Legal																	
Prior referrals	Number Mean =	1.6		1.3		0.9		0.8		1.96		2.15		1.49		2.66	
Court authority	0=No	1543	76	1832	93	1633	91	1259	89								
	1=Yes	477	24	134	7	166	9	164	11								
Charges	Number Mean =	1.3		1.1		1.1		1.3		1.27		1.32		1.35		1.52	
Crime severity	0=Misdemeanor	1559	77	1690	86	1390	77	1006	71	2941	94	2379	91	3404	90	2490	83
	1=Felony	461	23	277	14	408	23	417	29	203	7	240	9	395	10	499	17

[a] When necessary, race will be treated as a dummy variable with white as the reference category.

[b] School status will be treated as a dummy variable with attending-no problems as the reference category.

(continued)

Table 1. Case-Level Characteristics, Codes, and Distributions by Jurisdiction and Time Period, *continued*

	Code	Time 1 (N=7,207)								Time 2 (N=12,553)							
		BlackHawk		Woodbury		Polk		Scott		BlackHawk		Woodbury		Polk		Scott	
		N	%	N	%	N	%	N	%	N	%	N	%	N	%	N	%
Crime type[c]	0=Other	442	22	454	23	355	20	279	20	1040	33	1009	39	1123	30	1011	34
	1=Property	1027	51	1100	56	966	54	813	57	1251	40	892	34	1500	40	1101	37
	2=Person	260	13	153	8	325	18	245	17	536	17	548	21	790	21	575	19
	3=Drugs	290	14	258	13	152	8	85	6	317	10	171	7	387	10	303	10
Dependent Variable																	
Intake	0=Release	241	12	364	19	949	53	186	13	1074	34	2620	70	1136	30	1253	43
	1=Diversion	1088	54	1360	69	571	32	823	58	1257	40	475	18	1641	43	665	22
	2=Court referral	691	34	242	12	278	15	414	29	813	26	308	12	1022	27	1072	35

[c] Crime type will be treated as a dummy variables with other as the reference category.

Note: Time 1 represents data for 1980–1990, Time 2 for Black Hawk and Scott data for 1998–2008, for Woodbury and Polk, data for 2004–2008. Family status, school status, and court authority not part of data for Time 1. Intake will be treated as release/diversion vs. court referral for the analyses.

research, intake is defined as release/diversion versus court referral. The most common outcome in all four jurisdictions and in both time frames is release/ diversion. Results from cross-tabulations reveal differences in the distributions among the variables by jurisdiction within and across each time frame. These results are available upon request.

Analytic Procedures

Multivariate analysis in the form of logistic regression was used to model decision-making at intake. To discover the individual and joint effects of race on decision-making once legal and extralegal factors were controlled, the analysis was performed in several steps. An equation was first estimated to examine the presence of statistically significant additive effects for the legal and extralegal factors including race on the dependent variable, followed by the estimation of race interaction effects with each independent variable and intake. If a race interaction effect was found to be statistically significant at p < .01, separate models for each racial group was then run and will be presented. If no such effect was found to exist, separate models for each race group will not be detailed as part of the results.

Results

Black Hawk

The logistic regression results for intake decision-making differentiated by Time 1 and Time 2 is presented in Table 2. In this jurisdiction, African American juveniles are more likely to receive a court referral at intake than similarly situated white juveniles and this relationship is not conditioned by time (compare column 1 and column 2). African Americans at intake in Time 1 had a 12 percent higher likelihood of receiving the more severe outcome while at Time 2 they are two times more likely. Estimations of race interaction relationships with each independent variable within each time frame failed to produce evidence of statistically significant effects with intake decision-making.

Gender is a statistically significant predictor of intake decision-making at Time 2 but not Time 1. In the period capturing decision-making in 1998 to 2008, females receive leniency relative to her male counterpart. Being older increases the odds of receiving an intake court referral at Time 1. At Time 2, age has an inverse relationship with the dependent variable. Not attending school is a positive determinant of intake decision-making at Time 1 but evidence of such an effect at Time 2 does not exist.

Table 2. Logistic Regression Results for Intake for Blackhawk, Differentiated by Time

Variable	Time 1 Full Model (1)	Time 2 Full Model (2)
Social characteristics		
Race	.50**	.71**
	(.19)	(.09)
Gender	.06	−.48**
	(.15)	(.10)
Age	.11**	−.04*
	(.04)	(.02)
Family status	.06	
	(.12)	
School		
Attending, but problems	.08	
	(.15)	
Not attending	.62**	
	(.20)	
Legal		
Number of prior referrals	.26**	.20**
	(.03)	(.02)
Court authority	1.37**	
	(.14)	
Number of current charges	.26**	.23**
	(.08)	(.05)
Crime severity	1.74**	1.30**
	(.15)	(.16)
Property	.20	−.02
	(.16)	(.11)
Person	.58**	.29*
	(.20)	(.13)
Drugs	.19	.35*
	(.20)	(.16)
−2 log likelihood	1876.85	3139.56
N	2020	3144

Note: Time 1 (1980–1990) Time 2 (1998–2008). Regression coefficients, standard error ( ). Bold indicates statistically significant. Family status, school status, and court authority not part of data for Time 2. Estimations of race interaction effects with each independent variable and the dependent variable failed to yield the presence of a statistically significant relationship at $p < .01$.

* $p < .05$. ** $p < .01$.

Of the legal variables, most explain intake decision-making at both time frames and are in the expected direction. That is, youth with greater prior referrals, those with a greater number of charges, youth charged with a felony, and juveniles involved in a person offense increase the likelihood of receiving a more severe intake outcome.

In summary, legal criteria and to some degree factors representing social traits explain intake decision-making in both Time 1 and Time 2. Unfortunately so too does race even after controlling for the legal and extralegal considerations. Thus, factors associated with differential offending and being an African American contributes to minority overrepresentation in the juvenile justice system. This relationship does not appear to be conditioned by Time.

Woodbury

An examination of the logistic regression results for intake in Woodbury shows race to have an impact on decision-making at both time frames (Table 3). In Time 1, whites with a greater number of prior referrals increased the chances of receiving a recommendation for further court proceedings by 16 percent relative to the other race groups (column 2). This joint relationship is made more evident by comparing the effects of prior referrals on intake for whites (column 3), African Americans (column 4), and Native Americans (column 5). As can be seen a positive statistically significant effect exists for whites but no such effect is present for African Americans or Native Americans. Race is also a predictor of intake decision-making at Time 2 (column 6). Being African American increases the odds of receiving the more severe outcome by 1.82; for Native Americans by 2.42. Hispanic is not a statistically significant determinant of the dependent variable.

In Time 1 and Time 2, gender has a statistically significant relationship with the dependent variable (column 1, column 6). Being male increases the likelihood of receiving the more severe intake outcome than being a female. Age is a determinant of intake decision-making in Time 1 but not Time 2 as is attending school with problems.

Legal criteria explain decision-making to some degree in both Time periods. The number of prior referrals is a predictor of the dependent variable at Time 2 while crime severity impacts decision-making at both time frames. Drug offending is also predictive but the effect is inverse at Time 1 and positive at Time 2. Interestingly for Time 1, the greater number of statistically significant effects on intake decision-making is evident for whites (column 3). For African Americans and Native Americans participating in a felony seems to be the central factor influencing the intake outcome (column 4, column 5).

Table 3. Logistic Regression Results for Intake for Woodbury Differentiated by Time

Variable	Full Model (1)	Interaction Model (2)	Time 1 White (3)	Black (4)	Native American (5)	Time 2 Full Model (6)
Social characteristics						
Race						
Black	−.02	−.32				.60**
	(.34)	(.35)				(.20)
Native American	−.44	−.29				.88**
	(.41)	(.40)				(.21)
Hispanic						.21
						(.16)
Gender	−.71**	−.67**	−.86**	.04	−.09	−.51**
	(.23)	(.23)	(.27)	(.94)	(.55)	(.16)
Age	.20**	.19**	.19**	.25	.16	.03
	(.04)	(.04)	(.05)	(.16)	(.10)	(.03)
Family status	−.08	−.15	−.12	−.06	−.09	
	(.17)	(.17)	(.19)	(.65)	(.50)	
School						
Attending, but problems	.81**	.83**	.81**	.73	1.08*	
	(.19)	(.19)	(.21)	(.78)	(.54)	
Not attending	.43	.39	.32	.83	.63	
	(.25)	(.25)	(.28)	(1.14)	(.75)	
Legal						
Number of prior referrals	.04	−.02	.15**	−.08	−.02	.16**
	(.02)	(.04)	(.04)	(.14)	(.04)	(.02)
Court authority	−.35	−.46	−.95**	.11	.47	
	(.28)	(.29)	(.38)	(.86)	(.59)	
Number of current charges	.29	.29	.49**	.27	−.17	.08
	(.17)	(.17)	(.19)	(.57)	(.47)	(.04)
Crime severity	2.05**	2.05**	2.12**	1.91**	1.81**	1.53**
	(.17)	(.17)	(.19)	(.75)	(.50)	(.17)
Property	.03	.01	.01	.05	.27	−.13
	(.21)	(.21)	(.23)	(.91)	(.68)	(. 16)
Person	.29	.21	.07	.34	.79	.26
	(.29)	(.29)	(.33)	(1.06)	(.85)	(.17)
Drugs	−.67*	−.74*	−.70*	−.52	−1.77	.64**
	(.34)	(.34)	(.37)	(1.86)	(1.49)	(.24)
White X prior referral		.16**				
		(.05)				
−2 log likelihood	1147.01	1136.56	927.25	66.75	129.88	1664.42
N	1966	1966	1594	98	276	2620

Note: Time 1 (1980–1990) Time 2 (2004–2008). Regression coefficients, standard error ( ). Bold indicates statistically significant. Hispanic youth were not part of data for Time 1. Family status, school status, and court authority not part of data for Time 2. Estimations of race interaction effects with each independent variable and the dependent variable at Time 2 failed to yield the presence of a statistically significant relationship at p < .01.

* p < .05. ** p < .01

In short, legal factors as well as some extralegal considerations explain intake decision-making in both time frames. Being white with a greater number of prior contacts with the system increased the chances of receiving a severe intake outcome in the period represented by the years 1980 through 1990 or Time 1. Likewise, African Americans and Native Americans are more likely than similarly situated whites and Hispanics to receive a court referral in the period represented by the years 2004 to 2008 or Time 2.

Polk

Table 4 provides the logistic regression results for intake decision-making in Polk. At Time 1, race has a positive statistically significant effect on the dependent variable. Being African American increases the chances of receiving a court referral by .07 times relative to being white once extralegal and legal factors are controlled. No such race effect exists at Time 2. In addition, there was no evidence of a statistically significant race interaction effects with intake decision-making in either Time frame.

In both time frames, legal considerations predict intake decision-making. In Time 1, age and evidence of school problems or not attending school are also predictors of the dependent variable. In Time 2, being male once again is found to increase the chances of receiving the more severe intake outcome than his female counterpart.

Overall, factors such as crime severity and involvement in person offenses explain decision-making at both time frames. While race was a determinant of intake outcomes in Time 1, this relationship no longer exists at Time 2.

Scott

While race does not directly affect intake decision-making in Scott in Time 1 (Table 5, column 1) there is a positive statistically significant interaction between race and family status with decisions to recommend further court proceedings once legal and extralegal factors are controlled (column 2). African American youth who live in single-parent household have a 16 percent increased likelihood of being subject to greater social control at intake than other youth. The interaction effect between race and family status is clearer when examining the results from separate models for each racial group (column 3, column 4). As can be seen, family status has effects for both racial groups, but the association is only statistically significant for African Americans ($p < .01$).

Of the remaining social characteristics, age has a positive effect on the likelihood of being referred for further court proceedings. Not attending school

Table 4. Logistic Regression Results for Intake for Polk Differentiated by Time

Variable	Time 1 Full Model (1)		Time 2 Full Model (2)
Social characteristics			
Race	**.44***	African American	.12
	(.20)		(.10)
		Hispanic	.20
			(.15)
Gender	−.24		**−.24***
	(.21)		(.09)
Age	**.12***		.02
	(.05)		(.02)
Family status	.04		
	(.15)		
School			
Attending, but problems	**1.66***		
	(.24)		
Not attending	**1.28***		
	(.20)		
Legal			
Number of prior referrals	**.11***		**.23***
	(.03)		(.02)
Court authority	**.84***		
	(.23)		
Number of current charges	.21		**.26***
	(.13)		(.04)
Crime severity	**1.92***		**1.47***
	(.16)		(.12)
Property	.24		**.20***
	(.25)		(.10)
Person	**.62***		**.45***
	(.28)		(.11)
Drugs	.20		**.51***
	(.36)		(.14)
−2 log likelihood	1183.06		3908.05
N	1798		3799

Note: Time 1 (1980–1990) Time 2 (2004–2008). Regression coefficients, standard error ( ). Bold indicates statistically significant. Hispanic youth were not part of the data for Time 1. Family status, school status, and court authority not part of data for Time 2. Race for Time 1 is differentiated by white vs. African American; for Time 2, white is reference group. Estimations of race interaction effects with each independent variable and the dependent variable failed to yield the presence of a statistically significant relationship at $p < .01$.

* $p < .05$. ** $p < .01$

Table 5. Logistic Regression Results for Intake for Scott Differentiated by Time

Variable	Full Model (1)	Time 1 Interaction Model (2)	White (3)	African American (4)	Time 2 Full Model (5)
Social characteristics					
Race	.01	−.44			**.87****
	(.17)	(.30)			(.10)
Gender	−.23	−.23	−.47	.16	**−.40****
	(.20)	(.20)	(.26)	(.33)	(.11)
Age	**.26****	**.27****	**.28****	**.26****	−.05
	(.04)	(.04)	(.05)	(.07)	(.23)
Family status	**.45****	.29	.30	**.95****	
	(.15)	(.17)	(.18)	(.31)	
School					
Attending, but problems	.05	.04	.15	−.28	
	(.18)	(.18)	(.21)	(.35)	
Not attending	**.62***	**.61***	.57	.78	
	(.29)	(.29)	(.35)	(.52)	
Legal					
Number of prior referrals	**.41****	**.41****	**.48****	**.29****	**.24****
	(.06)	(.06)	(.08)	(.09)	(.01)
Court authority	**.76****	**.76****	**.67****	**.91****	
	(.22)	(.22)	(.27)	(.38)	
Number of current charges	**.43****	**.42****	**.36****	**.85****	**.30****
	(.08)	(.08)	(.09)	(.23)	(.04)
Crime severity	**1.56****	**1.57****	**1.67****	**1.38****	**1.65****
	(.16)	(.16)	(.19)	(.29)	(.13)
Property	.16	.15	.10	.32	**.22****
	(.21)	(.21)	(.25)	(.43)	(.11)
Person	**.80****	**.80****	**.18****	**.88***	**.31****
	(.24)	(.24)	(.30)	(.45)	(.13)
Drugs	**1.34****	**1.31***	**1.33****	.99	.08
	(.31)	(.31)	(.33)	(.91)	(.16)
Race x family status		**.68***			
		(.36)			
−2 log likelihood	1253.73	1250.00	878.35	359.30	2957.75
N	1423	1423	995	427	2990

Note: Time 1 (1980–1990) Time 2 (1998–2008). Regression coefficients, standard error ( ). Bold indicates statistically significant. Family status, school status, and court authority not part of data for Time 2. Estimations of race interaction effects with each independent variable and the dependent variable at Time 2 failed to yield the presence of a statistically significant relationship at $p < .01$.

* $p < .05$. ** $p < .01$.

also increases the chances of greater social control at intake. Of the seven legal indicators, only property offending is insignificant. The other six have positive effects on the dependent variable.

At Time 2, race once again impacts decision-making but directly (column 5). African Americans are over two times more likely than similarly situated whites to receive the more severe intake outcome.

While the effect of age on intake decision-making at Time 1 is no longer present, gender is a statistically significant predictor. Being female decreases the chances of receiving a referral involving further court proceedings. Of the six legal variables, all but drugs are a determinant of the dependent variable.

Discussion

An objective of this research was to assess the extent changes, if any, occurred in reducing racial disparities in intake juvenile justice processing in four juvenile court jurisdictions in the state of Iowa. The backdrop for the study was the DMC mandate which was implemented in 1989 for the purpose of ensuring the equitable treatment of all youth within the juvenile justice system (Leiber & Rodriguez, 2011). We examined the extent to which race and legal and extralegal criteria influenced intake decision-making at two different time periods, one before (1980 to 1990) and another after the DMC mandate (1998 to 2008 for two jurisdictions and 2004 to 2008 for the other two jurisdictions) to provide some indication as to whether greater parity in delinquency proceedings occurred. The consensus perspective with an emphasis on the importance of legal criteria and to some extent extralegal factors, and interpretations of the conflict viewpoint with an emphasis on race stereotyping framed the present inquiry.

Overall, the results before and after the DMC mandate yield support for sentiments espoused by consensus theory that factors associated with differential offending (i.e., crime severity) and to varying degrees evidence of problematic behavior or circumstances (i.e., school problems) explain intake decision-making. The consensus perspective also explains some of the disproportionate overrepresentation of minority youth in each of the four jurisdictions justifiable. While this finding is a positive for ensuring equitable treatment of youth, there is little evidence that the overall effects of race on intake decision-making changed from the pre-DMC mandate period relative to the post-DMC mandate time frame.

During the 1980s, African Americans were more likely than whites to receive the more severe intake outcome in three of the four jurisdictions, even after consideration of legal and extralegal factors. With one exception, for the period representing the post-DMC mandate, race was found to still affect the treatment of youth. African American youth, and in one jurisdiction, Native American youth, were more likely than whites to receive a recommendation for further court proceedings. In one jurisdiction, race was reported to influence intake decision-making in the pre-period but no longer in the post-period. In total, these findings suggest that in three of these jurisdictions the equitable treatment of youth has not occurred and race continues to matter. Thus, both differential offending and selection bias seem to contribute to the overrepresentation of minority youth. This conclusion parallels those derived from prior research (Bishop et al., 2010; Engen et al., 2002; Huzinga, Thornberry, Knight & Lovegrove, 2007; Leiber et al., 2011; Peck et al., forthcoming; Pope & Leiber, 2005; Rodriguez, 2007; Tracy, 2005).

Although the DMC mandate focuses on race, the JJDP Act also attempts to address issues pertaining to gender and includes juvenile justice responses to female youth (Bishop & Frazier, 1992; Hsia, Bridges & McHale, 2004). While the DMC mandate is a part of the JJDP Act, other aspects of the act have focused on gender disparities in the juvenile justice system. The treatment of girls relative to boys has been typically addressed within the context of perspectives that focused on notions of chivalry and paternalism. Depending on the perspective, girls have been assumed to either receive more severe outcomes (the paternalistic position) or more lenient outcomes (the chivalry position) compared to boys (Bishop & Frazier, 1992, Leiber et al., 2009; Leiber & Peck, 2015; Mallicoat, 2007). In this research, disparate treatment appears to be given to females relative to males. In all four jurisdictions, females received a more lenient intake outcome than males even after taking into account legal and extralegal considerations and thus render support for the chivalry perspective.

The findings concerning the unequal treatment of youth over two time frames despite the DMC mandate and the JJDP Act raises at least two points for discussion. The first point of discussion centers on the explanations for the differences in the treatment of African Americans (severe) and females (leniency). The juvenile court consists of many stages that involve different decision-makers at each stage and different goals whereby the effects of racism and sexism may have more or less of an influence and/or play out differently at one stage compared to another (e.g., Bishop et al., 2010).

This explanation also provides a context for understanding the greater presence of race and gender effects on intake decision-making. At intake, there exists an array of actors (e.g., police, detention personnel, probation officers) who have goals that center on law enforcement, predictions of risk of dangerousness, and need of treatment. Decisions that are based on consideration of both treatment needs and predictions of dangerousness can be difficult to reconcile, and are also ripe for the interjection of racial and gender biases since these concerns tend to be ambiguous and broad in scope and easily lend themselves to stereotyping.

The possibility of biases influencing court outcomes is further enhanced because at intake an enormous amount of discretion exists whereas at other stages (i.e., petition and adjudication), legal criteria are more likely to guide decision making. Combine this issue with the reality that justice officials rarely have either the information or assessment tools on which to base reliable and valid predictions of a youth's dangerousness or amenability to treatment, decision-makers frequently utilize a "perceptual shorthand" grounded in stereotypes and attributions that are linked to offender characteristics (Steffensmeier, Ulmer & Kramer, 1998, p. 767). Examples of such scenarios are found in prior research where minority youth and in particular, young, African American males are seen as more dangerous and less suitable for treatment than other race/gender groups (Leiber & Johnson, 2008). Other instances find that girls are frequently typecast as more "needy" than boys (Gaarder et al., 2004). Although speculative, the results from the present study pertaining to intake suggest that African Americans are viewed as more of a threat to society than whites, and females are perceived as less dangerous than males.

The second point of discussion revolves around the policy implications concerning the effectiveness of the DMC mandate in bringing about greater equality for all youth in juvenile justice proceedings. The results would seem to lend further credence to those who have argued that the DMC mandate has failed to bring about change (Bell & Ridolfi, 2008; Tracy, 2005). On the one hand, Tracy (2005) has argued that the DMC mandate has not been effective because it is misguided and should focus on the prevention of delinquency among minority youth. On the other hand, Bell and Ridolfi (2008) contend that the DMC mandate has failed because there are not strong enough incentives or sanctions. A third position, which does not necessarily see the DMC mandate as a failed attempt, focuses on the broadening of the inquiry to include multiple facets. The causal factors associated with involvement in delinquency and increased social control along with the perpetuation of race stereotypes that further disadvantage minority youth relative to white youth should be examined simultaneously (Kempf-Leonard, 2007; Piquero, 2008).

We see value in this last position that it is imperative that *both* differential offending and system issues be part of the conversation on the implementation of the DMC mandate. However, we also believe the federal government and the Office of Juvenile Justice and Delinquency Prevention (OJJDP) in particular, should be given more recognition for at a minimum attempting to sensitize people to the issue of minority overrepresentation. Specifically, that certain laws legitimate legal and extralegal criteria relied upon by justice officials, and system procedures may disadvantage minority youth and the poor more so than their white and non-poor counterparts. While over twenty-five years have passed, we are still faced with DMC. Although there have been gaps in the implementation of the mandate, progress on this issue has also occurred in Iowa and nationwide (Chappell, Maggard & Higgins, 2013; Donnelly, forthcoming; Feyerherm, 2008; Leiber & Rodriguez, 2011; Maggard, 2015; Nellis & Richardson, 2010; Poulin, Orchowsky & Iwama, 2011). Efforts to bring about change with the DMC mandate as a case in point are slow, and as evident in the results presented in this study, results are complex and evolutionary. It should not be viewed as a zero sum situation but rather as an ongoing and interrelated process that hopefully will result in greater equality for all youth.

References

Bell, J. & Ridolfi, L. (2008). Adoration of the Question: Reflections on the Failure to Reduce Racial and Ethnic disparities in the Juvenile Justice System. San Francisco: The Haywood Burns Institute.

Bishop, D. & Frazier, C. (1988). The Influence of Race in Juvenile Justice Processing. Journal of Research in Crime and Delinquency, (25) 3:242–263.

Bishop, D. & Frazier, C. (1992). Gender bias in juvenile justice processing: Implications of the JJDP Act. Journal of Criminal Law and Criminology, 82, 1162–1186.

Bishop, D. & Frazier, C. (1996). Race Effects in Juvenile Justice Decision-Making: Findings of a Statewide Analysis. Journal of Criminal Law and Criminology, 86:392.

Bishop, D. (2005). The Role of Race and Ethnicity in Juvenile Justice Processing. Darnell Hawkins & Kimberly Kempf-Leonard (eds.) In Our Children, Their Children: Confronting Racial and Ethnic Differences in American Juvenile Justice (pp. 23–82). MacArthur Foundation Research Network on Adolescent Development and Juvenile Justice. The John T. and Catherine MacArthur Foundation. Chicago: The University of Chicago Press.

Bishop, D., Leiber, M. & Johnson, J. (2010). Contexts of Decision Making in the Juvenile Justice System: An Organizational Approach to Understanding Minority Overrepresentation. Journal of Youth Violence & Juvenile Justice, 8:213–233.

Bishop, D. & Leiber, M. (2012). Race, Ethnicity, and Juvenile Justice: Racial and Ethnic Differences in Delinquency and Justice System Responses in D. Bishop and B. Feld (eds.) Juvenile Justice (pp. 445–484). New York, NY: Oxford University Press.

Bridges, G. S. & Steen, S. (1998). Racial Disparities in Official Assessments of Juvenile Offenders: Attributional Stereotypes as Mediating Mechanisms. American Sociological Review, 63:4.

Bridges, G., Conley, D. Engen, R. & Price-Spratlen, T. (1995). Racial Disparities in the Confinement of Juveniles: Effects of Crime and Community Social Structure on Punishment. Minorities in Juvenile Justice, edited by K. Kempf-Leonard, C. Pope & W. Feyerherm. Thousand Oaks, CA. Sage.

Bureau of the Census. (1990). 1990 Census of Population: General Population Characteristics.

Champion, D. (2001). The Juvenile Justice System: Delinquency, Processing, and the Law. Upper Saddle River, NJ: Prentice-Hall, Inc.

Chappell, A., S. Maggard & J. Higgins. (2013). Exceptions to the Rule? Exploring the Use of Overrides in Detention Risk Assessment. 11(4): 332–348.

Coalition for Juvenile Justice. (1993). Pursuing The Promise: Equal Justice For All Juveniles. Washington, DC.

Cochran, J.C. & Mears, D. P. (2015). Race, Ethnic, and Gender Divides in Juvenile Court Sanctioning and Rehabilitative Intervention. Journal of Research in Crime and Delinquency, 52: 181–212.

Davis, J. & Sorensen, J. (2013). Disproportionate Minority Confinement of Juveniles: A National Examination of the Black-White Disparity in Placements, 1997–2006. Crime & Delinquency. Crime & Delinquency, 59(1): 115–139.

Donnelly, E.A. (forthcoming). The Disproportionate Minority Contact Mandate: An Examination of its Impacts on Juvenile Justice Processing Outcomes (1997–2011), Criminal Justice Policy Review, doi:10.1177/08874034 15585139.

Durkheim, E. 1964. The Division of Labor. The Free Press.

Engen, R., Steen, S. & Bridges, G. (2002). Racial Disparities in the Punishment of Youth: A Theoretical and Empirical Assessment of the Literature. Social Problems, 49(2):194–220.

Federal Register. (1991). Notice of FY 1991 Competitive Discretionary Grant Programs and Availability of the Office of Juvenile Justice and Delinquency Prevention Program Announcement Application Kit. Washington, DC: Office of Juvenile Justice and Delinquency Prevention.

Feld, B. (1999). Bad Kids Race and the Transformation of the Juvenile Court. New York: Oxford University Press.

Feyerherm, W. (1995). The DMC Initiative: The Convergence of Policy and Research Themes. In K. Kempf-Leonard, C. Pope & W. Feyerherm (Eds.), Minorities in Juvenile Justice (pp. 1–15). Thousand Oaks, CA: Sage.

Feyerherm, W. H., Snyder, H. & Villarruel, F. (2006). Identification and Monitoring. Disproportionate Minority Contact Technical Assistance Manual. 3rd ed. Rockville, MD: U.S. Dept of Justice. Office of Juvenile Justice and Delinquency Prevention.

Feyerherm, W. (2008). DMC and Multnomah County: A Play in Four Acts. Presented at the annual Justice Research and Statistics Association conference. Portland, Oregon.

Gaarder, E., Rodriguez, N. &. Zatz, M. (2004) Criers, Liars and Manipulators: Probation Officers' Views of Girls. Justice Quarterly 21(3):547–578.

Graham, S. & Lowery, B. (2004). Priming Unconscious Racial Stereotypes About Adolescent Offenders. Law & Human Behavior 28(5):483–504.

Guevara, L., Herz, D. & Spohn, C. (2006). Gender and Juvenile Justice Decision Making: What Role Does Race Play? Feminist Criminology, 1: 258–282.

Haynes, M. (2012) In Focus: Disproportionate Minority Contact. Office of Justice Programs. Washington, DC: Office of Juvenile Justice and Delinquency Prevention.

Hsia, H. (1999). OJJDP Formula Grants Program. Juvenile Justice Bulletin. Washington, DC: Office of Juvenile Justice and Delinquency Prevention.

Hsia, H., Bridges, G. & Mchale, R. (2004) Disproportionate Minority Confinement: 2002 Update. Washington, D.C. Department of Justice.

Hsia, H. (2009). Introduction. Disproportionate Minority Contact Technical Assistance Manual. 4th ed. Rockville, MD: U.S. Dept of Justice. Office of Juvenile Justice and Delinquency Prevention.

Huzinga, D., T. Thornberry, K. Knight & P. Lovegrove. (2007). Disproportionate Minority Contact in the Juvenile Justice System: A Study of Differential Minority Arrest/Referral to Court in Three Cities. Report. U.S. Department of Justice.

Jones, C. (2015). Is Disproportionate Minority Contact (DMC) Improving? An Exploratory Analysis of the Arrest, Confinement, and Transfer Stages in Rural and Urban Settings. Journal of Ethnicity in Criminal Justice. 1–18.

Juvenile Justice and Delinquency Prevention Act of 1974, as amended [Public Law 93-15], Section 23 [a][23].

Kempf-Leonard, K. (2007). Minority Youths and Juvenile Justice: Disproportionate Minority Contact After Nearly 20 Years of Reform Efforts. Youth Violence and Juvenile Justice, 5, 71.

Leiber, M. (2002). Disproportionate Minority Confinement (DMC) of Youth: An Analysis of State and Federal Efforts to Address the Issue. Crime & Delinquency, (48) 1, 3–45.

Leiber, M. (2003). The Contexts of Juvenile Justice Decision Making: When Race Matters. State University of New York Press. Albany: NY.

Leiber, M. & Mack, K. (2003). The Individual and Joint Effects of Race, Gender, and Family Status on Juvenile Justice Decision-Making. Journal of Research in Crime and Delinquency, 40(1):34–70.

Leiber, M. & Fox, K. (2005). Race and the Impact of Detention on Juvenile Justice Decision Making. Crime & Delinquency, 51(4):470–497.

Leiber, M. & Johnson, J. (2008). Being Young and Black: What Are Their Effects On Juvenile Justice Decision Making? Crime & Delinquency 54 (4):560–581.

Leiber, M., Brubaker, S.J. & Fox K. (2009). A Closer Look at the Individual and Joint Effects of Gender and Race on Juvenile Court Decision Making. Feminist Criminology. 4(4):333–358.

Leiber, M. & Fields, M. (2010) An Examination of the Factors that Influence Juvenile Justice Decision Making In Six Iowa Jurisdictions. Technical Report. Submitted to the Division of Criminal and Juvenile Justice Planning.

Leiber, M., Bishop, D. & Chamlin, M. (2011). Juvenile Justice Decision-Making Before and After the Implementation The Disproportionate Minority Contact (DMC) Mandate. Justice Quarterly, 28(3):460–492.

Leiber, M. & Rodriguez, N. (2011). The Implementation of the Disproportionate Minority Confinement/Contact (DMC) Mandate: A Failure or Success? Journal of Race and Justice, 1(1):103–124.

Leiber, M. & J.H. Peck (2015) Race, Gender, Crime Severity and Decision-Making in the Juvenile Justice System. Crime & Delinquency, 61(6): 771–797.

Leiber, M., Peck, J.H. & Beaudry-Cyr. (2016). The Likelihood of a "Youth Discount" in Juvenile Court Outcomes: The Influence of Offender Race, Gender, and Age. Journal of Race and Justice 6(1): 5–34.

Leonard, K. & Sontheimer, H. (1995). The Role of Race in Juvenile Justice in Pennsylvania. Pp. 98–127 in Leonard, K, Pope, C. & Feyerherm, W. eds., Minorities in Juvenile Justice. Thousand Oaks: Sage.

Mallicoat, S. (2007). Gendered Justice: Attributional Differences Between Males and Females in the Juvenile Courts. Feminist Criminology, 2:4–30.

Maggard, S.R. (2015). Assessing the Impact of the Juvenile Detention Alternatives Initiative (JDAI): Predictors of Secure Detention and Length of Stay Before and After JDAI. Justice Quarterly, 32(4): 571–597.

Mears, D. P., Cochran, J. C., Stults, B. J., Greenman, S. J., Bhati, A. S. & Green-wald, M. A. (2014). The 'True' Juvenile Offender: Age Effect and Juvenile Court Sanctioning. Criminology, 52: 169–194.

Moore, R. &. Kuker, D. (1993). A Description and Discussion of Minority Overrepresentation in Iowa's Juvenile Justice System. Paper prepared by the Division of Criminal and Juvenile Justice Planning, Des Moines, Iowa.

Morrow, W.J., Dario, L.M. & Rodriguez, N. (2015). Examining the Prevalence of a "Youth Discount" in the Juvenile Justice System. Journal of Crime and Justice, 34(4): 473–490.

Nellis, A. (2005). Seven Steps to Develop and Evaluate Strategies to Reduce Disproportionate Minority Contact (DMC). Juvenile Justice Evaluation Center., D.C.

Nellis, A. & Richardson, B. (2010). Getting Beyond Failure: Promising Approaches for Reducing DMC. Journal of Youth Violence & Juvenile Justice, 8:266–276.

Peck, J.H., Leiber, M., Beaudry-Cyr, M. & Toman, E.L. (2016). The Conditioning Effects of Race and Gender on the Juvenile Court Outcomes of Delinquent and "Neglected" Types of Offenders. Justice Quarterly, 33:1210–1236.

Piquero, A. (2008). Disproportionate Minority Contact. The Future of Children, 18(2):59–79.

Pope, C. & Feyerherm, W. (1993). Minorities and the Juvenile Justice System: Research Summary. Office of Juvenile Justice & Delinquency Prevention (OJJDP). Washington, D.C.

Pope, C., Lovell, R. & Hsia, H. (2002). Disproportionate Minority Confinement: A Review of the Research Literature from 1989 to 2002. Washington, DC: U.S. Department of Justice, Office of Juvenile Justice & Delinquency Prevention.

Pope, C. E., and Leiber, M. (2005). Disproportionate Minority Contact (DMC): The Federal Initiative. In D. Hawkins & K. Kempf-Leonard (Eds.), Our Children, Their Children: Confronting Racial and Ethnic Differences in American Juvenile Justice. Chicago: University of Chicago Press. Pgs. 351–389.

Poulin, M., S. Orchowsky & J. Iwama (2011). Assessing DMC Initiatives: A Case Study of Two States. N. Parsons-Pollard (ed.) Disproportionate Minority Contact: Current Issues and Policies. Durham, NC: Carolina Academic Press. Pgs. 97–121.

Puzzanchera, C.A. Sladky, and W. Kang. 2015. "Easy Access to Juvenile Populations: 1990–2014." Retrieved from http://www.ojjdp.gov/ojstatbb/ezapop/

Rodriguez, N. (2007). Juvenile Court Context and Detention Decisions: Reconsidering The Role of Race, Ethnicity, and Community Characteristics in Juvenile Court Processes. Justice Quarterly, 24, 629–656.

Rodriguez, N., Smith, H. &. Zatz, M. (2009). Youth Is Enmeshed in a Highly Dysfunctional Family System: Exploring the Relationship Among Dysfunctional Families, Parental Incarceration, and Juvenile Court Decision Making. Criminology. 47, 1:177–208.

Rodriguez, N. (2013). Concentrated Disadvantage and the Incarceration of Youth Examining How Context Affects Juvenile Justice. Journal of Research in Crime and Delinquency, 50(2): 189–215.

Roper v. Simmons. (2005).1125. W. 3d 397. Statute Cited.

Sampson, R. &. Laub, J. (1993). Structural Variations in Juvenile Court Processing: Inequality, the Underclass, and Social Control. Law & Society Review 27:285–311.

Snyder, H. (2005). Juvenile Arrests 2003. Juvenile Justice Bulletin. Washington, DC: OJJDP.

Steffensmeier, D., Ulmer, J. & Kramer, J. (1998). The Interaction of Race, Gender, and Age in Criminal Sentencing: The Punishment Cost of Being Young, Black, and Male. Criminology 36:763–797.

Steinberg, L. & Scott, E. (2003). Less Guilty by Reason of Adolescence: Developmental Immaturity, Diminished Responsibility and the Juvenile Death Penalty. American Psychologist 58:1009–1018.

Stevens, T. & Morash, M. (2015). Racial/Ethnic Disparities in boys' Probability of Arrest and Court Actions in 1980 and 2000: The Disproportionate Impact of "Getting Tough" on Crime. Journal of Youth Violence & Juvenile Justice, 13: 77–95.

Tittle, C. & Curran, D. (1988). Contingencies for Dispositional Disparities in Juvenile Justice. Social Forces, 67:23.

Tonry, M. (1995). Malign neglect: Race, crime and punishment in America. NY: Oxford University Press.

Tracy, P. (2005). Race, Ethnicity, and Juvenile Justice. In Our Children, Their Children. D. F. Hawkins, K. Kempf-Leonard, Edit. Chicago, IL; University of Chicago Press.

Chapter 5

Assessing DMC Initiatives: A Case Study of Two States

Mary Poulin Carlton, Stan Orchowsky, and Janice Iwama

Background

In 2007, the Justice Research and Statistics Association (JRSA) began a project funded by the Office of Juvenile Justice and Delinquency Prevention (OJJDP) to examine the strategies that have been implemented in Iowa and Virginia to reduce disproportionate minority contact (DMC) in the states' juvenile justice systems. We were especially interested in using these states as case studies of how states and localities are utilizing empirical information to: (1) identify the extent and nature of the DMC problem; and (2) assess the effectiveness of their efforts to reduce DMC. In each state, we sought to examine both state-level efforts, as well as ongoing efforts in two targeted localities, to address DMC. In Iowa, the two target localities were Johnson and Linn counties, and in Virginia they were the cities of Newport News and Norfolk.

We did not conduct an evaluation of efforts in these states, per se, but rather we used information and data available in each state to document the history and status of DMC efforts in Iowa and Virginia that have been implemented over the past several years, identify the issues faced in carrying out DMC efforts, identify if and how the states measured the results of these efforts, and, when possible, analyzed available data to illustrate how localities can examine the impacts of specific DMC interventions. This chapter offers a discussion about what we learned about implementation of the state and local efforts in these two states and offers recommendations to help OJJDP and the states enhance their ability to address DMC issues, collect data, and evaluate the results of their efforts.

Methods

There were two data collection steps. The first part involved documenting the DMC problem(s) in each state, the steps taken to assess DMC, and interventions implemented in the two states, how these interventions were carried out, and the outcomes of these efforts. The second part involved examining interventions in two localities to determine how existing data can be used to assess their effectiveness.

We assumed that the DMC activities and issues in these two states are typical of those facing states across the country. It should be noted, however, that Iowa and Virginia were selected in part because of their long-standing and ongoing efforts to address DMC, and not to be "representative," in the statistical sense, of all states in the country.

Moreover, we did not contact any other states to specifically determine to what extent the activities and issues in Iowa and Virginia have applicability to the rest of the country. However, based on our experience working in this area we believe that what we learned in Iowa and Virginia will have relevance to all states that are actively working to address this issue.

We began data collection for the project by conducting interviews with state and local stakeholders in both states. The purpose of the interviews, which were conducted from the fall of 2007 to the spring of 2008, was to obtain opinions on DMC issues in the state or locality in which efforts are focused and to gather information on DMC efforts not available in published reports. Interview respondents included state and local juvenile justice system staff, other state staff involved in justice issues, and representatives of community efforts focused on DMC. A snowball sampling technique was used to identify potential participants. Altogether, we interviewed 28 stakeholders.

Next we examined all available documents relating to DMC in both states, with a particular focus on those produced in the last five years. These included assessment studies, reports prepared by commissions and consultants, and the DMC components of the states' three-year plans for compliance with requirements of the federal Juvenile Justice and Delinquency Prevention Act (and annual updates). In addition, project staff attended meetings of local groups meeting to address DMC issues. In Virginia, we also participated in two statewide DMC conferences.

Finally, we requested and received data from the Iowa's Justice Data Warehouse, as well as data from one of the local court jurisdictions. These data were used to illustrate how localities can examine the impacts of specific DMC interventions. These two interventions we examined were the Court Community Liaison Program in Linn County and a Johnson County diversion effort.

Findings

Part One: Stakeholder Interviews and Document Review

Overall, we learned a fair amount about DMC efforts in Iowa and Virginia. We put together lists of past DMC studies, identified key stakeholders in the states, learned about the impetus for DMC efforts in the states, identified and conducted a review of identified problems and suggested causes of DMC in the two states, and tried to connect DMC activities to problems and suggested causes. We connected what we learned to the Relative Rate Index (RRI) data for the two states. Here we briefly summarize what we learned.

Iowa has well over a decade of history in identifying both statewide and county-specific DMC problems and causes and has implemented a wide range of DMC efforts designed to address the identified problems and causes. Available documentation regarding the implementation of these efforts varies, but, at a minimum, information on what, why, when, and where efforts were carried out is available. For some of the larger, longer-term efforts, more information is available, but little evaluation information exists to document the success of efforts. The statewide integrated database, the Justice Data Warehouse, has been enhanced substantially over the last few years to permit tracking of cases by race from the point of complaint (i.e., referral to the juvenile court) to disposition. These enhancements permit analyses of changes in rates of minority involvement in the juvenile justice system and could facilitate the evaluation of DMC efforts.

In Virginia, the history of efforts to address DMC began in earnest around 2001. However, studies conducted prior to this date indicated the presence of minority overrepresentation. A wide range of problems and causes have been identified, but not all of these studies have arrived at similar conclusions. Though problems and causes may vary across jurisdictions and points in the system, gaps in available system data to document the problem and studies that do not include system data likely contribute to disparate conclusions. Many of the efforts in Virginia have focused on the detention decision. Available documentation regarding the implementation of DMC efforts varies, but, at a minimum, information is generally available on what, why, when, and where efforts were carried out. Finally, little information is available to assess the success of efforts.

Though this process answered many questions for us about what DMC efforts these two states carried out and how it was documented, it raised many questions regarding why and how efforts, programs, and projects were carried out. We decided that we needed to have further conversations with key stakeholders in each state and conduct a more thorough review of documents. By doing so we could then place states' work in the larger context of guidance provided by OJJDP to address DMC because states use these components to organize both their formula grant applications to OJJDP and the DMC components of their three-year plans and updates. We also considered the DMC guidance provided by national organizations in our assessment. In order to facilitate understanding regarding what we learned, we organized our findings according to the phases of OJJDP's DMC reduction cycle; the phases that states are supposed to follow to address DMC (identification, assessment, intervention, and evaluation).

Identification

Examining the efforts undertaken to address DMC begins with a review of the identification of whether and where DMC exists in the system. The RRI index data required by OJJDP are supposed to help states identify questions to ask at the assessment stage; that is why DMC exists. Both Iowa and Virginia have completed RRI matrices for the past several years and provide information on RRIs for localities on their state web sites. These publicly available trend data are useful for understanding change over time. However, there are some areas of concern for both states regarding the available data and how the data are used. In Iowa use of the RRI for diversion provides only a rough indication of whether DMC exists because it includes only one type of diversion, Informal Adjustment Agreements. Virginia omits arrest data because of concerns about the quality of the information reported by localities. The absence of data at these stages puts these states at a disadvantage when trying to identify whether and why DMC exists. Neither state's DMC report provides any interpretation of the data presented. By "interpretation" we mean not simply a narrative that explains data shown in graphs (e.g., "the detention rate for African-American youth was double the rate for white youth"), but what the data mean for previous and future DMC activities. This latter information is missing from both states' reports. It is clear that states are putting considerable time and effort into generating and reporting RRI data. What is less clear is whether the states find these data useful for clarifying the extent and nature of the DMC problem.

Assessment

Assessment studies are used to help identify why an overrepresentation problem exists at a particular stage. There should be a clear relationship between what states learn at the identification stage and what they explore in assessment studies.

Iowa has conducted a number of assessment studies over the past 15 years or so, mostly in the form of multivariate statistical analyses of the relationship between race and decision-making. Studies have been conducted by both outside consultants and the state's Statistical Analysis Center.[1] These have included qualitative and quantitative studies and have focused on multiple counties across the state and multiple points of contact in the system. These generally involve complex statistical analyses (logistic regression, for example) designed to assess whether race affects decision-making at various stages of the juvenile justice system after other factors, such as seriousness of offense, are accounted for. The studies have included recommendations for interventions. Many of these recommendations have endorsed approaches that many states, such as Virginia, are already implementing, even without the benefit of carefully-conducted assessment studies. These recommendations include: reform detention admissions; use a risk assessment instrument; continue race (and gender) cultural sensitivity training; expand crime prevention programs; and conduct additional research on DMC. A related issue to consider for Iowa is whether the projects and programs match the recommendations made by external consultants. Although there are some connections between initiatives and recommendations, certain topics, such as cultural sensitivity training, research on DMC, intake and detention decision making, and prevention programs for youths, are repeated in reports published between 1993 and 2007. This suggests that, for whatever reason, these recommendations were not addressed, or only partially addressed, during this period.

Virginia has not, to date, conducted a formal assessment study, but there have been several reports that have discussed issues related to racial disparity in the juvenile justice system. In 2010 the state's Department of Criminal Justice Services (DCJS) issued a solicitation for an external consultant to conduct a state-wide DMC assessment study similar to those that Iowa has carried out. However, the solicitation seemed to lack several elements that would seem to be important if the state were to be able to connect the identification and assessment stages, and use the information from these efforts to plan interventions. These missing elements included: providing specific RRI data to be used to plan assessment activities; requiring that the assessment process be based on decision points that the identification process has targeted; and noting potential data sources or the problems with the state's arrest data that have caused DCJS, which reports the RRIs to OJJDP, to reject their use in calculating the RRIs.

---

1. Statistical Analysis Centers (SACs) are state agencies that collect, analyze, and disseminate justice data.

In summary, there seems to be a "disconnect" between the guidance in the DMC Manual, a publication provided by OJJDP to help states gain compliance with the DMC requirement of the Juvenile Justice and Delinquency Prevention Act, and what these two states are doing. We see little evidence that Iowa and Virginia are using RRI values to explicitly target localities and decision points for further examination in order to specify the mechanisms at work (although a case can be made that Iowa has in effect done this by virtue of its consistent focus over the years on a handful of localities and its funding of multiple assessment studies). We see no evidence, from Iowa's published reports or Virginia's assessment study solicitation, that "structural factors, such as urban versus rural settings, and the concentration of racial poverty and inequality" (Virginia Department of Criminal Justice Services, 2010, p. 2–17), have been used to select jurisdictions for study.

Intervention

Both Iowa and Virginia have carried out similar state-level activities over the past several years. These activities have included the following:

- Establishing web sites that include DMC information and RRI statistics;
- Funding an annual DMC conference and other training initiatives;
- Funding assessment studies or other DMC-related studies;
- Studying DMC and related issues through the establishment of statewide task forces, commissions, etc.;
- Providing funding for local initiatives/interventions;
- Implementing a statewide risk assessment instrument (VA; IA in progress); and
- Implementing legislative changes designed to address DMC-related issues.

Risk Assessment Instruments

Iowa began pilot-testing a risk assessment instrument in Johnson and Linn counties in 2007. The Iowa Delinquency Assessment (IDA) is based on the Washington State Juvenile Court Assessment instrument. The instrument measures dynamic and static recidivism risk and protective factors in 11 domains. A short-form, or "pre-screen" version of the instrument was implemented to more quickly assess a youth's level of risk early in the adjudication process. It appears that the IDA has been used for different purposes in different localities. In Johnson and Linn counties the IDA was used primarily to inform service delivery. There have also been reported difficulties with CJJP being able to extract the IDA data entered by localities. No formal assessment of the use of the IDA has been conducted to date. As part of the Juvenile Detention Alternatives (JDAI) process, the state has appointed a committee to develop a statewide detention assessment tool. How this tool will fit with the IDA is not clear at this point.

Virginia has a well-developed risk assessment instrument. In 2000, the Virginia General Assembly mandated the development and statewide use of a detention risk assessment instrument. The Department of Juvenile Justice implemented the Detention Assessment Instrument (DAI) in December of 2002. The DAI is an objective screening tool with seven weighted items used at intake to determine whether a juvenile should be released, placed in a detention alternative or placed in secure detention awaiting a court hearing. The seven items on the DAI include measures of the seriousness of the current alleged offense(s), number and nature of prior adjudications of guilt, number and nature of pending petitions, supervision status, and history of failure to appear or runaway/escape. DJJ conducted a study of the DAI's implementation in 2004 and a validation study in 2007 (Reiner et al., 2007). A recent study of the juvenile justice system by the Virginia State Crime Commission included a survey of juvenile court judges and Court Service Unit (CSU) directors found that 74% judges and 63% of CSU Directors rated the Detention Assessment Instrument as either "very" or "somewhat" effective in reducing DMC (Virginia State Crime Commission, 2008).[2] DJJ is currently working with Orbis Partners, Inc. to implement their Youth Assessment and Screening Instrument (YASI), which generates risk and assessment scores in 10 domains of functioning. The YASI will replace the Risk Assessment Form, an instrument used at intake to classify juveniles according to their relative risk of reoffending.

To summarize, both Iowa and Virginia are actively pursuing the development and improvement of structured decision-making tools, both for detention decisions and service delivery. Neither state has produced an assessment of how their use of such instruments has affected DMC.

Conferences and Training

In 2007, Iowa held a two-day cultural competency training for teachers and other school personnel and staff of community-based agencies who work with youth in the area. The training was organized by the DMC Resource Center in collaboration with several other local agencies, including the local DMC Committee. Since 2002, the DMC Resource Center has sponsored a statewide DMC conference that has involved workshops, nationally-recognized experts, and

---

2. The survey results are in the state's three-year plan.

breakout sessions on various topics. The Center's Web site includes conference programs and some of the presentations for all eight DMC conferences.

Since 2007, Virginia has held an annual one-day statewide DMC conference that has featured nationally recognized experts in keynote and breakout sessions. The conference is cosponsored by DCJS and coordinated and hosted by Virginia State University (VSU) in Petersburg, VA. No conference content, such as copies of agendas or presentations, is available on either the VSU or DCJS Web sites.

Local-Level Activities

There have been a number of county-level activities in Iowa. The Sixth Judicial District in Iowa, which includes Johnson and Linn counties, has carried out a number of DMC efforts in the past few years. Some of these efforts have been funded by the state and other efforts have included policy or practice changes developed and carried out by Juvenile Court Services (JCS) without any additional funding for development or implementation. These interventions include centralized intake processing, diversion of low risk offenders, and cultural competency training. Polk County has carried out efforts aimed at diverting youths out of the system and has worked with school and child welfare systems to address issues that affected DMC. A few counties have created their own DMC committees and held DMC conferences. Though funded by the state, several counties have offered direct interventions (e.g., after-school programs and substance abuse prevention) with youths in the community. Iowa has also recently begun working with the Casey Foundation's Juvenile Detention Alternatives Initiative (JDAI).

We could not locate documentation of specific local initiatives that have been implemented in Virginia. However, in Virginia, both the Annie E. Casey Foundation's Juvenile Detention Alternatives Initiative (JDAI) and the Burns Institute have been working with selected localities.

Juvenile Detention Alternatives Initiative

JDAI was initiated by the Casey Foundation in 1992 to reduce localities' reliance on secure detention without increasing the risk to public safety. JDAI promotes changes to policies, practices, and programs to reduce reliance on secure confinement, improve public safety, reduce racial disparities and bias, and stimulate overall juvenile justice reforms. According to a recent report, there are now 110 JDAI sites in 27 states and DC (Mendel, 2009). The Casey Foundation provides monetary support to JDAI sites for training, planning, and coordination as well as technical support, resource materials and tools, and opportunities to learn from other JDAI sites.

In Iowa, Black Hawk, Polk, and Woodbury Counties have been working with JDAI since the summer of 2008. Casey made site visits and provided two training sessions in 2008, and an additional training session on risk assessment in 2009. Committees have been established, and work is underway to develop JDAI plans and a detention risk assessment screening instrument.

JDAI was initiated in seven localities in Virginia in 2003 (Bedford, Hampton, Hopewell, Lynchburg, Newport News, Petersburg, and Richmond). Norfolk was added as a JDAI site in October 2005. In Newport News and Norfolk, JDAI provided funding for a coordinator position to organize committees of key players to look at ways of improving detention policies and practices. In Norfolk, the coordinator and committee have worked to collect admissions data and publish monthly newsletters with admissions data, news, and updates. They have also amended the violation of probation policy, reduced the number of truants referred to detention, developed a parental notification process to decrease the number of failure-to-appear violations, and increased community awareness through a town hall meeting held in the fall of 2009. Representatives from Norfolk presented data on their JDAI accomplishments at a national JDAI conference in the summer of 2009. The presentation cites reductions in: the average daily detention population; the number of pre-dispositional admissions to detention; the length of stay in detention; the number of days the detention center was over capacity; the number of failure to appear and probation violations; and the number of truants in detention. The presentation also notes a number of additional accomplishments, including the elimination of video arraignments, the development of guiding principles for the use of detention, hiring a Detention Expeditor and strict adherence to a Detention Assessment Instrument.[3] In Newport News, DMC work began in earnest soon after the creation of a DMC sub-committee under the JDAI collaborative. In their first year, the DMC sub-committee conducted a review of system and community factors that might result in DMC and issued recommendations to the collaborative for reducing DMC in the juvenile justice system. However, once three-year funding from Casey for the JDAI coordinator position ended, progress stalled. The DMC committee has not met regularly for two years, and little progress appears to have been made since 2007.

---

3. *The Norfolk (VA) JDAI Story.* PowerPoint presentation provided to JRSA August 18, 2009.

Burns Institute

The Burns Institute works with key agency and community stakeholders in a "data-driven, consensus-based approach to change policies, procedures and practices that result in the detention of low-offending youth of color and poor youth" (Burns Institute, 2009). The key elements of the Institute's approach to working with local jurisdictions include: a jurisdictional assessment; formation of a local "governing collaborative"; securing a local coordinator; establishing consistent meetings; developing a work plan; data collection and decision point analysis; collecting the appropriate data; analyzing and interpreting the data; establishing an institutional response; defining success and purpose of detention; objective decision-making; examining case processing issues; and creating alternatives to detention (Bell, Ridolfi, Finley & Lacey, 2009). According to its Web site, the Burns Institute "has worked in more than 40 jurisdictions nationally and achieved significant results in reducing racial and ethnic disparities" (www.burnsinstitute.org/article.php?id=56).

The Burns Institute began its work in Virginia in 2006, when several localities received funding from DCJS to work with the Institute. Readiness Assessment Consultation (RAC) reports, jurisdictional assessments providing recommendations for how to proceed with addressing DMC, were prepared for Norfolk and Newport News in December 2006 and January 2007, respectively (Finley, Lacey & Garry, 2006, 2007). Of the 32 recommendations in the Norfolk RAC and the 24 in the Newport News RAC, 23 are the same for both jurisdictions.

In July 2007, DCJS contracted with the Burns Institute to continue its work with Newport News and Norfolk. In Norfolk, Institute representatives have attended monthly meetings of the DMC Committee, analyzed data obtained by the DMC committee, and provided guidance to the committee in dealing with the DMC issue in general and implementing the RAC report recommendations in particular.

A similar process was instituted in Newport News, but it appears that it had not gotten far when the DMC committee stopped meeting regularly. Our interviews with key stakeholders in Virginia revealed positive assessments of the Institute's efforts in Newport News, in that they helped provide a framework for discussing the city's DMC problem. DCJS has terminated Newport News' grant with the Institute.

According to key stakeholders, the Burns Institute submits quarterly reports to DCJS directly without review or feedback from Norfolk. There is no evidence that any evaluation or assessment of the Institute's work is being conducted, nor has Norfolk's DMC committee been asked formally by the state to provide feedback regarding the Institute's work. Except for the RAC report they received in 2006, the DMC committee has not received any other documents from the Institute and is not expecting any in the future. Stakeholders we interviewed felt that the Institute has been helpful in providing the Norfolk DMC committee with guidance in its DMC work, and appreciated the Institute's support in participating in its 2009 town hall meeting on DMC.

Evaluation

Neither Iowa nor Virginia has any information about evaluation activities in their three-year plans. The Iowa plan suggests that a process is being developed for collecting data from detention centers and from the use of the assessment instrument, and that the analysis of those data will serve as a component of the evaluation of the state's DMC efforts. The Virginia plan provides no discussion of evaluation.

As noted previously, several localities in Iowa and Virginia are working with the Casey Foundation on their JDAI initiative, and Newport News and Norfolk in Virginia have also worked with the Burns Institute. While both of these initiatives have won praise from many quarters, there is very little information available on the effectiveness of either, and most of what is available comes from the organizations themselves.

In the JDAI summary report released in 2009, the Casey Foundation claims that JDAI has resulted in: smaller detention populations; improved public safety; cost savings; reductions in the number of minority youth in detention in a number of sites; improved conditions of confinement; and stimulating broader changes in juvenile justice systems (Mendel, 2009). Regarding DMC specifically, the report states that "[w]hile JDAI sites have not collectively reduced the overall disproportionality of their detention populations, many sites have substantially reduced the number of minority youth in detention" and that "[i]n a handful of sites, JDAI leaders have substantially reduced disparities in the detention rates of white youth and youth of color" (Mendel, 2009, p. 22). In support of the first claim, the report notes that 61 JDAI sites reported detaining 873 fewer minority youth (an average of just over 14 youths per site) in 2007 than they did prior to their becoming JDAI sites. In a separate report citing the effectiveness of detention reform in reducing DMC, the Casey Foundation notes that three model JDAI sites have reduced disproportionate minority contact by a) lowering the proportion of youth of color in secure detention; b) evening the odds that young people of color are detained following arrest; and c) reducing the number of youth of color in detention (Annie E. Casey Foundation, 2009) and provides statistics to support these claims.

On the Burns Institute's web site, the Institute provides statistics regarding reductions in the use of secure detention with four localities. The Institute has not issued an evaluation report or data on the results of its efforts. According to its 2009 Annual Report, the Institute has "continued to work in jurisdictions across the country and have achieved results that demonstrate that our approach works. We recently shared those results with more than 18 jurisdictions in our first Racial and Ethnic Disparities Training Institute" (W. Haywood Burns Institute, 2009). No information on the Training Institute is available on the Burns Institute web site.

Part Two: Assessment of Local DMC Interventions

Again, of the interventions that we learned about in both states, there was little information documenting the success of the intervention. In some cases, written, public information on the logic and design of the intervention was also limited. This was particularly the case with local interventions that were not funded by the state as DMC initiatives. We sought data on interventions that we thought could be easily assessed using available system data. It was not our goal to conduct a comprehensive assessment of these programs; rather, we provide this information to illustrate the type of analysis that we would like to see localities, with assistance from states and OJJDP, undertake to assess their DMC initiatives. We also offer descriptions of "ideal" assessments of the two initiatives; that is, how we believe that the initiatives should have been evaluated under ideal circumstances. These ideal assessments would have taken far more resources and more advanced planning than was possible. However, we offer the ideal assessments as models that jurisdictions should strive toward when attempting to determine the success of DMC efforts that are similar to those assessed here. We do not have the space here to provide a full accounting of what we did to assess these efforts and the conclusions that we drew from this process. This discussion is available in the final report from the project entitled, "A Review of the Status of Disproportionate Minority Contact (DMC) Efforts in Iowa and Virginia." Here we provide an overview of the analysis, discuss challenges encountered when conducting the analyses, and describe the ideal assessments.

We found examples of local initiatives that we could reasonably assess in Iowa's Sixth Judicial District. One of these is the Court Community Liaison initiative, designed to increase the number of informal adjustment agreements and decrease the number of petitions filed for African-American youth. We obtained de-identified data from the Justice Data Warehouse and attempted to assess the impacts of this intervention and another in Johnson County designed to assess an effort to divert low-risk minority youths.

Linn County: Community Liaison Diversion Program

Overview of Program

The Juvenile Court Services (JCS) office serving Linn County reports that a greater number of African-American youths with low-level charges reject offers for Informal Adjustment Agreements (IAA) when compared to Caucasian youths. An IAA is essentially a contract requiring the juvenile admit to the charges on the complaint and requires the juvenile to abide by certain conditions of behavior in exchange for not being formally processed by the court. If the juvenile does not follow the conditions, they will receive a petition and be formally processed by the court. In response to this problem of African-American youths being more likely than Caucasian youths to reject IAA offers, in September 2007 Linn County hired a Community Liaison. Following referral from a juvenile court officer, the Community Liaison conducts a one-time visit to the homes of African-American youths who are offered an IAA prior to a determination by the court of whether to hold a youth in secure detention. At the home visit the Court Community Liaison, who is African-American, attempts to convince the youth and family to accept the IAA rather than being processed formally by the court; explains diversion; and offers informal and voluntary referrals for services (e.g., mental health services, mentoring) outside of the juvenile justice system. A Community Liaison was selected as the solution to this problem because court staff believed that parents of African-American youths did not trust the juvenile justice system and therefore were more likely to deny charges (i.e., reject the IAA offer) or not show up for intake processing. Youths are eligible for an IAA and, consequently, a visit by the Community Liaison if they: are African-American; have low level charge(s); do not have active case with JCS; do not have any possession of alcohol charges; and do not have any first time shoplifting charges.

Ideal Evaluation Approach

Ideally, an assessment of the program would use an evaluation approach that would allow us to say, with little doubt, whether the hiring of the community liaison helped increase the number of African-American youths who accept IAAs or holds for further review at intake. Such an assessment would have begun prior to the hiring of the community liaison and started with demonstrating the nature and extent of the problem of African-American youths being more likely than white youths to reject offers for IAAs exists.

To document the problem we would have started with a review of recent Relative Rate Indices (RRIs) data to see whether there is evidence that African-American youths are less likely to be diverted than white youths in Linn County. The RRI provides a preliminary indication of the existence of DMC; it does not provide information to indicate why DMC exists at a particular stage (e.g., differential offending patterns, bias). In Iowa, use of the RRI for diversion provides only a rough indication of whether DMC exists because it includes only one type of diversion, Informal Adjustment Agreements. For diversion, if the RRI is less than 1.0, there is evidence of DMC (underrepresentation) at that decision point. Using RRI data, during at least a few years prior to the implementation of the IDA, fewer African-American youths were diverted or released from the system than white youths and that the race of the youth, rather than selected legal and extralegal factors, is a significant predictor of this decision.

Having established that a problem does exist at diversion, the next step in the ideal assessment would be to look at racial differences in acceptance of the IAA offer, tracking why the youth and family accepted or rejected the offer. Some of the required data for such an analysis would have required additional data collection.

Following empirical verification of the problem and hiring of the community liaison, the assessment would continue with the data collection begun at the problem identification stage in order to help monitor program implementation as well as outcomes. One major difference between the analysis at the problem identification stage (when the RRI data were used) and the analysis at this stage is that program implementation and outcomes analysis would include case-level tracking. Acceptance of the IAA (or having a case held open) would be used as an outcome measure, while tracking offers for IAA would be a process measure. Program completion status would also be tracked as a process measure in order to determine which youths who were referred to the program subsequently received the home visit by the community liaison and showed up for the intake interview. Tracking program completion status is important because it is expected to impact whether the youth accepts the IAA.

An ideal evaluation design for this intervention would involve all African-American youths eligible for IAAs being randomly assigned to participate in the community liaison program or receive standard court processing. This experimental design would be an excellent approach to explain the impact, if any, on reducing minority overrepresentation by hiring a community liaison. If this experimental design was not feasible we would opt for a time series analysis, tracking the data collected at the problem identification stage for several months preceding the hiring of the community liaison and several months following the hiring of the community liaison. The time series approach, while not as rigorous as the experimental design, would still provide strong empirical evidence regarding the success or lack of success of the intervention.

Actual Program Assessment

The analysis we actually did conduct is not as compelling as the more ideal approach outlined above. Examining available data after the fact limited our ability to draw conclusions regarding the intervention. In order to assess whether the visits by the community liaison had the desired effect, official Juvenile Court Services (JCS) complaint and case event data were used as well as other JCS data collected for the purposes of implementing the program.

To determine whether there was any change in intake decisions following the hiring of the Community Liaison, we examined intake decisions occurring for unique complaints for youths with eligible charges who did not have an open JCS case over an 11-month period preceding the hiring of the community liaison and compared these to decisions made over a comparable time period following the hiring of the Community Liaison.[4]

Court data include only the actual intake decision made; they do not include data on offers, such as an IAA, that may have been made and subsequently refused. Court data do not specify certain types of charges that would exclude youths from being eligible for the program (e.g. shoplifting) making it difficult to identify these charges.[5] Further, JCS does not have a formal definition of a low level charge, which can be used to assess eligibility for the program. Therefore we examined the charge classes of youths who were referred to the program and defined low-level charges based on the charges of youths who were referred to the program. Though only African-American youths are eligible for the Community Liaison visit, we examined both African-American and Caucasian youths over the same two periods of time before and after the hiring of the Community Liaison to see if any changes in intake decisions experienced by African-American youths were experienced by Caucasian youths.

Analyses and Conclusion

Based on this analysis, we concluded that this program appears to hold promise when youths who were served by the program are examined, but it is important to study if and why apparently eligible youths are not referred to

---

4. We chose to begin with complaints preceding the hiring of the Community Liaison because of the lag in processing time from a complaint to the intake decision. Youths with complaint dates in August 2008 received visits by the Community Liaison.

5. There are 19 African-American and 69 Caucasian youth cases included the analyses which may have included a charge for a first time shoplifting offense.

the program. We also recommend carrying out a more complex analysis that includes a longer pre- and post-program time period to permit a larger number of cases, includes offers for IAAs, and excludes all youths with shoplifting charges. This will help determine whether the findings reported here are artifacts of the limited data available for analyses. When one examines all apparently eligible youths, the data appear to suggest that the program was not successful. After all, even though there was a decrease in the proportion of program-eligible African-American youths who proceeded further into the system by being petitioned, there was also a decrease in the proportion of program-eligible African-American youths who received IAAs or had their cases held open. Further, at the same time that there was a decrease in program-eligible African-American youths who proceeded further in the system by being petitioned, there was also a decrease in eligible white youths who proceeded further into the system by being petitioned, and there was an increase in the proportion of eligible Caucasian youths who received IAAs or had their cases held open. Consequently, it is hard to say whether these changes in intake decision making were due to the Court Community Liaison or some other factor. There were also many cases in which apparently eligible African-American youths were not referred to the program (66%). Though, of those cases of eligible African-American youths who entered and completed the program, 68% did receive the desired intake decision (i.e., received an IAA or had their case held open). Clear definition of the term "low level" charges would help address questions about eligibility for the program.[6] Further, it is possible that an unintended, yet desirable, consequence of the Community Liaison program is an increase in the proportion of cases diverted or dismissed. It is important to carry out a study that considers whether this has occurred as well as consider whether the change is due to an effort which began just two months following the start of the Community Liaison program to divert low risk youths from the system.

Johnson County Diversion Program

Overview of Program

According to the JCS office serving Johnson County, minority youths charged with low risk offenses are more likely than Caucasian youths charged with low risk offenses to be formally processed in court and, consequently, receive technical violations that result in a return to the justice system for more

---

6. JCS reports that this issue has been addressed and that they now use a risk assessment instrument to aid screening.

supervision. Prior to November of 2007, assessments of youths' risk of reoffending and needs were based on an interview with a Juvenile Court Officer (JCO). Though the assessment topics themselves were semi-structured (they addressed family, school, substance abuse, mental health, and court charges), the decision to petition a youth was based on a JCO's gut feeling, an informal assessment of needs, and the seriousness of the charge. Youths with a "serious" charge or "high" needs, terms without formal definitions, were reportedly more likely to get petitioned or an IAA with multiple conditions.

In November 2007 Johnson County began an effort to divert low risk youths from the system by basing diversion decisions on the score received on a risk (to reoffend) and needs assessment tool. The risk and needs assessment tool, the Iowa Delinquency Assessment (IDA), was implemented in Johnson County in January 2007. Every youth who receives a face-to-face intake receives the short version of the IDA and the score received on this tool is used to make the diversion decision. The short version of the IDA contains questions pertaining to criminal and social history. Youths whose cases proceed to court following the intake decision work with a JCO to complete the long version of the form. Some youths, such as first time offenders with certain charges and those with an active case in the juvenile justice system, are not eligible for face-to-face intakes. Eligible youths will receive a face-to-face intake and complete the IDA short form. If the IDA risk score is low, the youth is unlikely to be petitioned unless they have been charged with a sex offense or an OWI (operating while intoxicated). As of November 2007, youths who are classified as low risk, unless they are charged with a sex offense or OWI, are supposed to be diverted by having their case "held for further review." They should not receive a formal IAA and when the case is held for further review they are not under court supervision.

Ideal Evaluation Approach

Here again, an ideal assessment of the effort to divert low risk youths would have used an evaluation design that would have permitted us to report on, with little doubt, the impact of the use of the IDA on diversion decisions. We would have begun with documenting the problem prior to use of the IDA. This would have included:

- reviewing recent RRI data to see whether there is evidence that African-American youths are less likely than white youths to be diverted in Johnson County;
- reviewing Leiber et al.'s 2006 study to see if, when compared to white youths and after controlling for legal and extralegal factors (prior court

history, current offense information, age, and gender), African-American youths are less likely to be diverted;

- documenting how JCOs define "low risk" and "high needs" to determine whether variation in definitions of these terms is a contributor to the problem;
- creating RRI data split by risk level and race to see whether there is evidence that low risk African-American youths are less likely to be diverted (whether for IAA, having their case held open, or some other diversion type) than low risk white youths.

To document the problem, we would have begun with a review of recent RRIs, to see whether there is evidence that African-American youths are less likely to be diverted than white youths in Johnson County. Of the four years of RRI data preceding the intervention only in one year, 2006, does it appear that African-American youths were less likely than white youths to be diverted from the system (again, considering only IAAs and not other types of diversion). However, it is possible that neither of these DMC identification or assessment tactics would have been able to recognize the perceived problem if it relates only to low-risk African-American youths. If the problem only affects this sub-group of youth, it is possible that it would not be identified as a significant problem at diversion for African-American youths. Further, not all diversion types were included in the RRI calculation for diversion. Consequently, a more precise and inclusive approach is needed to identify if the hypothesized problem actually exists. This approach, as noted above, would involve documenting how JCOs define "low risk" and "high needs," and creating RRI data split by risk level and race to see whether there is evidence that low risk African-American youths are less likely to be diverted. Data collection and analysis for these two steps, if it was carried out prior to the implementation of the IDA, might have helped to clarify the nature of the DMC problem as it relates to diversion in this locality.

Following the documentation of the problem and implementation of the IDA, the assessment would have continued with the data collection begun at the problem identification stage in order to help monitor program implementation as well as outcomes. Again, case-level tracking would be required, both to monitor use of the IDA (that is, program implementation) and to measure outcomes (that is, the diversion of eligible low risk youths). Further, we would have examined the impact of technical violations as described in the assessment we actually carried out.

Data collection for this assessment would have begun several months preceding the implementation of the IDA and continued for several months following implementation. We would have carried out a time series analysis to look at the impact of the use of the IDA. Analyses would have addressed issues regarding use of the IDA that we discuss in the actual assessment of this effort. We would also want to examine whether any other program, policy, or practice changes (e.g., new diversion program) were implemented during the time of the analysis of this effort that may explain whether or not a youth was diverted from the system.

Actual Program Assessment

Official Juvenile Court Services (JCS) complaint and case event data, as well as short-form IDA scores obtained from JCS, were used to assess whether 1) youths with unique complaints from January 1 to June 30, 2008 who were classified as low risk were actually diverted by having their case held for further review at intake rather than being formally processed by the court; and 2) whether there were any differences in diversion decisions for complaints for low risk youths by race.[7]

Analyses and Conclusions

Regardless of race or charge (that is, regardless of charge eligibility for the program), the most common intake decisions for complaints for low risk youths was an IAA followed by the filing of, or a request for, a petition. Eligible African-American youths were twice as likely as Caucasian youths to have their cases held open, but eligible African-American youths were also more likely to have a petition requested or filed than Caucasian youths. IAA remained the most common intake decision when only cases eligible for diversion via having the case held open are examined, and eligible Caucasian youths remained more likely to receive an IAA than eligible African-American youths.

Using available data, it is difficult to explain why more eligible low risk youths, regardless of race, did not have the desired intake decision of "hold for further review." Further, it is unknown whether there has in fact been an increase in the proportion of low risk youths, particularly low risk minority youths, who had their cases held open for further review following the implementation of the diversion effort. Finally, we do not know why less than half of the cases we identified as eligible for the IDA actually received an IDA assessment.

Given some of the challenges in the available data we do not know the extent of the minority overrepresentation problem prior to the implementation of this

---

7. In this analysis, a case is represented by a unique complaint. Youths with multiple complaints were counted each time they presented with a unique complaint. A youth with multiple charges, but one complaint was counted only once.

diversion effort. Eligible low risk African-American youths had a petition requested or filed to a greater extent than eligible low risk Caucasian youths up to eight months following the start of the diversion effort. However, following the implementation of the diversion effort eligible low risk African-American youths were also more likely than similar Caucasian youths to have their cases held open (the least possible amount of contact with the court system), whereas eligible low risk Caucasian youths were more likely to receive an IAA than eligible African-American youths. This indicates that following the implementation of the diversion effort, eligible low risk African-American youths were more likely than similarly situated Caucasian youths to receive either the most serious response (a request for a petition) or the least serious response (having their case held open), but less likely to receive a moderately serious response (an IAA). So, there continues to be variation in intake decisions by race for low risk youths.

Three issues should be explored to understand use of the IDA. JCS should consider conducting case reviews and/or surveys of JCOs to examine whether and/or why: 1) many youths who are, according to standards set for the IDA, supposed to receive an IDA do not actually receive it; 2) issues or information other than the IDA score are used to make the intake decision; and 3) the IDA is only one of many pieces of information used to make the intake decision. JCS reports that diversion in Johnson County really began working as intended in November 2008. Assuming that is the case, analyses carried out here should be re-done and the time period from January to October 2008 should be treated as a pre-program time period and the following ten months should be treated as the post-program time period. This would permit a stronger assessment of the effect of the diversion effort because it would use a stronger research design (pre- and post-test), data on IDA scores would be available for the pre- and post-test time periods, and it would, hopefully, include a larger number of cases for the post-program analysis.

State Update: 2016

Iowa

DMC continues to be an issue for the state of Iowa. Relative Rate Indices (RRIs) for 2011 show overrepresentation of African-American youth at the points of arrest, detention, cases petitioned, and confinement (https://www.humanrights.iowa.gov/cjjp/disproportionate-minority-contact/data). Staff maintain that RRIs are a useful indicator of overrepresentation, particularly in a state like Iowa that has a small minority population.

Iowa has not conducted recent assessment studies. According to staff, this is mostly due to the time and expensive associated with these studies. Iowa has established and maintains a Justice Data Warehouse, and the hope has been to be able to use these data to track individual youth through all phases of the juvenile justice system, but this capacity does not yet exist at the state level.

The state continues to use the Iowa Delinquency Assessment (IDA), a risk/ need assessment tool. Recently, the state redesigned and revalidated the Detention Screening Tool (DST) with the goal of standardizing detention decision-making. The state is working on integrating an automated version of the DST with the Iowa Courts Information System.

Iowa has cut back significantly on conferences and training. It no longer maintains the DMC Resource Center, a university-based entity that sponsored annual DMC conferences and other training. The state has sent teams from three localities to the *Reducing Racial and Ethnic Disparities in the Juvenile Justice System*, a five-day training workshop sponsored by Georgetown University's Center for Juvenile Justice Reform. According to staff, the training is viewed as very valuable, but expensive ($3,000 per person).

Black Hawk and Woodbury Counties continue to work on JDAI initiatives. These efforts have produced demonstrable reductions in detention in general and minority detention in Woodbury County. Black Hawk County saw reductions in detention for all youth, but smaller reductions for minority youth (CASPPAC, 2014).

In 2013, Iowa applied for and received a Community and Strategic Planning (CASP) grant from OJJDP. The purpose of the CASP grant was to support the development of a strategic action plan to reduce DMC in Iowa's delinquency system. The CASP Project Advisory Committee (CASPPAC) produced a report in 2014 entitled *Recommendations and Action Plan for Reducing Disproportionate Minority Contacts in Iowa's Juvenile Justice System*. The report calls for: local schools to reduce court referrals; local law enforcement agencies to reduce DMC in arrests, particularly for non-violent offenses; widespread use of the juvenile detention screening tool and the use of a "dispositional matrix" to assist with determining appropriate outcomes for youth who come before the courts; and regular data and reports to monitor progress on the recommendations (CASPPAC, 2014).

Virginia

RRI data for 2012 indicate that DMC continues to be an issue at all stages of the juvenile justice system, with the problem most severe for referrals to juvenile court, secure detention, and confinement (Virginia continues to fail to report an RRI calculation for juvenile arrests) (http://www.dcjs.virginia.gov/juvenile/dmc/).

Virginia contracted with Development Services Group (DSG) in 2010 to conduct a DMC assessment study. The project included qualitative interviews with juvenile justice practitioners and quantitative analysis on the processing of juveniles at various juvenile justice contact points in Fairfax, Norfolk, and Richmond City. The findings and recommendations from the assessment report are not posted online nor are they included in the most recently posted update to the state's three-year plan (which states that they are available from the Department of Criminal Justice Services upon request).

The state's most recent three-year plan (2012–2014) calls for funding to implement alternatives to the use of school disciplinary and zero-tolerance policies that result in arrest and/or school suspension or expulsion.

The 2013 update to the three-year plan notes that "no formal process and/or outcome evaluations are conducted at the state level other than monitoring RRIs." It also notes that due to funding constraints, the DMC coordinator position was not full-time. The report does not mention work with either the Burns Institute or the Casey Foundation's JDAI initiative.

Conclusions and Recommendations

Having reviewed the DMC efforts in Iowa and Virginia we identified a number of areas which we believe will help OJJDP and the states enhance their ability to address DMC issues, collect data, and evaluate the results of their efforts. Here, we focus our attention on conclusions and recommendations related to evaluation and assessing the performance of DMC initiatives since that was the primary concern of our study. In developing these recommendations, we acknowledge that we have taken a somewhat narrow view of the DMC issue in several respects. We have not addressed any of the myriad issues associated with doing work in this area — for example, sensitivities around race. In focusing directly on DMC-specific interventions, we exclude many important programmatic initiatives, such as early childhood intervention and prevention programs. Further, we recognize that there are other important outcomes of DMC intervention efforts besides DMC reduction, most especially reducing the actual numbers of youth of color involved in aspects of the juvenile justice system such as detention. Finally, while our focus is on "hard data" and outcomes, we acknowledge the value of raising awareness of the DMC issue among key stakeholders through mechanisms such as annual conferences and meetings. DMC is a difficult and delicate problem, and the professionals who are working to find solutions are to be commended for their efforts. Many of our recommendations are aimed at OJJDP because for 20 years OJJDP has been the single entity responsible for DMC reduction efforts. To address the issue of how effectively states and localities are dealing with DMC we must assess, to some degree, the guidance they are provided by OJJDP.

Conclusions

Both JDAI and the Burns Institute stress the need for systematic data collection and analysis in their approaches to addressing DMC, and their work with localities seems to result in increased use of data as local jurisdictions consider their DMC problems. Similar emphasis must be placed on assessing the outcomes of local DMC interventions.

In addition to collecting and analyzing performance data, states and localities must be encouraged to document these efforts so that results can be shared with others and assessed by a wider audience. We identified a number of local initiatives that have been undertaken in Iowa to address DMC over the years. However, we found no information on the effectiveness of these interventions, and in fact just finding information on the interventions themselves was a challenge. We suspect that this is the case in many states, and that potentially useful information is being lost because of lack of documentation. We offered the ideal assessments of two DMC initiatives in Iowa as models that jurisdictions should strive toward when attempting to determine the success of DMC efforts that are similar to those assessed here. When the designs discussed in the ideal assessments are not possible jurisdictions should, at a minimum, carry out the steps listed below to assess their efforts.

- Use RRI data over several time periods (annually or more frequent time periods such as quarterly) to document that a problem exists.
- Use a recent assessment study (within the past few years) to explain why the problem exists. If a recent assessment study is not available, offer reason(s) why it is thought that the problem exists.
- Clearly describe the effort prior to its implementation. Include the target population, all the components/activities of the effort and the indicators of whether these activities are implemented as planned, how long the effort should take (if applicable), and what the indicators of success are.
- Ensure data are available to document the implementation and outcomes of the effort prior to its implementation.
- Use the data collected to assess the success of the effort.
- Document all of these steps and make the results publicly available.

Our assessment of the accumulated evidence on DMC interventions is that there is some evidence to suggest some promising DMC interventions, almost exclusively at the detention stage. Systemic interventions, such as JDAI and the Burns Institute approaches, seem to have the benefit of energizing, at least temporarily, local efforts to address the DMC issue, and both efforts offer some numbers that suggest reductions in DMC. However, there is no evidence that meets any reasonable standard of scientific validity and objectivity that shows either JDAI or the Burns Institute approach to be successful in reducing DMC. Certainly, evidence for effectiveness does not currently exist in the two states under study here. This situation is not unique to these two national initiatives, however. Overall, few DMC interventions have been objectively and rigorously evaluated, and there is little objective evidence that interventions designed to reduce DMC actually do so.

Recommendations

Based on these conclusions we offer a number of recommendations to enhance knowledge about DMC.

1. Any evaluation of a DMC initiative should have as its primary outcome measure the reduction of DMC.

While other outcomes, such as a reduction of the number of minority youth in secure confinement, may be desirable, DMC-reduction initiatives should be expected to actually reduce disproportionality.

2. OJJDP should more clearly define its expectations for states and localities regarding evaluation of DMC initiatives.

While the DMC Manual contains a great deal of useful information about evaluation, it is not clear who the audience for this information is. Few local interventions are likely to have the ability to collect and analyze data on DMC interventions and states may not have the resources to assist localities in these efforts. There should be consensus on the roles of key stakeholders in evaluating DMC initiatives.

3. OJJDP and the states should provide more detailed and specific information to localities on identifying and measuring the performance of DMC-related initiatives.

States and localities need to understand what to measure for their specific initiatives and how to collect data on these measures. They need knowledgeable researchers and evaluators to provide expertise in developing objective measures and methodologies for assessing the performance of DMC initiatives. OJJDP should explore options for providing this information, including training aids and individual consultations.

4.   Jurisdictions carrying out DMC initiatives, regardless of their funding source, should monitor the implementation and outcomes of these initiatives.

To build the evidence-base on what works to reduce DMC states and localities should be encouraged to carefully document what they are doing and what the outcomes are for the DMC initiatives they implement. At a minimum, they should be encouraged to collect process and outcome measures for DMC initiatives.

5.   OJJDP should fund comprehensive national evaluations of JDAI and the Burns Institute's approach to dealing with DMC.

Although JDAI and the Burns Institute have been working with a number of localities across the country, neither of these initiatives has been adequately evaluated by an objective source. We would suggest that OJJDP seek funding for such an evaluation.

In summary, there are a number of steps that both OJJDP and jurisdictions can take to improve knowledge about what is being done to reduce DMC and the outcomes of these efforts. Some of the steps will be more challenging and require more resources than others, but we believe that if each of these is implemented in good faith, they will contribute to DMC reduction.

Conclusions and Recommendations: 2016 Update

To update this chapter, we considered whether we would revise any of these recommendations regarding enhancing knowledge on DMC. We reviewed information publicly available on the Office of Justice Program's (OJP) and OJJDP's web sites and two National Research Council's (NRC) reports: "Reforming Juvenile Justice: A Developmental Approach" (NRC, 2013) and "Implementing Juvenile Justice Reform: The Federal Role" (NRC, 2014).

Since we made these recommendations in 2010, OJJDP has funded various projects to address DMC and identify what works to reduce DMC and has continued to provide assistance to states to address DMC. OJJDP has held a number of online trainings, meetings, and provided information on DMC efforts in the states, but these have provided little new information about effective

DMC practices[8]. Though there is an increase in the amount of state and national level DMC data documenting the problem, there is no evidence that guidance to States has changed. OJJDP's DMC Technical Assistance Manual (2009), the guidance associated with carrying out their five phase DMC reduction model, has not been updated since this chapter was first published. The most recent publication from OJJDP describing the DMC efforts of the states uses data submitted in fiscal year 2011 and shows that only four states have conducted an evaluation of a DMC reduction effort (OJJDP, 2012).[9]

The two NRC reports support our findings and call for significant changes in how DMC is addressed. Authors of the 2013 NRC report agreed with our statement in this chapter that there is little objective evidence that interventions designed to decrease DMC actually do so. The report provides recommendations regarding specific topics that should be the focus of DMC reduction efforts and how DMC reform should be addressed at the state, local, and national level. The 2014 NRC report concludes that OJJDP's approach for reducing disproportionate minority contact is ineffective and calls for a new OJJDP approach to reducing racial and ethnic disparities (NRC, 2014).

We remain steadfast on these recommendations. Though efforts to address DMC have continued over the past several years, we have not seen any substantial increases in the knowledge of effective DMC reduction efforts to warrant revisions to these recommendations.

References

Annie E. Casey Foundation (2009). *Detention Reform: An Effective Approach to Reduce Racial and Ethnic Disparities in Juvenile Justice*. Detention Reform Brief #3.

Bell, J., Ridolfi, L.J., Finley, M. & Lacey, C. (2009). *The Keeper and the Kept: Reflections on Local Obstacles to Disparities Reduction in Juvenile Justice Systems and a Path to Change*. San Francisco: W. Haywood Burns Institute.

Community and Strategy Planning Project Advisory Committee (CASPPAC) (2014). *Recommendations and Action Plan for Reducing Disproportionate Minority Contacts in Iowa's Juvenile Justice System*. Des Moines, IA: Iowa Department of Human Rights.

---

8. See https://www.nttac.org/index.cfm?event=trainingCenter.traininginfo&eventID= 38&from=training and http://www.ojjdp.gov/newsletter/245451/sf_5.html

9. This publication does not reference the JRSA work on DMC evaluation efforts in Virginia or Iowa.

Department of Juvenile Justice (2004). 2003 *Evaluation Report of the Detention Assessment Instrument (DAI): Implementation Phase.* Richmond, VA: Author.

Feyerherm, W. & Butts, J. (2003). *Proposed Methods for Measuring Disproportionate Minority Contact (DMC)* [Powerpoint Slides]. Retrieved from: http://ojjdp.ncjrs.gov/dmc/pdf/dmc2003.pps#1).

Finley, M., Lacey, C. & Garry, L. (2006) *Readiness Assessment Consultation (RAC) Report: Norfolk, VA.* San Francisco: W. Haywood Burns Institute.

Finley, M., Lacey, C. & Garry, L. (2007) *Readiness Assessment Consultation (RAC) Report: Newport News, VA.* San Francisco: W. Haywood Burns Institute.

Mendel, R.A. *Two Decades of JDAI: From Demonstration Project to National Standard.* Baltimore, MD: The Annie E. Casey Foundation., 2009. Retrieved from: www.aecf.org/majorinitiatives/juveniledetentionalternativesinitiative.aspx.

National Research Council. (2013). *Reforming Juvenile Justice: A Developmental Approach.* Committee on Assessing Juvenile Justice Reform, Richard J. Bonnie, Robert L. Johnson, Betty M. Chemers, and Julie A. Schuck, Eds. Committee on Law and Justice, Division of Behavioral and Social Sciences and Education. Washington, DC: The National Academies Press.

National Research Council. (2014). *Implementing Juvenile Justice Reform: The Federal Role.* Committee on a Prioritized Plan to Implement a Developmental Approach in Juvenile Justice Reform, Committee on Law and Justice, Division of Behavioral and Social Sciences and Education. Washington, DC: The National Academies Press.

Office of Juvenile Justice and Delinquency Prevention (2008). *Formula National-Level Performance Data Summary Report.* Washington, DC: Author.

Office of Juvenile Justice and Delinquency Prevention (2009). *Disproportionate Minority Contact Technical Assistance Manual (4th edition).* Retrieved from: http://www.ncjrs.gov/html/ojjdp/dmc_ta_manual/index. html.

Office of Juvenile Justice and Delinquency Prevention. (2012). *Disproportionate Minority Contact.* Washington, DC: Author. Retrieved from: http://www.ojjdp.gov/pubs/239457.pdf

Orchowsky, S., Poulin, M. E. & Iwama, J. (2010). *A Review of the Status of Disproportionate Minority Contact (DMC) Efforts in Iowa and Virginia.* Washington, DC: Justice Research and Statistics Association. Retrieved from: http://www.jrsa.org/pubs/reports/dmc-final-report.pdf.

Pope, C.E., Lovell, R. & Hsia, H.M. (2002). *Disproportionate Minority Confinement: A Review of the Research Literature From 1989 Through 2001.* U.S. Department of Justice: Office of Juvenile Justice and Delinquency Prevention.

Poulin, M.E., Iwama, J., and Orchowsky, S. (2008). *Interim Report: A Review of the Status of Disproportionate Minority Contact (DMC) Efforts in Iowa and Virginia.* Washington, DC: Justice Research and Statistics Association. Retrieved from: http://www.jrsa.org/pubs/reports/dmc-preliminary-report -final.pdf.

Reiner, S., Miller, J.B. & Gangal, T. (2007). Public Safety Outcomes of Virginia's Detention Assessment Instrument. *Juvenile and Family Court Journal,* 58(3), 31–41.

Virginia Department of Criminal Justice Services. (2010). *Virginia DMC Assessment.* Retrieved from http://www.dcjs.virginia.gov/procurement/docume nts/RFPStatewideDMCAssessment.doc.

Virginia Department of Criminal Justice Services (2013). *Virginia's Three-Year Plan 2012–2014: 2013 Update.* Richmond, VA: Author.

Virginia State Crime Commission (2008) *HJR 113: Final Report: Study of Virginia's Juvenile Justice System.* Richmond, VA: Author.

W. Haywood Burns Institute. (2009) *2009 Annual Report.* Retrieved from: www .burnsinstitute.org/article.php?id=58.

Chapter 6

Understanding Disproportionality and Child Welfare

Marian S. Harris

The child welfare system continues to be in a crisis when one examines race and poor outcomes for children of color. Race is a highly significant factor that impacts a decision to place a child in the foster care system. Racial disproportionality occurs when the population of children of color in any system including the child welfare system is higher than the population of children of color in the general population. Racial disparity occurs when the rate of disproportionality of one racial group (e.g., African American) exceeds that of a comparison group (e.g., White Americans). On September 20, 2013, there were approximately 402,378 children in foster care. The percentage of African American children in foster care decreased between FY 2004 and FY 2013, while there was an increase in the percentages of White children, Hispanic children, children of other races or multiracial children, and children of unknown race (Child Welfare Information Gateway, 2015). This decrease in the number of African American children in the child welfare system in 2013 is a stark contrast to their high rate of representation in foster care in 2002, i.e., 17.4 per 1,000 compared to 4.6 per 1,000 among White children (U. S. Department of Health and Human Services, 2013). Research has repeatedly demonstrated that children of color when compared to White children are removed from the care of their birth families and placed in foster care at higher rates, experience longer stays in care, and receive less services as well as a lower caliber of services than White children; their contact with child welfare caseworkers is also less (Barth, 1997; Child Welfare Watch, 1998; Harris & Skyles, 2005; Harris & Hackett, 2008).

Racism plays a large part in the social context of family situations that bring children into care. In a study of urban families referred for child

neglect, the most startling finding was economic disparity between
African American and White families. Although almost all of families
in the sample were poor, African American families suffered even
more from economic inequality than those in the general population (Downs, Moore, McFadden & Costin, 2000b, pp. 319–320).

Institutional racism has existed for decades in the child welfare system and
has adversely affected children of color and their families. Billingsley and
Giovannoni (as cited in Hill, 2004) delineated the following forms of racism
in their study of African American children: devaluing the culture and functioning of African American children and families, providing inequitable services, and excluding African Americans from participating in the decision-
making processes that impact their children and families. Latino children are
frequently removed from the care of their Spanish speaking birth parents and
placed with foster parents who only speak English. For example, a judge in Texas
threatened a young Latina birth mother by saying that he would remove her
child and place the child with her father unless she refrained from speaking
Spanish in her home and only spoke English (Verhovek, 1995).

Although racial disproportionality is most severe for African American
children, Native American children also experience higher rates of disproportionality in the child welfare system than do children of other races or ethnicities. Native American children have been removed from their families since their
initial contact with Europeans including Columbus. The colonial policies of
England, Spain, France and other countries were designed to eliminate the
"Indian problem" (Beane, 1989). A reduction in the size of many Tribes as
well as in the reservation population resulted when Native American children
were removed from the care and custody of their families. Indian agents
removed children from their families within the age range of five to twenty
years and sent them to boarding schools. Many racist practices existed in boarding schools; for example, children could not speak their native language or
practice traditional customs, were required to wear uniforms, had their hair
cut and experienced military discipline and regimens (George, 1997). When
the number of boarding schools began to decline in the 1930s and 1940s, the
Bureau of Indian Affairs searched for other out-of-home placements for
American Indian and Alaska Native children (George, 1997). The Child Welfare League of America and the Bureau of Indian Affairs started the Indian
Adoption Project with the goal of changing the image of American Indian
children in order to make them more adoptable. The Child Welfare League of
America sanctioned the practice of removing American Indian children from

their families and sending them to European American communities for adoption placements that were far away from their birth families.

In 2001, CWLA President and CEO, Shay Bilchik acknowledged "sincere and deep regret" for CWLA's role in the Indian Adoption Project; "no matter how well intentioned and how squarely in the mainstream this was at the time, it was wrong, it was hurtful, and it reflected a kind of bias that surfaces feelings of shame" (Kreisher, 2002).

In 2004, Native American children represented less than 1 percent of the total child population in the United States; however, 2 percent of children in foster care were Native American; Hispanic/Latino children represented 19 percent of the child population and 17 percent of the children in foster care (Washington State Racial Disproportionality Advisory Committee, 2008). However, there has been a decrease in the number of American Indian/Alaska Native children entering the foster care system as of September 30, 2012, i.e., 14.3% (U. S. Department of Health and Human Services, 2013).

Asian and Pacific Islander children and families have also been impacted by racial disproportionality in the child welfare system. Reports of maltreatment for Asian/Pacific Islander children are more likely to be substantiated than reports of maltreatment for White children (Johnson, Clark, Donald, Pedersen & Pichotta, 2007). A key problem in research with these families has been combining/identifying the varied ethnic and national groups as Asian. According to Pekczarski and Kemp (2006), there are over 20 different ethnic groups in the Asian and Pacific Islander census group; these groups have varied/distinct languages, countries of origin, and socioeconomic statuses. It is a misnomer to compile an "Asian" report/summary; any report/summary should clearly identify the specific Asian and Pacific Islander children and their respective families. There is not a simple explanation for the disproportionate representation of children of color in the child welfare system. However, it is important to examine key child welfare decision points as well as any bias that might exist in the decision making process.

Key Child Welfare Decision Points

Children are initially brought to the attention of the child welfare system when a call is made to Child Protective Services (CPS). Anyone can report suspected child abuse, neglect or maltreatment. This call/report of alleged child abuse and/or neglect comes from a variety of sources including family members, concerned neighbors, physicians, teachers, police officers, school counselors, community members, nurses, etc. The majority of the reports to the child welfare system come from "mandated reporters" who are in every state. Mandated reporters are required to report suspected child abuse, neglect or maltreatment or cause a report to be made, when, in their professional roles, there is reasonable cause to suspect abuse, neglect or maltreatment. Reasonable cause to suspect child abuse, neglect or maltreatment means that the professional utilizes her/his professional training and experience and observations and decides that a parent or other individual responsible for a child has harmed a child or placed a child in imminent danger or risk of abuse, neglect or maltreatment. The following are mandated reporters: (a) physicians; (b) dentists; (c) medical examiners; (d) child care workers; (e) social workers; (f) nurses; (g) medical examiners; (h) school teachers; (i) school counselors; (j) school officials; (k) coroners; (l) emergency medical personnel; (m) district attorney or assistant district attorney; (m) psychologists; (o) mental health professionals; (p) substance abuse counselors; (q) police officers; and (r) any employees or volunteers in residential care facilities for children. Child welfare workers assess each report to determine if an investigation is warranted. According to Lemon, D'Andrade, and Austin (2005), cases involving children of color are opened for an investigation at a higher rate than cases involving White children. There is the possibility of racial bias by mandated reporters at this major front end decision point. Findings from a study by Bowser and Jones (2004) revealed that when health and school officials suspect abuse, neglect, or violence against a child of color disproportionate rates of reporting increase.

There is a vast discourse in the literature regarding bias in the reporting process. Chand (2002) states that "exposure bias" rather than racial prejudice is the reason for the disproportionate high rate of reports.

> According to this view, because children from African American and Native American families are more likely to be poor, they are more likely to be exposed to mandated reporters as they turn to the public social service system for support in times of need. Problems that other families keep private become public as a family receives Temporary Assistance to Needy Families (TANF), seeks medical care from a public clinic, or lives in public housing (Cahn & Harris, 2005, p. 6).

Exposure bias is also referred to as visibility bias and has been extensively explored in child welfare referrals from mandated reporters from the medical profession. "Though several studies have shown the prevalence of addiction is the same for all races and social classes, hospitals serving poor families are more likely to conduct routine drug screening on women giving birth and on newborns, thereby increasing the likelihood of entry into the child welfare system for families served by such hospitals" (Cahn & Harris, 2005, p. 6). According to Chasnoff, Landress, and Barrett (1990), physicians tend to believe that substance abuse is more prevalent during pregnancy in women of color who are poor and reside in urban areas; consequently, physicians tend to suspect, test, and report African American women more than White women. During a six-month study in Pinellas County, Florida findings indicate that 10 times as many African American women as White women were reported to Child Protective Services as White women following the birth of their babies, although they were equally likely to test positive for drug abuse (Chasnoff, Landress & Barrett, 1990; Karp, 2001; Drug Policy Alliance; 2005).

Research has shown that "exposure bias" is evident at each decision point within the child welfare system. Investigators are more likely to err on the side of substantiation for African American children who have received child abuse reports in the past. Workload among caseworkers also affects their day to day decision-making and the time they are able to allocate for an investigation before making a final decision. The following pose problems in timely permanency planning for all children regardless of race: (a) high worker turnover; (b) conflicting requirements for multiple oversight systems (TANF), housing, child welfare; (c) absence of substance abuse or mental health treatment programs that can ensure parental recovery from addiction and mental illness within time-lines stipulated by policy; and (d) failure to communicate hope or respect by child welfare workers (Cahn & Harris, 2005).

After Child Protective Services receives a report about an allegation of child abuse, neglect or maltreatment a decision is made regarding whether or not to investigate the allegation and whether or not to substantiate the allegation after the investigation. Although several national studies have demonstrated that substance abuse has been the major cause of child neglect among African Americans, findings from a study by Bowser and Jones (2004) demonstrated no higher rate of abuse and neglect in families of color. Although research has consistently shown no differences in rates of abuse and neglect by families of color, racial differences are continuously prevalent in the high rates of cases opened for investigation and in rates of cases substantiated (Lane, Rubin, Monteith & Christian, 2002; Cahn & Harris, 2005; Harris & Hackett, 2008; Harris & Skyles, 2005; Johnson et al., 2007). Reports of child maltreatment for Latino or Hispanic children are more likely to be substantiated than reports of maltreatment for non-Hispanic White children (Church, 2006; Church, Gross & Baldwin, 2005).

Several factors have been reported to increase the number of African American children who enter the foster care system: (a) lack of affordable housing;

(b) lack of substance abuse services; (c) limited access to family support services to prevent entry and re-entry into foster care; and (d) limited or inadequate legal representation of birth parents (GAO Report, 2007). In the Bowser and Jones study (2004) substantiation rates were high due to a lack of investigators as well as shorter time lines for making decision; findings also revealed that investigators tended to substantiate allegations rather than determine allegations to be unfounded or inconclusive because of liability issues. A decision regarding placement is made after an allegation has been substantiated by Child Protective Services.

Once an allegation of child abuse, neglect or maltreatment is substantiated children of color are more likely to be removed from the care and custody of their parents and placed in out-of-home care; these children remain in care longer, experience numerous moves, and have lower reunification rates when compared to White children (U. S. Children's Bureau, 1997; Cahn & Harris, 2005; Harris & Hackett, 2008). According to Lemon, D'Andrade, and Austin (2005), fifty-four percent of African American children were placed in foster care as compared to thirty-eight percent of White children in their study of placement outcomes for children in Illinois. Johnson et al. (2007) studied children in the Minnesota child welfare system; their findings showed that when a White child and an African American child were placed in foster care for the same reason, their odds for reunification were remarkably different; the odds of family reunification for an African American child were 1.19 times the odds of family reunification for a White child. Harris and Courtney (2003) studied a sample of children in the California child welfare system; the following are their findings regarding family reunification:

1. Males were slightly less likely to be reunified than females.
2. Infants and adolescents were reunified slower than children of other ages.
3. Children removed from home because of neglect returned home at a slower rate than children removed for other reasons.
4. Child health problems slowed the rate of reunification.
5. Children in kinship foster homes and foster family homes returned home more slowly than children in other placement types.
6. African American children were reunited at a slower rate than other children.
7. Children from two-parent families were returned home faster than children from single-parent homes, regardless of the gender of the single parent (p. 423).

Children and families of color need the same services and supports as White children and families to facilitate timely family reunification when their children are removed from their care and placed in out-of-home care.

Several studies have shown service disparities based on race rather than any other factor in the quantity and quality of services provided to children and families of color (Harris & Hackett, 2008; Courtney, Barth, Berrick, Brooks, Needell & Park, 1996; Saunders, Nelson & Landsman, 1993; Close, 1983). "Research on the delivery of services to children and their families in the child welfare system consistently demonstrates that African American children are at a disadvantage regarding the range and quality of services provided, the type of agency to which they are referred, the efficiency with which their cases are handled, the support their families receive, and their eventual outcomes" (Harris & Skyles, 2005, p. 95). Hill (2001) examined six studies that clearly substantiated disparities in services for children of color (Jeter, 1963; Fanshel, 1981; Olsen, 1982; Katz, Hampton, Newberger & Bowles, 1986; Maluccio & Fein, 1989; Courtney et al., 1996). When compared to other ethnic groups Native American families are the least likely to be recommended for services (Olsen, 1982). Although African American birth parents tend to be referred for substance abuse treatment at higher rates, they receive a lower quality of substance abuse services (Walker, Zangrillo & Smith, 1994).

African American children are disproportionately represented in kinship care placements when compared to White and Asian children (GAO Report, 2007). According to Hill (2004), African American children are twice as likely to be in kinship care placements when compared to White children (29% vs. 14%). Most children are placed in kinship care because their birth parents have substance abuse problems. Kinship care placements tend to last longer than non-kinship care placements. Many states do not have the resources to provide substance abuse treatment services and other types of services needed to expedite the reunification process (GAO Report, 2007). Lack of services to kinship caregivers and birth parents hampers the family reunification process for children of color and their families. For example, Needell et al. (2004) found that African American children remained in kinship care placements at least five or more days with a median length of stay of 854 days; White children were in care 546 days; Latino children were in care 649 days and Asian children were in care for 539 days. Kinship care placements also present several challenges to kin caregivers including no financial resources, little knowledge about social service and/or educational systems, limited or no child care, and no health care insurance nor health care services (Harris & Skyles, 2008). It is very clear that changes are warranted at key decision points in the child welfare system to address racial disproportionality and disparities when children of color are removed from the care and custody of their birth parents and placed in foster care.

Addressing Disproportionality in Washington State

Several states are taking a proactive approach to address disproportionality including Texas, Michigan, Illinois, and Washington. Two legislators from Washington State (Representative Eric Pettigrew and Senator Claudia Kauffman) sponsored Substitute House Bill 1472 and it was signed by Governor Christine Gregoire on May 14, 2007. The bill gave the Secretary of the Department of Social and Health Services (DSHS) the responsibility of convening an advisory committee to determine whether racial disproportionality and racial disparity exist in the child welfare system. The legislation also stated that the advisory committee shall examine and analyze the following: (a) the level of involvement of children of color at each stage in the state's child welfare system including the points of entry and exit, and each point at which a treatment decision is made; (b) the number of children of color in low-income or single-parent families involved in the state's child welfare system; (c) the family structures of families involved in the state's child welfare system; and (d) the outcomes for children in the existing child welfare system (Substitute House Bill 1472: 2007). The advisory committee had to submit a report of the aforementioned analysis to the Secretary of the Department of Health and Social Services by June 1, 2008.

The committee will include no more than fifteen members who are experts in social work, law, child welfare, psychology or related fields, at least two tribal representatives, a representative of the governor's juvenile justice advisory committee, a representative of a community-based organization involved with child welfare issues, a representative of the Department of Social and Health Services, a current or former foster care youth, a current or former foster parent, and a parent previously involved with Washington's child welfare system. The Washington State Racial Disproportionality Advisory Committee (WSR-DAC) began work in November 2007. The WSRDAC made a decision to focus on increasing public awareness of racial disproportionality in child welfare. Therefore, it was crucial to have input and feedback from community stakeholders and American Indian Tribes in developing any remediation plan. The committee engaged in numerous remediation, outreach and education activities throughout Washington State.

The primary goal of the WSRDAC is "the elimination of racial dispropor-tionality and racial disparities in the state child welfare system without com-promising child safety or lowering the quality of services; key indicators are the following: (a) Race will not be a predictor of how a child will fare in Wash-ington's child welfare system; (b) Race will not be a factor when decisions are made about children by the child welfare system; and (c) All children will have equitable access to culturally appropriate services and supports delivered by culturally competent and sensitive staff and service providers" (Washington State Racial Disproportionality Advisory Committee, 2008, p. 2).

The Washington State Institute for Public Policy (WSIPP) served as techni-cal staff to the WSRDAC and utilized 2004 data from the child welfare system for the required analysis. Major findings from the study/analysis are as follows:

1. American Indian, Black and Hispanic children are referred into the Washington State child welfare system at disproportionate rates.
2. Cumulative disproportionality increases as American Indian and Black children move through the system.
3. American Indian children are three times as likely as White children to be referred to Child Protective Services; they are six times as likely to be in an out-of-home placement for over two years.
4. Black children are almost twice as likely as White children to be referred to Child Protective Services; they are nearly three times as likely to be in out-of-home placements for over two years.
5. Hispanic children have a 34% likelihood of referral than White children and are 7% more likely to have an accepted referral and 15% more likely to be placed in out-of-home care.
6. Asian American children enter the child welfare system at lower rates than White children. From accepted referral to placement, Asian Amer-ican children are not as likely to be in the Washington State child wel-fare system.
7. Children from low income families are more likely to be in the Wash-ington State child welfare system than children from affluent families. Children of single-parent families are more likely to be in the Wash-ington State child welfare system than children from two-parent households.
8. When income and family structure are considered as factors influenc-ing disproportionality at different key decision points in the child welfare process, race still emerges as the primary factor in dispropor-tionality (Washington State Racial Disproportionality Advisory Com-mittee, 2008, pp. 6–7).

The Washington State Racial Disproportionality Advisory Committee was mandated by the legislature to develop and submit a remediation plan to the Secretary of the Department of Social and Health Services if the analysis indicated disproportionality or disparity exists for any racial or ethnic group in any region in the state. The remediation plan shall include the following: (a) recommendations for administrative and legislative actions related to appropriate programs and services to reduce and eliminate disparities in the system and improve the long-term outcomes for children of color who are served by the system; and (b) performance measures for implementing the remediation plan (Substitute House Bill 1472: 2007). The WSRDAC has the responsibility for "ongoing evaluation of current and prospective policies and procedures for their contribution to or effect on racial disproportionality and disparity" (Washington State Racial Disproportionality Advisory Committee, 2008, p. 5).

The Washington State Racial Disproportionality Advisory Committee decided to develop annual remediation proposals. Inherent in each proposal are recommended actions designed to reduce racial disproportionality and improve outcomes for children of color at three key decision points: (a) referral to Child Protective Services; (b) removal from home; and (c) length of stay over two years. The major impetus for selecting these key decision points was findings from the 2008 WSRDAC Report. The WSRDAC and stakeholders who participated in the community engagement process indicated a need for an increase in culturally appropriate services delivered by culturally competent and sensitive providers at key decision points.

In 2009 the major recommendations implemented from the remediation plan included consultation with other states (Texas and Michigan) that are currently engaged in work to reduce racial disproportionality. Other work included studying issues regarding the Indian Child Welfare Act and American Indian racial disproportionality. A comprehensive examination of differences in disproportionality between Reservation Indians, Rural Indians and Urban Indians was also done. The goals and benchmarks recommended in 2009 were developed to help measure progress in reducing disproportionality at the three key decision points and disparities in service design, delivery and availability. As of January 1, 2010, Substitute House Bill 1472 requires the Secretary of the Department of Social and Health Services to provide annual reports to the appropriate committees of the legislature regarding the implementation of the remediation plan, including any measurable progress made to reduce and eliminate racial disproportionality and disparity in the state's child welfare system.

On the basis of recommendations by the WSRDAC the Washington State Institute for Public Policy per directive of the Legislature studied the effects of

Family Team Decision Making (FTDM) and Structured Decision Making (SDM) on racial disproportionality in 2011. The Family Team Decision Making Model includes birth families, foster parents, child welfare caseworkers and community members in all placement decisions to make sure that children and the adults who care for them have a network of support when they are involved in the child welfare system.

> Instead of being excluded from the process, the family, private service providers, and community representatives can participate in a discussion and partnership designed to keep the community's children safe. Where foster care is indicated, placements are more stable if foster parents participate as team members. Team decision making helps improve communications among individual service providers, who often speak only their own language. Services designed with the cooperation and input of families in terms that the family understands are more effective when offered to the family. The goals of team decision making are to improve the agency's decision making process; to encourage the support and "buy-in" of the family, extended family, and the community to the agency's decisions; and to develop specific, individualized, and appropriate interventions for children and families (Annie E. Casey Foundation, 2002, pp. 8–9).

This practice model was implemented in the six regions several years ago. It is applicable to two key decision points (removal from home and length of stay). The Washington State Department of Health and Human Services had 6,600 FTDM meetings for approximately 8,000 children in 2008. Findings from the 2001 research study revealed that FTDM had no effect on out-of-home placement, time to permanency, or new referrals.

An examination of outcomes by racial groups demonstrated three positive findings, 1) Latino children experienced decreased rates of placement, 2) Asian children achieved permanency more quickly than those in non-FTDM offices, 3) Black children exiting to permanency were less likely to be the alleged victims of new accepted CPS referrals (Washington State Institute for Public Policy, 2011, p. 1).

Structured Decision Making (SDM) is a case management model; this model is designed to assist Child Protective Services workers to make decisions regarding child safety and the risk associated with a child remaining in a home. Structured Decision Making is applicable to one key decision point in the remediation plan i.e. removal from home. Structured Decision Making was implemented by the Washington State child welfare system in 2007. The results of the preliminary SDM Study were presented to the WSRDAC on April 21, 2010, and indicate that Black children are negatively impacted by the SDM actuarial risk assessment tool. Additionally, when all races were analyzed the findings by the Washington State Institute for Public Policy (2011) reported the following:

- SDM had no effect on out-of-home placements.
- SDM had no effect on new reports to CPS.
- SDM had no effect on placements or new CPS reports for White, Indian, Asian, and Latino children in separate analysis for each race (Washington, State Institute for Public Policy, 2011, p. 1).

Family dynamics are different in each case of child abuse and neglect. Are child welfare workers using culturally appropriate and culturally sensitive engagement skills when interviewing Black families for SDM risk assessments? Although most of the items on the SDM assessment are objective, some items rely on the clinical judgment of the child welfare worker. Are child welfare workers using SDM correctly? Have child welfare workers been appropriately trained in the use of SDM? No assessment tool has the capability of predicting child welfare outcomes all the time; child welfare workers are free to use their discretion to reassign risk to a higher classification than is indicated on the tool. Whether or not a child is removed from her/his family and placed in the care and custody of the child welfare system varies based on the child welfare worker assigned to investigate the case (Rossi, Schuerman, & Budde, 1996).

Other States

The ongoing problem of poor outcomes for children of color in the child welfare system is being addressed across the nation. Many states including Minnesota, Oregon, and Texas have convened public meetings in an effort to understand the myriad of issues and poor outcomes for children of color and their families. It is important to understand the role played by organizations in perpetuating poor outcomes among children and families. Miller and Esenstad (2015) identified several themes in their recent report including:

- Racial equity work must be seen as fundamental to improving child welfare systems.
- An expanded commitment to racial justice required an explicit focus on understanding the influence of race and racism on children, families, communities and institutions.

- The active involvement of community members and community-based organizations provides accountability and supports the sustainability of this work across leadership tenures.
- Executive leaders from the child welfare and/or human service system, as well as other partnering systems, must be active champions of racial equity within their systems.
- Disparity-reduction efforts must be guided by data analyses at as many different levels as possible.
- Legislative and executive mandates are important catalysts for institutionalizing and resourcing this work.
- An organizational structure and dedicated resources are important considerations for supporting staff and this work over time.
- Additional resources are needed to support research and evaluation.

These themes highlight the need for research and evaluation and the importance of resources to address the problem at multiple levels in the child welfare system.

Conclusion

There continue to be concerted efforts to reduce racial disproportionality and disparity in the child welfare system in the United States. Miller and Esenstad (2015) identified the seven prominent types of disparity-reduction efforts that are currently being used in varied geographical locations across the country:

1. The use of **legislative directives and/or mandates** to initiate and monitor ongoing work to identify racial disparities and take actions to reduce them.

2. The creation of **operational structures within the child welfare agency and key child-and family-serving systems with responsibility to advance a racial equity agenda.**

3. **A range of data development and analysis strategies** with many states beginning their work by applying race/ethnicity and decision points' analysis to better understand the extent and nature of racially disparate outcomes.

4. **Training workforce development and capacity-building** actions that deepen an understanding among staff at multiple levels of an organization of how race and racism impact the lives of children, families

and communities, as well as the institutions that are charged with supporting them.

5. **Structuring new partnerships** with other public and private agencies, communities and families to assist with and support disparity-reduction efforts.

6. **Engagement with tribal governments** around compliance with the Indian Child Welfare Act and reduction of poor outcomes among tribal communities.

7. **Community engagement strategies** that support improved understanding between the public child welfare agency and community-based institutions and families within the racial and ethnic communities most impacted by the child welfare system (pp. 7–8).

Children of color continue to be disproportionately represented in the child welfare system in many states, especially African American, Native American, and Latino children. Numerous studies have shown that once children of color and their families become involved with the child welfare system they experience poorer outcomes than White children and families. For example, "Findings in a December 2011 Applied Research Center (ARC) report titled *Shattered Families* revealed that the detained or deported families of approximately 5,100 children currently placed in foster care were experiencing 'insurmountable barriers'" in their family reunification efforts (Harris, 2014, p. 43). Racial disproportionately has existed for decades in the child welfare system, a system designed to protect children and to do what is in their best interest. Is it in the best interest of children of color to have them repeatedly enter a child welfare system in disproportionate numbers, experience service disparities once they enter the system, exit the system slower, and experience failures of the system to provide services needed to expedite reunification with their birth families? Although there has been a decrease in the number of Black or African American children in the foster care system as of 2013, the number of Hispanic children, children of other races or multicultural children and children of unknown race has increased (Child Welfare information Gateway, 2013). It is a national travesty that many policies, programs, and practices continue to perpetuate racial disproportionality and disparity in the child welfare system.

Many states have finally recognized that racial disproportionality is a serious problem that demands immediate action and are working to eliminate the problem; however, other states continue to blame the victims, i.e., children and families of color and/or prefer to attribute the cause of the problem to other factors (poverty, substance abuse, and family structure) and simply maintain the status quo. It is time to utilize a collaborative approach that includes children and families of color as well as policy makers, administrators, and practitioners if the child welfare system is truly serious about finally eliminating racial disproportionality and disparity. It is time for the child welfare system to focus on providing equitable services to all children in the system and not to a select few based on race. Racial equity work is crucial to improve outcomes for all children involved in the child welfare system. Children and families of color pay a high social cost because of racial disproportionality and disparity in the child welfare system as well as in other systems that are plagued by this problem (education, health care, mental health, juvenile and criminal justice). "As long as disproportionality is viewed as an individual or personal issue of African Americans and Native American children or other children of color, the solutions to disproportionality will not be focused in the public domain of the child welfare system, a system that created and has continued to perpetuate disproportionality" (Harris & Hackett, 2008, p. 202). It is imperative to recognize and understand how race and racism impact the child welfare system, children, families, community members, community agencies and organizations and to take a proactive approach to achieve racial equity and improve outcomes for all children and families involved in the child welfare system in America.

References

The Annie E. Casey Foundation. (2002). *Team decision making: Involving the family and community in child welfare decisions: Building community partnerships in child welfare* (pp. 1–31). Baltimore, MD: Author.

Barth, R. (1997). Family reunification. *Child Welfare Research Review, 2*, 109–122.

Beane, S. (1989). History and policy implications. In E. Gonzalez & A. Lewis (Eds.), *Collaboration: The key—A model curriculum on Indian child welfare*. Tempe. AZ: Arizona State University.

Billingsley, A. & Giovannoni, J. (1972). *Children of the storm: Black children and American child welfare*. New York: Harcourt Brace Jovanovich.

Bowser, B. P. & Jones, T. (2004). *Understanding the over-representation of African Americans in the child welfare system: San Francisco*. Hayward, CA: The Urban Institute.

Cahn K. & Harris, M. S. (2005). Where have all the children gone? A review of the literature on factors contributing to disproportionality: Five key child welfare decision points. *Protecting Children, 20*(1), 4–14.

Chand, A. (2000). The over-representation of black children in the child protection system: Possible causes, consequences and solutions. *Child and
Family Social Work, 5,* 67–77.

Chasnoff, I. J., Landress, H. J. & Barrett, M. E. (1990). The prevalence of illicit-
drug or alcohol use during pregnancy and discrepancies in mandatory
reporting in Pinellas County, Florida. *New England Journal of Medicine,
322,* 1202–1206.

Child Welfare Information Gateway. (2015). *Foster care statistics 2013.* Washington, DC: U. S. Department of Health and Human Services, Children's
Bureau.

Child Welfare Watch. (1998). *The race factor in child welfare.* New York: Center
for an Urban Future.

Church, W. T. (2006). From start to finish: The duration of Hispanic children
in out-of-home placements. *Children and Youth Services Review, 28,*
1007–1023.

Church, W. T., Gross, E. R. & Baldwin, J. (2005). Maybe ignorance is not always
bliss: The disparate treatment of Hispanics within the child welfare system. *Children and Youth Services Review, 27*(12), 1279–1292.

Close, M. M. (1983). Child welfare and people of color: Denial of equal access.
Social Work Research and Abstracts, 19(4), 13–20.

Courtney, M. E., Barth, R. P., Berrick, J. D., Brooks, D., Needell, B. & Park, L.
(1996). Race and child welfare services: Past research and future directions.
Child Welfare, 75(2), 99–137.

Downs, S. W., Moore, E., McFadden, E. J. & Costin, I. B. (2000). Foster care: A
service for children and their families. In *Child welfare and family services:
Policies and practices* (6th ed., pp. 307–380). Boston, MA: Allyn & Bacon.

Drug Policy Alliance. (2005). Women of color. In *Affected communities: Race
and the drug war.* Retrieved June 15, 2010 from http://www.drugpolicy.org/
communities/race/womenofcolor.cfm.

Fanshel, D. (1981). Decision-making under uncertainty: Foster care for abused
and neglected children? *American Journal of Public Health, 71*(7), 685–686.

George, L. J. (1997). Why the need for the Indian Child Welfare Act? *Journal of
Multicultural Social Work, 5*(3/4), 165–175.

Harris, M. S. & Courtney, M. E. (2003). The interaction of race, ethnicity, and
family structure with respect to the timing of family reunification. *Children
and Youth Services Review, 25*(5/6), 409–429.

Harris, M. S. & Skyles, A. (2005). Working with African American children and
families in the child welfare system. In K. L. Barrett & W. H. George (Eds.),
Race, culture, psychology & law (pp. 91–103). Thousand Oaks, CA: Sage
Publications, Inc.

Harris, M. S. & Hackett, W. (2008). Decision points in child welfare: An action research model to address disproportionality. *Children and Youth Services Review, 30*(2), 199–215.

Harris, M. S. & Skyles, A. (2008). Kinship care for African American children: Disproportionate and disadvantageous. *Journal of Family Issues, 29*(8), 1013–1030.

Harris, M. S. (2014). Best/promising practices. In *Racial disproportionality in child welfare* (pp. 36–90). New York: Columbia University Press.

Hill, R. (2001). *Disproportionality of minorities in child welfare: Synthesis of research findings.* Washington, DC: Westat, 30.

Hill, R. (2004). Institutional racism in child welfare. *Race and Society, 7*(1), 19–33.

Jeter, H. (1963). *Children, problems and services in child welfare programs.* Washington, DC: U. S. Department of Health, Education and Welfare.

Johnson, E. P., Clark, S., Donald, M., Pedersen, R. & Pichott, C. (2007). Racial disparity in Minnesota child protection system. *Child Welfare, 86*(4), 5–20.

Karp, S. (2001, February). "Crack babies:" Black children defy stereotypes, face bias — the tragedy of "crack babies." *The Chicago Reporter.* Retrieved June 15, 2010, from http://www.findarticles.com/p/mi-mOJAS/IS-21-30 -730965/ print.

Katz, M., Hampton, R., Newberger, E. H. & Bowles, R. T. (1986). Returning children home: Clinical decision making in child abuse and neglect. *American Journal of Orthopsychiatry, 56*(2), 253–262.

Kreisher, K. (2002, March). *Coming home: The lingering effects of the Indian adoption project.* Retrieved October 1, 2010, from http://www.cwla.org /articles/cv0203indianadopthtm.

Lane, W. G., Rubin, D. M., Monteith, R. & Christian, C. W. (2002). Racial differences in the evaluation of pediatric fractures for physical abuse. *JAMA, 288*(13), 1603–1609.

Lemon, K., D'Andrade, A. & Austin, M. (2005). *Understanding and addressing disproportionality in the front end of the child welfare system* (pp. 4–20). Berkeley, CA: Bay Area Social Services Consortium.

Malluccio, A. & Fein, E. (1989). An examination of long-term foster care for children and youth. In J. Hudson & B. Galaway (Eds.), *The state as parent* (pp. 387–400). Dordrecht, The Netherlands: Kluwer Academic.

Miller, O. & Esenstad, A. (2015). *Strategies to reduce racially disparate outcomes in child welfare: A national scan* (pp. 1–75). Washington DC: Center for the Study of Social Policy.

Needell, B., Webster, D., Curraco-Alamin, S., Armijo, M., Lee, S., Lery, B., Shaw, T., Dawson, W., Piccus, W., Magruder, J. & Kim, H. (2004). *Child welfare*

services reports for California. Retrieved August 20, 2010, from http://cssr
.berkeley,edu/CWSCMSreports/.

Olsen, L. (1982). Services for minority children in out-of-home care. *Social Services Review, 56,* 572–585.

Pelczarski, Y. & Kemp, S. P. (2006). Patterns of child maltreatment referrals among Asian and Pacific Islander families. *Child Welfare, 85*(1), 5–31.

Rossi, P., Schuerman, J. & Budde, S. (1996). *Understanding child maltreatment decisions and those who make them.* Chicago, IL: Chapin Hall Center for Children, University of Chicago.

Saunders, E. J., Nelson, K. & Landsman, M. J. (1993). Racial inequality and child neglect: Findings in a metropolitan area. *Child Welfare, 72,* 341–354.

S. B. 1472, 60th Legis., (2007) (enacted).

The United States Children's Bureau. (1997), *National study of protective, preventive, and reunification services delivered to children and families.* Washington, DC: U.S. Department of Health and Human Services.

U. S. Department of Health and Human Services. (2013). *Recent demographic trends in foster care.* Washington, DC: Administration for Children and Families, Administration on Children, Youth and Families, Office of Date, ANALYSIS, Research, and Evaluation.

The United States Government Accountability Office. (2007). *African American children in foster care: Additional HHS assistance needed to help states reduce the proportion in care.* Washington, DC: Author.

Verhovek, S. H. (1995, August 30). Mother scolded by judge for speaking Spanish. *The New York Times.* Retrieved April 30, 2008, from http://www
.nytimes.com/.

Walker, C. D., Zangrillo, P. & Smith, J. M. (1994). Parental drug abuse and African American children in foster care. In R. Barth, J. D. Berrick & N. Gilbert (Eds.), *Child welfare research review* (pp. 109–122). New York: Columbia University Press.

Washington State Racial Disproportionality Advisory Committee. (2008). *Racial disproportionality in Washington State committee report* (pp. 1–112). Olympia, WA: Author.

Washington State Racial Disproportionality Advisory Committee. (2008). *Racial disproportionality and disparity in Washington state child welfare: Remediation plan* (pp. 1–27). Olympia, WA: Author.

Chapter 7

What's Fueling DMC? The Role of School Discipline Decisions on Disproportionality in the Juvenile Justice System

Cherie Dawson-Edwards, Nadia Nelson and Katie Nuss

Introduction

"Getting in trouble" at school is a social process that involves addressing a perceived violation of rules or norms by establishing and executing strategies designed to preserve a notion of justice and to prevent repeat offenses (Irby, 2014). Often, "getting in trouble" in school results in an office discipline referral, which can lead to classroom exclusion in the form of suspension or expulsion ranging from one class period to several days. The various forms of classroom exclusion "serve as the standard forms of punishment employed by schools throughout the United States" (Noguera, 2003, p. 342). Nationally, African American and Latino students are disciplined at a much greater rate than their white peers, with African American students experiencing the largest disparity (Johnston, 2000).

These school-based disparities appear to spill over into the juvenile justice system and are increasingly recognized as factors that contribute to disproportionate minority contact (DMC). While the Office of Juvenile Justice and Delinquency Prevention (OJJDP) has been providing avenues to address DMC in the juvenile justice system, their reliance on the DMC reduction model does not require jurisdictions to go beyond what they deem the front of the system — arrest. Based on evidence from identifying then assessing why DMC exists in a community, more and more jurisdictions are looking into the crossover youth that fall into both the educational discipline track and the juvenile justice system (see Frabutt, Cabaniss, Kendrick & Arbuckle, 2008). A dual system of punishment appears to be operating in many districts where numerous children receive a semblance of double jeopardy for school-based behaviors, some of which were historically handled internally by schools (see Hirschfield, 2008). While minority students only comprise 39% of the U.S. public school population, they make up 75% of law enforcement referrals and 79% of arrests for offenses occurring at school (U.S. Department of Education Office for Civil Rights, 2014).

Trends in school discipline disproportionately appear to mirror the toughening of sanctions in the criminal justice system. As the nation's criminal justice system moved towards a "tough on crime" approach, social controls in the juvenile justice system also followed suit. Simultaneously, the school discipline practices became more punitive and criminalized. Similar to the coercive mobility of concentrated incarceration, punitive school discipline has collateral consequences for the student, their family, their classmates and even their community. According to Perry and Morris (2014), these criminalized school discipline policies have caused students to be more likely to receive suspensions, expulsions, alternate school placements, or juvenile detention.

Minority Overrepresentation in School Discipline

One study analyzing discipline trends from 1991–2005 found since the early 1990s, minority students — Black, Hispanic, and American Indian — have experienced a trend of disproportionate discipline (i.e., sent to the office or detained after school) as compared to their White and Asian counterparts (Wallace, Goodkind, Wallace & Bachman, 2008). According to the same study, suspension and expulsion rates "are highest among Black boys, followed first by American Indian and Hispanic boys, and then by Black girls" (Wallace, Goodkind, Wallace & Bachman, 2008, p. 54). Another study conducted in Texas found that not only were minority students likely to be overrepresented in disciplinary actions, but that they were also more likely to be disciplined and/or placed due to discretionary rather than mandatory reasoning (Tajalli & Garba, 2014). The authors of this study stated, "the numbers imply concerted and nationwide racial discrimination toward minority students" (Tajalli & Garba, 2014, p. 621).

Discipline disproportionality can occur at two major points within the discipline process: at the point of the referral, or at the point of the administrative decision regarding discipline (Skiba, Horner, Chung, Rausch, May, & Tobin, 2011), they found overrepresentation of children from minority groups occurs at both points. Specifically, in grades K-6, "African American students appear to be overrepresented, relative to their proportion in the population, among those referred to the office" (Skiba et. al, 2011, p. 93), with the trend continuing to grades 6–9 as well. African American and Latino students "are overrepresented in suspension/expulsion rates relative to White students at both K-6 and 6–9 levels," but are underrepresented in less severe administrative decisions such as detention at all grade levels (Skiba et. al, 2011, p. 95).

There is no research that supports separating out the "bad" students from the "good" as a way to maintain order and control in a classroom or school. In fact, schools with large numbers of suspensions, attributed to either a large number of individual occurrences or a small number of students with numerous incidences, typically spend a great deal of time dealing with discipline and control issues and have little remaining time to address issues involving instruction and learning (Noguera, 2003). These widespread disproportionate disciplinary practices may be contributing to the "lowered academic performance among the group of students in greatest need of improvement" (Gregory et. al, 2010, p. 60). In order to close the discipline gap, and in turn hopefully address the achievement gap, the orientations and practices of both educational and juvenile justice institutions and their respective practitioners within the institutions must be reshaped (Johnston, 2000).

Zero Tolerance Policies and Practices

Zero tolerance policies have largely been blamed for the trends of racial disproportionality in school discipline and have been implemented notoriously as a form of school discipline in the United States. In its basic form, zero tolerance "assigns explicit, predetermined punishments to specific violations of school rules, regardless of the situation or context of the behavior" (Boccanfuso & Kuhfeld, 2011, p. 1). Zero tolerance policies were designed to have a deterrent effect on students; however, over the years the implementation and execution, these policies have proven troublesome resulting in students receiving severe punishments, even for some times minor offenses, including suspension, expulsion, and arrest for misbehavior.

Initially, these policies were not necessarily introduced as an approach for curbing student behavior. Rather the policy was introduced as a method for addressing habitual illegal behavior in the criminal justice system, ultimately resulting in harsher penalties for the chronic criminal. However, with the implementation of the Gun Free Schools Act of 1994, student punishment for bringing a firearm and/or weapon onto school grounds introduced a mandatory expulsion for such behavior and the practice has been mimicked nationally (US Department of Education, 1994). Zero tolerance policies vary by state, county, and school but their use has spread vigorously and their affect can be directly related to the number of youth engaged in the juvenile justice system.

Responding to the public outcry about increased violence at the hands of America's youth, the Gun Free Schools Act paved the way for an attack on the supposed terroristic behavior of youth. However, that behavior was not defined in a manner that considered contributing factors of youth. Instead, children — the very individuals whose minds are developing and need to be molded — became no more than descriptive behaviors outlined in black and white. In the late 1990s zero tolerance policies would begin a rolling surge and started to include more than just bringing guns, knives, and weapons to school. Around this time misconduct began to outweigh the issues of weapons in school and this direction was supported by the introduction of security officers, random searches, metal detectors, and stricter school based regulations — outside of those required by the Department of Education.

In 1994, the rate of juvenile violent crime peaked briefly, but immediately started a steady decline as reported for the next ten years, including a 3.8% decline in juvenile arrests from 2013 to 2014 — the last year of statics available (FBI, 2014). The enforcement of zero tolerance policies is a drastic change from the disciplinary practices, which used to occur within educational settings years ago. While the discipline of earlier days may have included corporal punishment, modern day discipline seems to no longer directly aim to mold the student's behavior through deterrence — but rather, it seems, to nullify the students' behavior by removing the student from the learning environment.

Discipline has become more formal and often no longer occurs between the student-teacher-parent structures. Instead, disciplinary responses quickly climb the administrative ladder and introduce the legal system into school situations at the onset of minor infractions. Additionally, due to the overzealous urge to keep schools *safe*, zero tolerance policies have reduced the discretionary responsibility from teachers and administrators with little reverence to how those actions affect students and the once ultimate mission of educating our youth. As such, zero tolerance discipline tactics have contributed to the blurring of lines between the juvenile justice system and the adult criminal system (Dupper, 2010).

Additionally, zero tolerance policies are not isolated to actual laws and district wide codes of conduct. Rarely mentioned in discussions is the idea of zero tolerance *practices*. Zero tolerance practices stem from policies but may be at the school level rather than district level. Practices are responses to behavior that may fit into the gray areas of district codes of conduct but are only practiced at the school level. For instance, in Jefferson County Public Schools in Kentucky, there are zero tolerance policies that align with the Gun Free Schools Act but there are also zero tolerance practices (i.e., automatic suspension for fighting) that are enforced at the school level. These practices lead to disparities in school discipline because the demographic of the school and the discipline style of the school leader could impact which students receive the harsher penalty.

Arguably, the expansion to more punitive applications of discipline has encouraged and developed a now distinct trajectory for students known as the *school-to-prison pipeline*. Researchers have defined the school-to-prison pipeline as a reduction in educational opportunities for students being punished by the school system, and the likelihood that these same students will further become removed from educational environments once their misconduct transitions to the juvenile justice system (NAACP, 2005). With the harsh discipline practices mandated by zero tolerance policies and the lack of resources, suspended and/or expelled students become disengaged and are more likely to drop out of school—all of which are contributing factors in their engagement in delinquent behavior (Wald & Losen, 2003, p. 11). The "school-to-prison pipeline" is the term assigned to this continued system of failure based on flawed policies and procedures, which push at-risk youth out of the school system towards the juvenile justice system, before considering any forms of alternative sanction.

The school to prison pipeline is filled with students of color. Studies have shown that not only are students disciplined differently by race but that there is also relationship with the type of offense. Other research shows that minority youth are disciplined for more subjective behaviors while white students are disciplined for objective behaviors. Many districts' discipline data reflects that disproportionality shows up with minor, but subjective, behavior such as deliberate disruption or willful defiance/disruption. This behavior is defined as:

> " . . . disrupting school activities or otherwise willfully defying the valid authority of school staff." This broad definition has included suspensions for everything from a student failing to follow directions or bring materials, to wearing a hat in class or talking back to a teacher (Fix School Discipline, 2014).

Due to the egregious nature of minority overrepresentation for subjective behaviors qualified under willful defiance, California recently took legislative action to remedy the issue. In 2014, Assembly Bill 20 prohibits California from suspending K-3 students for willful defiance. The statewide legislation followed local district policy changes. In the 2013–2014 academic year, San Francisco eliminated suspensions for willful defiance. Subsequently, Los Angeles Unified School District and Oakland Unified School District followed suit in 2014 and 2014, respectively. California's policy changes were a result of increasing evidence that willful defiance persistently impacted exclusionary discipline. Frey (2014) reported that prior to the legislation, willful defiance made up 43 percent of California's suspensions. Nineteen percent of willful defiance suspensions were African-American students though they only comprised of six percent of California's student enrollment (Frey, 2014).

Theoretical Explanations for School-Based DMC

School discipline disparities and DMC appear to be inextricably related. Scholars have noted that while the topics are parallel in nature, they are largely understudied as connected issues (Nicholson-Crotty et al., 2009). Instead, school discipline research and DMC research reflect the larger issue of the two systems not working in tandem but operating in silos. While empirical relationships have been tested, there is still little literature available that clearly and consistently connects the two issues. One notable study that addresses the dearth in the literature was conducted by Nicholson-Crotty and colleagues (2009), who argued that DMC in juvenile court referrals mirror the disproportionate discipline patterns of schools. The genesis of their thesis derived from previous works that noted that troubled youth in both the education and juvenile systems tend to have similar risk factors. DMC research shows the following as risk factors for contact with juvenile justice system:

- Economically disadvantaged and unstable communities and neighborhood social contexts (Fite, Wynn, and Pardini, 2009; Sampson, Morenoff, and Raudenbush, 2005; Moak, Shaun, Walker, and Gann, 2012);
- Low-performing institutions, especially public schools (Sharkey and Sampson, 2010);
- Delinquent peers (Fite, Wynn, and Pardini, 2009);
- Family risk factors such as unmarried or single parents, incarcerated parents, poor parent-child communication, and harsh, lax, or inconsistent discipline (Fite, Wynn, and Pardini, 2009; Vespa, Lewis, and

Kreider, 2013; Sampson, Morenoff, and Raudenbush, 2005; Jarjoura, Roger, DuBois, Shlafer, and Haight, 2013);
* Greater exposure to violence (Kilpatrick, Saunders, and Smith, 2003) (see: Office of Juvenile Justice Delinquency and Prevention Model Programs, nd)

The cumulative nature of these risk factors prompted the National Research Council (2013) to state the following:

> ... minority youth are born into and raised in severely compromised familial, community, and educational environments that set the stage for a range of adverse behaviors and outcomes, including problems in school, relationships, and engaging in prosocial behavior (p. 224).

Other explanations for DMC propose that minorities may be treated differently based on perceived threats to cultural, social, economic and political dominance (Thomas, Moak & Walker, 2012). In order to protect their dominance, the racial threat hypothesis asserts that Whites will increasingly utilize formal control tactics such as arrest, detention and confinement. Minority or racial threat suggests that as dominant power structures are seemingly diminished by increased proportions of minorities, then those in power (i.e., Whites) develop mechanisms for control such as punitive legal policies (Rocque & Paternoster, 2011). Symbolic threat relies more on the idea that Black communities suffer from social disorganization and extreme violence due to intentional institutional racism. As a result, Black communities can be socially isolated thus leading to the rejection of mainstream norms, values and beliefs. Since African-Americans appear to oppose mainstream culture, Whites perceive them to be threatening to normative social order. Controlling this threat may come in the form of crime control measures, which serve to "legally enforce community values and morality and protect the interests of the majority group" (Thomas et al., 2012, p. 245)

Policy research on racial disparities can be explained through a threat hypothesis lens. This framework is important in a discussion of disproportionality of social controls (both in the educational and juvenile justice systems). Decision-makers in both systems have the potential to make their decisions based on the perceived threat of minority youth (Leiber & Fox, 2005). The National Research Council (2009) has argued that in response to threats to normative social order, Whites have historically and consistently developed mechanisms to control minority populations. These "peculiar institutions" began with chattel slavery and include: Black codes/Convict leasing, Jim Crow,

Ghettos and Prisons (Wadhwa, 2016). Wadhwa (2016) states that schools and their racial discipline gaps are now part of the historical "peculiar institutions" that have served to isolate, exclude and ostracize Blacks in the US. More specifically, she states:

> Just as people who are not valued in the service economy have been socially excluded and contained in prisons, young people who are unable to perform on grade level or adhere or to behavior norms are often excluded through suspension and expulsion and contained in alternative schools or juvenile detention centers (Wadhwa, 2016, p. 24).

Welch and Payne (2010), in the first study to consider racial threat as an explanation to school discipline disparities, applied the theory from a crime related perspective. They cite evidence that racial threat, or its proxy—racial composition of place—has been shown to be related to punishment based justice decisions, such as: corrections (Jacobs & Helms, 1999), rates of incarceration (Leiber & Fox, 2005), and executions (Tolnay, Beck & Massey, 1992). They suggested that crime-related racial threat may operate in school disciplinary structures in the same manner that it has proven to increase the punitiveness in criminal justice policies. Welch and Payne (2010) extended the hypothesis to disproportionality in school discipline by positing that evidence of racial threat in schools would negatively impact their usage of harsh disciplinary techniques. They found that school racial composition impacted the punitiveness of school disciplinary policies. More specifically, they found that schools with larger numbers of black students utilize harsher punishments in response to misbehavior.

Rocque and Paternoster (2011) also extended the racial threat hypothesis to the realm of school discipline by claiming that while minority students may not be a political or economic threat to whites, that they could be a considered a "cultural threat" (p. 636). The cultural threat hypothesis is evident when minority students reject the predominant White school culture of academic success and an "appearance of docility" (Rocque & Paternoster, 2011, p. 636). They suggest that as white educators perceive this rejection, then they are more likely to respond more punitively and formally to minority youth in comparison to their fellow white classmates. They propose:

> School discipline can be understood within the context of racial threat theory because teachers . . . with their culture of academic success and need for control over the school environment, may easily perceive black students as a source of trouble or a threat to their ability to control the cultural context of what goes in school (p. 639).

Nicholson-Crotty, Birchmeier and Valentine (2009) tested the racial threat hypothesis to show that student behavior alone cannot explain the disparities in school discipline. They calculated a relative rate for each school as well as the relative rate for the juvenile justice decision point. Their findings support that disproportionality in suspensions was related to the DMC in referrals to court. Controlling for factors such as; poverty, unemployment and urbanization, they still found the relationships existed. Among all of the variables they tested, Nicholson-Crotty et al. (2009) found that population density was most predictive of a relative referral rate for African-American youth.

Paradigm Shifting: Zero Tolerance to Restorative Practices

Although many school districts continue to use zero tolerance practices, research shows that their effectiveness in curbing student misbehavior is non-existent. Additionally, students are disproportionately being negatively affected by these policies resulting in an influx of youth exposure to the juvenile justice system — especially as it regards students from minority backgrounds (Farmer, 2010). Alternatively, there are some non-punitive approaches to dealing with problems of misconduct within the school environment, which have shown promise. These alternative approaches to school discipline are expected to have positive impacts on students and directly influence their ability to excel in the academic environment. Current trends in addressing discipline disparities include restorative approaches that focus on "social, behavioral, and cognitive skill-building, character education, and/or targeted behavioral support for students who are at risk for violent or illegal behavior" (Boccanfuso & Kuhfeld, 2011, p. 4). They all show promise for changing school climate and culture; addressing racial disparities in school discipline; and curbing school-based arrests and juvenile court referrals.

Restorative practices (RP) in schools derive from justice system strategies focused on repairing harm by including the offender, victim and community in resolving conflict. Restorative practices focus on building relationships, which help address conflict and accountability. School districts use a range of restorative practices strategies to effect student behavior. The RP continuum ranges from affective language to restorative conferences. It is a discipline model that strives to "repair harm and create whole school community environment, while reducing the frequency and severity of school violations" (Payne & Welch, 2015, p. 540). Research has shown that students are receptive to RP and prefer restorative discipline solutions over the traditional punitive responses such as detention, suspension and expulsion (Payne & Welch, 2015). Theoretically, implementing RP should serve to reduce the use racial disparities in exclusionary discipline strategies; however, whether or not it will adequately reduce discipline disparities is still up for debate due to criticisms of evaluative studies.

Several school districts have seen dramatic differences in their exclusionary discipline numbers after adopting restorative practices policies. Gonzalez (2012) reported that in Oakland, CA, the introduction of restorative practices at Cole Middle School reduced suspensions from fifty suspensions per 100 students to six suspensions per 100 students after three years. She also cites the success of Peoria, Illinois schools, which implemented restorative justice in an effort to curb suspensions and referrals to law enforcement. Before restorative justice, Manual High School was plagued with police presence for minor infractions and referrals to juvenile court. After the implementation of peer juries, they saw a 43% decrease in referrals for African-American students (Gonzalez, 2012).

While not explicitly restorative, schools are increasingly introducing related ideas such as Positive Behavior Intervention and Supports (PBIS) and Trauma Informed Care (TIC). PBIS operates on a school-wide level and focuses on improving the ability for a school (as a whole) to teach its students about positive behavior expectation and provide those students the necessary support for adhering to the defined behavior (Sprague & Horner, 2006; Vincent, Sprague & Gau, 2013). At PBIS schools, discipline plans aim to evaluate the complementing mechanisms of behavioral problems and are school-wide but student-specific (Buffalo County Public Schools, 2015). This multi-tier program contains levels that each aim to address the issues of behavior from a positive standpoint: first, by setting expectations, then targeting at-risk students, then providing intense intervention for the most egregious behavior. While PBIS is a relatively new endeavor for many school districts, some are seeing positive effects on discipline disparities. Skiba, Arrendondo, and Rausch (2014) report that schools have reported "some reductions in disciplinary exclusions for Hispanic/Latino and American Indian/Alaska Native students, but not for African-American students" (p. 4).

Trauma informed care has helped some schools see successes in reducing suspensions and expulsion by seeking to understand the underlying issues causing misconduct and insubordination in and out of the classroom. Trauma informed care "means that every adult who interacts with a child at school understands and responds appropriately to the impact of trauma on the child" (Children's Defense Fund Ohio, 2015, p. 7). This is particularly important due to reports that an estimated two in every three youth report they have experienced psychological trauma (Bath, 2008; Copeland, Keeler, Angold & Costello, 2007).

Relationships with adults that are supportive and responsive are shown to prevent and reverse the adverse effects of trauma. Researchers have noted that healing from traumatic events is not relegated only to mental health settings. Greenwald (2005) suggested that "parents, counselors, teachers, coaches, direct care workers, case managers, and others are all in a position to help a child heal" (Bath, 2008, p. 17). As it relates to school discipline, TIC considers that children who experience trauma may display symptoms of post-traumatic stress disorder (PTSD) and their misbehavior may be a manifestation of the trauma. In addition, the ACEs Study found that "associations between early trauma and increased drug use and abuse, disease, disability, and social problems across a person's lifetime. Low-income students and students of color are particularly vulnerable, in part because of differential access to mental health care" (Children's Defense Fund Ohio, 2015, p. 6).

A more trauma informed approach for schools would refer students to prevention or treatment. For example, in Orange County Public Schools (2015) the administration has the choice of referring students to a prevention or treatment program for a range of infractions from open defiance and bus disruption to trespassing and fighting (p. 27). Oftentimes, students are exhibiting negative behavior due to issues occurring outside of the school environment. Problems in the home, abuse, neglect, and mental health are often triggers for their behavior but not discussed or unrecognized by teachers and staff. Interventions aimed at helping youth deal with the trauma they are experiencing within their lives are effective methods for reducing disruptive behavior while also providing counseling and coping techniques that can be used throughout their lives.

Loose Coupling, Schools and Disproportionate Minority Contact

Zero tolerance policies entered the academic environment on the coat tails of a federal mandate directly relating to the reduction of school violence at the hands of youth. While the implementation of the Gun Free Schools Act was developed at a time immediately following a brief surge in juvenile school violence, its barriers were far reaching and resulted in the abundance and widespread use of zero-tolerance policies across that nation. Zero-tolerance policies now warrant disciplinary action amongst students for things as minor as insubordination and as significant as weapons violations. Although teachers and administrators may appreciate the ease of use and accessibility of support in their decisions to suspend, expel, and or transfer students to juvenile justice services, the research on their effectiveness is still lacking—while the evidence of their negative effect on student development is abundant (Porter, 2015).

Several studies link classroom exclusion to low academic achievement. Morrison et. al (2001), for example, found a relationship between suspensions and academic performance, noting that students with office referrals and suspensions had lower grade point averages (GPAs) than did their peers without such disciplinary consequences. Miles and Stipek (2006) noted that repeated experiences with low academic performance can lead to student frustration and disengagement, as well as low self-confidence, which contribute to classroom disruptions. Perhaps most enlightening of all, in a study about the academic, social, and emotional repercussions of classroom exclusion, Brown (2007) reported that the students themselves noted the negative effects of missed instructional time on their overall academic achievement.

Though both the discipline and achievement gaps have been widely documented, little research attempts to find a relationship between the two. The loss of instructional time due to suspensions or expulsions can lead to lower academic achievement, as evidenced above, and has been documented, but the disproportionate disciplinary practices meted out by schools to minority students are infrequently linked to minority students' lower academic achievement. Gregory et. al (2010) synthesize "the research on racial and ethnic patterns in school discipline" (p. 59) in order to suggest the influence of the racial discipline gap on "racial patterns in achievement" (p. 59). By examining patterns in academic achievement, neighborhood characteristics, behavior, and contact with the justice system, this study states that no one solution will work to address such a multi-faceted problem, and that significantly more research must be done to address such a complex and urgent matter.

It is the responsibility of both the justice and educational systems to understand the juvenile justice system begins before arrest and referral. Decisions in schools mimic the sanctions of the justice system. In a school setting, each classroom is a courtroom and each teacher is a judge. They are the arguably the true gatekeepers to the justice system. The manner in which discipline is handled even at the classroom level may have implications for whether or not that child ends up in the juvenile justice system. Gregory and colleagues (2014) stated that one school suspension or referral is all it takes to escalate the probability that a student will drop out of school or experience academic failure. Research has proven that "youth who are disciplined or court-involved are at increased risk of dropping out and becoming involved in the juvenile justice system" (Fowler, 2011, p. 17). The Advancement Project (2005) reported that punitive responses to school misbehavior have contributed to the "tripling of the national prison population from 1987–2007" (Gonzalez, 2012, p. 283).

It is this type of evidence that should pull together the stakeholders in both systems to develop effective and continuous solutions that cross systems. Bishop and colleagues (2010) suggested that the juvenile justice system consists of loosely coupled organizations. They studied DMC in the juvenile justice system by examining the actions from a focal concerns perspective and organizational coupling. Their application of organizational theory to racial disproportionality is a framework important for understanding change. Related to their framework, Singer (1996) acknowledged:

> . . . modern bureaucracies perpetuate themselves by establishing and applying separate spheres of knowledge. When they work together, they seldom reach consensus. More often than not, the purposes and goals of each organization are engrafted onto a decision that may not appear rational or internally consistent, but which reproduces the interests of each party to the decision. Collective deference sustains organizational legitimacy and minimizes interorganizational conflict. Thus, concerns about incompatibilities among the objectives that are embodied in any decision tend to give way to the goal of supporting and endorsing the specialized interests and expertise of each party to the decision (p. 17).

The organizational approach is intriguing and necessary. Far too much time is spent on data about disproportionality and arguably not enough time is allotted to the decision makers and their organizational context. Bishop et al. (2010) argues that juvenile justice is a nonsystem. Further, they argue "there are important consequences of processing young people through a justice system in which the multiple agencies involved in decision making are independent, governed by different rules and mandates, and oriented toward goals and objectives that are frequently different from and sometimes incompatible with the priorities of other organizational units" (Bishop et al., 2010, p. 216).

Using this lens, it is important to acknowledge that a nonsystem can include components that are not traditionally included. Schools are a system of their own; however, more and more research is showing that students are also the youth that crossover into the juvenile justice system. While Bishop et al. (2010) do not include schools in their analysis, the study's approach and findings are illustrative for this chapter. They found that there is a host of misinformation, miscommunication and apathy amongst the systems to adequately address the interconnectedness.

It is important for juvenile justice professionals to understand that schools have a duty to use the most effective means to provide a safe learning environment for its students and staff. But it is equally as important for school officials to recognize the justice implications presented when codes of conduct are unnecessarily punitive. Accordingly, methods for discipline should steer away from the binary procedures outlined in zero tolerance policies and move toward programs like those of positive behavioral change, treatment, and restorative practices for those students who need assistance. The school environment is one of significance for a student in the developmental stages of life and the alternatives outlined in this chapter suggest there are indeed other ways besides zero tolerance that can successfully keep the school environment safe while also providing youth the opportunity to learn, grown, and excel in their academic achievements and disrupt their pipeline to prison.

References

Advancement Project (2005). Education on Lockdown: The Schoolhouse to Jailhouse Track. Retrieved April 27, 2016 from http://www.advancement project.org/sites/default/files/publications/FINALEOLrep.pdf.

Arcia, E. (2006). Achievement and Enrollment Status of Suspended Students: Outcomes in a large, multicultural school district. *Education and Urban Society, 38*(3), 359–369.

Bath, H. (2008). The three pillars of trauma informed care. *Reclaiming Children & Youth,* 17(3), 17–21.

Bishop, D. (2005). The role of race and ethnicity in juvenile justice processing. In D. Hawkins & K. Kempf-Leonard (Eds.), *Our children, their children: Confronting racial and ethnic differences in American juvenile justice* (pp. 23–82). MacArthur Foundation Research Network on Adolescent Development and Juvenile Justice. The John T. and Catherine MacArthur Foundation. The University of Chicago Press.

Bishop, D.M., Leiber, M. Johnson, J. (2010). Contexts of decisionmaking in the Juvenile Justice System: An organizational approach to understanding disproportionate minority contact. *Youth Violence and Juvenile Justice,* 8(3), 213–233.

Boccanfuso, C. & Kuhfeld, M. (2011). *Multiple responses, promising results: Evidence-based, nonpunitive alternatives to zero tolerance.* (Research Brief 2011-09) Retrieved April 27, 2106 from http://childtrends.org/wp-content/uploads/2011/03/Child_Trends-2011_03_01_RB_AltToZeroTolerance.pdf.

Brown, T. M. (2007). Lost and turned out: Academic, social, and emotional experiences of students excluded from school. *Urban Education, 42*(5), 432–455.

Buffalo Public Schools — New York. (2015). *Standards for Community-Wide Conduct and Intervention Supports.* Retrieved April 6, 2016 from http://www.buffaloschools.org/StudentServices.cfm?subpage=57596.

Children's Defense Fund Ohio. (2015). Issue Brief: Addressing Children's Trauma: A Toolkit for Ohio Schools Children's Defense Fund — Ohio. Retrieved April 27, 2016 from, http://www.cdfohio.org/research-library/2015/addressing-childrens-trauma.pdf

Copeland, W.E., Keeler, G., Angold, A. & Costello, E.J. (2007). Traumatic events and posttraumatic stress in childhood. Archives of General Psychiatry, 64, 577–584.

Dupper, D. R. (2010). Does the Punishment Fit the Crime? The Impact of Zero Tolerance Discipline on At-Risk Youths. *Children & Schools.* pp. 67–69.

Farmer, S. (2010). Criminality of Black youth in inner-city schools: 'moral panic', moral imagination, and moral formation. *Race, Ethnicity & Education, 13*(3), 367–381. doi:10.1080/13613324.2010.500845.

Fite, P.J., Wynn, P. & Pardini, D.A. (2009). Explaining discrepancies in arrest rates between black and white male juveniles. *Journal of Consulting and Clinical Psychology, 77*(5), 916–927.

Fix School Discipline, (2014). Fact Sheet: Fix School Discipline Bills: AB 420. Retrieved on April 27, 2016 from, http://fixschooldiscipline.org/wp-content/uploads/2014/11/AB-420-Fact-Sheet-Implementation.pdf

Fowler, D. (2011). School discipline feeds the "pipeline to prison." *Phi Delta Kappan, 93*(2), 14–19.

Frabutt, J.M., Cabaniss, E.R., Kendrick, M.H., Arbuckle, M.B. (2008). A community-academic collaboration to reduce disproportionate minority contact in the juvenile justice system. *Journal of Higher Education Outreach and Engagement, 12*(3), 5–21.

Frey, S. (2014). Agreement reached on 'willful defiance' bill. Retrieved on April 27, 2016 from, http://edsource.org/2014/agreement-reached-on-willful-defiance-bill/65671

Gonzalez, T. (2012). Keeping kids in schools: Restorative justice, punitive discipline, and the school to prison pipeline. *Journal of Law and Education, 41*(2), 281–335.

Greenwald, R. (2005). *Child Trauma Handbook: A Guide for Helping Trauma-exposed Children and Adolescents.* New York: The Haworth Maltreatment and Trauma Press.

Gregory, A., Skiba, R. J. & Noguera, P. A. (2010). The Achievement Gap and the Discipline Gap: Two sides of the same coin. *Educational Researcher, 39*(1), 59–68.

Irby, D.J. (2014). Trouble at School: Understanding school discipline systems as nets of social control. *Equity & Excellence in Education, 47*(4), 513–530.

Jarjoura, G.R., DuBois, D.L., Shlafer, R.J. & Haight, K.A. (2013). Mentoring children of incarcerated parents: A Synthesis of Research and Input from Listening Session Held by the Office of Juvenile Justice and Delinquency Prevention and White House Domestic Policy Council and Office of Public Engagement. Retrieved April 27, 2016 from, http://www.ojdp.gov/about/MentoringCOIP2013.

Jefferson County Public Schools — Kentucky. (2015). *Code of Acceptable Behavior and Discipline and the Student Bill of Rights.* Retrieved April 7, 2016 from http://www.jcpsky.net/Pubs/codeofconduct.pdf.

Johnston, R.C. (2000). Federal data highlight disparities in discipline. *Education Week, 19*(41).

Kilpatrick, D.G., Saunders, B.E. & Smith, D.W. (2003). *Youth Victimization: Prevalence and Implications.* Washington, DC: Office of Justice Programs, National Institute of Justice, U.S. Department of Justice.

Kim, C.Y., Losen, D.J., & Hewitt, D.T. (2010). *The School-to-Prison Pipeline: Structuring Legal Reform.* NYU Press: New York, NY.

Leiber, M. & Fox, K. (2005). Race and the impact of detention on juvenile justice decision making. *Crime and Delinquency*, 51, 470–490.

Miles, S. B. & Stipek, D. (2006). Contemporaneous and longitudinal associations between social behavior and literacy achievement in a sample of low-income elementary school children.*Child Development, 77*, 103–117.

Moak, S.C., Shaun, T.A., Walker, J.T. & Gann, S.M. (2012) The influence of race on preadjudication detention: Applying the symbolic threat hypothesis to Disproportionate Minority Contact. *OJJDP Journal of Juvenile Justice, 2*(1), 73–89.

Morrison, G.M., Anthony, S.L, Storino, M. & Dillon, C. (2001). An examination of the disciplinary histories and the individual and educational characteristics of students who participate in an in-school suspension program. *Education and Treatment of Children, 26*(1), 276–293.

NAACP. (2005). *Interrupting the School to Prison Pipe-line.* Washington DC.

National Research Council. 2013. *Reforming Juvenile Justice: A Developmental Approach.* Washington, D.C.: The National Academies Press.

Nicholson-Crotty, S., Birchmeier, Z. & Valentine, D. (2009). Exploring the impact of school discipline on racial disproportion in the juvenile justice system. *Social Science Quarterly*, 90(4), 1003–1019.

Noguera, P.A. (2003). Schools, Prisons, and Social Implications of Punishment: Rethinking disciplinary practices. *Theory Into Practice, 42*(4), 341–350.

Office of Juvenile Justice Delinquency and Prevention Model Programs (nd). Literature Reviews: Disproportionate Minority Contact. Retrieved April 27, 2016 from, http://www.ojjdp.gov/mpg/litreviews/Disproportionate_Minority_Contact.pdf.

Orange County Public Schools — Florida. (2015). *Code of Student Conduct.* Retrieved April 7, 2016 from https://ocps.net/SiteCollectionDocuments /Docs%20Continually%20 Updated/Code%20of%20Conduct.pdf.

Perry, B.L. & Morris, E.W. (2014). Suspending progress: Collateral consequences of exclusionary punishment in public schools. *American Sociological Review*, 79(6), 1067–1087.

Porter, T. R. (2015). The School-to-Prison Pipeline: The Business Side of Incarcerating, Not Educating, Students in Public Schools. *Arkansas Law Review (1968-Present)*, *68*(1), 55–81.

Rocque and Paternoster (2011). Understanding the antecedents of the school-to-jail link: The relationship between race and school discipline. *The Journal of Criminal Law and Criminology,* 101(2), 633–665.

Sampson, R.J., Morenoff, J.D. & Raudenbush, S. (2005). Social anatomy of racial and ethnic disparities in violence. *American Journal of Public Health*, 95(2), 224–232.

Sharkey, P. & Sampson, R.J. (2010). Destination effects: Residential mobility and trajectories of adolescent violence in a stratified Metropolis. *Criminology*, 48(3), 639–681.

Singer, S. (1996). *Recriminalizing Delinquency: Violent Juvenile Crime and Juvenile Justice Reform.* New York: Cambridge University Press.

Skiba, R. J., Arredondo, M. I., Rausch, M. K. (2014). New and developing research on disparities in discipline. Bloomington, IN: The Equity Project at Indiana University. Retrieved April 26, 2016 from http://rtpcollaborative. indiana.edu/briefing-papers/.

Skiba, R. J., Horner, R. H., Chung, C., Rausch, M. K., May, S. L & Tobin, T. (2011). Race Is Not Neutral: A national investigation of African American and Latino disproportionality in school discipline. *School Psychology Review*, *40*(1), 85–107.

Skiba, R. J., Michael, R. S., Nardo, A. C. & Peterson, R. L. (2002). The Color of Discipline: Sources of racial and gender disproportionality in school punishment. *The Urban Review, 34*(4), 317–342.

Sprague, J.R. & Horner, R.H. (2006). Schoolwide positive behavioral supports. in S.R. Jimerson & M.J. Furlong (Eds). The Handbook of School Violence and School Safety. (pp. 413–427). Mahwah, NJ: Erlbaum.

Tajalli, H. & Garba, H. A. (2014). Discipline or Prejudice? Overrepresentation of Minority Students Disciplinary Alternative Education Programs. *Urban Review , 46*, 620–631.

Thomas, S.C., Moak, S.A. & Walker, J.T. (2012). The influence of race on pre-adjudication detention: Applying the symbolic threat hypothesis to Disproportionate Minority Contact. *Journal of Juvenile Justice*, 2(1). Retrieved on April 26, 2106 http://www.journalofjuvjustice.org/JOJJ0201/article06.htm

Tolnay, S.E., Beck, E.M. & Massey, J.L. (1992). Black competition and white vengeance: Legal execution of black as social control I the cotton south, 1890–1929. *Social Science Quarterly*, 73, 627–644.

U.S. Department of Education. (1994). *Gun Free Schools Act*. Retrieved April 7, 2016, from http://www2.ed.gov/policy/elsec/leg/esea02/pg54.html.

U.S. Department of Education. (2014). Data Snapshot: School Discipline. Retrieved April 27, 2016, from http://ocrdata.ed.gov/Downloads/CRDC-School-Discipline-Snapshot.pdf.

Vespa, J., Lewis, J.M. & Kreider, R.M. (2013). America's Families and Living Arrangements: 2012. Washington, DC: US Census Bureau. Retrieved April 27, 2016 from, http//www.census.gov/prod/2013pubs/p20-570.pdf

Vincent, C.G., Sprague, J.R. & Gau, J.M. (2013). The Effectiveness of School-wide Positive Behavior Interventions and Supports for Reducing Racially Inequitable Disciplinary Exclusions in Middle Schools. Retrieved on May 16, 2016 from, https://civilrightsproject.ucla.edu/resources/projects /center-for-civil-rights-remedies/school-to-prison-folder/state-reports /copy6_of_dignity-disparity-and-desistance-effective-restorative-justice -strategies-to-plug-the-201cschool-to-prison-pipeline/vincent-SWPBIS -effectieveness-ccrr-fonf-2013.pdf.

Wallace, J. M., Goodkind, S., Wallace, C. M. & Bachman, J. G. (2008). Racial, Ethnic, and Gender Differences in School Discipline among U.S. High School Students: 1991–2005. *Negro Educational Review , 59* (1/2), 47–62.

Wacquant, L. (2000). The new "peculiar" institution: On the prison as surrogate ghetto. *Theoretical Criminology*, 4(3), 377.

Wadhwa, A. (2016). *Restorative Justice in Urban Schools: Disrupting the School-to-Prison Pipeline*. Routledge: New York, NY.

Welch, A.A. & Payne, W. (2010). Racial threat and punitive school discipline. *Social Problems*, 5, 25–48.

Chapter 8

Criminal Justice, Race and the War on Drugs

Ojmarrh Mitchell and Michael J. Lynch

Introduction

As this book illustrates, a significant body of extant research examines issues of racial bias in criminal justice processes and law. Taken as a whole this body of research suggests that race affects a variety of criminal justice processes. To be sure, the strength of the evidence on racial disparity varies across specific issues, time and geographic space in the U.S., and can even depend, in some cases, on the method of analysis or the variables included within the analysis. Despite these observations, the relationship between race, law and criminal justice is the most pronounced and consistent with respect to drug crimes. Historically, the race-drug connection has been illustrated by various "wars" on drugs: the opiate wars in the U.S. from the 1870s through the early 1900s revolved around the use of these drugs among Asian populations; the focus on marijuana and black Americans became part of law enforcement's campaign against drug use in the 1930s, spearheaded by Harry Anslinger, the first Commissioner of the Federal Bureau of Narcotics; the emergence of racial differentiation in sentencing in the 1986 *Controlled Substances Act* which provided penalties for crack cocaine, a drug more widely used in minority communities, that were 100 times as severe as the penalties for powdered cocaine, a drug more often used by affluent whites; to the long-running "war on drugs" that has influenced criminal legislation and crime control in the U.S. since the Civil Rights Movement.

This chapter focuses specific attention on the contemporary era of the war on drugs (WoD) and race associated with President Reagan and Nancy Reagan's national crusade against drugs (Reagan, September 14, 1986) and passage of the Anti-Drug Abuse Act of 1986. The contemporary WoD targeted low-level drug dealers and users for arrest by encouraging law enforcement officers to target these offenders and through increased drug sanctions for convicted drug offenders (e.g., long mandatory minimum prison sentences). These policies have had, as did earlier drugs wars, an especially detrimental effect on racial and ethnic minorities, but particularly on African-Americans (Musto, 1999).

To place this claim in context, consider that in 1980, prior to the WoD, the drug arrest rate was roughly twice as high for African-Americans (491 per 100,000) compared to whites (238 per 100,000). At the height of the drug war (1989) this ratio had increased to 4 to 1 and stimulated the expansion of racial disparities in imprisonment (Western, 2006). And while the WoD affected the growth of imprisonment for both blacks and whites, Blumstein and Beck (1999:25) estimated that the effect lead to a 17% increase in incarceration for whites but a 36% increase in incarceration for blacks between 1980 and 1996.

Reflecting on this and similar evidence, Michael Tonry (1995:82, our emphasis) argued that "The War on Drugs was a *calculated effort*" to increase the percentage of young black men in prison. In contrast, John P. Walters (2001:19), U.S. drug czar under President George W. Bush and WoD proponent, stated that the idea of the criminal justice system "unjustly punishing young black men" is one of the "great urban myths of our time."

The remainder of this chapter addresses whether African-Americans have been unjustly punished by policies instituted under the auspices of the WoD, or whether racial disparities in criminal justice outcomes are the consequence of differential drug use across racial groups.

The Contemporary War on Drugs: Background

As noted, the WoD was set in motion by Ronald Reagan and passage of the Anti-Drug Abuse Act of 1986. During the late 1980s, a "media frenzy" focusing on drug use, especially crack cocaine (Reinarman and Levine, 1997a) began when two young black athletes, Len Bias and Don Rogers, died within a week of one another after ingesting cocaine. Following these deaths, thousands of stories about cocaine appeared in the nation's newspapers (Trebach, 1987) and TV news (Diamond, 1991), and touted the dangers of crack and the mayhem surrounding the "crack epidemic."

This spate of news coverage emphasized four primary issues. First, that crack was highly addictive (e.g., see *Newsweek*, March 17, 1986). Second, that addicted mothers gave birth to addicted babies who would suffer from a variety of maladies including brain damage and low IQs (Baum, 1996). Third, that crack markets generated other crimes, especially violent crime (for discussion see Brownstein, 1997). And finally, that crack use had reached epidemic proportions in America's inner cities and was spreading to middle-class suburbs (e.g., *Newsweek*, March 17, 1986). In retrospect, many of these themes proved to be inaccurate (Frank, Augustyn, Knight, Pell, and Zuckerman, 2001; Goode, 2005; Goldstein, 2001; USSC, 2007).

More important than these media themes was the link the media made between African-Americans and crack use (Reeves and Campbell, 1994). Prior to the WoD, Reeves and Campbell found that 60% of cocaine users/sellers shown on television news were white. After 1986, however, news accounts involving cocaine users most often showed non-whites (66%). Thus, television news shows left viewers with the image of cocaine offenders as blacks. This message was not lost on media consumers. A study by Burston, Jones and Roberson-Saunders (1995) found that 95% of respondents in a Washington, D.C. area survey described both the typical drug user and trafficker as black.

Politicians, including U.S. presidents Reagan and G. H. W. Bush, reinforced media themes of crack's dangers, and used these to demonstrate their commitment to law and order. In a well known incident, President George H.W. Bush held up a bag of crack confiscated by federal agents, and noted that crack was "turning our cities into battle zones and murdering our children," and that "the gravest domestic threat facing our nation today is drugs . . . in particular, crack" (Bush, 1989). Congressman E. Clay Shaw (Republican, Florida) declared drugs "the biggest threat that we have ever had to our national security" (Baum, 1996: 231).

Media and political focus on the crack "epidemic" had a dramatic impact on public opinion. For example, in 1985 public opinion polls, only 1% of respondents identified drug use as "the most important problem facing the country today." In 1986, after the Bias and Rogers deaths and the ensuing political and media frenzy, this figure increased to 10% (Reinarman and Levine, 1997b: 24). In September of 1989, following President Bush's national address declaring drugs "the gravest domestic threat," 64% of respondents believed that drugs were the country's most important problem (Reinarman and Levine, 1997b: 24) despite the fact that drug use, including cocaine use had been dropping for several years prior to 1989.

To address the public concern they in part had stimulated, Congress passed a series of laws that spurred aggressive drug enforcement, significantly increased penalties for federal drug offenses, and provided federal financial support to states to fund law enforcement activities and build new prisons. The two central pieces of legislation that initiated the latest WoD were the federal Anti-Drug

Abuse Acts of 1986 and 1988. The Anti-Drug Abuse Act of 1986 included several new drug regulations and penalty provisions such as deportation penalties for alien drug traffickers, the prohibition of interstate commerce in drug paraphernalia, and the death penalty for certain drug offenses. The hallmark of this Act, however, were long mandatory minimum prison sentences for drug trafficking. The most controversial was the "100-to-1 ratio" that required, for example, first-time offenders to serve 10-year mandatory minimum prison sentences for the distribution of 5,000 grams (11.02 pounds or 177.32 ounces) or more of powder cocaine, or 50 grams (0.1102 pounds or 1.763 ounces) or more of crack cocaine. Under this law, the punishment for trafficking 100 grams (3.52 ounces) of powdered cocaine was effectively equivalent to those for trafficking 1 gram (0.0352 ounces) of crack cocaine. The 1988 Act escalated earlier provisions, and included among other penalties a five-year mandatory minimum sentence for the *simple possession* of 5 grams or more of crack cocaine. This provision made crack the only drug that required a mandatory penalty for a first-time possession.

Much has been written about the increased sentences for drug offenses created by Anti-Drug Abuse Acts, particularly the 100-to-1 crack/powder cocaine ratio. Considerably less attention has been given to what we believe is a bigger policy change—the targeting of street-level drug distributors and users. The Reagan/Bush administrations touted the need to focus drug enforcement activities on neighborhood level drug offenders as opposed to high level and international drug distributors targeted by previous administrations. The first National Drug Control Strategy (ONDCP, 1989) clearly reflected this thinking: "*[S]treet-level enforcement remains the best tool* we have for restoring a sense of order and civility to neighborhoods where drugs. . . . The first priority of local drug enforcement, then, is to employ effective police methods capable of fighting drugs at the neighborhood level" (p. 21, our emphasis). The Strategy also made clear the intended result of street-level drug enforcement: "Making streets safer and drug users more accountable for their actions requires the criminal justice system to expand and reform in an unprecedented way. *Effective street-level enforcement means dramatically increasing the number of drug offenders arrested*" (ONDCP, 1989: 24, our emphasis).

The seismic shift in federal drug policy established under the WoD was accompanied by billions of dollars in federal funds to states adopting law enforcement activities consistent with this new philosophy. The strings attached to the federal funds distributed to states had the effect of changing drug policy at the state level. States adopted more punitive sentences for drug offenders. For example, 31 states enacted mandatory minimum drug sentences by 1994 (Bureau of Justice Assistance, 1996). And at least fifteen states created sentencing policies that distinguished crack cocaine from powdered cocaine and reserved harsher sentences for the former substance (USSC, 2007). The end result of these changes were sharp increases in average time served for drug offenses; average time served went from 14 months in 1983 to 24 months in 2001—a 70% increase (Western 2006). Without a doubt these changes in drug sentencing were dramatic; yet, they pale in comparison to WoD's effects on drug arrests.

The War on Drugs and Arrests

The initial effects of the WoD can be seen in increased arrests for drug offenses between 1980 (pre-WoD) and 1990 (post-WoD). During this time period, drugs arrests increased by 87.6% (from 580,900 to 1,089,500). Arrests for violent and property crimes also expanded during this period, but at much reduced levels—48.5% for violent crimes and 19% for property crimes. Drug arrests continued to increase significantly during the 1990s, and from 1990–2000, drug arrest rose by 45% compared to a decline in both violent crime arrests (−11.4%) and property crime arrests (−26.9%). In the new millennium (2000–2008) drug arrests continued to increase, though by only 15.4 percent. Property crime arrests rose as well, but by only 4.1%, while violent crime arrests declined (4.8%). Over the entire time period (1980–2008) drug arrests expanded by 191% while violent crime arrest increased by 25.2% and property crime arrests declined 9.4%.

Increasing arrests for drug offenses are also evident when examining arrest ratios between drug, violent and property crimes. For example, in 1980 there were 3.21 property crime arrests for every drug arrest. By 2008, this trend had reversed itself, and there were 1.01 drug arrests for every property crime arrest. A similar picture emerges when examining the ratio of drug to violent crime arrests. In 1980, there were 1.22 drug arrests for every violent crime arrest but by 2008 this ratio grew to 2.86.

To illustrate the effect of the WoD on race and drug crime arrests, *Human Rights Watch* (HRW; http://www.hrw.org/en/reports/2009/03/02/decades disparity) collected data on drug arrests by race of offender from 1980 through 2007 from the Uniform Crime Reports for adults. In 1980, 27% of drug arrests involved blacks but by 1988, after the initial spread of the WoD, 40% of drug arrestees were black. The percentages of drug arrestees who were black peaked in both 1989 and 1991 at 42%, and declined slowly to 35% by 2007.

To get a more complete picture of the extent of racial differences in arrest, it is useful to employ race-based offending rates adjusted by population (for discussion of various uses and misuses of these measures see: Lynch, 2002). In

1980, HRW reports (Figure 1) that the drug arrest rate for whites was 190 per 100,000 and 554 per 100,000 for blacks—a disparity ratio that is 2.9 times higher for blacks. By 1988, the drug arrest disparity had increased to 5.1 times higher for blacks.

Race-based drug arrests rates for both whites and blacks grew as a result of the WoD. Between 1980–1988 the drug arrest rate grew 58.4% (to 301/100,000) for whites, *but expanded by 179% for blacks* (to 1,547/100,000). The disparity ratio reached 5.5 in both 1989 and 1991 (i.e., there were 5.5 times as many blacks arrested for drug offenses compared to whites), and declined slowly since to 3.6. Still, in 2007, the drug arrest rate for blacks was 1,721 per 100,000 or 211% higher than in 1980, while the drug arrest rate for whites rose by approximately 151% during this same period. Thus, while the WoD led to increased arrests for both blacks and whites, the effect was much greater for blacks than whites.

Figure 1. U.S. Adult Drug Arrest Rates per 100,000 by Race, 1980–2007

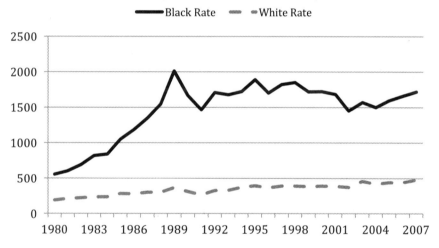

Source: Human Rights Watch, http://www.hrw.org/en/node/81105/section/4

The effect of the WoD is by no means uniform across locations in the U.S. Disparity ratios, for example, vary widely across states. Still, there is no state in which whites are arrested for drug offenses more often than blacks per 100,000 population (see Human Rights Watch). For the 48 states for which this information is available for 2007, the mean disparity ratio was 4.98. Thirty-one states had disparity ratios below that mean (Hawaii had the lowest disparity ratio, 2.0), with 17 states above the mean (both Iowa and Minnesota had mean disparity ratio of 11.3).

The War on Drugs and Imprisonment

The punitive shift associated with the WoD also impacted the U.S. prison system, increasing the number of prisoners serving time for a drug offense. In 1985 prior to implementation of the WoD there were 48,391 drug offenders incarcerated in the United States; by 2003 this figure has grown to 326,700 — a 575% increase (Mitchell, 2009). While this punitive shift affected Americans of every race, it particularly affected black Americans (Western, 2006; Lynch 2007). As an example of this racial imbalance, consider that in 1985, of the roughly 22,000 newly admitted inmates with a drug offense as their most serious conviction, 39% were black and 38% were white; in contrast, in 2003, of the nearly 112,000 inmates who fell into this category, 53% were black and 30% were white (Mitchell, 2009). These are just a few of the statistics that illustrate the racially disparate impact of the WoD, but they are far from the only such statistics. There is a significant literature addressing this issue, and it is sufficient for our purposes to note that the WoD has been shown to have a large impact on imprisonment and on racially disproportionate prison admissions (Tonry, 1995; Blumstein and Beck, 1999; Western, 2006; Lynch, 2007). Rather than repeat this evidence, we turn our attention to the following question: given that blacks are arrested, convicted, and incarcerated at rates that greatly exceed those of whites, can these racial disparities be explained by differences in drug offending?

Explanations for Racial Disparity in Drug Sanctioning

There are three competing, but non-contradictory, hypotheses used to explain the growing racial disparities in drug arrests and incarcerations. We refer to the first explanation as the "differential involvement" hypothesis. According to this hypothesis growing racial disparities in criminal justice outcomes have emerged due to growing racial disparities in drug offending. Simply put, the increase in black drug arrests reflects their growing drug offending. Scholars adhering to this hypothesis note that black/white economic inequality grew during the 1980s and as a result blacks were increasingly tempted by "employment" in illicit drug markets and/or downtrodden blacks were increasingly likely to be heavy drug users as a means to cope with their situations (Currie, 1993; Duster, 1997).

The second explanation contends that blacks and whites are equally likely to engage in drug offending, but blacks are subject to greater police scrutiny due to racial differences in the nature of drug offending; hence, we refer to this as the "differential scrutiny" hypothesis. Scholars utilizing this perspective (e.g., Blumstein, 1993; Goode, 2002; Tonry, 1995) note that blacks' lower economic standing leaves them with less access to private space and as a consequence drug offending in black communities is more likely to occur in public (e.g., street corners) and semi-public places (e.g., crack houses), involve smaller, more frequent transactions, and that police patrols are often concentrated in black communities. All of these factors expose drug offending in black communities to heightened police surveillance.

The third explanation centers on racial bias on the part of criminal justice policy-makers and/or criminal justice decision-makers (e.g., police, judges, prosecutors). In this view, racial disparities in drug arrests and incarcerations are due to racial bias on the part of policy-makers who constructed new policies that consciously or subconsciously targeted black drug offenders, including racial disparities in drug crimes produced by changes in law enforcement or sentencing practices that sanction black drug offenders more often and more harshly than whites.

It should be noted that racial bias does not need to be overt or even conscious to affect decision-making (Lynch and Patterson, 1996). Psychological research indicates that prevailing racial stereotypes can affect one's actions, even if one holds no conscious racial animus, as cultural stereotypes that link minorities to drugs, crime, and other socially undesirable behaviors are pervasive, and, thus, may affect decision-making at a subconscious level (Fridell, 2008). For example, Devine's research (1989) into the psychology of racism revealed that individuals who exhibit "low prejudice" on the Modern Racism Scale were as knowledgeable of racial stereotypes as "high prejudice" individuals. When asked to identify the components of black stereotypes, "the most common theme in subjects' protocols was that blacks are aggressive, hostile, or *criminal-like*" (Devine, 1989:9, our emphasis). Devine also found that when given a task that tapped automatic cognitive processes both low- and high-prejudice respondents reacted in a manner consistent with racial prejudice. Although the subconscious component of racism is extremely difficult to evaluate empirically, this notion is important because it highlights that one need not be a "racist" to make racially biased decisions.

Examining the Differential Involvement Hypothesis

With these hypotheses in mind, we return to the question: Is racial disparity in drug arrests a product of differential drug use patterns across blacks and whites? As noted, available data indicates that even prior to the WoD, blacks had higher drug arrest rates than whites. This finding clearly indicates that racial disparity in drug arrest did not originate with the WoD. Evidence also suggests, however, that the WoD exacerbated racial disparities in drug arrests (Mauer, 2009). These disparities peaked in 1991 before subsiding, though they remain at levels above the pre-WoD period. For either of these patterns to explain the racial differences observed in drug arrests, black use of drugs would need to exceed white use of drugs by a significant margin.

To examine these expectations, we draw on data from the National Survey of Drug Use and Health (NSDUH) and restrict our analysis to 2008, though any year of these data could be employed. The NSDUH estimates drug use from a national sample, and is, in our view a more appropriate data sources than school-based drug use surveys, which are tainted by the omission of school drop-outs and chronic absentees. Moreover, because the data are based on households instead, of students, they include a wide age range. Here we use the portion of NSDUH related to adults (those 18 and over).

Table 1 displays the findings from the NSDUH survey. That table shows the number of drug users for each drug use category (first row for each drug category) and the percent of each racial group reporting use of a particular drug category (second row). If we consider percent usage within each racial group, self reported drug use for blacks exceeds self reported drug use for whites in three categories: all drugs (16.8 to 13.9%); marijuana (13.7 to 10.1%); and crack (0.6 to 0.5%). These percentages appear to suggest that racial differences in drug arrests are possible given that within these racial groups, black drug use exceeds white drug use. These percentages are misleading, however, because they fail to take into consideration the fact that whites far outnumber blacks in the population. To reflect this fact, table one also includes the estimated number of users for each drug type based on the reported use rates and the population of whites and blacks in the U.S. These data reveal a vastly different picture of drug use.

Reexamining Table 1 and focusing on row one for each drug type, it is clear that for every category of drug use, white users far outnumber black users in the prior year. For example, while 16.8% of blacks admit to using any drug in the prior year compared to 13.9% of whites, numerically there were nearly 26 million self admitted white drug users but only about 6.4 million black self reported drug users. In other words, for every one black self-reported drug user there are 4 self-reported white drug users. Adjusting for population size, then, in each drug use category there are far more white users than black drug users, and 80.3% of all reported drug use involves whites.

Table 1. Estimated Number of Self Reported Drug Users by Race for Non-Hispanics, 2008, Past Year Use, and Percent Reporting Use in the Past Year (in parentheses)**

	Whites	Blacks	W/B Ratio*	Percent Users Who Were White
All Drugs	25,926,960	6,356,497	4.08	80.3
	(13.9)	(16.8)		
Marijuana	18,839,014	5,183,572	3.63	78.4
	(10.1)	(13.7)		
Cocaine	4,290,073	832,398	5.15	83.9
	(2.3)	(2.2)		
Crack	932,625	227,018	4.11	80.4
	(0.5)	(0.6)		
Hallucinogens	2,611,349	264,854	9.86	90.8
	(1.4)	(0.7)		
Inhalants	3,730,998	151,345	24.65	96.1
	(2.0)	(0.4)		

* The W/B Ratio is the number of white self reported drug users for every one self reported black drug user.

** These data were derived from the U.S. Department of Health and Human Services, National Household Survey on Drug Abuse, 2008 data. The most recent data released under NHSDA can be found at: http://www.oas.samhsa.gov/nsduhLatest.htm/

With these observations about drug use in hand, let us return to a consideration of arrest data. At the WoD's peak in 1991 42% of drug arrestees were black. Yet, NSDUH data indicates that approximately 80% of all drug users are white. In other words, if the NSDUH estimates are accurate, then blacks are arrested twice as often as their use rates would predict.

The NSDUH data can also be employed to examine the expectation of increasing disparities in drug use by race over time (see Mitchell, 2009). In regards to any drug use, the black-white drug difference was more than 3 percentage points in 1979, dropped to less than 1 percentage point by the late-1980s, and by the millennium drug use rates were virtually identical (see Figure 2). In effect, the NSDUH indicate that over time, black and white drug use rates have converged or become more similar within racial groups. These findings are at odds with expectations of a sharp increase in black drug use during the late-1980s and a marked increase in white drug use in the early-1990s. Simply stated, these drug use trends, which indicate increasing similarity in drug use by race, do not comport with drug arrest trends, which show sustained and growing disparities by race. (For additional analysis relevant to drug use patterns and race see Mitchell, 2009.)

Figure 2. Drug Use by Race and Type, 1979–2003

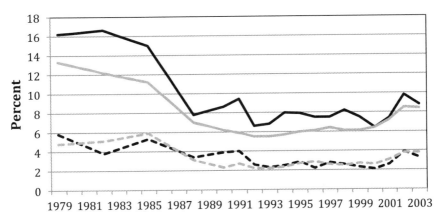

Source: National Househould Survey of Drug Use and National Survey of Drug Use and Health, various years.

The results in Figure 2 indicate that the massive increase in black drug arrests cannot be explained by blacks' greater involvement in drug use. Perhaps this escalation in black drug arrest rates is due to blacks' greater involvement in drug distribution. Recent analyses of race and drug distribution data, however, indicate that racial differences in drug distribution also cannot explain racial disparities in drug arrests. Using the National Longitudinal Survey of Youth, Mitchell (2009) found that "between 1997 and 2006 whites were significantly more likely to be involved in drug distribution than blacks; 23.4% of whites and 19.1% of blacks had ever sold or helped sell any illicit drug. And whites and blacks were equally likely to have sold hard drugs, 10.2% vs. 8.9%, respectively. Yet, blacks were more likely than whites to have been arrested on a drug distribution charge, 4.3% vs. 2.5%" (Mitchell 2009: 62). More disturbing is that Mitchell discovered a large difference in self reported arrests among drug distributors by race: 28.8% of black drug dealers report being arrested compared to 12.4% of white drug dealers. Mitchell also found that white drug dealers were less likely to be convicted of a drug sales offense compared to blacks: 3.2%

compared to 12.7%. Thus, the differential involvement hypothesis is not supported by data examining drug use or drug distribution.

The research of Beckett, Nyrop, and Pfingst (2006) also refutes the differential involvement hypothesis. These authors examined racial disparities in drug distribution arrests in Seattle. This research asked participants in a needle exchange program to describe the race/ethnicity of their suppliers, and compared the results Seattle Police Department drug arrest data. The survey data indicated that for all drugs except crack (47% black, 41% white) the majority of low-level methamphetamine, heroin, and ecstasy dealers were reported as white. Yet, black dealers were disproportionately arrested for every drug type in the police data. For example, while 47% of reported crack dealers were black, 79% of arrested crack dealers were black. Similarly, while 7.2% of methamphetamine dealers were black, 17.2% of those arrested for methamphetamine delivery were black. Beckett and colleagues attribute the over-representation of black drug dealers at arrest to the fact that police focus on: 1) crack, a drug with a greater proportion of black drug dealers; 2) outdoor drug transactions, instead of indoor transactions; and, 3) open-air drug markets that have a large percentage of minorities, instead of other open-air drug markets that have predominantly white dealers. Clearly, Beckett et al.'s work supports the differential scrutiny hypothesis and refutes the differential involvement hypothesis.

Examining the Differential Scrutiny Hypothesis

The structure of law and law enforcement, including the content of law, police tactics and sentencing patterns, have been widely discussed as explanations for racial disparities observed in the criminal justice system. With respect to the WoD, concern over drug use was, at first, stimulated by news coverage. This was the first phase in launching the attack against minority drug users, and it drew on and at the same time manipulated public perceptions and widely shared stereotypes of minorities identified in the psychological literature. Politicians used these media messages to demonstrate their concern with the rising crime problem associated with drug use, and elevated these concerns to a national campaign by producing a set of stringent Anti-Drug Acts and by providing funding for anti-drug initiatives. These new drug control strategies included specific policies that perhaps indirectly targeted minority drug offenders, which lead to massive increases in the number of black drug offenders being arrested. Policing tactics such as "street sweeps" of visible drug markets that are disproportionately located in lower income and minority communities had a disparate effect on African-Americans. Police agencies also engaged in drug dealer and user "profiles," which were often based on faulty data assumptions (Lynch, 2002) to create guidelines that caused police to focus attention on "suspicious" minorities (Cole, 1999). By creating policies that disproportionately affected blacks, policy-makers and police re-enforced cultural stereotypes linking racial minorities to drug crime.

In the end, the public nature of black drug dealing combined with the WoD's policy decisions to focus on low-level drug offending produced stark racial disparities in police scrutiny, and in turn stark racial disparities in drug arrests. While it is impossible to empirically prove that *race* directly affected any of the decisions that set the WoD and its racially biased outcomes in motion, social psychological research supports the contention that internalized cultural racial stereotypes connecting blacks to crime, especially drug crime, could have played an important role in this process. Further, the racial disparate effects of the WoD's key policies easily could have been predicted, if policy-makers had exercised even a modicum of due diligence.

Thus, the most cogent explanation of the worsening racial disparity in drug arrests is that police, in part at the behest of federal policy-makers, adopted tactics designed to make abundant low-level drug arrests. Policy-makers and police chose to focus on low-level drug dealers instead of wholesalers and importers. They chose to focus on open-air drug markets located in urban areas, instead of closed-door transactions characteristic of suburban and rural dealers. They chose to wage a war using tactics that exploit ignorance of the law (e.g., "consent searches"). None of these decisions is intrinsically racially biased, but all of these decisions capitalize on stark racial inequality that spatially, socially, and politically isolate blacks from whites. In other words, the commonality underlying these decisions is that they navigate the boundary between socially advantaged and disadvantaged groups without making an overt reference to race, but they nevertheless culminate in severe racial inequities in drug arrests.

Explaining Racial Disparities in Drug Sentencing

Not only are black drug dealers arrested and convicted at higher rates than whites, but they are also more likely to be sentenced to a term of incarceration if convicted. For example, in 2004, 71% of African-Americans but only 63% of whites convicted on similar felony drug offenses were sentenced to prison, yet once sentenced, both groups received the same average prison sentence: 31 months (BJS, 2007). Can the difference in incarceration described above be explained by "legally relevant" factors such as offense seriousness and prior criminal record rather than by race alone?

There is sizeable empirical research that examines racial disparities in drug offender sentencing. Findings from seventeen studies where offense seriousness and prior criminal history were controlled simultaneously have been summarized in Mitchell (2005). He found that sixteen (94%) of these studies reported that blacks were punished more harshly than whites after controlling for legally relevant factors. The mean random effects odds ratio was 1.44 (95% CI 1.28–1.62), which means that if 50% of whites were sent to prison, then 59% of blacks would receive the same treatment. These studies, however, found little evidence of racial disparity in the length of prison terms given to black versus whites.

The findings from Mitchell's meta-analysis indicate that racial disparity in decisions to incarcerate convicted drug offenders cannot be explained by differences in the severity of current offense or by differences in prior criminal conduct. The question becomes: Why are blacks incarcerated more often than whites convicted of similar drug offenses and with similar criminal histories? Extant research suggests that race matters in drug sentencing for two primary reasons: 1) blacks fit the prevailing stereotype of a drug offender; and, 2) the appropriate sentence in drug cases is often ambiguous. This ambiguity allows court actors the requisite freedom to use their discretion, which appears to be affected by an offender's race.

Again, in the latest American drug war, the principal drug of concern has been cocaine, which has been "associated in public imagery with disadvantaged *minority* residents of the inner cities" (Tonry, 1995: 94, our emphasis). Blacks have become the stereotypical drug offender in the current crusade against drugs despite the fact that whites are more likely to use and sell drugs. These prevailing perceptions that link race, violence, and involvement in drug offending may affect court actors as well as the general public unconsciously. For example, when asked to describe a "dangerous drug offender" Washington State court personnel responses included black drug offenders twice as often as white drug offenders, 16% vs. 8% (Steen, Engen, and Gainey, 2005). The researchers also found that white drug offenders who fit the profile of a dangerous drug dealer were sentenced more harshly than white dealers who did not fit the profile. In contrast, however, "decision makers do not appear to make sharp distinctions between the most 'dangerous' black offenders and most other black offenders . . . For black offenders, decision makers appear to adjust all but the least-threatening cases upwards" (Steen, Engen, and Gainey, 2005, p. 461). This latter finding suggests that a drug offender's race, above and beyond other factors, is used as a marker of dangerousness and culpability.

In short, notions of a typical drug offender are steeped in contemporary racialized stereotypes, and the ambiguity of the appropriate sentence for such offenders allows court actors' decisions to be affected by these stereotypes and other racial biases that result in more punitive sanctions for blacks than whites.

Discussion

In this chapter we have demonstrated four outcomes. First, racial disparities in drug arrests and sentencing outcomes *cannot* be explained by differential involvement in drug offending. At the same time that cross race drug use has converged, drug arrests continued to diverge sharply. Second, the differential in drug arrests is not due to differential involvement of blacks in more serious forms of drug offending, including the type of drug used and with regard to the distribution of drugs. Third, racial disparities in sentencing cannot be explained by differences in offense seriousness or criminal history. Finally, we have demonstrated that the drug-race-disparity connection has been exacerbated by the WoD. Clearly, racial disparities in drug sanctions predate the WoD, but the WoD did substantially add to existing racial disparities. Thus, the WoD is not the cause of these disparities; rather, the WoD is, like other forms of racial disparity, a symptom of the processes that generate racial disparities more generally. In our view, the racial disparities linked to the WoD are more deeply rooted within the structural context of American society and are found in: general racial stereotypes concerning African-Americans; stereotypes that associate minorities and drug use and trafficking; an economic system where stereotypes and structural inequities continue to produce disadvantages for African-Americans; and, a political system that uses racialized issues to gain the political support of whites.

As noted, WoD policies were accompanied by federal financial aid that led law enforcement agencies to adopt tactics that more closely scrutinized the public and semi-public drug markets common in inner-city, lower class minority areas. The tremendous discretion allotted to authorities when enforcing these policies has allowed conscious and unconscious racial bias to influence drug control efforts. The end result is a pattern of elevated racial disparities in drug arrests and incarcerations that cannot be explained by racial differences in drug offending.

Some (Kennedy, 1997; Stith, 1993) have argued that the racial disparities associated with the WoD should be interpreted within the context of efforts to help minority communities combat drug and crime problems. While there is some evidence that Congress supported the WoD out of concern about drug and crime problems in urban, largely minority communities, a host of indicators undermine the general conclusion that the WoD was enacted to help black communities. First, this conclusion is at odds with historical evidence of racial bias in past drug control efforts such as Musto's (1999) observation that the history of U.S. drug control strategies has been most punitive when the drug of concern is associated with threatening racial or ethnic minorities—a pattern evident in the current drug war. Given America's long history of racial bias in drug control policy, its longer history of neglecting black victims of crime (both these histories are detailed extensively by Kennedy, 1997), and the contemporaneous rolling back of social programs designed to assist blacks, policy-makers' sudden concern for minorities and their communities is deeply puzzling.

Second, the policies and practices that Kennedy and others argue were designed to help black communities are most strongly disfavored by residents of those communities. In their national study of African-Americans, Bobo and Thompson (2006) found 66% believe that drug laws "are enforced unfairly against black communities," whereas nearly 80% of whites believe that drug laws are applied equally to "all would be drug users." More distressingly, nearly a quarter (24.8%) of African-Americans thought that the WoD was "just an excuse for police to harass and imprison the inner-city youth." These authors argued that current drug control strategies undermine the legitimacy of the criminal justice system in black communities. Specifically, they found that respondents who perceived unfairness in the WoD expressed reduced confidence in the police and a greater willingness to let a guilty defendant go free ("jury nullification") in cases where the defendant claimed to be a victim of racial bias. Taken together, the authors' results confirm that blacks are acutely aware of racial disparities in the WoD, they believe that the WoD is unfair, and this sense of unfairness affects their perceptions of the criminal justice system. If the WoD's policies were designed in large part to benefit black communities, then findings like these are difficult to explain.

Finally, if the WoD was launched to correct drug problems in minority communities, it should be challenged on these grounds as a failure. There is, in other words, little evidence that supports the effectiveness of the WoD as a useful drug reduction tool. Simply put, if policy-makers were truly concerned with effective drug control policy or the health of black communities, the WoD's policies would have been altered long ago.

In contrast to this "external aid" hypothesis, scholars argue that political expedience was a primary motivation for launching the WoD because alternative policies (e.g., drug rehabilitation and efforts to reduce social inequality) were perceived as "soft on crime," and made politicians who pushed such policies vulnerable in future elections (Tonry, 1995; Beckett, 1997). More controversially, several scholars (Edsall and Edsall, 1991; Tonry, 1995) argue that conservative politicians have used punitive criminal justice policies to appeal to the anti-black sentiment of some white voters and the resentment that some white voters have of the gains made by African-Americans (at white expense) since the Civil Rights Movement. These factors culminated in the creation of ineffective, costly, and unjust drug policies at the expense of the public coffers and the freedom of thousands of Americans, particularly African-Americans, while primarily benefitting the political ambitions of elected officials.

Because we view racial disparities within criminal justice processes as deeply entrenched within the structural, cultural economic, and political foundations of American society, there is no quick, easy or simple solution to this problem. In short, addressing racial bias as an outcome of social, cultural, economic, and political relationships and processes requires actions that eclipse traditional criminal justice policy reform. To address criminal justice processing biases, broad social and economic programs and reforms are required that eliminate the basis of these disparities as they exist outside the criminal justice system. These programs may include addressing the elimination or reduction of racial bias through educational programs that challenge racial stereotypes, enhancing inter-racial relationships through exposure and experience with diverse groups, economic reforms that address not only race based economic inequities, but economic disadvantage more generally, and political reforms that directly and openly discuss and address the critical, but often neglected, issue of race.

References

Anti-Drug Abuse Act of 1986, H.R. 5484, 99th Congress (1986).

Anti-Drug Abuse Act of 1988, H.R. 5210, 100th Congress (1988).

Baum, D. (1996). *Smoke and Mirrors: The War on Drugs and the Politics of Failure*. Boston, MA: Little, Brown and Company.

Beckett, K. (1997). *Making Crime Pay*. New York: Oxford University Press.

Beckett, K., Nyrop, K., & Pfingst, L. (2006). "Race, Drugs, and Policing: Understanding Disparities in Drug Delivery Arrests." *Criminology*, 44(105–137).

Blumstein, A. (1993). "Making Rationality Relevant—The American Society of Criminology 1992 Presidential Address." *Criminology*, 31(1), 1–16.

Blumstein, Alfred and Allen J. Beck. 1999. "Population Growth in—Prisons, 1980–1996." Pp. 17–61 in *Crime and Justice: A Review of Research*, vol. 26, Editors Michael Tonry and Joan Petersilia. Chicago, IL: The University of Chicago Press.

Bobo, L. D., & Thompson, V. (2006). "Unfair by Design: The War on Drugs, Race, and the Legitimacy of the Criminal Justice System." *Social Research*, 73(2), 445–472.

Brownstein, H. H. (1997). The Media and the Construction of Random Drug Violence. In L. K. Gaines, & P. B. Kraska (Editors), *Drugs, crime, and justice: Contemporary perspectives* (pp. 67–86). Prospect Heights, IL: Waveland Press.

Bureau of Justice Assistance. (1996). *National Assessment of Structured Sentencing*. Washington, D.C.: U.S. Government Printing Office.

Burston, B. W., Jones, D., & Roberson-Saunders, P. (1995). "Drug Use and African Americans: Myth Versus Reality." *Journal of Alcohol and Drug Education*, 40(2), 19–39.

Bush, G. H. W. (1989). Address to the nation on the National Drug Control Strategy, September 5, 1989. *The Public Papers of President George H.W. Bush*. http://bushlibrary.tamu.edu/research/public_papers.php?id=863 &year=1989&month=9.

Cole, D. (1999). *No Equal Justice: Race and Class in the American Criminal Justice System*. New York: The New Press.

Currie, E. (1993). *Reckoning: Drugs, the Cities, and the American Future*. New York: Hill and Wang.

Devine, P. G. 1989. "Stereotypes and Prejudice: Their Automatic and Controlled Components." *Journal of Personality and Social Psychology* 56(1):5–18.

Diamond, E. (1991). *The Media Show: The Changing Face of the News, 1985–1990*. Cambridge, MA: MIT Press.

Duster, T. (1997). Pattern, Purpose, and Race in the Drug War. In C. Reinarman, & H. G. Levine (Editors), *Crack in America: Demon drugs and social justice* (pp. 260–287). Berkeley, CA: University of California Press.

Edsall, T.B., & Edsall, M. (1991). Chain Reaction: The Impact of Race, Rights, and Taxes on American Politics. New York: W.W. Norton and Company.

Frank, D. A., Augustyn, M., Knight, W. G., Pell, T., & Zuckerman, B. (2001). "Growth, Development, and Behavior in Early Childhood Following Prenatal Cocaine Exposure: A Systematic Review." *Journal of the American Medical Association*, 285(12), 1613–1625.

Fridell, L. (2008). "Racially Biased Policing: The Law Enforcement Response to the Implicit Black-Crime Association." In M.J. Lynch, E. B. Patterson, and K. K. Childs (Eds.), *Racial Divide: Race, Ethnicity and Criminal Justice*. Monsey, NY: Criminal Justice Press (pp. 39–59).

Goldstein, A. (2001). *Addiction: From Biology to Drug Policy*. New York: Oxford University Press.

Goode, E. (2002). "Drug Arrests at the Millennium." *Society*, 39(5), 41–45.

————. (2005). *Drugs in American Society, Sixth Edition.* New York: McGraw-Hill.

Kennedy, R. (1997). *Race, Crime, and the Law.* New York: Vintage Books.

Lynch, Michael J. (2007). *Big Prisons, Big Dreams: Crime and the Failure of the U.S. Prison System.* Newark, NJ: Rutgers University Press.

Lynch, Michael J. (2002). "Misleading 'Evidence' and the Misguided Attempt to Generate Racial Profiles of Criminals: Correcting Fallacies and Calculations Concerning Race and Crime in Taylor and Whitney's Analysis of Racial Profiling." *The Mankind Quarterly.* 42,3:313–330.

Lynch, Michael J. and E. Britt Patterson. (1996). "Thinking About Race and Criminal Justice: Racism, Stereotypes, Politics, Academia and the Need for Context." In M.J. Lynch and E. B. Patterson (Eds.), *Justice With Prejudice.* Albany, NY: Harrow and Heston.

Mauer, Marc. (2009). *The Changing Racial Dynamics of the War on Drugs.* Washington, DC: The Sentencing Project. http://www.sentencingproject.org/doc/ dp_raceanddrugs.pdf.

Mitchell, O. (2005). "A Meta-Analysis of Race and Sentencing Research: Explaining the Inconsistencies." *Journal of Quantitative Criminology,* 21(4), 439–466.

Mitchell, O. (2009). "Is the War on Drugs Racially Biased?" *Journal of Crime & Justice* 32(2):49–75.

Musto, D. F. (1999). *The American Disease: Origins of Narcotic Control.* New York: Oxford University Press.

Newsweek. (1986). Kids and Crack: An Epidemic Strikes Middle America. Pp. 59–65.

Reeves, J. L., & Campbell, R. (1994). *Cracked Coverage: Television News, the Anti-Cocaine Crusade, and the Reagan Legacy.* Durham, NC: Duke University Press.

Reinarman, C., & Levine, H. G. (1997a). The Crack Attack: Politics and Media in the Crack Scare. In C. Reinarman, & H. G. Levine (Editors), *Crack in America: Demon drugs and social justice* (pp. 18–51). Berkeley, CA: University of California Press.

Reinarman, C., & Levine, H. G. (1997b). Crack in Context: America's Latest Demon Drug. In C. Reinarman, & H. G. Levine (Editors), *Crack in America: Demon drugs and social justice* (pp. 1–17). Berkeley, CA: University of California Press.

Steen, S., Engen, R. L., & Gainey, R. R. (2005). "Images of Danger and Culpability: Racial Stereotyping, Case Processing, and Criminal Sentencing." *Criminology,* 43(2), 435–468.

Stith, K. (1993). "The Government Interest in Criminal Law: Whose Interest Is It, Anyway?" Pp. 137–70 in *Public Values in Constitutional Law*, Editor Stephen E. Gottlieb. Ann Arbor, MI: University of Michigan Press.

Tonry, M. (1995). *Malign Neglect: Race, Crime, and Punishment in America*. New York: Oxford University Press.

Trebach, A. (1987). *The Great Drug War*. Philadelphia: Macmillan.

United States Office of National Drug Control Policy [ONDCP]. (1989). *National Drug Control Strategy*. Washington, D.C.: Office of the National Drug Control Policy, Executive Office of the President.

United States Sentencing Commission [USSC]. (2007). *Report to Congress: Cocaine and Federal Sentencing Policy*. Washington, D.C.: United States Sentencing Commission.

Walters, J. P. (2001). Drug Wars: Just Say No . . . to Treatment without Law Enforcement. 19. *The Weekly Standard*.

Western, B. (2006). *Punishment and Inequality in America*. New York: Russell Sage Foundation.

Chapter 9

After Ferguson, a Familiar Era of Race, Crime, and Policing: The Impact of Law Enforcement on Persistent Race-Differentiated Arrest Rates

John David Reitzel

In an earlier version of this chapter the goal was to explore some of the key causes and correlates of arrest disparities by race through the lens of two related empirical facts. First, African Americans are over-represented in some types of serious crime and violence, irrespective of the particular data collection methodology employed (Blumstein, Cohen, Roth & Visher, 1986; Elliott, 1994). Second, African Americans are disproportionately arrested for many of the most serious crimes (Bureau of Justice Statistics, 2010). In reviewing the literature and arrest statistics it has become clear however there is a lack of concrete findings, which would indicate bias, compared to that which would reflect earnest and fair law enforcement practices (Novak and Chamlin, 2012).

Although easy to point to the disparities and call it bias, this would leave out the very real involvement in crime among some blacks and the lack of systematic evidence about police-decision making, police policy, and community specific crime rates which structure police-public contacts. However, in the ensuing years since the first publication, a rash of incidents between police and African Americans from Staten Island, New York, to Ferguson, Missouri, to Waller County, Texas, drew an intense national spotlight on this and related issues, sparking not only mass protests around the country, but a vigorous, sometimes hostile public debate pitting black activists vs police, particularly the Black Lives Matter movement (#blacklivesmatter, 2013).

The attention generated anew public and media interest in policing black communities and the troubling specter of bias against blacks. This has been partly driven by the emergence of social media such as Twitter and Facebook and subsequent rise of hashtag activism, but also because a growing number of these incidents have been caught on ever increasingly ubiquitous smart phone videos. Where prior to smart phones controversial incidents were often left to police dash cams or security cameras, or the occasional bystander, technology has helped to place policing in the spotlight seemingly everywhere.

Perhaps no other case signifies the coalescing of these various developments than the August 9, 2014, shooting death of a black teenager named Michael Brown in the middle of a Ferguson, Missouri (St. Louis County), street by a white Ferguson Police Department officer named Darren Wilson. What this case has come to represent is that there are still deeply embedded problems between many police departments and the black communities they patrol, problems that might have been simmering just below the surface for years but now get national exposure. As controversial as the Ferguson case is, it certainly was not the first and will not be the last, yet is one of a growing number incidents that suggest a changing reality for many communities and the police departments that patrol them. These cases have also shaped a changing public discourse, one where African Americans and other supporters are forcing their voices to be heard while challenging the policing and political establishment to reform policing and criminal justice writ large (e.g., see the problems with race and mass incarceration) (Alexander 2011).

It is tempting to take this space to explore what the future holds within this new context, but it seems more appropriate to revisit the underlying issues that give much of the current controversy its thrust, that is, to reexamine the structural factors and trends associated with disproportionate minority contacts with police that lead to arrest and to the continued discord and distrust marking these interactions. This seems even more urgent now given that the police response to crime has never only been a matter of offending. Crime in the United States is a complicated affair that is often about the structural factors that color the daily interactions between police and the communities they patrol. Likewise, our formal response to crime that is how the criminal justice system responds to and punishes criminal offenders is complex. Arrest and imprisonment rates are influenced by considerable number of factors including social, political, and economic forces. Some of the unfortunate outcomes of this complication have led to disproportionate contact with the criminal justice system for some racial or ethnic groups compared to others (Bureau of

Justice Statistics, 2010). Nowhere in contemporary society is this more evident than with African Americans.

Race, Crime, and Policing

Although the residual effects of a long history of racism and discrimination continue to shape the race/crime issue, some important developments have occurred which have preceded the newfound public and media interest. Theories regarding the race/crime (and policing) intersect have gotten stronger, better reflecting complex empirical reality (Sampson and Bean, 2006; Peterson and Krivo, 2009). The empirical literature has grown steadily, providing new insights into the current state of race, crime, and policing.

In the public and political spheres, this issue has gone from the occasional topic to one that in the last three years has been covered regularly by both mainstream and non-mainstream media and has been addressed by political leaders including President Obama. Indeed, this has included the passage of the Fair Sentencing Act (Congressional Budget Office, 2010) that seeks to reduce mass incarceration, which is another problem in criminal justice marked by institutional racism. There is also as of this writing, a host of policy changes being negotiated in Congress, which show potential for criminal justice reform not witnessed since the 1960s. Yet, despite these noteworthy developments and the fact that rates of serious crime and violence having reached historic lows nationally, racial disparities in criminal justice remains a pervasive if confounding matter in American social life, one that most clearly manifests in its unequal presence among economically and socially disadvantaged African American communities.

At the same time, new developments in crime fighting strategies and technology have been given a sizable amount of credit for the dramatic reduction in crime (Harcourt & Ludwig, 2006; Willis, Mastrofski & Weisburd, 2003; Kelling and Sousa, 2001). In the mid-1990s, Broken Windows theory formed the basis for the New York City Police Department's (NYPD) implementation of what became the widely heralded and now widely emulated COMPSTAT program, which makes far greater use of technology and long standing organizational practices in developing novel proactive crime fighting strategies (Harcourt & Ludwig, 2006; Willis et al., 2003; Silverman, 1999). Other related initiatives emerged from police departments around the country during this time, such as hot spot policing (Sherman, Shaw & Rogan, 1995; Braga, Weisburd, Waring, Greene Mazerolle, Spelman, and Gajewski, 1999) and community and problem oriented policing (Chappell, MacDonald & Manz, 2006; Braga et al., 1999; Goldstein, 1990) which together, have been argued by some as also being primary reasons for the crime drop (Zimring, 2006; Sherman, 1997). But these crime-fighting successes have engendered more questions than answers. First, the literature on policing and crime reduction reveals that historically the police have had little, if any, effect on crime rates (Fyfe, 2004; Eck & Maguire, 2006; Klockars, 1983). Questions therefore arise about the more recent empirical evidence on the reductive effects police crime fighting strategies (Braga, Pierce, McDevitt, Bond & Cronin, 2008; Harcourt & Ludwig, 2006; Rosenfeld, Fornango & Baumer, 2005; Zimring, 2006; Levitt, 2004; Sherman et al., 1995). Second, unanswered questions also remain about the intended and unintended consequences of changing law enforcement practices that seem to have affected African American communities disproportionately than white communities (Gibson, Walker, Jennings & Miller, 2009, Batton & Kadleck, 2004). Third, macro level changes were also occurring in society that had little to do with specific changes to police practices. Sociological factors such as demographic changes and changes in drug markets might provide stronger explanations about racial, economic, and geographic differences in offending then changes in policing practices (Zimring, 2006; Hagerdorn & Rauch, 2004; Levitt, 2004).

Last, institutional processes within the criminal justice system other than policing, including changes in sentencing and imprisonment legislation, have stronger empirical support for their effects on crime (Zimring, 2006; Levitt, 2004). What links these phenomena together is a legacy of racial discrimination that helped create the current racially and economically stratified conditions with a concomitant historically troubled relationship between urban African American communities and the police. It is in this "race-space divide" (Peterson and Krivo, 2009) that African American criminality has come to signify a different, if often misunderstood, type of crime problem (Gabbidon and Greene, 2009). It is also within this divide that some of our most persistent social problems beyond crime have played out. Any investigation into racial differences in crime and punishment should not only take into account structural (and cultural) factors that produce them but also how the police might affect such differences. Where and how law enforcement agencies decide to place their resources and what types of crimes they focus on most heavily are not always race-neutral decisions (Wilkins & Williams, 2009, Chambliss, 1994). Such decisions are also not necessarily based upon empirical evidence (Wilkins & Williams, 2009). Rather, they are often borne out of assumptions regarding the criminogenic conditions of the communities in which they patrol and stereotypical beliefs about the criminal propensity of individual residents within those communities, of which race plays an inextricable role in shaping such attitudes (Chambliss, 1994). In order to minimize racial bias in policing, thus establishing a principle of racial egalitarianism, we are therefore left to determine what an equitable distribution of arrests (and imprisonment) are relative to race-specific crime rates (Wilson, Dunham & Alpert, 2004). It also means we must disentangle the effects of structural (and much thornier cultural factors) that can lead to significant racial differences in offending from the effects of differential policing and punishment that seems to unjustifiably target African Americans (Chambliss, 1994). This is, of course, not just an abstract exercise; the race/crime issue is of principal interest in the political arena where issues of justice and civil rights remain controversial topics that are fundamental to maintaining a robust democracy.

The rest of this chapter examines the key factors that linked to disparities in black disproportionate arrest rates. The discussion then turns toward examining how developments in modern police practices might have helped create racial differences in offending, at least those that might lead to disproportionate minority contact with the criminal justice system and the places these developments within the context of the increasing focus on potential racial biases in policing.

Correlates of Race and Crime

Criminological efforts to understand aggregate level differences in crime across racial groups generally fall into three areas: group-based and individual differences in arrest rates and group-based differences in punishment (Cohn, Barkan, and Halteman, 1991). The main thrust of racial differences in crime and violence typically derive from macro-structural explanations, such as economic inequality or extreme concentrated disadvantage but also include factors such as unemployment, human and social capital, and residential segregation and community disorganization (Peterson & Krivo, 2009; Clear, Waring, and Scully, 2005; Walker et al., 2006; Sampson & Wilson, 1995). Family structural and process factors including single parent and female-headed households and family size, also play a role (Sampson and Laub, 2004; Eggleston & Laub 2002; Moffitt, 1993), especially as it links to gang violence and drug use (Clear, Waring & Scully, 2005; Walker et al., 2006; Krivo & Petersen, 2000; Parker and McCall, 1999). From a socio-historical context, these covariates of crime, which link to geographic residency and economic inequality—broadly defined—per haps best frame our understanding of racial differences in crime and violence.

In his 1978 book, *The Declining Significance of Race*, William Julius Wilson wrote that the subordination of some blacks and the advancement of others is more a function of economic class than race. At the time, this was a controversial pronouncement, sparking widespread debate. Wilson's argument is no longer divisive. Since the 1960s, societal changes have measurably diversified the nature of the African American experience and economic inequality has been shown to be strongly associated with other types of inequality, particularly racial inequality (Bobo and Kluegal, 1993; Kluegal, 1990; Wilson, 1987). Race alone is still a critically important social force in American life, but the importance of economics, especially when it interacts with race is of equal importance. Yet, any progress made in recent decades has been hampered by the reality that too many segments of the African American population remain trapped in the pressing exigencies of concentrated poverty, de facto residential segregation, social and economic marginalization, and by their increasing over-representation in the criminal justice system (Sampson and Bean, 2006; Walker et al., 2006; Feagin, 2001; Krivo, Peterson, Rizzo & Reynolds, 1998). Nevertheless, the correlation between socioeconomic deprivation and heightened criminal offending is among the most widespread general findings in academic criminology (Fergusson, Swain-Campbell, and Horwood, 2004).

To better illustrate the interaction of race and economics nationally, it is helpful to examine changes in poverty rates and median-household income for African Americans compared to whites. Data from the U.S. Census Bureau (2006) show that between 1960 and 1995 the percentage of African Americans living below the poverty line decreased from about 55% to 32%. By 2000, this number decreased to 22%. At the same time, household income increased for all groups. In 1971, the median household income for African Americans was about 19,000 dollars compared to 32,000 dollars for whites. By 2005, median household income had increased to 34,500 dollars for African Americans and to 46,000 dollars for whites. However, in 2005 the disparity in median household income was nearly as large as it was forty years prior, which is particularly noteworthy when considering that African Americans had only achieved a median household income level by 2005 that equaled the white 1968 median household income (U.S. Census Bureau, 2006). Societal changes have improved the economic well-being for many Americans, especially those changes that brought a notable number of them out of poverty, did not operate evenly nor did they lessen the gap between median household incomes of African Americans relative to white Americans. National level economic trends bear import on race and crime, but smaller macro-level units, such as the neighborhood, actually provides a more nuanced perspective about the structural factors that correlate to race differentiated crime rates. For example, Sampson and Wilson (1995: 42) examined racial differences in neighborhood concentrated disadvantage in 171 cities with populations greater than 100,000 and found that the black/white racial disparity was so complete "that the 'worst' urban contexts in which whites reside are considerably better off than the average context of African American communities." This finding suggests that national level economic trends do not tell a complete story about changes in conditions for poor African Americans and that we need to look more closely at neighborhood differences that might lead to variations in offending.

According to Sampson and colleagues (2002), well over one hundred studies of neighborhoods have been conducted since the mid-1990s. Broadly, many of them examine structural factors such as concentrated disadvantage, population heterogeneity and density, high levels of single parent dwellings, social capital, access to resources such as hospitals and governmental agencies, and the percentage of young juvenile males. In addition, some recent studies have added to the neighborhood literature by investigating the spatial effects of disadvantaged neighborhoods that are surrounded by or overlap other disadvantaged neighborhoods (Peterson and Krivo, 2009). These studies have found significant correlations between disadvantaged neighborhoods geographically nested within other similarly disadvantaged neighborhoods with higher levels of crime and violence compared to similar neighborhoods that abut better neighborhoods (Peterson and Krivo, 2009; Morenoff, Sampson, and Raudenbush, 2001). In other words, crime in poor African American neighborhoods, which tend to be more segregated or even hyper-segregated from the rest of the community not only appear to increase due to neighborhood structural characteristics, they are exacerbated by spatial dynamics that make many of these neighborhoods hotspots of urban violence and decay. Peterson and Krivo (2009) speculate that this is because poor African American neighborhoods might be cut off from the political and economic institutions and social networks that can help alleviate such problems, thus leaving crime and violence to fester. While we know with some confidence that neighborhood factors do very well in explaining race differentiated crime rates, there is still much work to be done. Those one hundred studies that Sampson referred to are just scratching the surface of a difficult issue that requires even more research than it has gotten. The problems inherent in these communities run deep, with crime being only one of the negative outcomes.

Distribution of Arrests by Race

Whatever limits in knowledge that persist regarding disparities in African American criminal justice outcomes, it is nonetheless safe to say that the disparities themselves raise questions on two fronts. One, what is the true nature of criminal behavior African Americans and is it really that different than it is for Whites or other groups? And two, is the approach by criminal justice authorities biased against blacks? The statistics might answer both, but with the latter question, we cannot make such a determination from them alone. This raises another question about the statistics themselves. What would be a fair statistical distribution of arrests by race? Ideally, every group it would be the same or very close to the numerical representation of a group's population. Consider the numbers. There are over three hundred and twenty-one million people living in the United States today. Non-Hispanic/Latino White Americans comprise a racial majority at just over one-hundred and ninety-six million people or about 63.70% percent of the US population, while Non-Hispanic/Latino Blacks comprise a little over thirty-seven million or about 12.7% of the US population (U.S. Census Bureau, 2016), yet the differences in each group's share of arrest is considerable.

Table 1. Total, Mean, and Percent Arrests by White, Black, and Total for All UCR Part 1 and Weapons and Drug Crimes 2009–2015

	Murder			Rape			Robbery		
	Total	Mean	Percent	Total	Mean	Percent	Total	Mean	Percent
Total	51,840	8,640	100.00	90,203	15,034	100.00	503,269	83,878	100.00
White	24,709	4,118	47.63	59,276	9,879	65.70	215,448	35,908	42.78
Black	25,965	4,328	50.10	28,684	4,781	31.82	279,375	46,563	55.55

	A.Assault			Burglary			Larceny		
	Total	Mean	Percent	Total	Mean	Percent	Total	Mean	Percent
Total	1,835,597	305,933	100.00	1,297,340	216,223	100.00	5,989,131	998,189	100.00
White	1,164,387	194,065	63.42	870,526	145,088	67.13	4,104,688	684,115	68.53
Black	618,513	103,086	33.68	401,971	66,995	30.93	1,714,239	285,707	28.63

	Auto			Weapons			Drugs		
	Total	Mean	Percent	Total	Mean	Percent	Total	Mean	Percent
Total	328,814	54,802	100.00	708,699	118,117	100.00	7,359,281	1,226,547	100.00
White	212,327	35,388	64.70	410,313	68,386	57.90	4,930,504	821,751	67.02
Black	107,883	17,981	32.70	285,617	47,603	40.30	2,306,041	384,340	31.30

	Violent Crime Index			Property Crime Index			All Crimes		
	Total	Mean	Percent	Total	Mean	Percent	Total	Mean	Percent
Total	2,480,909	413,485	100.00	7,666,971	1,277,829	100.00	57,503,966	9,583,994	100.00
White	1,463,820	243,970	58.98	5,225,733	870,956	68.18	39,807,298	6,634,550	69.22
Black	952,537	158,756	38.37	2,236,244	372,707	29.15	16,188,959	2,698,160	28.15

*Data come from the Federal Bureau of Investigations (FBI) Uniform Crime Reports (UCR) for Arrests 2009–2015

Table 1 shows the arrest statistics for White and Black Americans for seven of eight index crimes (less arson), for weapons and drug crimes, for Violent and Property Crime Indices, and Total Arrests for All Crimes listed in Table 43a in the UCR. Taking the White arrest numbers first, the mean arrest percentages for all crimes is 69.22%, which is 5.20% greater than their population. Limiting it to just Part I crimes, Whites were arrested for 60.78% of the time, which is 2.92% less than their representation in the population. Conversely, the numbers for African Americans tell quite a different story; one that has been ongoing for some time. African Americans comprise about just less than 13% of the population, yet they were over-represented in arrests for all serious crime and in total crime. This disparity in arrests ranged from 15.45% for All Crimes (28.15%) to 37.40% for Murder/Non-Negligent Homicide (50.10%) and 42.85% for Robbery (55.55%). Put differently, African American arrests for seven of the most serious crimes averaged from 28.63% for Larceny to 55.55% for Robbery, putting the average arrest disparity at over 23%.

As a policy matter, racial disparities provide great cause for concern since they demonstrate deep-seeded problems that are outcomes of systemic inequality and other structural disadvantages (Durlauf, 2005). A fair distribution of arrests should therefore include only those behaviors or factors under individual control, of which an individual's racial group is not among them (Durlauf, 2005). In addition, part of the problem in measuring race differences in crime is that crime and race are both social constructions. How we define crime and criminals are outcomes of complicated processes that bring together perceptions of criminal propensity and decision-making about the groups in which individuals belong at each step of the criminal justice system (Leiber, Reitzel, and Mack, 2010; Steffensmeier, Ulmer & Kramer, 1998). The relative proximity to actual characteristics of either the group or the individual affects equity in treatment under the law and can have far-reaching implications from simple contact with the police through post imprisonment. Some researchers, however, have turned toward more relative benchmarks, such as with cross-national crime comparisons (Messner and Rosenfeld, 2006; Lynch, 2002) But here too, there are three problems that are of immediate importance:

1. Most of the other developed countries that we compare ourselves to do not have the type of racial issues that the U.S. faces.
2. Cross-national comparisons are somewhat burdened by additional methodological dilemmas relative to cultural and legal differences in defining crime and with variations in the operation of their criminal justice systems.
3. Even after controlling for such differences, comparisons might only inform us about the magnitude of our crime problem relative to other nations, not about inter-racial group differences in offending.

Notwithstanding the lack of a truly objective comparison measure, we can draw some tentative conclusions about the arrest numbers within the context of what is already known about crime. Setting aside the overall level of crime as a potential, African Americans have comprise 31% of all arrests between 2009 and 2014. But there is another wrinkle here that needs to be factored in. Since crime peaked in the early 1990s, the black arrest rates have plummeted. Figure 1 shows that the arrest rates for all crimes, and for Violent and Property Index Crimes have plummeted since the early/mid-1990s. In fact, the average decrease is over is nearly 50% with violent crime arrests decreasing over 55% since it peaked in 1994. This stunning decline, which initially caught researchers off-guard is something that still has not been adequately fleshed out considering that even though crime remains a plague on many black communities, that there is over 50% is many of them must mean improvements in safety and well being for such communities.

Figure 1. Black Arrest Rate Trends 1980–2012

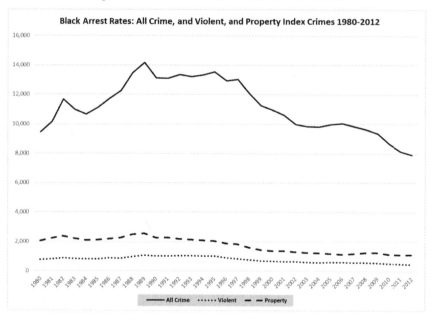

Whereas the 1980s and early 1990s were marked by crack cocaine epidemic and drug turf wars, in many urban centers around the country from New York City to Richmond, Virginia, to Los Angeles, have decidedly changing outlooks with respect to criminal activity and the implications are many including that those most at risk for criminal behavior are simply less violent and criminal, generally. Second, these decreased numbers leave no doubt that politically loaded rhetoric about superpredators (Dilulio, 1995) should be put to rest once and for all. Not only have successive waves of African Americans reaching peak offending age not been superpredators, but their offending rates have declined to the point where they are beginning to look much more like their White counterparts, especially if one accounts for socioeconomic class and neighborhood residency. This might seem like hyperbole, think about it for a moment. In 1993, Blacks were responsible for a nearly unbelievable 13,301 of 23,400 homicides (FBI, 1993) yet by 2014, blacks were arrested for less than 4,250 homicides, which is over 68% decrease in homicides! In contrast, Whites were responsible for 9,693 murders in 1993 and 5,288 in 2014. The decidedly more precipitous decline is similar across multiple index and non-index crime types, and together demonstrates a changed reality for African Americans.

Yet, at the same time there has been a paradoxical four-fold increase in the number of people on probation or parole and in jail or prison (Bureau of Justice Statistics, 2016). In 1980, there were slightly more than 1.8 million people under some manner of formal supervision but by 2008, the number increased to over 7 million. Statistics on federal and state prison populations show that there were 319,000 incarcerated or 139 for every 100,000 persons in 1980 but by 2000 there were over 1.4 million people in prison or jail. African American disproportionate imprisonment follows a similar pattern of arrest. African Americans comprise over 39% of the 1,947,000 people who were in prison, jail, or probation by year's end 2014.

Based on first arrest statistics, one in every three African American men will have been imprisoned in federal or state facilities during their lifetime (Bureau of Justice Statistics, 2006; Travis, 2005). Some researchers have estimated that nearly 10% of all African American males less than thirty years of age were in prison in the year 2000 (Travis, 2005; Beck and Harrison, 2002). Haney and Zimbardo (1998) and Mauer (1999) calculated that more black males were in prison than in college (see also Travis, 2005). The disparity in both arrest and imprisonment (and other punishments) really paint a grim portrait for many African Americans, yet as disturbing as these numbers are, they only tell us about outcomes, not causation or correlation. The racial composition of arrest and imprisonment also shapes our perceptions and understanding of crime, raising some concerns about how we interpret the disparities. The first is that arrest statistics, while useful, are misleading (Gabbidon and Greene, 2009). With the exception of homicide, in absolute numerical terms, whites are still arrested twice as much for serious violent and property crimes than are African Americans. This merits reinforcing. Whites are more than twice as likely to be arrested for serious violent and property crimes, as are African Americans. Thus, even while African Americans are disproportionately arrested and imprisoned, relative to their population size, a majority of those arrested overall are white.

In contrast, popular beliefs and misconceptions about crime developed over decades from the effects of mass media fascination and cultural glorification of inner city urban violence, along with the opportunism of racial politics, has contributed to the racialization of crime (Gabbidon and Greene, 2009). By reinforcing misconceptions or even creating complete myths about African American criminal behavior, it puts a black face on crime. This has led to the legitimization and even reification of negative stereotypes about African Americans and further, to the emergence of dubious law enforcement practices such as racial profiling that has a basis in such stereotypes. The racialization of crime also creates an ecological fallacy by casting criminal suspicion on individual African Americans based upon the characteristics or features of the group, regardless of whether these characteristics have any basis in reality or whether the individual in question shares anything more than a superficial link to such characteristics (Gabbidon and Greene, 2009; Bursik, 1988; Robinson, 1950). This process, perhaps, has likely helped elevate African American crime rates beyond structural and other factors since it suggests that the police are more likely to make a priori assumptions about the guilt of African Americans compared to whites. Gabbidon and Greene (2009) make a strong case about this, arguing that our fixation on violent crime distorts the fact that there are more similarities than differences in offending across racial groups.

Terry Stops

Over time, the oft-difficult relationship between the police and African Americans has led to deep distrust in communities (Batton & Kadleck, 2004). It is also a product of real or alleged law enforcement practices such as racial profiling and differential drug enforcement strategies targeting African American communities; and from specific events such as the shooting of an African American suspect whether or not that person was guilty of a crime; and even how police patrol neighborhoods that residents rate high on incivilities (Piquero, 1999). Put simply, the relationship between African Americans and law enforcement is a history of real and perceived differential treatment that has been reinforced over time by the mounting anecdotal and empirical evidence.

Each shooting of an unarmed African American man and each case where an African American perceives a police stop (frisk or search) as targeting them for no other apparent reason except for the color of their skin can undermine the legitimacy of the police and can further erode relations and any potential gains that might have been made (Gibson et al., 2009; Hickman & Piquero, 2009; Tyler & Wakslak, 2004). The police interact with citizens in many different ways and although not all of the law enforcement practices employed in African American communities are problematical, there are a number of different types of interactions in which police contact with African Americans have garnered a great deal of attention. Two overlapping practices are discussed here, not only because they are controversial, but rather, because they are linked together by alleged racial profiling and because they appear to have the strongest criminal justice effect on disproportionate African American arrest rates.

One way in which the police patrol the streets is to stop and frisk persons that they suspect of having committed a crime. For this type of proactive street encounter, called an "investigative detention" or "Terry stop," after the 1968 *Terry v. Ohio Supreme Court* decision, police need only reasonable suspicion of criminal activity rather than probable cause, while also having the legal right to pat down frisk a person for a weapon (Katz, 2004). Stop and frisk is a regular staple of policing, giving maximum discretion to the individual police officer because of the lower standard of suspicion (Katz, 2004). At the street level, police stops and frisks are among the most divisive of all practices. Despite being in "public," the street is where charges of police harassment and abuse seem to proliferate, even if they go unreported. And though police have been found to stop and frisk people of all racial and ethnic backgrounds, in many cities, African Americans seem to withstand the worst of this practice, which has led to charges of racial and ethnic profiling (Gibson et al., 2009).

Racial Profiling

Police stop, frisk, and search practices are often viewed synonymously with the profiling of African Americans and other minorities. Although racial and ethnic profiling has long been a practice employed in law enforcement (Piliavin & Briar, 1964), in the past decade it has received decidedly more academic attention (Gibson et al., 2009; Reitzel and Piquero, 2006; Russell, 2001). In every respect, racial profiling is indistinguishable from other forms of racial discrimination or bias. It emerges from the same racialized stereotypes about African American criminality and can have the same negative effects, starting with the presumption of criminality simply because of skin color or ethnic background, or worse, perhaps even without any consideration of criminality (Batton & Kadleck, 2004; Kennedy; 1997). It is what Kathryn Russell (2001: 721) poignantly termed as blackness becoming "an acceptable risk factor for criminal behavior." In recent years, however, it has been treated as a somewhat independent social and academic issue, and as such, racial profiling ensues in a relatively new academic niche within a broader exploration of systemic racial bias in the criminal justice system (Reitzel and Piquero, 2006). Early discussion about racial profiling centered on whether it was profiling if race was used alone in police decision-making in stops and searches or in conjunction with other, more objective behavioral factors (Reitzel and Piquero, 2006; Batton & Kadleck, 2004). Though in recent years, it seems that it no longer matters. If race is used as a factor in decision-making by the police, it is racial profiling. Whatever definition one chooses, it remains that profiling is a practice that can occur in nearly all areas of police work.

The literature on racial profiling has found significant over-representation of African Americans in cities and departments around the country with little conflict between findings (Gibson et al., 2009; Reitzel and Piquero, 2006). In fact, the findings were pretty consistent whether studies focused on police stop and frisks in the street (NYCLU, 2010; Ridgeway, 2007; Fagan & Davies, 2000), or used as a factor in police traffic stops and searches (Engel & Calnon, 2004, Warren, Tomaskovic-Devey, Smith, Zingraff & Mason, 2006; Lamberth, 1997).

An instructive empirical example of how police stop and frisk practices link to racial profiling comes from a study by Fagan and Davies (2000). Examining stop and frisk data from New York City, the authors found that, overall, African Americans were significantly more likely to be stopped and frisked by the New York City Police Department (NYPD) compared to whites and to Hispanics/Latinos. The racial pattern of stop and frisks held even after controlling for resident's race, 'crime-specific' crime rates, and the racial distribution across New York's 77 police precincts. More tellingly, their analysis found that in precincts where African American residents comprised less than 10% of the resident population, they were over twice as likely to be stopped for weapons offenses compared to their arrest rate. On the other hand, whites were less than one time more likely to be stopped compared to their arrest rate. Examining the effects across all precincts, African Americans were considerably more likely to be stopped for alleged weapons violations and violent crimes. In racially mixed precincts, their findings were even more significant. African Americans were more than twice as likely to be stopped for violent crimes and nearly three times more likely to be stopped for weapons violations in these neighborhoods (Fagan & Davies, 2000).

In 2007, the Rand Corporation published a technical report on the NYPD's stop and frisk practices that diverges from the earlier findings by Fagan and Davies, the report did not reach the depth of analysis as the Fagan & Davies study (Ridgeway, 2007). In this report, they found only nominal disparities in stops and frisks of African Americans, while also finding that the contraband hit rates for whites was actually higher than for African Americans. Although the Rand report suggested that even though overall they found little racial difference in stops and searches (and use of force), there were locations in New York City in which African Americans were significantly over-represented (Ridgeway, 2007). Incidentally, in 2010, the New York Civil Liberties Union (2010) published a report on the NYPD's stop and frisk practices. Preliminary analysis by the NYCLU found that from 2004–2009, the overall number of police stops and frisks significantly increased by over 250,000 from 315,483 to 575,304. African Americans averaged over 50% of those stopped and frisked even though they comprise only about 16% of the New York City residential population. Comparatively, whites, who comprise nearly 45% of the population, averaged 10% of stops and frisk over that same time period. Although further analysis is needed to draw firmer conclusions about the NYCLU findings, it appears that at a minimum, African Americans are still being targeted by the NYPD and at worst; they might be targeted more now than in 1999. Although the above three studies focus on one police department only (NYPD), they reflect a growing body of research that has found some consistency finding minority over-representation, particularly African American over-representation, in police stops and searches (Gibson et al., 2009). Whether these studies reflect institutional or individual officer profiling of African Americans and other minorities is still an open empirical question, but it is not with respect to the courts. In an important development in 2012, Judge Shira Scheindlin found that the NYPD's Stop & Frisk practice to be unconstitutional (Center for Constitutional Rights, 2012).

War on Drugs

There are few things in criminal justice, from policing to imprisonment, which has done more to exacerbate the pervasive problems in disadvantaged communities, African American or otherwise, then how the government has prosecuted drug crimes. Starting with President Johnson's declaration of war on crime in the 1960s and launched into overdrive under President Reagan's war on drugs campaign, U.S. drug crime policy has been disastrous in innumerable ways (Tonry, 1995; Walker, 2006). Most of all, though, the war on drugs has created a situation where communities are torn apart, family members are pitted against each other, assets are seized, and criminal justice officials are corrupted, all without much significant change in drug sales or usage. Jerome Miller called it a "search and destroy mission aimed at African Americans" (Walker 2006; Miller, 1996). I would call it a search and destroy mission aimed at all Americans, with African Americans being the most unfortunate victims.

Figure 2. Black and White Drug Arrest Rates 1980–2012

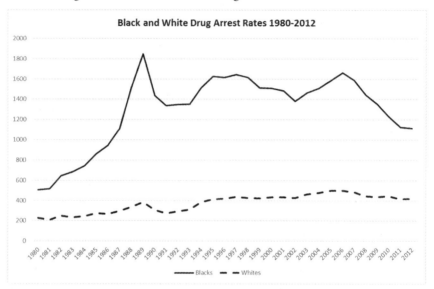

Though no social group has been unaffected by the war on drugs, it has disproportionately affected disadvantaged communities of color. As shown in Figure 2, since the early 1980s, even while the overall number of arrests has dropped dramatically, drug related arrest rates (and imprisonment rates) have skyrocketed (Bureau of Justice Statistics, 2016). Some research found that about 20% of the increased incarceration rate is directly attributable to non-violent drug offenders receiving prison sentences (Tonry, 1995). Though we have a long history of combating drug and alcohol use using the criminal justice system, it is the more recent war on drugs that began in earnest when Congress passed the 1986 Anti-Drug Abuse Act, establishing harsh sentences for drug use, possession and sale and creating a racially biased sentencing structure (i.e., "100:1 ratio for crack vs. powder cocaine") (Kennedy, 1997).

Admittedly, by the end of the 1980s the crack and gang epidemic was in full force, however, the alleged justification for the draconian sentencing legislation, made worse through the creation of a moral panic by the media/political establishment nexus (Chambliss, 1994) and by the 1988 Anti-Drug Abuse Act (similar justifications were used in New York during the 1970s in passing the "Rockefeller Drug Laws"), was to go after "drug kingpins." Instead, it unleashed the police, bringing the full might of state and federal governments to bear in prosecuting drug related crimes (Walker, 2006). In disadvantaged African American communities, drug sales are more likely to take place in the street (compared at least to drug sales in more affluent communities of any color or ethnicity) while becoming hotspots of crime and subsequent targets of increasing militarized police operations (Walker, 2006). Figure 2 shows the increase in imprisonment by race and the increase in drug related arrests, respectively. Though not conclusive, the patterns reveal that while overall arrests declined in the 1990s, imprisonment rates skyrocketed.

African American imprisonment rates increased three times as much as the white imprisonment rate, which was largely due to both increased arrest and imprisonment for violent crimes followed by arrest and imprisonment for drug crimes. In one way, we can view both the modern version of racial profiling in stop and frisk practices as being an outcome of the war on drugs and how the police, and the entire criminal justice system, reorganized itself in its wake (Johnson, Golub & Dunlap, 2006; Chambliss, 1994). If anything, the empirical and voluminous anecdotal evidence clearly shows a watershed period in the criminal justice system that commenced full force in the 1980s, which disproportionately hurt disadvantaged minorities. The other side of this coin though, which has been alluded to a few times in this chapter, is how this has not had the same effect on middle and upper class communities of any color, and in some respects, have advantaged them.

Conclusion

The goal of this chapter was to explore the intersection of racial disparities in arrest rates and police practices that have been shown to or are believed to contribute to such disparities, while placing the uneasy relationship between African Americans and police within the context of recent incidences such as those in Ferguson, Missouri. This is necessary given how the public debate about police practices, including the use of deadly force, has led to many acrimonious exchanges between the blacks and police that signify a troublesome new era of what has been a centuries long problem. Complicating this debate has been a media and police driven claims of police being under siege and that speaking out about such controversial practices has led to what has been termed a "Ferguson Effect" which is empirically unsupported, but nonetheless claim that protesting police violence and disparate treatment against blacks has caused more violence and crime to rise in the United States (Rosenfeld, 2016). There has additionally been the suggestion that protesting police has led to a spike in ambush killings of police officers, putting all police at risk and ruining the relationships between police and black communities in various cities around the country.

Yet, much of this was said without any evidence whatsoever except that there was heightened tensions and some serious violence linked to protests in various cities including Ferguson, New York, and Baltimore, as well as others. But like any claim, we must turn to the available evidence and thus far, it does not seem to support that this effect was real or anything more than localized variation in crime rates under acute circumstances. For instance, in analysis by Rich Rosenfeld for the Sentencing Project, found that where evidence of a spike in homicide rates did occur in St Louis and other cities that should probably not be attributed to simple random variation, neither did he find evidence of an effect. Likewise, in my own analysis of the fifteen largest cities, I too found increasing homicide rates 13 of the 15 largest cities in the US, though Detroit (−1%) and Boston (−22%) witnessed homicide decreases. The mean increase without Detroit or Boston was 21%. But as important as homicide rates are to understanding crime, we cannot just consider only one crime. And while the statistics for 2015 are not available, it is important to note that in nearly all of the cities that witnessed increases in homicides did not see similar increases in other violent crimes such as aggravated assaults or robberies, nor other serious property crimes. In other words, whatever underlying forces are at work in shaping national and local homicide rates, seems to be limited only to homicides, while also calling into question just what the Ferguson effect is?

Notwithstanding media created effects, arrest and imprisonment statistics and the growing literature on race, crime, and policing portray a criminal justice system that has targeted African Americans, both directly and indirectly. The numbers reflect this conclusion and the empirical studies across numerous criminological contexts substantiate it. Yet, there is more to this issue that needs to be examined and more context that needs to be added if we are to move beyond the misconceptions, untruths, and biased policies. With that, I will use the remainder of this space to briefly discuss two important points that frame this issue.

First, Gabbidon and Greene (2009) made the argument that there are more similarities than differences in crime across races and ethnicities. This is true generally speaking, but specifically, their claim has been borne out by crime statistics. Even though serious crime and violence amongst is still considerably higher for Blacks than it is for Whites, the dramatic reduction over the last two decades might be the most important story here (were it not for the pernicious effects of bias and institutional racism). On the other hand, so as not to compound one misconception with another, it does not negate the fact that there is a very real crime problem in many poor African American communities, but it differs from both other African American communities and other white and minority communities. Yet the devil, as they say, is in the details. We can turn toward a number of literatures to illuminate some of them. For instance, in the life-course criminology literature, the empirical evidence clearly shows that although most people have committed crimes in their lives, serious crime is overwhelmingly concentrated among only a small percentage of active offenders (Piquero, Farrington & Blumstein, 2003; Wolfgang, Figlio and Sellin, 1972). This is to say that most people, even in the high crime communities, are law abiding citizens.

Likewise, in studies of racial profiling and stops and frisks by the police, hit rates are also very small, seeming to average less than 15% (NYCLU, 2010; Ridgeway, 2007; Engel & Calnon, 2004; Fagan & Davies, 2000). Such a low hit rate demonstrates that police rarely able to find contraband or have much reason to make arrests relative to most stops. Within the context of the race/crime issue, the basest stereotypes applied to African Americans and the racialization of crime that reinforces these stereotypes, thus applying the propensity of high rate African American offenders to the larger African American community. This needs to be put to rest. Even while crime and violence rates are significantly disproportionate compared to whites, nowhere does the evidence show that anything approaching the disproportionate arrest rates for a small subset of African Americans is typical of the entire African American population.

Last, we would make the same error in thinking about police that we do about African Americans if we claimed that all police officers are racially biased against African Americans because some officers actively discriminate. The answer to policing's problem with the African American community does not start with individual officers, who are in a real way, the lowest bureaucratic agents in the criminal justice hierarchy (see Goldstein, 1977). Rather it starts with the organizational structure of the police. Police agencies, through their charge as law enforcement agents, are provided an enormous amount of power, but similar to many other large and dynamic organizations, they suffer from the same institutional biases and inertia that makes eradicating entrenched racial bias incredibly tough. As a result, while the police might be more inclined towards proactivity rather than reactivity in combating crime, their organizational responses to crime are affected by many different factors, most prominently, legislation and public pressure and fear about some types of crime versus others. Thus, while racially discriminatory policing has long been a problem for law enforcement, in the modern era, it has taken on the additional racial baggage from the war on drugs and other exogenous forces. In this way, it is the racially biased drug policies passed by state and federal legislatures in the 1970s and 1980s, and reinforced across the political spectrum that bears some responsibility for institutional racism in policing. Unfortunately, fault matters little when the outcomes for the African American community remain the same. In sum, the relationship between race, crime, and policing is a difficult issue that has been distorted by an ongoing racially charged public discourse which gives too much credence to stereotypes and myths about African Americans and too much political power to the formal criminal justice institutions that erroneously (though sometimes deliberately) use those stereotypes as a basis for shaping its response to crime. The combined effects make it increasingly harder for many African Americans to avoid becoming ensnared in the widening net cast by the criminal justice system, even in an era when crime in the United States has precipitously decreased. And recent incidents have shown a spotlight on just how problematical things are between police departments and many black communities. Until such time that policies truly address the causes of racial and economic stratification, and until such time that criminal justice practitioners such as the police recognize their own role in perpetuating racial and economic problems suffered most prominently in disadvantaged African American communities the longer the distrust and acrimony will remain, and in that sense, no one wins.

References

Alexander, C. (2010). *The New Jim Crow: Mass Incarceration in the Age of Color Blindness*. New York City: The New Press.

Batton, C. & Kadleck, C. (2004). Theoretical and methodological issues in racial profiling research. Police Quarterly, 7, 30–64.

Beck, A. J. & Harrison, P. M. (2002). Prisoners in 2000. Washington D.C.: Bureau of Justice Statistics.

Black Lives Matter. (2016). Retrieved from blacklivesmatter.com.

Blumstein, A., Cohen, J., Roth, J. & Visher, C. (Eds.). (1986). Criminal careers and "career criminals" (Vols. 1–2). Washington D.C.: National Academy Press.

Bobo, L. & Kluegal, J. R. (1993). Opposition to race-targeting: Self-interest, stratification ideology, or racial attitudes? American Sociological Review 58:443–464.

Braga, A. A., Pierce, G. L., McDevitt, J., Bond, B. J. & Cronin, S. (2008). The strategic prevention of gun violence among gang-involved offenders. Justice Quarterly, 4, 1, 132–162.

Braga, A. A., Weisburd, D., Waring, E. & Green Mazerolle, L. (1999). Problem solving in violent crime places: A randomized controlled experiment. Criminology, 37(3), 541–580.

Bureau of Justice Statistics. (2010). Retrieved from http://bjs.ojp.usdoj.gov. (Last accessed on January 5, 2016).

Bursik, R. J. Jr. (1988). Social disorganization and theories of crime and delinquency: Problems and prospects. Criminology, 26, 519–551.

Chambliss, W, J. Policing the ghetto underclass: Politics of law and law enforcement. (1994). Social Problems, 41, 2, 177–194.

Chappell A., MacDonald J. & Manz P. (2006). The organizational determinants of police arrest decisions. Crime & Delinquency, 52(2), 287–307.

Clear, T. R., Waring, E. & Scully, K. (2005). Communities and reentry. In Jeremy Travis and Christy Visher (Eds.), Prisoner reentry and crime in America. Cambridge, UK: Cambridge University Press.

Cohn, S. F., Barkan, S. E. & Halteman, W. A. (1991). Punitive attitudes toward criminals: Racial consensus or racial conflict? Social Problems, 38, 287–296.

Congressional Budget Office (2010). Cost Estimate: S. 1789 Fair Sentencing Act of 2010. S. 1789. Retrieved from http://www.cbo.gov/ftpdocs/114xx/doc11413/s1789.pdf.

Durlauf, S. N. (2005). Racial profiling as a public policy question: Efficiency, equity, and ambiguity. The American Economic Review, 95, 2, 132–136.

Eck, J. E. & Maguire, E. R. (2006). In A. Blumstein and J. Wallman (Eds.) The crime drop in America. New York: Cambridge University Press.

Eggleston, E. P. & Laub, J. H. (2002). The onset of adult offending: A neglected dimension of the criminal career. Journal of Criminal Justice, 30, 603–622.

Elliott, D. (1994). Serious violent offenders: Onset, developmental course, and termination — The American Society of Criminology 1993 Presidential Address. Criminology, 32, 1–21.

Engel, R. S. & Calnon, J. M. (2004). Comparing benchmark methodologies for police-citizen contacts: Traffic stop data collection for the Pennsyl vania State Police. Police Quarterly, 7, 97–125.

Fagan, J. & Davies, G. (2000). Street stops and broken windows: Terry, race, and disorder in New York City. Fordham Urban Law Journal XXVIII (December), 457–504.

Feagin, J. R. (2001). Racist America: Roots, Current Realities, and future reparations. New York: Routledge.

Fergusson, D., Swain-Campbell, N. & Horwood, J. (2004). How does childhood economic disadvantage lead to crime? Journal of Child Psychology and Psychiatry 45:956–966.

Fyfe, J. (2004). Good policing. In S. Stojkovic, J. Klofas & D. Kalinich (Eds.), The administration and management of criminal justice organizations: A book of readings. Belmont, CA: Wadsworth.

Gabbidon, S. L. & Taylor Greene, H. (2009). Race and crime. Thousand Oaks, CA: Sage Publications Inc.

Gibson, C. L., Walker, S., Jennings, W. G. & Miller, J. M. (2009). The Impact of Traffic Stops on Calling the Police for Help. Criminal Justice Policy Review, 21, 2, 139–159.

Goldstein, H. (1977). Policing a free society. Cambridge, MA: Ballinger Publishing Company.

Goldstein, H. (1990). Problem-Oriented Policing. Philadelphia: Temple University Press.

Hagerdorn, J. & Rauch, B. (2004). Variations in urban homicide: Chicago, New York City and global urban policy. Chicago: Harry F. Guggenheim Foundation.

Haney, C. & Zimbardo, P. (1998). The past and future of U.S. prison policy: Twenty-five years after the Stanford Prison experiment. American Psychologist 53, 709–727.

Harcourt, B. E. & Ludwig, J. (2006). Broken windows: New evidence from New York City and a five-city social experiment. The University of Chicago Law Review, 73, 1, 271–320.

Hickman, M. J. & Piquero, A. R. (2009). Organizational, administrative, and environmental correlates of complaints about police use of force: Does minority representation matter? Crime & Delinquency, 55, 1, 3–27.

Johnson, B., Golub, A. & Dunlap, E. (2006). The Rise and fall of hard drugs, drug markets, and violence in inner-city New York. In, A. Blumstein & J. Wallman (Eds.), The Crime Drop in America. Cambridge University Press.

Katz, L. R. (2004). Terry v. Ohio at Thirty-Five: A Revisionist View. Mississippi Law Journal. Retrieved from http://www.olemiss.edu/depts/ncjrl/pdf/katzMSLJ04.pdf.

Kelling, G. L. & Souza, W. H. (2001). Do Police Matter? An analysis of the impact of New York City's police reforms. The Manhattan Institute, No. 22.

Kennedy, R. (1997). Race, crime and the law. New York: Pantheon.

Klockars, C. (1983). Thinking about police. New York: McGraw Hill.

Kluegal, James R. (1990). Trends in whites' explanations of the black-white Gap in socioeconomic status, 1977–1989. American Sociological Review, 55, 512–525.

Krivo, L. J. & Petersen, R. D. (2000). The structural context of homicide: Accounting for racial differences in process. American Sociological Review 65, 547–559.

Krivo, L. J., Peterson, R. D., Rizzo, H. & Reynolds, J. R. (1998). Race, segregation, and the concentration of disadvantage: 1980–1990. Social Problems, 45:61–80.

Lamberth, J. (1997). Report of John Lamberth, Ph.D. American Civil Liberties Union. Retrieved from www.aclu.org/court/lamberth.html.

Leiber, M. J., Reitzel, J. D. & Mack, K. (2010). Probation officer recommendations for sentencing relative to judicial practice: The implications for African Americans. Criminal Justice Policy Review. doi:10.1177/088740 3410374230.

Levitt, S. D. (2004). Understanding why crime fell in the 1990s: Four factors that explain the decline and six that do not. Journal of Economic Perspectives, 18,1,Winter, 163–190.

Lynch, J. (2002). Crime in international perspective. In J. Q. Wilson and J. Petersilia (Eds.) Crime: Public policies for crime control. Oakland, CA: ICS Press.

Mauer, M. (1999) Race to incarcerate. New York: The New Press.

Messner, S. F. & Rosenfeld, R. (2006). Crime and the American dream. Belmont, CA: Wadsworth.

Miller, J. (1996). Search and Destroy: African American males in the criminal justice system. New York: Pantheon.

Moffitt, T. E. (1993). Adolescence-limited and life-course persistent antisocial behavior: A developmental taxonomy. Psychological Review, 100, 674–701.

Morenoff, J. D., Sampson, R. J. & Raudenbush, S. W. (2001). Neighborhood inequality collective efficacy, and the spatial dynamics of urban violence. Criminology, 39, 3, 517–560.

New York Civil Liberties Union. (2010). Racial Justice. Stop and frisk fact sheet. Retrieved from http://www.nyclu.org/issues/racial-justice/stop-and-frisk practices.

Novak, K. J. & Chamlin, M.B. (2012). Racial Threat, Suspicion, and Police Behavior: The Impact of Race and Place in Traffic Enforcement. Crime & Delinquency, 58(2) 275–300. DOI: 10.1177/0011128708322943

Parker, K. F. & McCall, P. (1999). Structural conditions and racial homicide patterns: A look at the multiple disadvantages in urban areas. Criminology, 37, 447–477.

Peterson, R. D. & Krivo, L. J. (2009). Segregated spatial locations, race-ethnic composition, and neighborhood violent crime. The Annals of the American Academy of Political and Social Science, 623, 93–107.

Piliavin, I. & Briar, S. (1964). Police encounters with juveniles. American Journal of Sociology, 45, 229–243.

Piquero, A. R., Farrington, D. P. & Blumstein, A. (2003). The criminal career paradigm. In Michael Tonry (Ed.), Crime and Justice: A Review of Research. Chicago: University of Chicago Press.

Piquero, A. (1999). The validity of incivility measures in public housing. Justice Quarterly, 16, 4, 793–818.

Reitzel, J. & Piquero, A. (2006). Does it exist? Studying citizens' attitudes of racial profiling. Police Quarterly, 9:161–183.

Ridgeway, G. (2007). Analysis of racial disparities in the New York Police Department's stop, question, and frisk practices. Santa Monica: Rand Corporation.

Robinson, W. S. (1950). Ecological correlations and the behavior of individuals. American Sociological Review, 15, 351–357.

Rosenfeld, R., Fornango, R. & Baumer, E. (2005). Did Ceasefire, COMPSTAT, and Exile, reduce homicide? Criminology & Public Policy, 4, 3, 419–450.

Russell, K. (2001). Racial profiling: A status report of the legal, legislative, and empirical literature. Rutgers Race & the Law Review (61) 1–16.

Sampson, R. J. & Bean, L. (2006). Cultural mechanisms and killing fields: A revised theory of community-level racial inequality. In R. P., Lauren Krivo & John Hagan (Eds.) The many colors of crime: inequalities of race, ethnicity and crime in America. New York: New York University Press.

Sampson, R. J. & Laub, J. H. (2004). Shared beginnings, divergent lives: Delinquent boys at age 70. Cambridge, MA: Harvard University Press.

Sampson, R. J., Morenoff, J. D. & Gannon-Rowley, T. (2002). Assessing "neighborhood effects: Social processes and new directions in research. Annual Review of Sociology, 28, 443–478.

Sampson, R. J. & Wilson, W. J. (1995). Toward a theory of race, crime, and urban inequality. In John Hagan and Ruth D. Peterson (Eds.) Crime and inequality. Stanford CA: Stanford University Press.

Sherman, L. W. (1997). Preventing Crime: What works, what doesn't, what's promising. A report to the United States Congress. National Institute of Justice. Washington DC.

Sherman, L. W., Shaw, J. W. & Rogan, D. P. (1995). The Kansas City Gun Experiment. Washington DC: National Institute of Justice.

Silverman, E. B. (2001). NYPD battles crime: Innovative strategies in policing. Boston: Northeastern University Press.

Steffensmeier, D., Ulmer, J. & Kramer, J. (1998). The interaction of race, gender, and age in criminal sentencing: The punishment cost of being young, black, and male. Criminology, 36, 763–797.

Tonry, M. (1995). Malign neglect. New York: Oxford Press.

Travis, J. (2005). But they all come back: Facing the challenges of prisoner reentry. Washington DC: The Urban Institute Press.

Tyler, T. R. & Wakslak, C. J. (2004). Profiling and police legitimacy: procedural justice, attributions of motive, and acceptance of police authority. Criminology, 42, 253–81.

U. S. Census Bureau. (2016). U.S. Department of Economics and Statistics Administration. Retrieved from http://www.census.gov/.

U. S. Census Bureau. (2000). Income and Poverty, 2000. Washington D.C.

U.S. Department of Economics and Statistics Administration. (2016). http://www.census.gov/.

Walker, S. (2006). Sense and nonsense about crime and drugs: A policy guide. Belmont, CA: Wadsworth.

Walker, S. (2001). Searching for the denominator: Problems with police traffic stop data and early warning system solution. Justice Research and Policy, 3, 63–95.

Walker, S., Spohn, C. & Delone, M. (2006). The color of justice: Race, ethnicity, and crime in America. Belmont, CA: Wadsworth.

Warren, P., Tomaskovic-Devey, D., Smith, W., Zingraff, M. & Mason, M. (2006). Driving while black: Bias processes and racial disparity in police stops. Criminology, 44, 709–738.

Wilkins, V. M. & Williams, B. N. (2009). Representing blue: Representative bureaucracy and racial profiling in the Latino community. Administration & Society, 40, 775–798.

Willis, J., Mastrofski, S. & Weisburd D. (2007). Making Sense of COMPSTAT: A Theory-Based Analysis of Organizational change in Three Police Departments. Law and Society Review, 41, 1, 147–188.

Wilson, W. J. (1987). The Truly disadvantaged: The inner city, the underclass, and public policy. University of Chicago Press, Chicago.

Wilson, W. J. (1978). The Declining significance of race: Blacks and changing American institutions. Chicago: University of Chicago Press.

Wilson, G., Dunham, R. & Alpert, G. (2004). Prejudice in police profiling. American Behavioral Scientist, 47, 7, 896–909.

Wolfgang, M. E., Figlio, R. M. & Sellin, T. (1972). Delinquency in a birth cohort. Chicago: University of Chicago Press.

Zimring, F. E. (2006). The great American crime decline. New York: Oxford University Press.

Chapter 10

Increasing Police Legitimacy Through Body-Worn Cameras

Amy Kyle Cook, Shana Mell, and William V. Pelfrey, Jr.

Introduction

Recent highly-publicized encounters between police and citizens such as those in New York City, Ferguson, Baltimore, Chicago, Charleston, and Cleveland, have left African-Americans, particularly those in high-crime, urban neighborhoods, questioning treatment by the police. Incidents like these are nothing new for those living in socially disadvantaged communities as racially biased law enforcement practices have a well documented history. From the brutal narrative of slavery that was followed by a system of legally condoned Jim Crow laws, Blacks were restricted to a segregated existence despite civil rights victories (Unnever & Gabbidon, 2011). In 1966, the Black Panther Party identified a ten-point program to educate and revolutionize Black communities due to being exploited at the hands of the government, namely, the police (Newton, 1973). The first program they emphasized was point number seven, "We want an immediate end to POLICE BRUTALITY and MURDER of Black people" (Newton, 1973, p. 346). In his platform, Newton (1973) went on to describe that the police had never been protectors of Black communities but rather they oppressed and continually brutalized Blacks. As a further protest to existing conditions, in 1967 during the height of the civil rights movement, violent riots erupted in 128 American cities as a result of feelings of frustration, discrimination, and prejudice on behalf of African-American rioters (Briggs, 1968).

To evaluate the racial divide between Blacks and Whites that precipitated the riots, President Lyndon B. Johnson established the National Advisory Commission on Civil Disorders (NACCD) also known as the Kerner Report in

1968 (Embrick, 2015). The committee investigated aspects of social, economic, and psychological inequality and police practices experienced by Blacks (Briggs, 1968) and concluded that "Our nation is moving toward two societies, one black, one white—separate and unequal" (as cited in Embrick, 2015, p. 837). The nation would be reminded once again in 1991, of the reach of police brutality in the beating of Rodney King in Los Angeles that was caught on tape by a bystander. In 1999, the fatal shooting of Amadou Diallo, a Black Immigrant, by four White officers from the New York City Police Department (NYPD) was another highly publicized incident calling into question the mistreatment of Blacks and the topic of racial profiling by the police (Fridell, 2008; Forst, 2004). According to the police, Diallo matched the description of a rape suspect, ran from the police when they approached him, failed to follow police commands, and was tragically killed when he reached for his wallet, an act which officers interpreted as reaching for a weapon.

As Fridell (2008) notes, there were likely a number of reasons that the officers may have believed that Diallo's behavior was dangerous such as he did not respond to police commands to stop, he was in a violent neighborhood, and he was seen reaching for something perceived to be a gun. None of the officers involved in these incidents were convicted. In 2009, an Oakland man, Oscar Grant was killed by a Bay Area Rapid Transit officer. Although the officer was the first in California to be charged with murder, he was convicted of involuntary manslaughter and sentenced to two years in prison, with time served (Armaline, Vera Sanchez & Correia, 2014). These anecdotes do not diminish the experiences of others who have suffered at the hands of police but provide context of the history of the relationship between the police, race, and the communities they serve.

Allegations of police misconduct foment feelings of hostility between police and their constituency. In poor, minority communities, the lack of trust in police is so entrenched that interactions between police and citizens creates anger and resentment, negatively effecting feelings of equity (Gill, Weisburd, Telep, Vitter & Bennett, 2014). National polls provide some insight into the relationship between race relations and law enforcement. According to a 2014 Gallup poll, confidence in the police was significantly lower among Blacks as compared to Whites—37 percent and 59 percent, respectively. More specifically, Blacks (25 percent) had very little to no confidence in the police as compared to Whites (12 percent). Moreover, when asked about perceptions of treatment by the police, young Black males between the ages of 18–34 reported higher levels of mistreatment by police within the past 30 days as compared to older Black males. Black respondents rated police officers lower than White respondents when they assessed honesty and ethics among police officers.

Other polls have produced similar findings. In a nationally representative sample, 70 percent of those polled believed Blacks were not treated fairly by the police (Gabbidon & Higgins, 2009). Likewise, 88 percent of Blacks as compared to 59 percent of Whites were more likely to believe Blacks were not treated fairly by the police (National Bar Association, 2015). Perhaps one of the most notable findings from both Gabbidon and Higgins' study and the National Bar Association's 2015 poll was that Southern residents believed Blacks were treated less fairly by the police than Whites. These findings are not surprising given the history of the racial caste system implemented by Whites and enforced by the police, especially in the South.

Given the critical nature of policing as a profession, understanding perceptions of citizens is an important part of improving police-community relations. Research has shown that citizens are not able to accurately assess police on issues of legality. That is, citizens are not familiar with police policies and practices; however, citizens are able to assess police on how they treat them and others— a concept known as police legitimacy (Police Executive Research Forum (PERF), 2014). Legitimacy gives consideration to the belief that law enforcement officers are able to exercise their authority to maintain order, manage conflicts, and solve problems in the communities they serve (Schulhofer, Tyler & Huq, 2011; Tyler, 2004, 2009, 2011; Tyler & Jackson, 2013).

Police Legitimacy and Procedural Justice

Police legitimacy is a measure of perceptions of the police and reflects three important ideals (1) the public trusts and has confidence in the police and believes they are honest, (2) the willingness of citizens to defer to the law and accept police authority, and (3) the belief that the police are morally justified and appropriate in their actions (PERF, 2014). As Forst (2004) explains, legitimacy is primarily about the public's perceptions about what is just and effective. Legitimacy is also the existence of a system void of corruption and public malfeasance (Forst, 2004). Citizens' attitudes about whether police behave legitimately are generally based on personal experiences or larger law enforcement matters (Tankebe, 2009; Tyler & Huo, 2002; Tyler & Wakslak, 2004).

In a qualitative study of 40 residents in West Oakland, personal and vicarious narratives shed light on aggressive and corrupt police practices (Armaline et al., 2014). Specifically, residents shared experiences with researchers that were thematically centered around the belief that the police do not protect and serve or treat them in a fair and just manner. Moreover, their experiences were shaped by race; residents believed they were subjected to aggressive and corrupt practices because of their skin-color. Since legitimacy relies on the public's trust and confidence in the police, strategies used by the police cannot be effective in solving crime because legitimacy is a primary driver of citizen cooperation and engagement (Tyler, Goff & MacCoun, 2015). Citizens that believe the police are legitimate are more likely to comply with the law and cooperate with officers.

The Police Executive Research Forum (2014) suggests that procedural justice is the means to achieving police legitimacy. Trust is a critical component to procedural justice and a loss of trust threatens legitimacy (Katz, W., 2015). The idea of procedural justice first appeared in Thibaut and Walker's (1975) innovative research suggesting that undesired outcomes will be accepted when police practices are considered fair. Kunard and Moe (2015) offer a relatively straight forward way of explaining procedural justice. The researchers assert that one's assessment of an interaction with an officer is based on the *outcome* of an encounter and the *process* they encounter. More specifically, *outcome* is concerned with the decision the officer makes while *process* is concerned with the way the officer came to make the decision and whether the officer explained his/her decision. There are four distinct principles of procedural justice identified as tools that build mutual respect and trust between the police and the public (Kunard & Moe, 2015). When these strategic behaviors are applied by law enforcement officers, community support for the police is more likely to occur:

Fairness and consistency of rule of application. This is the notion that the processes used to reach an outcome matters more so than the outcome itself. Decision making, having a respectful conversation with citizens, and the process by which an outcome is arrived at matters.

Voice and representation in the process. Having a voice is an important aspect of feeling as though one's opinion matters. It is the idea that they are being listened to and that some consideration is being given to their concerns.

Transparency and openness of process. When decisions are made in a transparent manner, meaning they are made in the open, the public is more likely to understand the ultimate result of a decision. Decisions that are as transparent as possible are more likely to be accepted even if the decision is an unfavorable one.

Impartiality and unbiased decision making. Impartial decisions are made based on evidence not opinion, speculation, or guesswork. When data is used to explain decisions, understanding and acceptance are more likely to follow.

When the public perceives the intentions of the police as fair, they tend to possess higher levels of legitimacy (Kunard & Moe, 2015; Tankebe, 2009; Tyler & Wakslak, 2004). Legitimacy is conferred on those acting in a procedurally just manner (President's Task Force on 21st Century Policing, 2015). Research has shown that two themes emerge regarding perceptions of fair police practices. First, public perceptions of fair treatment are strongly related to police legitimacy (Schulhofer et al., 2011; Tyler, 2004, 2009, 2011; Tyler & Fagan, 2008) and legitimacy is consistently correlated with desired outcomes such as citizens' heightened willingness to cooperate, obedience to the law, providing assistance and information when needed, and empowering the police to function in the scope of their duties (Sunshine & Tyler, 2003; Tyler & Fagan, 2008). Second, citizens who reported fair treatment by the police were more likely to comply with police requests, accept the outcome of the encounter, provide police with necessary information, and assist with case closure (Mastrofski, Snipes & Supina, 1996; McCluskey, 2003; Paternoster, Brame, Bachman & Sherman, 1997; Tyler & Huo, 2002).

Examining sources of trust in the police, procedural justice and perceived collective efficacy were important factors in explaining trust; however, researchers highlight the fact that procedural fairness was more important in shaping levels of trust toward the police (Nix, Wolfe, Rojek & Kaminski, 2015). It comes as no surprise that persons living in areas low in collective efficacy and more disadvantage were less inclined to believe the police were fair and, as a result, residents were more cynical of both the police and the law (Nix et al., 2015). These results echo that of previous researchers who found that higher levels of community disorder were related to lower levels of confidence in the police (Ren, Cao, Lovrich & Gaffney, 2005). Since the police spend much of their time in disadvantaged neighborhoods these findings are especially important because they underscore the critical need for the police to practice high levels of respect, politeness, and fairness when performing their duties (Nix et al., 2015). The bottom line is that citizens will only trust police when they believe the police are treating them respectfully and fairly.

Negative and hostile police-citizen encounters are the norm for many African-Americans living in socially disadvantaged and violent neighborhoods (Jones & Raymond, 2012). In a qualitative study of one citizen's effort to document the vast amount of police brutality occurring right in front of them, one of the residents and videographer explained "There was a need for it because there was just so much police brutality going on, I mean, right in front of us, and you couldn't prove it because it was their word against ours" (Jones & Raymond, 2012, p. 110). Six years of video-taped interactions with the police provided the proof these citizens needed to show that the police were abusing their power — evidence which was submitted to state and federal level court systems (Jones & Raymond, 2012). Stories like these and the many accounts of poor police-community relations justify Embrick's (2015) argument that after 47 years the relationship between Blacks and Whites and police violence toward Blacks has not improved since the Kerner Report was issued.

Indeed, the deterioration of police-community relationships in minority communities has resulted in tarnished images of justice, increased levels of mistrust and hostility, and even violence perpetrated against police officers. These severe negative consequences beg the question, how can the relationship between the police and the communities they serve be repaired? One answer may lie in technology. In the age of 24-hour news coverage, social media frenzy, and citizen-recorded events that question the legitimacy of the police, law enforcement agencies are eager to increase levels of trust within their communities.

Equipping police officers with body-worn cameras (BWCs) has become a priority for departments attempting to enhance public safety and improve police community relations (Vorndran, Burke, Chavez, Fraser & Moore, 2014). According to the American Civil Liberties Union (ACLU) (2013), BWC programs are considered a best practice among law enforcement agencies. Additionally, the ACLU supports the use of BWCs as a check against both the abuse of police powers and as a protection against false accusations of abuse against police (ACLU, 2015). In *Floyd v. City of New York* (2013) Judge Shira Scheindlin ruled that the NYPD's stop and frisk program was unconstitutional and ordered the NYPD to implement a BWC program in one precinct from each borough. In her ruling, Judge Scheindlin asserted that BWC footage would provide an objective record of stop and frisks so that police conduct could be reviewed to determine whether minorities were stopped simply because of their race. She further explained that the videos should alleviate some of the mistrust that exists between police and Blacks and Hispanics.

While the literature is scant surrounding BWC effectiveness, one of the most highlighted aspects of BWC programs is the potential for improving relationships between police and residents. In addition, improving the integrity of the criminal justice system and the effective delivery of police services are noted as essential for the stability of communities (FACTSHEET: Strengthening Community Policing, White House, 2014). In December 2014, President Obama showed his commitment to increasing levels of trust between police and the communities they serve when he proposed $263 million to fund police purchase of BWCs, expand training for police departments, provide resources for reform in police departments, and increase the number of cities where the Department of Justice engages law enforcement agencies (FACTSHEET: Strengthening Community Policing, White House, 2014).

Over the past few years, BWC programs have received a significant amount of attention despite the relatively few published studies that have evaluated their effectiveness (Lum, Koper, Merola, Scherer & Reioux, 2015; White, 2014). Recent surveys have estimated that between one-fourth and one-third of local law enforcement agencies have adopted BWCs despite the fact that as of December 2015, only 12 studies on BWCs have been published in scholarly journals and three of those are from the same data sets (Lum, et al., 2015; Stanley, 2015). Regardless of the lack of extensive analyses, extant research and anecdotal evidence indicates that agencies implementing BWC programs demonstrate high levels of transparency and legitimacy, a reduction in citizen complaints and officer use of force, improved behavior among citizens, increased levels of trust among police, and enhanced communication with citizens (White, 2014). In addition, BWC programs may offer some levels of protection against police departments including a decrease in false allegations against the police, a decrease in litigation costs, a decrease in report writing time (Katz, Choate, Ready & Nuno, 2015). Given the seemingly promising outcomes of BWC programs, a review of the literature is warranted.

Police Use of Body-Worn Cameras

Police accountability, transparency, and public support. A perceived benefit of BWC programs is transparency, or the willingness of a police department to open itself up to outside scrutiny (White, 2014). It may be that transparency and citizen feelings of police legitimacy may be enhanced by BWC programs simply because BWC footage would be available and even though these claims have not been empirical tested, the technology itself would likely increase transparency. This is likely the very point Judge Scheindlin was making in her ruling in *Floyd v. City of New York* (2013). The fact that citizens may be able to request footage or if departments are willing to release footage of encounters with the police, levels of trust may be increased (Considering Police Body Cameras, 2015). Unfortunately, there are no definitive results on whether BWCs promote transparency. A public opinion survey in the United Kingdom (UK) found that 64 percent of respondents believe police should wear BWCs and the same number felt that BWCs would reduce crime and antisocial behavior (ODS Consulting, 2011). Between 37 and 49 percent of citizens reported that they would feel safer if police wore BWCs (ODS Consulting, 2011). Police officials have reported that their agencies have experienced fewer complaints and that police-citizen encounters have improved since wearing BWCs (Miller, Toliver & PERF, 2014). Public support for BWCs speaks to the potential for increased accountability and transparency (Considering Body Worn Cameras, 2015). White (2014) contends that issues of transparency and citizen perceptions of BWCs are lacking.

Reducing complaints through improved officer behavior. Using a randomized controlled experiment where half of the department's officers were assigned to an experimental group (officers wore BWCs) or a control group (did not wear BWCs), a study conducted in Rialto, California tested the effects of officer use of force and citizen complaints against police (Ariel, Farrar & Sutherland, 2015). The experimental group experienced a reduction in both use of force incidents and complaints against police whereas use of force in the control group was twice as high. Another study using the Rialto data specifically examined the impact of BWCs on self-awareness and socially desirable behavior and found that there was a 50 percent reduction in the total number of use of force incidents (Farrar & Ariel, 2013). Ariel and colleagues (2015) note the importance of the impact of BWCs on police behavior, especially when there are rules that should be followed. Police Chief William Farrar of Rialto stated, "Whether the reduced number of complaints was because of the officers behaving better or the citizens behaving better — well, it was probably a little of both" (Miller, Toliver & PERF, 2014). In-depth interviews with state troopers regarding the implementation of in-car cameras have revealed similar findings. Troopers repeatedly commented that it is human nature to behave to the best of one's ability when you know you are being watched (Westphal, 2004).

Ready and Young (2015) examined 100 officers from Mesa, Arizona's Police Department to evaluate officer behavior on performing stop and frisks and arrests. The researchers found that officers wearing BWCs were less likely to perform stop and frisks and make arrests; however, those same officers were also more likely to write citations. In addition, officers wearing BWCs initiated more contacts with citizens and reported BWCs as helpful during encounters with the public. Ready and Young (2015) found that there was a reduction in use of force incidents and citizen complaints by 75 percent and 40 percent, respectively.

In a study of the Orlando Police Department, Jennings, Lynch, and Fridell (2015) used random assignment of BWCs to an experimental group or a control group to compare officer response-to-resistance and citizen-generated complaints for aggressive, threatening, and/or intimidating behavior, and/or excessive use of force. Their results indicated that officers randomly assigned to wear BWCs had a significantly lower prevalence of response-to-resistance and received significantly fewer complaints as well as a significantly lower prevalence of complaints compared to those that did not wear BWCs. When considering general perceptions of improved officer behavior, Jennings et al. (2015) reported twenty-five percent of officers in their study agreed or strongly agreed that the implementation of the BWC program directly impacted their behavior in the community. Only about 20 percent of officers believe BWCs would improve their own behavior whereas 29 percent agree that the BWC would make them behave "by-the-book" (Jennings, Fridell & Lynch, 2014). Furthermore, Jennings et al. (2014) and Jennings et al. (2015) provide strong evidence that officers support the use of BWCs in the course of their job duties. Jennings et al. (2014) also reported that 77 percent, a majority of the officers surveyed, would feel comfortable wearing BWCs.

As part of the *Smart Policing Initiative* (SPI), Katz et al. (2015) examined the impact of BWCs on officer's perceptions, officer complaints, and domestic violence case processing and outcomes using a quasi-experimental design in the Phoenix, Arizona, Police Department. Officers were initially ambivalent about using BWCs; however, post-implementation, officers believed the cameras were easier to use than they previously expected and believed the program should be expanded to other departments. Among the officers wearing BWCs, citizen complaints significantly declined and complaints against officers wearing BWCs were less likely to be sustained. Katz et al. (2015) also found that officer productivity was enhanced as evidenced by a significant increase in the number of arrests made by officers wearing BWCs. According to reports from police officials, officers with a history of complaints have requested BWCs to protect themselves against future problems (Miller, Toliver & PERF, 2014). Critics of BWC programs contend that reductions in citizen complaints cannot necessarily be attributed to improved police conduct (Considering Police Body Cameras, 2015). It could be that citizens consciously decided against filing a complaint and not due to improved police conduct; it will be important not to confuse the two when evaluating the efficacy of other programs (Considering Police Body Cameras, 2015).

Case resolution. Technology may provide an objective and timely resolution of complaints against officers. Video and audio recordings of interactions between police and the public provides additional evidence that can be used in investigating and rapidly resolving complaints of police misconduct (Vorndran, et al., 2014; Westphal, 2004). White (2014) notes that frivolous complaints may be less likely for officers wearing BWCs because video footage can immediately refute their claim. Evidence from BWC footage in the United Kingdom provided the support police officers and wardens needed as a result of the complaints filed against them, vindicating the officers (ODS Consulting, 2011). Similarly, in-car cameras were beneficial in clearing officers in 96 percent of the complaints filed against them (Westphal, 2004). BWCs also provide reassurances to the officers involved, reduced the amount of time to resolve complaints, and reduced the amount of time police spend in resolving complaints (ODS Consulting, 2011).

Improved behavior among citizens. In order to promote citizen cooperation and engagement, the police must be viewed as legitimate (Tyler et. al., 2015). Proponents of BWCs argue that the mere presence of the camera will improve citizens' behavior because they will be more respectful and compliant (White, 2014). Feedback from a number of officers in the United Kingdom indicated that the BWC kept them from being assaulted with the additional benefits of protection, reassurance, security, and welfare against aggressive individuals (ODS Consulting, 2011). According to officers' perceptions, 28 percent of officers surveyed from the Orlando Police Department reported that BWCs impacted citizen behavior and 41 percent agreed that BWCs are capable of de-escalating confrontations with citizens they encounter (Jennings et al., 2015). Mayor Randy Brown of Evesham, New Jersey, echoed these sentiments when he commented to reporters about the usage of BWCs in Evesham, "People act better. It reduces altercations. This changes the game" (philly.com, 2014). In contrast, Katz et al. (2015) did not find that BWCs had an effect on suspect behaviors for resisting arrest.

Increased officer safety. Increased levels of police trust and legitimacy based on fair and just police practices may have a spill-over effect on officer safety; however, no studies to date exist to support this hypothesis. Less than a handful of studies have examined aspects of officer safety among those recording interactions with citizens. Increased officer safety was one of the positive impacts of the in-car camera program among a nationally representative sample of state troopers (Westphal, 2004). As for BWCs, although Jennings et al. (2014) showed that officers were generally supportive of BWC programs (62 percent), less than 20 percent of officers felt that they would actually feel safer wearing BWCs. Additional research is needed that explores aspects of officer safety especially considering the recent acts of violence perpetrated against police officers.

Training for law enforcement agencies. Police executives contend that BWCs have strengthened accountability and transparency within departments by identifying and correcting problems (Miller et al., 2014). Quite simply, BWCs serve as a training tool to improve officer performance (identifying officers who abuse their authority or by addressing questionable practices) by using footage to evaluate performance, provide scenario-based training, continuing educational programs, and to identify areas in which training is needed (Miller et al., 2014; Vorndran et al., 2014; Westphal, 2004). Miller and colleagues also contend that BWCs can help address structural problems such as racial profiling within departments. The added value of audio and video of an encounter will allow police administrators (and researchers) to more fully understand the relationship between police-citizen encounters and (a) whether racial profiling took place, (b) the patterns of behavior that were present, and (c) the frequency of occurrence (Miller et al., 2014). The Civil Rights Division of the Department of Justice has encouraged departments to employ BWCs to show the public they are engaged in constitutional policing (Miller et al., 2014). In summary, BWCs offer great promise as both a training tool and a more thorough review of police behavior during critical incidents (White, 2014).

Concerns. Despite the value and perceived benefits of BWC programs, there are a number of legitimate concerns regarding implementation, including: privacy for citizens and officers, officers' health and safety, departmental policies and training, cost of equipment, usage and maintenance, data storage and management, public disclosure policies, and civil liability (Miller et al., 2014; White, 2014). Additionally, the officers in the Katz et al. (2015) study shared day-to-day usage concerns about the length of download times, the extra time it took to complete reports, and the potential that their BWC footage could be used against them. Interpretation and objectivity of video footage present additional concerns (Kahan, Hoffman & Braman, 2009). Given the extent of these concerns and lack of empirical evidence, police departments planning to implement BWC programs need to invest considerable time into planning and training. Agencies must invest significant energy in policy development and training, particularly regarding citizen privacy. When a citizen reports a sexual assault, rape, or other sex crime victimization, recording that interaction with a BWC may be inappropriate. Likewise, citizens with mental health issues may reveal personal health information which should also be kept confidential. It is important to consider the complexities around revelatory police-citizen interactions, develop appropriate policies to address those potential scenarios, and train officers to know when to turn the BWC on, and when to turn it off. It is important to acknowledge that the literature highlights a number of other potential benefits for the use of BWCs throughout the criminal justice system and not just for the police; however, a discussion of those benefits is outside of the scope of this chapter.

Though a number of studies are currently underway, the research on BWC programs is sparse (see Lum et al., 2015). While the literature suggests a host of positive outcomes for both the public and law enforcement communities, the implementation of BWC programs does not address *how* police officers go about making decisions with whom they encounter (i.e., biases officers may have, intentional or not). According to Fridell's (2014) work on Fair and Impartial Policing, the national discussion on race and policing has involved outdated notions of how bias manifests, i.e. explicit bias such as racism. Changing norms, the Civil Rights Act, and legislative interventions made discrimination illegal and, consequently, overt forms of prejudice have declined (Dovidio & Gartner, 1999). However, as Fridell (2008) explains, social psychologists have found that "implicit or unconscious racial bias can impact what people perceive and do, even in subjects who consciously hold non-prejudiced attitudes" (p. 39).

Bias manifests as a result of the tendency to automatically categorize others. Man has an inclination to prejudice because all thinking involves categorization and the natural tendency to form generalizations even when the content is an oversimplification of experiences (Allport, 1958). Allport links prejudice with prejudgment. As Lawrence (1987) explains, the categorization of others is necessary in order to cope with daily experiences. Because of the unconscious nature of implicit biases and the decisions that result, implicit biases have been studied in a variety of contexts such as race and ethnicity, sexual orientation, religion, body shape, and age and among those working in healthcare, education, court systems, and law enforcement. Understanding the role that implicit bias plays in the decisions made by police officers is crucial if law enforcement agencies are committed to improving police-community relations. The following section discusses some of the research on implicit bias and perceptions of race and crime among citizens and police officers.

Implicit Bias

In her work on implicit bias Fiske (2008) emphatically stated, "Here's the first thing to understand: Modern prejudice is not your grandparents' prejudice" (p. 14). The reference to "your grandparents' prejudice" is the notion of explicit bias where racism and sexism were known quantities because people expressed themselves in a manner consistent with their thoughts (Fiske, 2008). Implicit bias refers to attitudes or stereotypes that affect understanding, actions, and decisions in an unconscious way (Staats, 2013). Simply put, negative biases can occur spontaneously, automatically, and without one's full awareness (Dovidio & Gartner, 1999). People of all races are influenced by implicit biases that have behavioral consequences (Richardson, 2011). Perhaps this is because prejudices may be hardwired in the brain; researchers have found that emotions are visible in magnetic resonance imaging (MRI) (Fiske, 2008).

In laboratory experiments, study participants were shown pictures of older people, those with disabilities, drug addicts, the homeless, rich businessmen, and Olympic athletes (Fiske, 2008). Participants then had to report the emotion they associated with each group. As expected, feelings of pity were associated with the disabled and the elderly, disgust for the homeless and the drug addicted, envy toward the businessmen, and pride for the Olympic athletes (Fiske, 2008, p. 15). Another set of participants were then put into a functional MRI scanner to observe their brain activity as they looked at the pictures. As soon as the participants saw the picture of the homeless man, their emotions produced a set of reactions associated with the insula, which is indicative of disgust, and avoidance, much like the feelings humans would have for garbage (Fiske, 2008). Fiske acknowledged being surprised to see how easily the physical characteristics of others evoked such deep-seated reactions among study subjects. Other studies of brain activity have shown spikes in the amygdala when White people viewed pictures of Black faces they judged as threatening (Fiske, 2008). According to Staats (2013), the amygdala activates when the brain perceives threat or anxiety and plays a major role in processing emotions such as fear (and pleasure) and is involved with identifying implicit attitudes. Interestingly enough, Fiske (2008) found that when the context of the photos changed, brain functions also changed suggesting that circumstances and other influences can alter the way people think.

The extant literature has shown that biases are unconscious, hardwired in the brain, inevitable and produce behavioral consequences. In the first experimental study of its kind, Payne (2001) examined race and its influence on the identification of weapons among a sample of undergraduate students. Participants were quicker to identify handguns over hand tools after they were primed with Black faces versus White faces. In addition, students misidentified hand tools as guns more often when Black priming occurred as compared to White priming. Correll, Park, Judd, and Wittenbrink (2002; 2007) tried to recreate the experiences of police officers by creating video games to simulate hostile conditions that are typically present in police shoot/don't shoot scenarios. In the first part of the Correll et al. (2002) 4-part study, participants shot Black armed suspects quicker than Whites. When participants were forced to make quicker decisions in part two, unarmed Blacks were shot more often than Whites. Part three revealed that shooter bias was stronger for those participants who believed there was a culture that characterized Blacks as aggressive, violent, and dangerous. The last part of the study revealed that Whites and Blacks displayed equivalent levels of bias during shooting simulations—that is, Whites and Blacks shot Blacks at higher rates than they shot Whites.

Media stories and racial stereotypes that portrayed Blacks as dangerous also influenced decisions to shoot. Having had stereotypes reinforced through news stories that Blacks are dangerous, shooters were more likely to shoot unarmed Blacks but failed to shoot armed Whites (Correll et al., 2007a). Repeated exposure to stereotypic congruent images exacerbated the shooting of Blacks quicker than Whites and led shooters to not shoot unarmed Whites as quick as they did unarmed Blacks. The results reinforced that bias is driven by the accessibility of danger stereotypes, race, and weapons. Blacks, like Whites, employ increased levels of shooter bias against high stereotypical

Blacks as compared to low-stereotypical Blacks in split-second decisions to shoot (Kahn & Davies, 2010). Low-stereotypical Blacks had a light skin tone, narrow nose, and thin lips whereas high-stereotypical Blacks had a dark complexion, broad nose, and thick lips (Kahn & Davies, 2010). Specifically, Black shooters in the study were more likely to have mistakenly shot unarmed high-stereotypical Blacks as compared to low-stereotypical Blacks. Blacks also mistakenly failed to shoot armed low-stereotypical Blacks more than armed high-stereotypical Blacks. As for White shooters in the study, a similar pattern emerged; because high-stereotypical Blacks were associated with danger, they were shot more often than low-stereotypical Blacks and Whites. Furthermore, White shooters mistakenly failed to shoot low-stereotypic Blacks and Whites armed with weapons (Kahn & Davies, 2010).

Studies specific to police officers have produced similar findings as that of undergraduate students. Based on computer simulated exercises, initial results of police officers revealed that they were more likely to shoot unarmed Blacks as opposed to unarmed Whites; however, the more exposed police officers were to the computer simulations, the more unbiased their decisions were in shoot/don't shoot decisions (Plant & Peruche, 2005). In later trials, police officers showed no signs of bias in their shooting decisions and they became more accurate (Plant & Peruche, 2005). The repeated exposure to simulations resulted in a more conservative shift in decisions to shoot (Plant & Peruche, 2005). In their 5-part study of undergraduate students (studies 1–3) and police officers (studies 4 and 5), Eberhardt, Goff, Purdie & Davis (2004) found that just like students, police officers more frequently categorized Blacks as criminal and thought of crime as Black. The officers were also more likely to falsely identify a more stereotypical Black face after being primed with crime images than when not primed with crime images (Eberhardt et al., 2004).

In contrast, a multi-pronged comparative study between community members and police officers showed that officers outperformed community members in a few important ways (study 1) (Correll et al., 2007b). First, police officers effectively demonstrated the ability to differentiate between armed and unarmed targets. Second, officers made the correct decisions to shoot quicker than others. Third, and arguably the most important finding, although police occasionally shot unarmed suspects, they were no more likely to shoot unarmed Blacks than they were to shoot unarmed Whites. The one area in which officers showed clear evidence of bias was in response time to shoot. Officers were quicker to shoot armed Blacks and quicker not to shoot unarmed Whites. According to Correll et al. (2007b), the results indicate that stereotypes influence decisions to shoot when confronted with Black targets. Conversely, stereotypes of Whites (as non-criminals) influence decisions not to shoot.

Part 2 of the study proved to be more challenging for both trained police officers and community members when researchers reduced the time in which participants had to shoot. Both groups exhibited difficulty in processing stereotypic incongruent targets as they were slower to make the correct decision on whether to shoot or not shoot when it came to unarmed Blacks and armed Whites. Unlike community members that were "trigger happy" and more likely to shoot Blacks, police officers more effectively distinguished between when to shoot and not to shoot. Police officers showed no bias in their decisions to shoot (Correll et al., 2007b). Correll et al. (2007b) concluded that police officers were quicker to respond, more accurate, and less biased with respect to their decisions to shoot or not shoot than the decisions made by community members.

These studies demonstrated that implicit or unconscious biases likely influenced study participants to associate high stereotypic Black features with dangerousness, aggressiveness, and violence which in turn caused them to mistakenly shoot unarmed Blacks, mistakenly not shoot armed Whites, and misidentify hand tools as weapons when primed with Black faces or images of criminality. Not surprisingly, the studies of police officers revealed that they were more thorough in their ability to distinguish when to shoot and when not to shoot (likely a result of their training) and their decisions to shoot were quicker than citizens. The difference in quickness may be a function of associating Blacks with crime and seeing crime as Black (see Eberhardt et al., 2004).

While the aforementioned studies were based on simulated exercises, Fryer's (2016) analyses explored racial differences among actual use of force incidents reported in four separate databases. Even after controlling for contextual and behavioral factors, Fryer found large racial differences among lower levels of use of force incidents; however, Fryer did not find any racial differences among those killed by police officers. Fryer notes two important points about use of force data and the policies geared toward those involved in what he refers to as low levels of use of force incidents such as misusing hands or pushing citizens. The first is that few departments collect data in regard to lower levels of force and second, that many departments do not punish or hold officers accountable for lower levels of use of force. Holding officers accountable for these lower levels of use of force incidents "may be more amenable to policy change" (Fryer, 2016 p. 36).

The data from these studies simply does not exist to condemn community members or police officers as prejudice against Blacks; however, the differences in the results are highly likely to be the result of culturally based stereotypic associations (Correll et al., 2002). With respect to police officers, while they may be very well intentioned, according to Richardson (2011), "In the policing context, implicit stereotypes can cause an officer who harbors no conscious racial animosity and who rejects using race as a proxy for criminality to unintentionally treat individuals differently based solely upon their physical appearance" (p. 2039).

While psychologists acknowledge that implicit biases are widespread and shape what people do (Correll et al., 2002), psychologists also contend that people can override or reduce prejudices. Research suggests that bias awareness increases one's ability to accept feedback of personal biases and to take action to reduce biases (Perry, Murphy, Dovidio, 2015). When people are made aware of their biases, they can override their automatic responses with controlled responses that produce non-prejudiced behaviors (Fridell, 2008). As Correll et al. (2002) and Plant & Peruche (2005) noted, training scenarios such as those that work to distinguish guns from other items such as hand tools (or other items) are likely to help reduce the stereotypes that result in shooter bias. In addition, positive contacts with those that are stereotyped (Pettigrew & Tropp, 2006) and the presentation of broad-ranged counter stereotypic information (Dovidio & Gartner, 1999) have reduced intergroup prejudice. Recognizing the role of implicit biases and implementing fair and impartial strategies to overcome such biases in policing is of utmost importance for police executives because of the split-second, life or death decisions police officers face. By employing fair and impartial policing strategies there is the opportunity to enhance police legitimacy through increased levels of trust, respect, and cooperation from the public.

Fair and Impartial Policing

A relatively new approach for law enforcements agencies is the implementation of Fair and Impartial Policing (FIP), a scientific approach to training police officers in a bias-neutral fashion (Fridell, 2014). FIP is based on the following fundamental principles:

- All people have biases
- Biases are normal to human functioning
- Implicit biases influence decisions without conscious thinking
- Policing decisions based on stereotypes are unsafe, ineffective, and unjust
- FIP is fundamental for procedural justice and important for the achievement of police legitimacy
- Officers can learn to reduce and manage biases

- Supervisors can learn to identify biased behavior and take corrective action when they detect biased policing
- Law enforcement executives and command level staff can implement a comprehensive agency wide program to produce FIP

The FIP curriculum was developed by distinguished experts in the areas of human biases, biased policing, along with police executives, supervisors and officers, and community stakeholders (Fridell, 2014). Police departments nationwide have adopted FIP perspectives. The Special Litigation Unit of the Department of Justice (DOJ), a unit that investigates agencies engaging in unconstitutional and biased policing practices, provides FIP training to agencies experiencing problems (FIP, 2015). Fridell (2008) opines that the single act of adopting a FIP perspective is not sufficient to produce unbiased performance among police officers—they must implement a multi-faceted approach. She offers several practical recommendations for law enforcement agencies attempting to counter bias policing.

First, agencies must examine their *recruiting and hiring practices* to produce a diverse workforce and hire officers that can police in a bias-neutral manner. A diverse police force sends the message to the public that equity is a core value and that the agency understands the perspective of minorities. Fridell (2008) recommends departments consider the extent to which applicants have interacted positively with minorities in other settings. Second, *training* plays a crucial role in minimizing racially biased policing. Training should include an awareness of personal biases so that officers can learn to override automatic responses with controlled responses and unlearn the Black-crime association that has been implicated in simulated shooting exercises. Third, *policies* must clearly articulate what constitutes racially biased policing. Fridell (2008) explicitly argues against the use of "solely" policies (those that prohibit race or ethnicity as the sole factor to be used in developing probable cause or reasonable articulable suspicion) because they lack meaningful guidance and are detrimental to efforts to promote fair and impartial policing. In other words, "solely" policies do not encompass many other inappropriate uses of race or ethnicity.

Fourth, appropriately selected and well-trained *supervisors* are necessary to promote adherence to policies. Fridell (2008) asserts that supervisors should also be able to reflect on their own biases, be effective managers, and strong role models. Supervisors should be aware of patterns of discriminatory police actions and be willing to respond to officers' inappropriate behavior. Fifth, the *style of policing* employed by departments has implications far beyond enforcement. For example, the principles of community policing recognize the strength of cooperative interactions among citizens and police to reduce bias and highlight the potential value of problem-oriented policing whereby the police work with residents to identify and solve problems that contribute to crime and disorder. As stated by Tyler et. al. (2015), "If the police can buy into a change from a 'warrior culture' to a 'guardian culture' and from a police 'force' to a police 'service' in their own definition of what gives them legitimacy, then officers, as well as the community, can gain" (p. 76).

While much of the research, including media attention, has focused on negative aspects of police-citizen interactions, little research has examined the impact of negative media attention on police self-legitimacy, the notion of an officers' confidence in their authority. Nix and Wolfe (2015) found that negative publicity was associated with self-legitimacy. Officers reported that negative publicity made policing more difficult and dangerous, hindered proactive policing, made it difficult to be motivated at work, made officers less likely to want to work with community members to solve crime, and made a career in policing less enjoyable. These findings have important policy implications for law enforcement agencies and the communities they serve because police self-legitimacy is an integral part of the police-citizen dialogue (Nix & Wolfe, 2015; Wolfe & Nix, 2015). If the police lack confidence in their ability to serve, communities suffer.

Negative publicity was not the only factor that contributed to police officers' willingness to engage in community partnerships (Wolfe & Nix, 2015). Organizational justice was a significant factor as well. According to Wolfe and Nix (2015), organizational justice includes the respectful and fair treatment of officers by command staff regardless of gender, race or ethnicity. Additionally, law enforcement agencies were believed to be just when command staff explained their decisions and the reasons for policy changes (Wolfe & Nix, 2015). Regardless of the negative publicity received, officers who believed in their authority to police (self-legitimacy) and that their agency was fair (organizational justice), were more likely to partner with the public to solve crimes. Organizational justice minimized the effects of negative publicity (Wolfe & Nix, 2015) thereby protecting officers from internalizing negative publicity. These findings are profound for police administrators because they underscore the important role of treating officers justly so that in turn, officers will treat the public justly.

Conclusion

The President's Task Force on 21st Century Policing (2015) highlights the recent shift in policing philosophy from crime fighting to one of public trust and confidence. The mission of the task force was to outline the best policing practices and to provide recommendations on how those practices would be able to reduce crime while building trust. As a result, task force members recommended six action items presented in the form of pillars that they believe will bring about long-term improvements to police-community relations—these recommendations include building trust and legitimacy and the increased use technology such as BWCs. Given the contentious relationship between police and many minority communities, BWC programs may be the manner in which police are able deliver safer communities, safer police, and improved police-community relationships. It is popular to talk about how the police do not embrace change but the police are leading the charge for change (Schultz & Coldren, 2015). Fridell (2008) believes the implementation of research-guided reforms may serve as role models for other professions. It should be clear that the implementation of BWC programs alone will not be the answer to improved police legitimacy. Police executives must acknowledge their role in creating just organizations and address the role of implicit biases in officers' decision making to ensure that policing is carried out in a fair and impartial manner. As Martin Luther King, Jr. so profoundly wrote in a letter from his Birmingham, Alabama jail cell on April 16, 1963, "Injustice anywhere is a threat to justice everywhere."

References

Allport, G.W. (1958). The nature of prejudice. Anchor Books, Garden City.

American Civil Liberties Union. (2013). *Strengthening CBP with the use of body-worn cameras*. Washington, DC.

Ariel, B., Farrar, W.A. & Sutherland, A. (2015). The effect of police body-worn cameras on use of force and citizens' complaints against the police: A randomized controlled experiment. *Journal of Qualitative Criminology, 31,* 509–535.

Armaline, W.T., Vera Sanchez, C.G., Correia, M. (2014). 'The biggest gang in Oakland': Re-thinking police legitimacy. *Contemporary Justice Review, 17*(3), 375–399.

Briggs, Jr. V.M. (1968). Report of the National Advisory Commission on Civil Disorders: A review article. *Journal of Economics Issues, 2,* 200–210.

Considering Police Body Cameras. (2015). *Harvard Law Review, 128*(6), 1794–1817.

Correll, J., Park, B., Judd, C.M. & Wittenbrink, B. (2002). The police officer's dilemma: Using ethnicity to disambiguate potentially threatening indi viduals. *Journal of Personality and Social Psychology, 6,* 1314–1329.

Correll, J., Park, B., Judd, C.M. & Wittenbrink, B. (2007a). The influence of stereotypes decisions to shoot. *European Journal of Social Psychology, 37,* 1102–1117.

Correll, J., Park, B., Judd, C.M. & Wittenbrink, B., Sadler, M.S. & Keesee, T. (2007b). Across the thin blue line: Police officers and racial bias in the decision to shoot. *Journal of Personality and Social Psychology, 92*(6), 1006–1023.

Dovidio, J.F. & Gaertner, S.L. (1999). Reducing prejudice: Combating inter-group biases. *Current Directions in Psychological Sciences, 8*(4), 101–105.

Eberhardt, J.L., Goff, P.A., Purdie, V.J. & Davies, P.G. (2004). Seeing black: Race, crime, and visual processing. *Journal of Personality and Social Psychology, 87*(6) 876–893.

Embrick, D.G. (2015). Two nations, revisited: The lynching of black and brown bodies, police brutality, and racial control in "post-racial" Amerikkka. *Critical Sociology, 41*(6), 835–843.

Fridell, L. (2014, December). Fair and impartial policing: A science based per-spective. Presentation to Henrico Division of Police and Richmond Police Department, Richmond, VA.

Farrar, W. & Ariel, B. (2013). Self-awareness to being watched and socially desir-able behavior: A field experiment on the effect of body-worn cameras and police use of force. Washington, DC: Police Foundation.

Fiske, S.T. (2008, Summer). Are we born racist: Look twice. *Greater Good, 14*–17.

Forst, B. (2004). Errors of justice: Nature, sources, and remedies. Cambridge University Press.

Floyd v. City of New York, 959 F. Supp 2d 540 (2013).

Fridell, L.A. (2015). *Fair and Impartial Policing.* Retrieved from Fair and Impar-tial Policing website: http//www.fairandimpartialpolicing.com/Extended_About+FIP_2015.pdf

Fridell, L.A. (2008). Racially biased policing: the law enforcement response to the implicit black-crime association. In Lynch, M. J., Patterson, B., Childs, K.K. (Eds.), *Racial divide: Racial and ethnic bias in the criminal justice sys-tem* (pp.39–59). Monsey, NY: Criminal Justice Press.

Fryer, Jr., R.G. (2016). An empirical analysis of racial differences in police use of force (Working Paper 22399). Retrieved from National Bureau of Eco-nomic Research website: http://www.nber.org/papers/w22399

Gabbidon. S.L. & Higgins, G.E. (2009). The role of race/ethnicity and race rela-tions on public opinion related to the treatment of blacks by the police. *Police Quarterly, 12*(1), 102–115.

Gallup (2014). *Black and white attitudes toward police. Retrieved from* http://www.gallup.com/poll/175088/gallup-review-black-white-attitudes-toward-police.aspx

Gill, C., Weisburd, D., Telep, C., Vitter, Z. & bennett, T. (2014). Community ori-ented policing to reduce crime, disorder and fear and increase satisfaction and legitimacy among citizens: A systematic review. *Journal of Experimental Criminology, 10*(4), 399–428.

Jennings, W.G, Fridell, L.A. & Lynch, M.D. (2014). Cops and Cameras: Officer perceptions of the use of body-worn cameras in law enforcement. *Journal of Criminal Justice, 42,* 549–556.

Jennings, W.G., Lynch, M.D. & Fridell, L.A. (2015). Evaluating the impact of police body-worn cameras (BWC) on response-to-resistance and serious external complaints: Evidence from the Orlando Police Department (OPD) experience utilizing a randomized controlled experiment. *Journal of Criminal Justice, 43,* 480–486.

Jones, N. & Raymond, G. (2012). "The camera rolls": Using third-party video in field research. *The Annals of the American Academy of Political and Social Science, 642,* 109–123.

Kahan, D.M., Hoffman, D.A. & Braman, D. (2009). Whose eyes are you going to believe? *Scott v. Harris* and the perils of cognitive illiberalism. *Harvard Law Review, 122,* 838–906.

Kahn, K.B. & Davies, P.G. (2010). Differentially dangerous: Phenotypic racial stereotypically increase implicit bias among ingroup and outgroup members. *Group Processes & Intergroup Relations, 14*(4), 569–580.

Katz, C., Choate, D., Ready, J. & Nuno, L. (2015). Evaluating the impact of officer worn body cameras in the Phoenix Police Department, Phoenix, AZ. *Center for Violence Prevention & Community Safety, Arizona State University.*

Katz, W. (2015). Enhancing accountability and trust with independent investigations of police lethal force. *Harvard Law Review, 128,* 235–245.

King, Jr., M.L. (1963, April 16). [Letter to Fellow Clergymen]. African Studies Center, University of Pennsylvania. Retrieved from http://www.africa.upenn.edu/Articles_Gen/Letter_Birmingham.html

Kunard, L. & Moe, C. (2015). *Procedural justice for law enforcement: An overview.* Washington, DC: Office of Community Oriented Policing Services.

Lawrence, C.R. (1987). The Id, Ego, and equal protection: Reckoning with unconscious racism, *39*(2), 317–388.

Lum, C., Koper, C., Merola, L., Scherer, A. & Reioux, A. (2015). *Existing and ongoing body worn camera research: Knowledge gaps and opportunities.* Report for the Laura and John Arnold Foundation. Fairfax, VA: Center for Evidence-Based Crime Policy, George Mason University.

Mastrofski, S.D., Snipes, J.B. & Supina, A.E. (1996). Complace on demand: The public's response to specific police requests. *Journal of Research in Crime and Delinquency, 33,* 269–305.

McCluskey, J.D. (2003). Police requests for compliance: Coercive and procedurally just tactics. New York, NY: LFB Scholarly.

Mesa Police Department. (2013). On-officer body camera system: Program evaluation and recommendations. Mesa, AZ: Mesa Police Department.

Miller, L., Toliver, J. & Police Executive Research Forum. (2014). Implementing a Body-worn camera program: Recommendations and Lessons Learned. Washington, DC: Office of Community Oriented Policing Services.

National Bar Association Poll. (2015). Retrieved from http://www.tallahassee.com/story/news/local/2015/09/09/poll-says-blacks-whites-agree-police-treat-blacks-differently/71918338/

Newton, H. (1973). The finding of the black panther party and patrolling. In C. Carson, D. Garrow, G. Gill, V. Harding, D. Clark Hine (Eds.), *The eyes on the prize civil rights reader: Documents, speeches, and firsthand accounts from the black freedom struggle* (pp.345–361).

Nix, J. & Wolfe, S.E. (2015). The impact of negative publicity on police self-legitimacy. *Justice Quarterly*, 2–24. doi: 10.1080/07418825.2015.1102954

Nix, J., Wolfe, S.E., Rojek, J. & Kaminski, R.J. (2015). Trust in the police: The influence of procedural justice and perceived collective efficacy. *Crime & Delinquency*, *61*(4), 610–640.

ODS Consulting. (2011). Body worn video projects in Paisley and Aberdeen, self evaluation. Glasgow: ODS Consulting.

O'Reilly, D. (2014, August 7). Evesham police chief calls cameras a 'game changer.' The Philadelphia Inquirer. Retrieved from http://articles.philly.com/2014-08-07/news/52519341_1_body-cameras-security-cameras-evesham-police-chief

Paternoster, R., Bachman, R., Brame, R. & Sherman, L.W. (1997). Do fair procedures matter? The effect of procedural justice on spousal assault. *Law & Society*, *31*(1), 163–204.

Payne, B.K. (2001). Prejudice and perception: The role of automatic and controlled processes in misperceiving a weapon. *Journal of Personality and Social Psychology*, *81*(2), 181–192.

Perry, S.P., Murphy, M.C. & Dovidio, J.F. (2015). Modern prejudice: Subtle, but unconscious? The role of bias awareness in whites' perceptions pf personal and others' biases. *Journal of Experimental Social Psychology*, *61*, 64–78.

Plant, E. A. & Peruche, B.M. (2005). The consequences of race for police officers' response to criminal suspects. *Psychological Science*, *16*(3), 180–183.

Peruche, B.M. & Plant, E. A. (2006). The correlates of law enforcements officers' automatic and controlled race-based responses to criminal suspects. *Basic and Applied Psychology*, *28*(2), 193–199.

Pettigrew, T.F. & Tropp, L.R. (2006). A meta-analytic test of intergroup contact theory. *Journal of Personality and Social Psychology, 90*(5) 751–783.

Police Executive Research Forum. (2014). *Legitimacy and procedural justice: A new element of police leadership.* Washington, DC: U.S. Department of Justice, Bureau of Justice Services.

Police Executive Research Forum. (2015). Lessons learned from the 2015 civil unrest in Baltimore. Washington, DC.

President's Task Force on 21st Century Policing. (2015). *Final Report of the President's Task Force on 21st Century Policing.* Washington, DC: U.S. Department of Justice, Office of Community Oriented Policing Services.

Ready, J.T. & Young, J.T. (2015). The impact of on-officer video cameras on police-citizen contacts: Findings from a controlled experiment in Mesa, AZ. *Journal of Experimental Criminology, 11,* 445–458.

Ren, L., Cao, L, Lovrich, N., Gaffney, M. (2005). Linking confidence in the police with the performance of the police: Community policing can make a difference. *Journal of Criminal Justice, 33,* 55–66.

Richardson, S.L. (2011). Arrest efficiency and the Fourth Amendment. *Minnesota Law Review, 95,* 2035–2098.

Roy, A. (2014). on-officer video cameras: Examining the effects of police department policy and assignment on camera use and activation. *Master's Thesis Presented to the Graduate Supervisory Committee at Arizona State University.*

Staats, C. (2013). State of the science: Implicit bias review, 2013. The Kiran Institute, Ohio State University, Columbus, Ohio.

Schulhofer, S.J., Tyler, T.R., Huq, A.Z. (2011). American policing at a crossroads: Unsustainable policies and the procedural justice alternative. *The Journal of Criminal Law & Criminology, 101,* 335–374.

Schultz, A. & Colder, Jr., J.R. (2015, August). *CNA out front: Policing in the 21st century—the changing role of police in our democratic society.* Retrieved from https://www.cna.org/CNA_files/PDF/CIM-2015-U-011039-FINAL.pdf

Stanley, J. (2015). Police body-mounted cameras: With right policies in place, a win for all, Version 2.0. ACLU. Retrieved from https://www.aclu.org/sites/default/files/assets/police_body-mounted_cameras-v2.pdf

Sunshine, J. & Tyler, T.R. (2003). The role of procedural justice and legitimacy in shaping public support for policing. *Law & Society Review, 37,* 513–548.

Tankebe, J. (2009). Public cooperation with the police in Ghana: Does procedural fairness matter? *Criminology, 47*(4), 1265–1293.

Thibaut, J. & Walker, L. (1975). Procedural justice. Mahwah, NJ: Lawrence Erlbaum.

The White House. (2014, December). *Fact sheet: Strengthening community policing.* Washington, DC: Office of the Press Secretary. Retrieved from

https://www.whitehouse.gov/the-press-office/2014/12/01/fact-sheet
-strengthening-community-policing

Tyler, T.R. (2004). Enhancing police legitimacy. *The Annals of the American Academy of Political and Social Science, 593,* 84–99.

Tyler, T.R. (2009). Legitimacy and criminal justice: The benefits of self-regulation. *Ohio State Journal of Criminal Law, 7,* 307–359.

Tyler, T.R. (2011). Why people cooperate: The role of social motivations. Princeton, NJ: Princeton University Press.

Tyler, T.R. & Fagan, J. (2008). Legitimacy and cooperation: Why do people help the police fight crime in their communities? *Ohio State Journal of Criminal Law, 6,* 231–275.

Tyler. T.R., Goff, P.A. & MacCoun, R.J. (2015). The impact of psychological science on policing in the United States: Procedural justice, legitimacy, and effective law enforcement. *Psychological Science in the Public Interest, 16*(3), 75–109.

Tyler, T. R. & Huo, Y.J. (2002). Trust in the law: Encouraging public cooperation with the police and courts. New York, NY: Russell-Sage Foundation.

Tyler, T. & Jackson, J. (2013). Future challenges in the study of legitimacy and criminal justice. Yale Law School, Public Law Working, 264.

Tyler, T.R & Wakslak, C.J. (2004). Profiling and police legitimacy: Procedural justice, attributions of motive and acceptance of police authority. *Criminology, 42*(2), 253–281.

Unnever, J.D. & Gabbidon, S.L. (2015). Do blacks speak with one voice? Immigrants, public opinions, and perceptions of criminal injustices. *Justice Quarterly, 32*(4), 680–704.

Vorndran, K., Burke, P.A., Chavez, I.M., Fraser, K.M. & Moore, M.A. (2014). Enhancing police accountability through an effective on-body camera program for MPD officers. *Report and Recommendations of the Police Complaints Board to Mayor Vincent C. Gray, the Council of the District of Columbia, and Chief of Police Cathy L. Lanier.*

Westphal, L.J. (2004). The in-car camera: Value and impact. *The Police Chief, 71*(8), Retrieved from http://www.policechiefmagazine.org

White, M.D. (2014). Police officer body-worn cameras: Assessing the evidence. Washington, DC: Office of Community Oriented Policing Services.

Wolfe, S.E. & Nix, J. (2015). The alleged "Ferguson Effect" and police willingness to engage in community partnership. *Law and Human Behavior.* doi:10.1037/lhb0000164.

Chapter 11

Privileged Mexicans: Race and Class Effects on Support for Crime Control[1]

George Wilson, Bryan Lagae, and Alex R. Piquero

Pursuant to the growing socio-economic heterogeneity of minorities in the U.S. in recent decades, social scientists have paid increasing attention to how minority status acts in concert with privileged class position (routinely referred to as a "middle class" position) to structure ideological orientations (for reviews see Shelton and Wilson, 2012; Wilson, 2001; Gilliam and Whitby, 1989). Such an exercise is crucial in resolving important assimilation issues in the context of assessing how the changing racial/ethnic composition of the privileged population will be associated with stances on sociopolitical issues. To date, studies have tended to focus on one privileged minority population, African Americans, and have examined a limited range of political orientations, namely, focusing on aspects of political identification such as political party affiliation (Guterbock & London, 1983; Jackman & Jackman, 1983) and ideological compatibility with presidential candidates/national civic leaders (Dillingham, 1981; Jackman & Jackman, 1983) as well as support for redistributive policy initiatives to ameliorate socioeconomic inequality in America (Gilliam & Whitby, 1989; Herring, 1989; Innes & Sittig, 1996; Jackman & Jackman, 1983; Parent & Stekler, 1985; Welsh & Foster, 1987; Wilson, 2001). Overall, these studies have reached consistent results: a racial schism is present among the middle class. Specifically, minority status rivals privileged class position in causal importance, which produces adherence to ideological tenets that are more liberal (e.g., higher levels of Democratic or liberal party support=liberal; support

1. Thanks are expressed to Merlin Greenberg for making constructive comments on an earlier draft of this paper.

for more interventionist policies=liberal) than the White middle class but more conservative than working class, co-racial group members.

These contributions to be sure, are meaningful, but we need to undertake additional analyses of the race/class basis of the political ideology of privileged segments of minority populations. Absent in existing studies, for example, are examinations of the ideological profile of other minority groups, including, most conspicuously, Latinos/Latinas—the most numerically preponderant minority group in the U.S. (Farley, 1996). These examinations, particularly when they are sufficiently refined to focus on sub-Latino populations, such as Mexicans, incorporate at least one highly politicized dynamic that is not a dominant factor in analyses of African Americans, namely, immigration status. Immigration, i.e., spending formative years of one's life outside of the U.S., for Latinos, generally, and Mexicans, specifically, is a documented conservatizing force along a range of ideological tenets. For example, it enhances susceptibility to both Republican party affiliation and adopting an "individualistic, Horatio Alger" (Steinberg, 1981) orientation to issues of stratification beliefs such as the causes of poverty/wealth, and gives rise to perceptions that blocked opportunities are inconsequential as causes of socioeconomic inequality in America (Portes, 1992; Lee, 2008; Masuoka, 2008; Panjota & Gershon, 2006; Manforti & Sanchez, 2010). Analyses of Mexicans are also timely: despite long being the sub-Latino population with the lowest mean income and highest poverty rate, evidence is now emerging that they are experiencing socioeconomic differentiation at a rate that rivals other historically more economically successful sub-Latino populations including, most notably, Cubans.

In addition, existing race/class studies of privileged segments of minority populations have not assessed ideological stances toward a range of topical social issues in American society. Along these lines, one "hot" topical social issue, ignored in race/class analysis that is replete with ideological overtones, is the control of crime (Wilson & Dunham, 2001; Gilens, 1996). In this vein, the ideologically laden nature of crime control is manifest (Flanagan, McGarrell & Lizotte, 1989) in the "fundamental antinomy regarding efforts to control crime" (Wilson & Dunham, 2001:46), that is, the debate about whether to adopt a classically liberal "preventive" approach that places a premium on addressing social ills thought to underlie criminal behavior such as deficient schools, impoverishment, and joblessness/underemployment, or alternatively adopt a classically conservative "punitive" approach to crime control that emphasizes individual responsibility for crime, advocating, for example, the importance of catching, convicting, and incarcerating criminals (Browning & Cao, 1992;

Unnever & Cullen, 2010). In fact, this antinomy is the basis of radically divergent—and hotly debated—alternative policy prescriptions that affect the appropriation of significant amounts of resources—both material and human—that is predicated on determinations of assigning responsibility for criminal behavior (Beckett & Sasson, 2000; Flanagan, 1996).

In short, the scope of race/class sources of stratification ideology among minority middle classes—in terms of minority groups examined and the range of ideological tenets examined—needs to be broadened. We do this in this study, specifically, utilizing nationally representative data from the 2011 and 2013 National Election Study (NES) to assess predictions from three perspectives concerning the additive and interactive effects of minority status and position in the class structure in explaining support of the Mexican middle class toward the punitive versus preventive stance on crime control.

Theoretical Perspectives

The Class Perspective

Class theory, the first perspective, maintains that position in the stratification system is the sole basis of ideological sentiments related to issues of crime control in American society. Class theory, in fact, represents a distillation of studies from disparate theoretical orientations that have in common the notion that successive rises in structural position in society are associated with greater ideological support for policies that maintain the socioeconomic status quo. Accordingly, this first perspective posits that the Mexican middle class—by virtue of their relatively privileged location in the class structure—should express support for agents of the state to invoke harsh and punitive enforcement of criminal activity. Under the umbrella of class theory are two versions of class theory. First, class theory grounded in Marxist and Neo-Marxist theory assert that across racial lines economic interest created by membership in structural categories based on degrees of ownership of, and supervisory control over, the means of production in the economies of advanced capitalist societies dictate levels of ideological commitment towards the state apparatus to maintain existing social and economic arrangements (Humphries & Greenberg, 1993; Wright & Cho, 1992; Wright, 1988, 1985). Second, a more Weberian conception of class theory asserts that individuals from different racial groups who occupy roughly similar degrees of privilege based on socioeconomic criteria adhere to similar ideological stances toward issues—such as the appropriate form of social control exercised by the state—that impacts on their shared, broad-based interests (Herring, 1989; Parkin, 1971).

The Race Perspective

Race theory constitutes the second perspective: it provides a basis for predicting that attitudes along the punitive-preventive crime control continuum among the Mexican middle class should be a product of minority status and, thus, operate independently of social class. Significantly, however, among relatively privileged Mexicans, this perspective would appear to have two iterations depending on, in particular, immigrant status. The first iteration applies to privileged Mexicans who spent their formative years in the U.S. This segment of the Mexican population is viewed as similar to African Americans who represent a "classic liberal minority" in that they assert, for example, relatively high levels of perceived discrimination and prejudice in American society (Sizemore & Milner, 2004; Moghaddon, Taylor & Lambert, 1995). In fact, several studies have found that at all class levels, race effects regarding ideological issues of crime control among African Americans are driven by beliefs that racial discrimination is widely practiced in the criminal justice system (Unnever, 2008). For example, the police are viewed as using excessive force in African American communities (Brooks, 1993; Huang & Vaughn, 1996; Lasley, 1994;) and courts engage in unduly harsh sentencing of African Americans (Gerber & Engelhardt, 1996; Hagan & Albonetti, 1982; Schwartz, Guo & Kerbs, 1993). In fact, this view among African Americans—and by extension the same view by Mexicans raised in the U.S.—underlies the rejection of a conservative or "get tough" criminal justice ideology (Browning & Cao, 1992) and the adoption of a more classically liberal solution to crime control that involves addressing the social and economic roots of crime (Lasley, 1994; Unnever, Cullen & Jones, 2008).

A second iteration of race theory is viewed as operating among privileged Mexicans who were not raised in the U.S. This group is viewed as likely to express a lower level of perceived racial discrimination (Portes, 1992) and adopts a group identity based on a "traditional immigrant mentality" (Steinberg, 1981); they adhere to a form of individualism premised on notions of self-reliance and moral responsibility that, ultimately, places the blame for crime disproportionately on the voluntary behavior, or individual choice, of criminals. This orientation, overall, is viewed as consistent with a "get tough" criminal justice ideology that emphasizes punitive sanctions and harsh enforcement, a classically conservative orientation to the solution of crime (Browning & Cao, 1992).

The Ethclass Perspective

A third formulation—the ethclass perspective—represents a synthesis of the race and class perspectives. Most systematically enunciated by Gordon (1964), the ethclass perspective maintains that, similar to class theory, relatively privileged minority group members are drawn to the status quo by virtue of their position in the class structure. However, operating simultaneously is a sense of shared fate as a member of a racial minority. Specifically, identification with their minority status serves to operate independently of the effect of social class (Dillingham, 1981; Gilliam & Whitby, 1989; Gordon, 1964). Accordingly, groups such as privileged Mexicans should experience a "dual consciousness" in which race and class should exert both independent effects and a shared effect across a wide range of issues including those related to the control of crime.

Significantly, however, manifestations of ethclass dynamics—similar to race theory—is posited as having two iterations depending on immigrant status. Specifically, among privileged Cubans raised within the U.S.—who have a more traditionally liberal attitude than Mexicans raised outside of the U.S.—ethclass dynamics are manifest in adhering to a stance along the preventive-punitive continuum that is more liberal than the White middle class but more conservative than the Mexican working class. Further, among middle class members raised outside of the U.S., a "get tough" attitude towards crime control is manifest if they have more liberal orientations along the preventive-punitive continuum of crime control than the Mexican working class but are more conservative along the continuum than the White middle class.

In the sections that follow, we assess the merits of these perspectives in the context of dissecting a nationally representative sample that includes a sufficient number of Mexicans—at both middle and working class levels—to sustain quantitative analyses.

Data and Methods

Data from the 2011 and 2013 survey years of the National Election Study (NES) are utilized to assess the issues of interest. The NES is a full probability sample of English speaking adults living in households in the United States (for a full description of the NES see Miller, Kinder & Rosenstone, 1993). Overall, the sample for this study consists of 565 Mexicans and 1,436 Whites who satisfy selection criteria along lines of race and social class. The socio-demographic profile of sample members is in Table 1.

Table 1. Sample Profile

	Whites (N=1436)	Mexicans Raised in U.S. (N=315)	Mexicans Not Raised in U.S. (N=250)
Age (Years)	38.1	36.3	37.8
Education (Years)	11.7	11.7	11.6
Middle Class (%)	60.8	50.7	49.3
Male (%)	49.5	53.3	52.3

Dependent Variable

Crime Control Measure

All survey respondents were asked, "Do you think the best way to reduce crime is to address social problems or to make sure criminals are caught, convicted, and punished, or that we should do something in between?" This variable was operationalized along a continuum with higher values expressing a more classically liberal crime control policy: 2=address social problems, 1=something in between, and 0=criminals are caught, convicted, and punished.

Independent Variables

Race and Social Class

Race is coded as 1=Mexican and 0=White. Social Class is coded as 1=middle, 0=working and is based on occupational criteria. The current occupation of sample members is coded into one of four 1990 census-based occupational categories. Those whose occupation is in the Managerial-Professional category constitute the middle class. Sample members whose current occupation falls in three other categories: a) Service, Precision, Production, (b) Repair, Operators, Fabricators, and (c) Laborers constitute the working class. Utilizing an occupationally based measure of social class is highly appropriate: stratification research has demonstrated a causal link between class-based occupational experiences and the formation of a wide range of values. For example, research in the tradition of "work and personality" (Kohn 1969; Kohn and Schooler 1982) has documented that class-based work conditions are related to the formation of attitudes about self-direction vs. conformity and the degree of intellective functioning developed and, more specifically, has speculated that work experiences are associated with the learning and subsequent generalization of orientation about, for example, political orientations about income redistribution (Shelton and Wilson, 2012) and state sanctioning of punitive behavior (Wilson and Dunham, 2001).

Additional Variables

Several other categories of variables are examined primarily as controls. We include two status variables—earnings (in year preceding interview) and educational attainment (in years), which are conventionally used to measure position in the stratifications system but are modestly correlated with occupationally-based conceptions of social class (Kohn & Schooler, 1982; Wright, 1985). We also include socioeconomic characteristics, namely, gender (dummy variable for female with male as reference), age (years), marital status (1=married, 0=single), and region of residence (dummy variables for North, South, West with Midwest as reference). The inclusion of the variables is based on the documented influence of stage of the life-span (Setterston & Mayer, 1997), gender as an ascriptive characteristic (Jackman, 1994) and region of residence (Firebaugh & Davis, 1988) on a broad range of ideological-based social issues, including crime, abortion, school busing, and support for affirmative action policies. Along these lines, those who are younger, female, and reside outside of the South adhere to more conventionally liberal postures.

Analytic Strategy

This study performs separate analyses of Cubans who grew up in the U.S. and those who did not grow up in the U.S., relative to Whites. In both analyses, descriptive and multivariate techniques are utilized to assess the crime control attitudes of the Mexican middle class relative to the Mexican working and White middle and working classes. Sequentially, analyses proceed as follows: first, mean-level differences are assessed with respect to crime control posture and whether differences across groups are statistically significant. Next, ordinary least squares regression (OLS) is used to assess the effect of race and social class on attitudes toward crime control. In this regard, the simple multivariate model is constructed to assess the independent effects of race and social class on attitudes about crime control. Then, a hierarchical F-test procedure is employed to examine whether the combined or interactive effects of race and social class explain variation in crime control attitudes above and beyond all independent effects in the models. Finally, if race/class interactive terms are significant, regression equations are "solved." In this vein, predicted scores are derived on the dependent variable for particularly important observed cases among the middle and working classes for both Mexicans and Whites. Significantly, this procedure most closely specifies the precise magnitude and direction of interaction effects for both groups.

Results

Table 2 presents mean levels of support for crime control for the race/class groups (descriptive statistics for all variables are contained in the Appendix). The results suggest that among the Mexican middle class, race/class dynamics vary by immigrant status. First, among middle class members raised in the U.S., there is support for the liberal iteration of the ethclass perspective. Specifically, prima facie evidence of an interaction effect among middle class Mexican derives from the mean values (1.5) along the preventive-punitive continuum being significantly lower, and, thus, more conservative, than those of the Cuban working class (1.9) but higher, and, thus, more liberal than the White middle class (1.4). Second, among those members of the Mexican middle class not raised in the U.S., there is more support for the conservative iteration of the race perspective. Specifically, mean values of the Cuban middle class are identical to those of the Cuban working class (1.2) and are more conservative than Whites (1.4 to 1.7).

These descriptive results are suggestive but they must be supplemented with multivariate analyses to establish stronger links. Accordingly, Table 3 presents

Table 2. Mean Levels of Support For Crime Control Strategies

	Middle	Working
Mexican—U.S. Raised	1.5	1.9
Mexican—Non-U.S. Raised	1.2	1.2
Whites	1.4	1.7
T-Test Middle Class		
Mexican-U.S. Raised—White	4.18*	
Mexicans Non U.S. Raised—White	4.12*	
T-Test Working Class		
Mexican-U.S. Raised—White	4.22*	
Mexicans Non U.S. Raised—White	5.72**	

* p < .05, ** p < .01

results from OLS regressions that assess the additive effects of all variables in the model and the interaction effects of race and social class. The results build on those reached in the descriptive analyses. First, an iteration of the ethclass formulation constitutes the most appropriate theoretical lens through which to interpret support among Mexican raised in the U.S. Two findings, in particular, are noteworthy: race and social class have measurable independent effects on levels of support for crime control (race, $B=.17$, $p<.05$; class $B=.18$, $p<.05$). Further, the inclusion of the race/class interaction term significantly enhances the explained variance in the regression equation. Accordingly, the multivariate analyses provide confirmation that with respect to crime control attitudes, both minority status and the structural imperatives associated with a privileged class position pull on this category of middle class Mexicans to determine posture toward crime control. Second, an iteration of the race perspective provides the best interpretation for the crime control attitudes of middle class Mexicans who were not raised in the U.S. Specifically, minority status is the most significant predictor in the main effects model ($B=.24$, $p<.01$) and the race/class interaction term is not statistically significant.

Finally, regarding the segment of the Mexican middle class raised in the U.S, we are interested in more closely determining the directionality and magnitude of the interaction effect. Accordingly, the regression equation is solved for the occupational category within the middle and working classes that have the most individuals — managers-professionals and laborers — among Mexicans and Whites in the sample. Table 4 reports the unstandardized coefficients for the interaction terms, which reflect predicted scores on the preventive-punitive crime control continuum.

Findings are straightforward and support the liberal iteration of the ethclass formulation. Specifically, the Mexican middle class has values along the continuum that are lower than those of working class Cubans (1.4 to 1.7) so the middle class is more conservative but are higher than middle class Whites (1.6 to 1.7), so the Mexican middle class is more conservative, as they have lower scores (more punitive) on the crime control measure.

Conclusion

Social science examinations of the race/class basis of ideological orientations among middle class segments of minority populations have been limited in two fundamental ways, namely, (1) focusing on only one minority population, namely, African Americans, and, (2) focusing on a limited range of ideological domains, for example, paying little attention to the crucial domain of crime

Table 3. OLS Regressions of Attitudes Toward Crime Control among Two Groups of Mexicans

Variable	Mexicans Non-U.S. Raised			Mexicans U.S. Raised		
	B	b	T-Ratio	B	b	T-Ratio
Race	.24**	.23	6.36	.17*	.13	4.93
Class	.09	.05	1.67	.18*	.123	
Income	−.02	−.01	1.34	−.05*	−.02	4.18
Education	.02*	.01	3.81	.01	.01	1.31
Gender	.03	.04	1.33	.12*	.07	4.13
Age	−.05*	−.03	3.75	−.01	−.01	1.56
Marital Status	.02	.02	1.40	.05	.03	1.63
North	.03	.03	1.23	.04	.03	1.22
South	.04	.02	1.18	.06	.04	1.24
West	.02	.05	1.14	.03	.02	1.30
Race * Class (hierarchical F Test)						
R2 Additive Model	.027	.022				
R2 (Inclusion of Interaction)	.027	.030				
T Ratio	1.82	3.76*				

* $p < .05$, ** $p < .01$

control. This study addresses these limitations by assessing the race/class basis of adherence to a fundamental distinction found within the domain of crime control—"preventive," that is, addressing the perceived roots of crime such as bad schools, joblessness, poverty, etc., versus "punitive," that is, capturing, convicting, and incarcerating criminals as solutions to crime control. Most important, we focused on Mexicans, a sub Latino-population who has not been subject to much research on their crime control perceptions.

Findings from our NES sample indicate that race/class dynamics among the Mexican middle class are complex. In this regard, most notable is that immigrant status is a fundamental cleavage that defines how ideological orientations about crime control unfold. In particular, Mexicans raised in the U.S. operate as a "traditional minority group" so they are similar to African Americans in adopting a posture that is in accord with a liberal iteration of the ethclass perspective, that is, their views are intermediate between the more conservative (i.e., greater support for punitive measures) White middle class and the more liberal (i.e., greater support for preventive measures) Mexican working class. In contrast, privileged Mexicans not raised in the U.S. operate as a "traditional immigrant group," that is, adhering to a view that is in accord with a conservative iteration of the race perspective: they lean more towards supporting

Table 4. Joint Effects of Race and Class on Crime Control
Attitudes: Mexicans Raised In the U.S.

	Middle Class Score	Working Class Score
Mexican	1.4	1.7
White	1.6	1.7

preventive measures than Whites and this support is identical across class categories.

These findings have fundamental implications for theory and research. Going beyond the traditional "Black-White" paradigm in race relations research and assessing a "new immigrant group" demonstrates — at least in the context of crime control ideology — the potential complexity of race/class dynamics: more than one dynamic operates within a minority group. In fact, in the case of the Mexican middle class, immigrant status appears to be a dividing line that separates the most traditionally liberal and the most traditionally conservative crime control postures. Apparently, a causal dynamic, presumably experiential by way of institutional, media, or parent/peer influences, leads to the simultaneous liberalizing and conservatizing of crime control ideology among, respectfully, those raised in the U.S. and those raised outside of the U.S. (Panjota & Gershon, 2006; Manforti & Sanchez, 2010). In addition, findings indicate that the crime control issue may not be as unambiguous a source of division across racial lines, as, for example, when only Whites are compared to African Americans (see Wilson & Dunham, 2001; Gilens, 1996). In particular, the internal division within the Mexican middle class serves to mute the impact of race. Ironically, however, this division may well serve to limit the influence of Cubans in effectuating crime control policy. Sociological research on the socio-historic roots of policy implementation, mostly in the area of civil rights legislation in the post-1965 period, has found that state and federal legislative bodies of government are responsive to politically influential segments, i.e., the middle class, of sizable constituencies (Edsall & Edsall, 1991; McAdam, 1982). Accordingly, the lack of consensus within a relatively small population — privileged Mexicans — may well serve to limit their policy input, particularly relative to a much larger population, notably the White middle class.

This study should serve as the impetus for further research on race/class dynamics of crime control among minority middle class populations. First, we need to know if the complex dynamics found here are also found in other sub-Latino groups such as Dominicans, Puerto Ricans, and Colombians, as well as, for example, Asian and sub-Asian groups such as the Chinese, Japanese and

Koreans, all of whom have experienced unprecedented socioeconomic differentiation in recent decades. Second, with respect to these analyses, the demonstrated multidimensionality of crime control attitudes necessitates that additional dimensions be explored. These dimensions include "the use of force" (how much force by crime control agents is permissible), the "scope" of crime control (the breadth of behavior to be controlled), and "crime control spending" (how much financial commitment the government should make to eradicating crime) (see Wilson & Dunham, 2001, for a review of these dimensions). Third, in all future analyses, the role of forms of political and stratification ideology versus, for example, personal experience with agents of crime control will help to shed further light on the underpinnings of race/class dynamics among privileged minority populations. These research efforts, in sum, promise to enhance our understanding of how minority status and structural location, two classic stratification factors, shape notions about a crucial ideological domain, namely, how criminality in America should be addressed.

References

Beckett, K. & Sasson, T. (2000). *The politics of injustice.* Thousand Oaks, California: Pine Forge Press.

Brooks, L. (1993). Police discretionary behavior: A study in style, pp. 19–33. In R. Dunham & G. Alpert (Eds.) *Critical issues in policing: Contemporary readings (pp.19–23).* Prospect Heights: Waveland Press.

Browning, S.L. & Cao, L. (1992). The impact of race on criminal justice ideology. *Justice Quarterly* 9:685–699.

Cao, L., Frank, J. & Cullen, F.T. (1996). Race, community and confidence in the police. *American Journal of Police* 15:3–22.

Cohn, S., Barkan, S. & Halteman, W. (1991). Punitive attitudes towards criminals: Racial consensus or racial conflict. *Social Problems* 38:387–395.

Cullen, F.T., Cao, L., Frank, J., Langworthy, R.H., Browning, S.L., Kopache, R. & Stevenson, T.J. (1996). Stop or I'll shoot: Racial differences in support for police use of deadly force. *American Behavioral Scientist* 39:449–460.

Dillingham, G. (1981). Race, class, and political identity. *Ethnic and Racial Studies* 8:25–41.

Edsall, T. & Edsall, M. (1991). *Chain reaction: The impact of race, rights, and taxes on American politics.* New York: W.W. Norton.

Farley, R. (1996). *The New American Reality.* New York: Russell Sage.

Firebaugh, G. & Davis, K. (1988). Trends in anti-black prejudice, 1972–1984: Region and cohort effects. *American Journal of Sociology* 94:251–272.

Fishman, L. (1998). Images of crime and punishment. In C. Mann & M. Katz. (Eds.), *Images of color, images of crime* (pp. 40–57). Los Angeles: Roxbury Press.

Flanagan, T.J., E.F. McGarrell, and A.J. Lizotte. (1989). Ideology and crime control policy positions in a state legislature. *Journal of Criminal Justice* 17:87–101.

Flanagan, T. (1996). Public opinion and public policy in criminal justice. In Flanagan, T. & D. Longmire (Eds.) *Americans view crime and justice: A national public opinion survey* (pp. 151–158). Thousand Oaks: Sage Publications.

Frank, J., Brandl, S.G. & Cullen, F.T. (1996). Reassessing the impact of race on citizens' attitudes toward the police: A research note. *Justice Quarterly* 13:321–334.

Gerber, J. & Engelhardt-Greer, S. (1996). Just and painful: Attitudes toward sentencing criminals. In T. Flanagan & D.R. Longmire (Eds.), *Americans view crime and justice: A national public opinion survey* (pp. 62–74). Thousand Oaks: Sage Publications.

Gilens, M. (1996) *Why Americans Hate Welfare*. Princeton: Princeton University Press.

Gilliam, F. & Whitby, K. (1989). Race, class, and attitudes toward social welfare spending: An Ethclass interpretation. *Social Science Quarterly* 70:88–100.

Gordon, M. (1964). *Assimilation in American life: The role of race, religion, and national origins*. New York: Oxford University Press.

Guterbock, T. & London, B. (1983). Race, political orientation, and participation: An empirical test of four competing theories. *American Sociological Review* 48:439–453.

Hagan, J. & Albonetti, C. (1982). Race, class and the perception of criminal injustice in America. *American Journal of Sociology* 88:329–355.

Hamm, M.S. (1995). *The Abandoned Ones: The Imprisonment and Uprising of the Mariel Boat People*. Boston: Northeastern University Press.

Henderson, M.L., Cullen, F.T., Cao, L., Browning, S.L. & Kopache, R. (1997). The impact of race on perceptions of criminal injustice. *Journal of Criminal Justice* 25:447–462.

Herring, C. (1989). Convergence, polarization or what? Racially based changes in attitudes and outlooks. *The Sociological Quarterly* 30:261–281.

Huang, W. S. & Vaughn, M. (1996). Support and confidence: Public attitudes toward the police. In Flanagan, T. & Longmire, D.R. (Eds.) *Americans view crime and justice: A national public opinion survey* (pp. 31–45). Thousand Oaks: Sage Publications.

Humphries, D. & Greenberg, D. (1993). The dialectics of crime control. In D. Greenberg (Ed.), *Crime and capitalism: Readings in Marxist criminology* (pp. 463–508). Philadelphia: Temple University Press.

Inness, L. & Sittig, J. (1996). Race, class and support for the welfare state. *Sociological Inquiry* 66:175–196.

Jackman, M. & Jackman, R. (1983). *Class awareness in the United States.* Berkeley: University of California Press.

Kohn M. & Schooler, C. (1982). Job conditions and personality: A longitudinal assessment of their reciprocal effects. *American Journal of Sociology* 87:1257–1286.

Kohn, M. (1969). *Class and conformity.* Homewood. Illinois: Dorsey Press.

Lasley, J.R. (1994). The impact of the Rodney King incident on citizen attitudes toward police. *Policing and Society* 3:245–255.

Lee, T. (2008). Race, Immigration, and The Identity-To-Politics Link. *Annual Review of Political Science* 11:457–478.

Moghaddam, F., Taylor, D. and Lambert W. (1995). Attitudes and Discrimination: A Study of Whites, Blacks, and Cubans in Miami. *Journal of Cross-Cultural Psychology* 26:209–220.

Manforti, J. and Sanchez G. (2010) The Politics of Perceptions: An Investigation of the Presence and Sources of Perceptions of internal discrimination Among Latinos. *Social Science Quarterly* 91:245–265.

Masuoka, N. (2008). Defining The Group—Latino Identity and Latino Politics in the U.S. *American Politics Research* 36:33.61.

McAdam, D. (1982). *Political process and the development of black insurgency.* Chicago: University of Chicago Press.

Miller, W, Kinder, D. & Rosenstone, S. (1993). *American National Election Study.* Inter-University Consortium for Political and Social Research. Ann Arbor.

Panjota, A. and Gershon, S. (2006). Political Orientations and Naturalization Among Latinos and Latina Immigrants. *Social Science Quarterly* 87:1171–1187.

Parent, W. & Stekler, P. (1985). The political implications of economic stratification in the Black community. *Western Political Quarterly* 38:521–537.

Parkin, F. (1971). *Class Inequality and The Political Order.* New York: Sage.

Piquero, A.R. (2008). Disproportionate minority contact. *The Future of Children* 18:59–79.

Portes, A. (1992). *City on the Edge.* Berkeley: University of California Press.

Quadagno, J. (1994). *The Color of Welfare.* New York: Oxford University Press.

Schwartz, I., Guo, S. & Kerbs, J.J. (1993). The impact of demographic variables on public opinion regarding juvenile justice: Implications for public policy. *Crime and Delinquency* 39:5–28.

Setterston, R. & Mayer, K. (1997). The measurement of age, age structuring, and the life course. *Annual Review of Sociology* 23:233–261.

Shelton, Jason and George Wilson (2012) Black Attitudes Toward Redistribution Policy. *Sociological Perspectives* 34: 25–43.

Short, J. (1997). *Poverty, Ethnicity, and Violent Crime*. Boulder, Colorado: Westview Press.

Sizemore, D and Milner W. 2004. Hispanic Media Use and Perceptions of Discrimination. *The Sociological Quarterly* 45:765–784.

Steinberg, Steven. (1981). *The Ethnic Myth*. New York: Routledge.

Unnever, J.D. (2008). Two worlds far apart: Black-white differences in beliefs about why African-American men are disproportionately imprisoned. *Criminology* 46:511–538.

Unnever, J.D. & Cullen, F.T. (2010). The social sources of Americans' punitiveness: A test of three competing models. *Criminology* 48:99–129.

Unnever, J.D., Cullen, F.T. & Jones, J.D. (2008). Public support for attacking the 'root causes' of crime: The impact of Egalitarian and racial beliefs. *Sociological Focus* 41:1–33.

Welsh, S. & Foster, L. (1987). Class and conservatism in the Black community. *American Politics Quarterly* 4:445–470.

Wilson, G. & Dunham, R. (2001). Race, class, and attitudes toward crime control: The views of the African American middle class. *Criminal Justice and Behavior* 28:259–278.

Wilson, G. (2001). Support for redistributive policies among the African American middle class: Race and class effects. *Research in Social Stratification and Mobility* 18:97–114.

Wright, E. & Cho, D. (1992). State employment, class location, and ideological orientation: A comparative analysis of the United States and Sweden. *Politics and Society* 20:167–196.

Wright, E. (1985). *Classes*, London: Verso Press.

Chapter 12

The Prison Industrial Complex: Contributing Mechanisms and Collateral Consequences of Disproportionality on African American Communities

Isis N. Walton and Shanieka S. Jones

Introduction

"An inmate at a private prison is like a guest at a hotel and the economic incentive is to book every available room and encourage every guest to stay as long as possible."

Eric Schlosser (1998)

Conversations, writings, policies and practices have been permeated by the constant discussion surrounding mass incarceration and the prison industrial complex (PIC). However, the directional relationship between the PIC and mass incarceration is still unclear. Is the PIC responsible for the mass incarceration binge or is the mass incarceration binge responsible for the ever-expanding prison industrial complex? The answer—does it really matter? Of greater significance and importance is the collateral damage and consequences that are resultant from both, particularly to African American communities.

Long gone are the days of reducing crime and suffering as goals of crime control efforts. Economic gain is the moving force in this process! The primary culprit of this is the prison industrial complex or better known as the PIC, one of the fastest growing industries in the United States. Although other industries are also contributing to the economic industry of crime control and the growing numbers of incarcerated individuals, perhaps one of the most pervasive is the increasing use of technology in the "war against crime." The main targets of this war seem to be inner-city minorities, a dispensable population; a controllable and relegated surplus population with capital producing benefits. The prison industrial complex is arguably both a coincidental outcome and a continuous, purposeful pursuit that results in collateral damages to African-Americans and the communities in which they reside. This chapter will begin by providing a backdrop of the prison industrial complex, contributing mechanisms and policies that have sustained the collateral damage of African American communities by creating a feedback loop of perpetual disproportionate incarceration. Further, the chapter will amalgamate into an intense and necessary critical analysis highlighting some of the collateral damage/consequences of the booming prison industry and its mass incarceration of African-Americans. Moreover, the ecological effects of the PIC will be examined specifically focusing on the social and generational effects of mass incarceration on communities of color.

In the Money: The Business of Punishment — The Prison Industrial Complex

Although there is no single pivotal event that led to the development of the prison industrial complex (a term first coined by Angela Davis in 1998), there are however several historical events that come together to amalgamate its development. Some argue that the prison industrial complex (PIC) is a modern version of the convict leasing system which was developed post slavery and culminated the return of the lucrative market for prison labor (Blackmon, 2008; Browne, 2007; Davis, 2003). Others indicate the toughening of drug laws (Mauer & King, 2006; Roberts, 2004; Schlosser, 1998) and the rise of privatization (Mauer & King, 2007; Davis, 2003, 1998; Schlosser, 1998) and the establishment of the "New Jim Crow" (Alexander, 2010) are the other major contributors of the PIC. The PIC has been defined as interest groups that represent organizations that do business in correctional facilities, which some people believe are more concerned with making more money than actually rehabilitating criminal offenders or reducing crime rates. Moreover, the PIC is a confluence of government interests and private businesses, where the punishment industry has become a main concern of private capital.

According to Schlosser (1998),

> The "prison-industrial complex" is not only a set of interest groups and institutions; it is also a state of mind. The lure of big money is corrupting the nation's criminal-justice system, replacing notions of safety and public service with a drive for higher profits. The eagerness of elected officials to pass tough-on-crime legislation — combined with their unwillingness to disclose the external and social costs of these laws — has encouraged all sorts of financial improprieties. (p. 55)

The PIC has gained momentum with the increase of tougher criminal laws and sentencing policies (detailed later in the chapter) which are part of the favors officials provide to support the PIC (Thompson, 2012; Schlosser, 1998). To illustrate the structural relationship between the PIC, private industry and governmental interests, the following (Figure 1) is presented.

Figure 1. The "Iron Triangle"

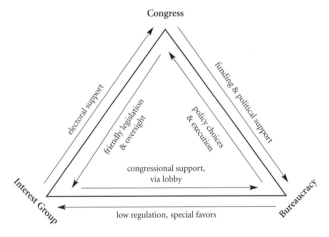

Figure 1, the Iron Triangle, is used to characterize the various players of the PIC that represent governmental interest and private business by which the three points represent: (1) legislative bodies (i.e., Congress, state General Assemblies, etc.); (2) interested parties (private corporations); and (3) the 'bureaucracy' (i.e., governmental agencies); all working to support the PIC. The gist: the prison industrial complex consists of legislative bodies that pass 'tough on crime' policies that contribute to increases in incarceration such as policies established by Nelson Rockefeller in the early 1970s and those that followed, like three-strikes, mandatory-minimums (MMs), and truth-in-sentencing laws (Mauer & King, 2007). These policies as well as others are supported by the interested parties, such as private prison corporations who build and profit from the construction of prisons (i.e., Corrections Corporation of America — CCA) and for-profit businesses (i.e., IBM, Dell Computers, Toys R' US, Victoria's Secret, etc.) who use cheap prison labor to cut costs (McCormack, 2012; Smith & Hattery, 2006; Davis, 1998). The interested parties are afforded favors by governmental organizations such as a state-level Department of Corrections offering prison space (i.e., cheap rent) for the private companies to house their operations. For instance, Lockhart Technologies closed its doors and laid off 150 employees only to reopen and restart their operations inside the state prison (Whyte & Baker, 2000). Further, the profits gained from inmate's cheap labor, and the sale of surveillance and monitoring products garner millions for private industries. The 2010 merger between private correctional companies GEO, Cornell Companies, and BI Incorporated resulted in 1.5 billion dollars in annual revenues for GEO Group and they became the world's leading provider of privatized correctional, detention and treatment services (Corrections Corporation of America Annual Report, 2011). As a result of the merger, GEO, owned 32 behavioral health facilities with a capacity of 5,000 beds and 97 detention and correctional facilities with a capacity of 76,000 beds. Since the merger, the GEO Group has seen continual growth in its annual revenue. According the Geo Group's Annual Report (2014), "over the last five years, GEO has developed and acquired more correctional, detention, and community reentry facilities than any other correctional organization in the world, with approximately 30,000 built or acquired beds in that time period." According to the GEO Chairman and CEO, George C. Zoley, they are positioning "the company to meet the ongoing demand for correctional and detention beds" (Corrections Corporation of America Annual Report, 2014). A demand that will ultimately be met by funneling inmates into prison through tougher legislation, zero tolerance school policies and the presence of New Jim Crow laws. The collateral consequences of these policies and the persistence of the mass incarceration craze will continue to cripple and deteriorate communities that have record numbers of people removed and sent to prison.

The other relational flow of the triangle in regards to the PIC consists of legislative bodies offering legislation that is beneficial to the interested parties;

interested parties then lobby and funnel money to governmental agencies for support of congressional initiatives and other considerations. The cycle perpetuates with the "you rub my back, I'll rub yours" principle. In the ever-expanding prison industrial complex and the increased desire of interested private entities and businessmen, which also includes politicians, to have a "piece of the pie" and make profits, is the support, establishment and passage of policies that severely criminalize and penalize behaviors that ordinarily would be less criminal and more a societal concern (i.e., minor drug offenses).

Astonishingly, nearly half of the people sent to state prisons in 2011 were for non-violent drug, property or public order crimes (The Sentencing Project, 2014). Convicted drug offenders constituted 17% of state inmates in 2010 in comparison to 48% of federal prison inmates in 2011. Half of males (50%) and more than half of females (59%) in federal prison were serving time for drug offenses on September 30, 2014 (The Bureau of Justice Statistics, 2014). Comparatively on the global frontier, similar crimes in other countries would either not be considered a criminal act and/or would result in fines, community service or drug treatment (Schlosser, 1998). However, the position taken by the United States to use prison as the answer to many social ills, despite what they are; is an answer that is by far the most expensive and least productive in terms of punishment.

The authors believe that to see the above structural analysis, you have to connect the dots between a number of economic, political and social patterns that are usually observed in isolation which may call one to question some of his or her own actions and attitudes. For one to see the connections is a colossal undertaking, as the PIC is a huge conglomerate framework that expands far and wide. Thus, unknowingly, many of us participate in the prison industrial complex. However, in challenging one's self to analyze the massive nature of the PIC and its effects critically, we can change the course of generational incarceration and social debt. Hence, the objective in this de-construction of the PIC is twofold: (1) this work is extremely relevant given the record high numbers of incarcerated African Americans and the impact it has on communities; and (2) it will begin the process of demonstrating the multiple layers of interdependence and symbiotic relationship of the government and private industry as capitalist profiteers in the business of punishment. Although both are important, this chapter's main focus is to delineate the collateral damage to African American communities as a direct result of mass incarceration and the PIC. This discussion will not concentrate on the traditional subject of disenfranchisement of the offender, but will focus on the invisible punishment that happens as a result of removing record numbers of persons from already socially and economically disadvantaged communities.

Politics, Policies, and Prison Labor: The Convergence of the PIC

Theoretically, most PIC analysis should examine the multidimensional reasons for the prison expansion and mass incarceration. This analysis begins with a look at "The War on Drugs" the latest contributor in the conglomeration of the PIC, which was coined and spearheaded by former President Richard Nixon in 1972. However the infamous "War" did not gain its full momentum until President Ronald Reagan took office. Although the criminalization of certain drugs and substances began in the mid-20th century, President Reagan's "War on Drugs" was pivotal because of its felonization of certain drug offenses and tougher legislative policies (King & Mauer, 2006). For example, truth-in-sentencing policies have created longer prison terms for mostly non-violent offenders, additionally; three-strike legislation has equally had the same effect on booming prison populations (King & Mauer, 2006). MMs and structured sentencing guidelines have also played a tremendous part in the United States becoming the reigning leader of incarceration, more than any other industrialized country.

Specifically, the 1986 Drug Abuse Act and other legislation to follow were significant for a variety of reasons as they collaterally:

- Established sentencing guidelines that required longer sentences, where the average sentence for crack cocaine defendants is 11 years (Meierhoefer, 1992).
- Established policies that re-categorized certain drug offenses, specifically making smaller possession convictions of crack cocaine felonies (from misdemeanor status) (Paleaz, 2014).
- Established MMs for possession of crack cocaine, where possession of five grams of crack cocaine mandated a 5-year minimum sentence (King & Mauer, 2006).
- Established "Three Strikes and You're Out" policy that puts habitual offenders away for 25 years to life on their third conviction. The policy becomes problematic in that in widens the net and catches non-violent offenders, and consequently three times as many drug offenders are becoming "lifers" (Paleaz, 2014).

As a result the "The War on Drugs" and the passage of get-tough policies, most of the populations in federal prisons grew enormously, and many prisons were (and still are) operating above capacity despite the recent release of almost seven thousand non-violent drug offenders by the Sentencing Commission in October 2015. These increases singularly were due to the influx of inmates convicted of drug offenses (Bureau of Justice Statistics, 2015; 2010; 2008, 2006, 2004). Along with the increasing numbers of inmates was the mounting number of prisons built (and needed) to house the surplus population, which is disproportionately African American. The considerable impact is far reaching, (and often invisible) as it affects more than the inmates themselves but families and communities in which they reside.

One of the most cited causes of disproportionality in incarceration rates between African Americans and Caucasian Americans can be credited to the inequity of the MMS passed by Congress in 1986 (Hammond, n.d.). Likewise, the imprisonment crisis in the U.S. was shaped by policing and sentencing laws created by war on drugs and the mass incarceration binge (Alexander, 2010; McTighe and Jervis, 2008). Overwhelmingly, the effects of these anti-drug policies are disproportionately felt by poor people of color where imprisonment has now become a "normative life experience" for the majority of young African Americans residing in urban communities (Chaike, Thomas & Ryan, 2008).

The criterion of Federal MMS includes the drug weight, and/or the presence of a firearm during a felony offense. Accordingly, the offender must serve 85 percent of the sentence, parole is not an option, and the judge must impose the sentence regardless of the role played by the defendant in the offense, any mitigating factors and/or rehabilitative likelihood (King & Mauer, 2006). Despite the similarity in chemistry and physiological effects of crack and cocaine, disproportionality exists in the laws regarding punishment. The possession of 5 grams of crack was subject to a MM of five years while it takes 100 times the amount of powder cocaine to receive the same MMS (Abrams, 2010). The Fair Sentencing Act of 2010, a new legislative policy (signed by President Obama on August 3, 2010) changed the prolific disparity in cocaine laws from the original ratio of 100 to 1 policy to 18 to 1 (FAMM, 2010). However, the bill passed was not initially made to apply retroactively, therefore, did not apply to persons previously sentenced (Washington Post, 2010). The impact of the disparate crack/cocaine laws has created a surplus of thousands of inmates experienced in prison industries, which leads to increased profitability for PIC and reduced wages and loss of critical jobs for the public. Hence, although the new bill is closer to equalizing both drugs, non-violent drug offenders who sell crack cocaine will still fuel the PIC. This disparity in policy and punishments seems to be one of the most prolific uses of racial profiling to date, as crack is predominately used by poor Blacks and Latinos while the white middle class often uses powder cocaine. Any mention of crack cocaine laws pertains to the 100:1 Crack Cocaine policy as it was (and still is) one of the greatest contributors of the disproportionality of incarceration and the mass incarceration boom of African Americans.

Privatizing Punishment: The Proliferation of Prison Labor Programs

Prison labor programs in their varying modes are responsible for the profits that private industries gain from inmate labor. Prison labor programs came back into favor with Chief Justice Burger's position that "housing inmates without teaching them skills is stupid" philosophy and eventually his quest for the establishment of "Factories with Fences" was fulfilled (FPI, 2009). Although a novel idea, it was initially postulated to provide inmates with tools for reentry while contributing to the economy, it has now evolved into a profit making business that teaches inmates unemployable skills and provides tremendous revenue for private companies.

Modern prison labor programs can come in a variety of forms:

1. Federal and state prisons employ inmates to produce goods for sale to the government and open market.
2. Private companies contract with prisons to hire prisoners.
3. Private prisons employ inmate labor for private profit, either for outside companies or the prison operators themselves.

It can be argued that the first arrangement can be seen as minimally beneficial to the prison and the inmates because the revenue made by this form of prison labor is funneled back into the system. Specifically looking at item one, the Federal Prison Industries (UNICOR) pays a more comparable wage to inmates as opposed to other sources of labor presented. The latter two arrangements are more exigent in that they both speak to the treatment of prisoners, which was one the key reasons that convict leasing was abolished.

As stated in the aforementioned section, prisons are becoming increasingly important to the U.S. economy and are the primary and/or the sole option of punishment for most criminal offenses, especially for drug offenders and, as a result, private prisons have flourished. According to Hammond (n.d.) "prison privatization is the most obvious example of opportunistic capitalism in the current development of the prison industry." Within the last three decades, the numbers of private prisons and net profits have grown. Whereas, unlike state and regional correctional facilities, prison labor is the sole contributor to the vast profits of these private facilities. There are several private companies in the punishment business that benefit from the exploitation of the burgeoning prison industry. Corporations benefit from prison labor because they are able to cut costs such as health care benefits and unemployment insurance to increase profits. Some of these corporations include Victoria Secret, IBM, J.C. Penny and Toys R Us (Davis, 2003; Whyte & Baker, 2000; Schlosser, 1998)

As indicated previously, there are many players in the prison industries play-ground; however, the most visible players of the growing "corporatization of punishment" are private prison companies (Davis, 1998). Adding to the finan-cial conglomeration of the PIC has been the demand for governmental con-tracts to build prisons, which have bolstered the construction industry. In so much that the major new niche according to the architectural community is prison design and is unquestionably why the Cornell and GEO Corporations decided to merge, notwithstanding the windfall of monetary gain for all involved (Correctional News, 2010).

Beyond the private prison construction businesses, there has been an influx of companies who create and sell products for the punishment industry as well. Westinghouse and similar companies are gaining their fair share of marketing products like "Hot Wire" fencing and "Night Enforcer" goggles, which are being sold to law enforcement agencies. Schlosser (1998) posits the significant growth of the punishment business (PIC) by calling our attention to the trade shows, conventions, websites and mail-order catalogs as strategies used to market items for the punishment industry. Additionally, he referred to the Corrections Yel-low Pages and its thousands of vendors and investors to include Wall Street financiers, food service companies, banks, architectural and construction firms as well as plumbing supply companies. Davis (1998) asserts "corporations that appear to be far removed from the business of punishment are intimately involved in the expansion of the prison industrial complex." For example, Mer-rill Lynch makes profits by investing in prison construction bonds. Phone companies have gotten in on the punishment industry by providing telephone service inside prisons, as it is estimated that a pay phone in prison could gen-erate as much as $15,000 per year (Schlosser, 1998). In addition to the extremely high price of prison calls, a subsidiary of Verizon Communications added a $3.00 surcharge to every call to California inmates (Schlosser, 1998). For exam-ple, Zero Plus Dialing, a phone company used in the United States Peniten-tiary Atlanta, charged $9.94 for a 15-minute call, plus a $5 service fee for inmate calls. This is a hefty price to pay—but who is being punished here? The authors contend it is both the family of the inmate and the inmate. The campaign for prison phone justice has been pursuing the issue for over ten years; and only recent on August 9th, 2015, the FCC passed a set of rules that drastically reduced the cost of interstate phone calls between prisoners and their family and con-tacts on the outside.

Lastly, high-tech industries and financiers are not the only ones getting income from imprisonment. Several departmental stores are profiting as well. For example, Nordstrom sells "Prison Blues," a line of jeans, t-shirts, etc., that are made in Oregon prisons with the advertising slogan "made on the inside to be worn on the outside" (Davis, 1998). Colleges, universities and state agencies also benefit from the PIC as they furnish their offices, classrooms and dorms with reduced cost furniture made from correctional enterprises, where inmates are paid low wages for making the furniture.

Any time a person is made to work in involuntary servitude, it constitutes slavery. So, when private companies make contracts about inmates' labor without their consent to the contractual terms, it in turn, is slavery. So, we have in fact, recreated slavery under the guise of imprisonment, with a new name but the same old faces of ghosts past. Case and point, the 13th amendment of the U.S. Constitution, which was passed and ratified in 1865, abolished slavery in the United States and asserts that "Neither slavery nor involuntary servitude, except as a punishment for crime whereof the party shall have been duly convicted, shall exist within the United States, or any place subject to their jurisdiction" (National Archives, Thirteenth Amendment).

The Profiteering of Slavery in Another Form: Convict Leasing

Perhaps the most insidious ideological thought that permeates through the prison industrial complex concerns the institutionalization of African American slavery. United States prison labor has its roots in slavery. Dubois (1906) wrote "The Spawn of Slavery," a critical essay on the convict leasing system of the South. In the essay, Dubois argued that the Post-Civil War South was using convict labor to replace the free labor that was enjoyed during slavery. Consequently, convict leasing was a system in which prisoners were hired out to continue the slavery tradition. During this time, petty offenses were brought against Blacks to produce the necessary numbers for convict labor. For example, Blacks were charged with petty theft such as stealing crops or not carrying out their sharecropping commitments. Once convicted, Blacks were hired out for picking cotton, building railroads and working in mines. States that were most noted in using black inmate (once again slave) labor were Georgia, Alabama and Mississippi. The notorious Parchman plantation, a prison farm, which existed until 1972, grew out of the demand for prison labor. Eighty-eight (88) percent of Georgia's hired out convicts between the years 1870 and 1910, were Black. In a disproportionately similar vein, 93% of Alabama's hired out miners were Black (Pelaez, 2014). Jim Crow segregation laws also imposed severe infractions and inmate slave labor for freed Blacks in the south. These laws infiltrated every fabric of human life in regards to schools, housing and marriage and many other aspects of daily life.

Despite the original goal of social control and the public's interest in fighting crime, prisons are now the resultant catalyst of monstrously profitable gains of the PIC made on the backs of disadvantaged populations. Angela Davis in her 1998 article "Masked Racism: Reflections of the Prison Industrial Complex," so poignantly states, "colored bodies constitute the main human raw material in this vast experiment to disappear the major social problems of our time." Further, Davis (1998) asserts "the prison industrial complex has thus created a vicious cycle of punishment which only further impoverishes those whose impoverishment is supposedly 'solved' by imprisonment."

Collateral Damage: The Vanquished Community

Most academic discourse about collateral consequences is tied to effects felt by the person convicted of the crime and sentenced to punishment (i.e., reentry, voting disenfranchisement, housing, public assistance). Recent literature has opened up the dialogue to include the effects on women, children, and collateral effects of the entire community that is left behind (Alexander, 2010; Hagedorn, 2010; Travis 2002; Mauer & Chesney-Lind, 2002; Braman, 2002; Mumola, 2000; Sudbury, 2000; Rose & Clear, 1998). Specifically indicating that communities of color are especially vulnerable to the fallout created by the trend of mass incarceration and tougher sentencing penalties as exorbitant numbers of an already marginalized population get caught in the prison-industrial web (Sudbury, 2000).

As we study the impact of expanding mass incarceration on those populations (i.e., African Americans) most noticeably affected by changes in criminal justice policies and practices, it is only befitting that attention is given to the socioeconomic characteristics of incarceration rates, the incarcerated population, and their communities over time and space. Hence, as of June 30, 2009, state and federal prisons and local jails had custody over almost 2.3 million inmates, which is a rate of one in every 131 U.S. residents (Bureau of Justice Statistics, 2010). While the 2009 end of year report has not been officially published to see if differing rates of incarceration exist for jail and prison inmates based on gender and race, the midyear 2009 report indicated disproportionality in incarceration rates by race and gender. Black males had an incarceration rate of 4,749 per 100,000, an incarceration rate more than six times than white males (708 per 100,000) and 2.6 times higher than Hispanic males (1,822 per 100,000) (Bureau of Justice Statistics, 2010). Although the incarceration rates for females have always been far lower than the incarceration rates of males, female rates of incarceration are the fastest growing population with the highest increases for black women. According to Bureau of Justice Statistics (2010)

Black females had an incarceration rate of 333 per 100,000, a rate more than two times as likely as Hispanic females (142 per 100,000) and almost four times higher than white females (91 per 100,000). Since yearend 2000, the nation's prison and jail custody populations have increased by approximately 20 percent (Bureau of Justice Statistics, 2009). The U.S. now holds the unprecedented highest incarceration rate of any industrialized nation and as the numbers grow so too does the racial disproportionality in incarceration. According to Elliott Currie (1998), "mass incarceration has been the most thoroughly implemented government social program of our time." The powers driving the PIC are creating the world in its image—one that promotes the exploitation of black labor by creating racial criminalization.

Collateral Impact of Racial Criminalization and PIC on African American Communities

There are collateral consequences that result from the removal of large numbers of people differentially from their communities. As the numbers of brown bodies permeate the cell block walls of the nations' prisons, the communities of these bodied people become desolate, absent of capable guardians, filled with a steady supply of motivated offenders and suitable targets. Cohen and Felson's (1979) use of Routine Activity Theory can be used a backdrop to analyze the level of damage being done in these already socially disorganized communities. Historically the theory postulated how the routine activities of individuals increase the probability of criminal activity. In this case, the authors suggest these same elements of the theory help to explain what can happen in communities when they suffer the loss of large numbers of individuals to the criminal justice system.

As mass incarceration becomes normalized for African Americans, so too does the inability for a community to survive. The crippling effect of this process follows. Although there are numerous effects of disproportionality that mass incarceration and the proliferation of the PIC have on communities of color, only a few will be illustrated here. Specifically, to be addressed are the social-political-economic consequences that have come as a result of the expansive imprisonment policies such as the "War on Drugs." Not surprisingly then, are those who have experienced the greatest impact of mass incarceration and disenfranchisement policies, are the poor and people of color. Equally disturbing is the exacerbated dilution and elimination of the political power within these already vulnerable communities.

As Stevenson (2006) indicates "the widespread incarceration of men in low-income communities has had a profound negative impact on social and cultural norms relating to family and opportunity." Further, he explains that the astonishing rate of imprisonment of poor minority women with children has had an equally devastating effect causing a disastrous level of displaced children and dependents. The effect on these communities has led to a "dispiriting culture of hopelessness and despair that has festered into cycles of violence, criminality, and failure" (Stevenson, 2006).

According to Travis (2002),

> the new wave of invisible punishments is qualitatively different as well. Taken together, the recent enactments, many of them passed by Congress, chip away at critical ingredients of the support systems of poor people in this country. Under these new laws, offenders can be denied public housing, welfare benefits, and the mobility necessary to access jobs that require driving, child support, parental rights, and the ability to obtain an education. . . . For many offenders, the social safety net has been severely damaged. (p. 18)

When individuals (or communities) have blocked access to the means, illegitimate forms of behavior will suffice to reach goals as explained by Merton's mode of adaptation. Disproportionately as African American men are incarcerated, women increasingly become the defenders, protectors and financial proprietors of the community, which ultimately positions them to participate in non-traditional often illegal forms of behavior. For example, they may become involved in the drug economy as a result of a debt owed by their husband or boyfriend or simply because it is a viable way to earn money for their family. Resultantly they may even be involved in gang activity for the establishment of protection for themselves or their children. Within these communities, there is the recruitment of young offenders, as young boys and girls can be influenced to join gangs and the drug enterprise for financial gain and/or protection. Adolescents are often are seduced into criminal activity because their mother's inability to financially provide and protect them. Additionally, the lack of consistent male role models to demonstrate legitimate forms of economic gains or to provide guidance on navigating through the distorted lines of racial, social and economic injustice that permeate many of these communities, leads to youth who are swallowed up in the belly of the beast. Inevitably, the cycle is repeated!

When crime flourishes in a community, the moral and social fabric often degenerates, and the depreciation of the value of punishment heightens. Despite the consequential effects of the removal of a continuous supply of individuals from a collective space, the effect of the punishment becomes muted and does not deter the majority from participating in criminal behavior. As incarceration becomes normalized in these communities, some individuals rationalize the crime and incarceration cycle because it is so prevalent. So there is no reaction to an adverse consequence of someone being sent to prison because of the normalcy of the cycle. Also, when there is the depreciation of the value of punishment, there is a devaluing of the roles the individual plays in the community that outweighs the role as an offender. At any given time the offender can act as a parent, neighbor, or a confidant but once the individual is incarcerated not only is a void left behind, but the offender can sometimes be immortalized and imprinted in the community as the sacrificial lamb.

Socially, the increased levels of mass incarceration of Black men have helped to create generational social debt for the youth that occupy these communities. The likelihood of them going to prison has just been increased tremendously. The level of responsibility has been heightened for both women and kids while burdening the caretaker to assume all the roles and responsibilities that should be shared. As a result, incarceration increases familial deficits and further strains already weak relationships.

On the economic landscape, mass incarceration reduces the funding in schools and other public services, increases social inequality, and expands future generational debt. For example, the Census is used to allocate resources based on numbers of individuals within communities, the amount of taxes paid and other quantitative items that are based on the number of people. These communities are negatively impacted as their voices have been muted due to the lack of politically able individuals that can vote, and/or the lacking number of homeowners, and/or the lack of the number of income earners that create a significant tax base within these communities. Despite current efforts to "ban the box" from employer discrimination and the restoration of voting rights by reducing the paperwork, barriers still exist. So as people are removed, so too does the decline of income, the population and political power which ultimately cause major economic disenfranchisement thereby creating future generational debt.

Conclusion

When analyzing the 2010 Census information about the population of African Americans in the U.S., there is a glaring disparity between the relative number, the percentage of African Americans in the U.S. (12%), and the number incarcerated. It is beyond belief that a population of people who *only* make up a small fraction of the total population are the ones overwhelming represented in the nation's prisons and jails. So, is it that Blacks commit more crime?

Or do the laws disproportionately select, target and incarcerate? In the previous sections, research was used to delve into the multidimensional layering of policies, practices and historical events that have unprecedentedly galvanized the normalcy of incarceration for an entire racial group. Reflecting on the previous statement of normalizing confinement and prisonization is painful and at the same time unethical because of the realization of its accuracy. Case in point, in a corrections class of forty-five African and Latino American sophomore level college students, all but 2 raised their hands when asked if they had a primary relative that has been or is incarcerated. More shocking is the response that followed, where the students who admitted to having a family member incarcerated considered and treated the two students who did not raise their hands as an aberration.

Previous research indicated that the level of incarceration for African American men was a significant issue. The Sentencing Project (1990) reported that one in four black men in the U.S. were under the control of the Department of Corrections, which included imprisonment, probation, and/or parole. The problem was further exacerbated by 1995 as the national rate had risen to one-in-three (Mauer & Hurling, 1995). So the question still remains . . . from when this book was first written in 2010 and now in its current revision in 2016 . . . why do we not appear to be any closer to crime justice reform and problem solving justice solutions to the expanding level of predictable and common experience of incapacitation of Blacks and Latinos in the United States? At one time, the development of the PIC and the evolution of its consequences seemed somewhat of a happenstance; however now it's seemingly a ruthless, deliberate and purposeful pursuit of extermination and capitalistic gain that desecrates and annihilates communities of color. After four decades of the imprisonment experiment, there has been too much time to rectify and solve some of the problems created to have done nothing. The impact has been far-reaching and catastrophic, so much so that we indoctrinate young kids of color to accept prison culture through the exportation of the prison lingo, culture and fashion, which further perpetuates and normalizes the incarceration of African Americans.

The exposure of the strategic design of social control that was purposeful in sustaining a racial caste system by the establishment of New Jim Crow Laws targeted towards offenders who were swept ferociously in prisons during the "mass incarceration craze" has led to heightened consciousness among many groups especially African Americans. No longer is mass incarceration seen as a criminal justice issue but it has been catapulted as the number one threat against the existence of African American communities including its sustainability. Mass incarceration is now seen as a racial justice and civil rights issues.

The collective efficacies of many groups (ACLU, CBC, etc.) has been brought into our everyday discussions by a palatable discussion presented by Michelle Alexander's *The New Jim Crow* and thus has been part of the catalyst for current criminal justice reform.

The toll of the PIC, mass imprisonment and the "War on Drugs" on African American communities has been a financial war exerted on the relationships of children, spouses, parents, partners and caretakers. A war that has led to the disruption of social and family networks, by weakening the already financially strapped, politically vanquished and emotionally fragile support systems of entire communities. Support systems that are the building blocks to strong and vibrant communities and that are usually indispensable and dependable in times of need. Recent discussions and writings specifically Michelle Alexander's book of living in a color blind and a post-racial society have functioned to emphasize the purposeful pursuit of maintaining and constructing a racial caste system that privileges whiteness and marginalizes people of color. These conversations have also defined the incapacitating structural effects and the legacy of how mass incarceration, the New Jim Crow unfairly impacts communities of color as well as the institutional and structural inequalities of race. If we are to advance as a nation, how can we continue to support a system that isn't built on justice but built on a profit making enterprise that benefit on human suffering? The *intoxication of incarceration* must end! If we are to get "high" let us do so through transformative justice by building human and social capital so that all communities matter.

References

Abrams, J. (2010). Congress passes bill to reduce disparity in crack, powder cocaine sentencing Retrieved July 29, 2010, from http://www.washington post.com/wpdyn/content/article/2010/07/28/AR2010072802969.html.

Addams, J. (1920/1960). Twenty Years at Hull-House. New York: Signet.

Alexander, Michelle. (2010) .*The New Jim Crow: Mass Incarceration in the Age of Colorblindness* .New York: The New Press.

American Friends Service Committee (1971). Struggle for Justice: a Report on Crime and Punishment in America. New York: Hill & Wang.

Blackmon, D. A. (2008). Slavery by Another Name: The Re-enslavement of Black People in America from the Civil War to World War II. New York: Doubleday.

Bonczar, T. (2003). Prevalence of Imprisonment in the U.S. Populations, 1974–2001. Bureau of Washington, D.C.: Bureau of Justice Statistics.

Retrieved August 31, 2010, from http://bjs.ojp.usdoj.gov/content/pub/pdf/piusp 01.pdf.

Bonczar, T. E and Beck A. J. (1997). Lifetime Likelihood of Going to State or Federal Prison. Washington, D.C.: Bureau of Justice Statistics.

Braman, D. (2002). Families and Incarceration. Mauer, M. & Chesney-Lind, M. (eds.). Invisible Punishment. New York: The New Press.

Bratton, W., Griffiths, W., Mallon, R., Orr, J. & Pollard, C. (1998). Zero tolerance: Policing a Free Society. London: IEA Health and Welfare Unit.

Browne, J. (2007). Rooted in Slavery: Prison Labor Exploitation. Race, Poverty & The Environment, 14(1).

Bureau of Justice Statistics. (2002). Recidivism of Prisoners Released in 1994. Retrieved August 31, 2010, from http://bjs.ojp.usdoj.gov/index.cfm?ty=pbdetail&iid=516.

Bureau of Justice Statistics. (2009). Growth in Prison and Jail Populations Slowing: 16 States Report Declines in the Number of Prisoners. Washington D.C.: Retrieved July 15, 2010, from http://www.ojp.usdoj.gov/newsroom/pressreleases/2009/BJS090331.htm.

Cooper M., Sabol, W.J. &. West H.C. (2009). Prisoners in 2008. Washington, D.C.: Bureau of Justice Statistics.

Corrections Corporation of America, *2011 Annual Report: Form 10-K.*

Corrections Corporation of America, *2014 Annual Report: Form 10-K.*

Couture H., Harrison, P.M., Sabol, W.J. (2007). Prisoners in 2006. Washington, D.C.: Bureau of Justice Statistics.

Currie, E. (1998). Crime and Punishment in America. New York: Metropolitan Books.

Culp, R. (2005). The rise and stall of prison privatization: An integration of policy analysis perspectives. Criminal Justice Policy Review, 16, (4).

Davis, A. Y. (1998). Masked Racism: Reflections on the Prison Industrial Complex. Colorlines Magazine.

Davis, A. Y. (2003). Are Prisons Obsolete? New York: Seven Stories Press.

Dubois, W.E. B. (1901). The Spawn of Slavery. The Missionary Review of the World, 14.

Factories with Fences: 75 Years of Changing Lives. (2009). Federal Prison Industries. Retrieved July, 1, 2010, from http://www.unicor.gov/information/publications/pdfs/corporate/CATMC1101.pdf.

Families Against Mandatory Minimums. The Case Against Mandatory Sentences. Retrieved April 28, 2010 from http://www.famm.org/Repository/Files/PrimerFinal.pdf.

Foucault, M. (1979). Discipline & Punish: The Birth of the Prison. New York: Vintage.

Fulbright, K., Ed. (1996). The Unintended Consequences of Incarceration. New York: Vera Institute of Justice.

GEO and Cornell Announce Merger. (2010). Retrieved July, 1, 2010, from http://www.correctionalnews.com/articles/2010/04/19/geo-and-cornell-announce-merger.

Glaze, L., Kaeble, D., Minton, T., and Tsoutis . A (2015). Correctional Populations in the United States, 2014. Washington, D.C.: Bureau of Justice Statistics. Retrieved on March 27, 2016 from http://www.bjs.gov/index.cfm?ty=pbdetail&iid=5519

Hagedorn, J. (2003). The Prison, Race, and the Community, pp. 1099–1101. The Enclyclopedia of Community. Sage Publications. Retrieved on June 25, 2010, from http://www.gangresearch.net/Archives/hagedorn/prisoncom.html.

Harrison, P. M. & Karberg J. C. (2003). Prison and Jail Inmates at Midyear 2002. Washington, D.C.: Bureau of Justice Statistics.

Hartnett, S. (c. 1997). Prison Labor, Slavery & Capitalism In Historical Perspective referencing, Novak, D.A., The Wheel of Servitude: Black Forced Labor After Slavery.

Justice Policy Institute, *Gaming the System: How the Political Strategies of Private Prison Companies Promote Ineffective Incarceration Policies* (Washington, DC: Justice Policy Institute, June 2011), 29.

King, R. S. &Mauer M. (2006). Sentencing with Discretion: Crack Cocaine Sentencing After Booker. Washington, D.C.: The Sentencing Project.

Lichtenstein, A. (1993). Good Roads and Chain Gangs in the Progressive South: The Negro Convict is a Slave. The Journal of Southern History, Athens, Georgia: Southern Historical Association.

Mahmood, M. (2004). Collateral consequences of the prison-industrial complex. Social Justice. Retrieved on July, 1, 2010, from: http://www.accessmylibrary.com/article-1G1-133752506/collateral-consequences-prison-industrial.html.

Mauer, M. (2006). Race to Incarcerate, revised and updated. New York: The New Press.

Mauer, M. (2003). Comparative International Rates of Incarceration: An Examination of Causes and Trends. Washington, D.C.: The Sentencing Project.

Mauer, M. & Chesney-Lind, M. (2002). Invisible Punishment: the Collateral Consequences of Mass Imprisonment. New York: New Press.

Mauer, M. & Hurling, T. (1995). Young Black Americans and the Criminal Justice System: Five Years Later. Washington DC: The Sentencing Project.

Mauer M. & King R. S. (2007). A 25-Year Quagmire: The 'War on Drugs' and Its Impact on American Society. Retrieved June 27, 2010, from http://www

.sentencingproject.org/Admin/Documents/publications/dp_25yearquag
mire.pdf.

McCormack, Simon. (2012). Prison Labor Booms As Unemployment Remains
High; Companies Reap Benefits. The Huffington Post, retrieved January 2016 from http://www.huffingtonpost.com/2012/12/10/prison-
labor_n_2272036.html

McTighe, L. & Jervis C. (2008). Confronting HIV and Mass Imprisonment: Two
Intersecting Epidemics. Retrieved July, 31, 2010, from http://www.champnet
work.org/media/unshackle/Confronting_HIV-Mass_Imprisonment.pdf.

Meierhoefer, B. S. (1992). The General Effect of Mandatory Minimum Prison
Terms: A Longitudinal Study of Federal Sentences Imposed. Washington
DC: Federal Judicial Center.

Morris, N. and D. J. Rothman, Eds. (1998). The Oxford History of the Prison:
The Practice of Punishment in Western Society. New York: Oxford University Press.

Mumola, C. J. (2000). Incarcerated Parents and Their Children. Washington,
D.C.: Bureau of Justice Statistics.

Pelaez V. (2014). The Prison Industry in the United States: Big Business or a
New Form of Slavery? Global Research. Retrieved March 27, 2016, from
http://www.globalresearch.ca/index.php?context=va&aid=8289.

Pew Center on the States, Public Safety Performance Project. (2008). One in
100: Behind Bars in America. Retrieved July, 25, 2010, from http://www.
pewcenteronthestates.org/uploadedFiles/8015PCTS_Prison08_
FINAL_2-1-1_FORWEB.pdf.

Pierre T. & Ryan, J. (2008). U.S. Prison Population Hits an All Time High, ABC
News, June 6, 2008. Retrieved June 27, 2010, from http://abcnews.go.com/
TheLaw/story?id=5009270.

Platt, A. M. (1969). The Child Savers: The Invention of Delinquency. Chicago
and London: University of Chicago.

Prison Labor Cheats Society. 2001. Retrieved on June 30, 2010, from http://
www.wpi.edu/News/TechNews/010327/prisonlabor.shtml.

Roberts, D. E. (2004). The Social and Moral Cost of Mass Incarceration in African American Communities. Stanford Law Review, 56.

Rusche, G. & Kirchheimer O. (1939). Punishment and Social Structure. New
York: Columbia University Press.

Sabol, W. J. & West, H.C. (2008). Prisoners in 2007. Washington, D.C.: Bureau
of Justice Statistics.

Schlosser, E. (1998). The Prison Industrial Complex. The Atlantic Monthly.

Shelden, R. G. (2005). Slavery in the 3rd Millennium Part II—Prisons and Convict Leasing Help Perpetuate Slavery. The Black Commentator, 142.

Smith E. & Hattery A. (2006). The Prison Industrial Complex. Sociation Today, 4(2). Retrieved on June 25, 2010, from http://www.ncsociology.org/socia tiontoday/v42/ outline8.htm.

Stevenson, B. A. (2006). Confronting Mass Imprisonment and Restoring Fairness to Collateral Review of Criminal Cases. Harvard Civil Rights-Civil Liberties Law Review, 41(1).

Sudbury, J. (2000). Transatlantic Visions: Resisting the Globalization of Mass Incarceration. Social Justice 27,(3).

The Fair Sentencing Act Corrects a Long-time Wrong in Cocaine Cases. Retrieved August 3, 2010, from http://www.washingtonpost.com/wpdyn/ content/article/2010/08/02/AR2010080204360.html.

The GEO Group and Cornell Companies Announce $685 Million Merger Creates $1.5 Billion Revenue Diversified Provider of Essential Government Services April 19, 2010. Retrieved April 20, 2010 from, http:// realcostofprisons.org/blog/archives/2010/04/geo_and_cornell.html.

The National Archives. Thirteenth Amendment to U.S. Constitution: Abolition of Slavery. Retrieved on October 8, 2010, from http://www.archives.gov/ historical-docs/document.html?doc=9&title.raw=13th%20Amend ment%20to%20the%20U.S.%20Constitution%3A%20Abolition%20 of%20Slavery.

The Sentencing Project. Facts about prisons and people in prisons. Retrieved January 2016 from http://www.sentencingproject.org/doc/publications/ inc_Facts%20About%20Prisons.pdf

Thompson, H. A. (2012). The Prison Industrial Complex. *New Labor Forum (Sage Publications Inc.), 21*(3), 38–47. doi:10.4179/NFL.213.0000006

Tonry, M. (1995). Malign neglect. New York: Oxford Press.

Travis, J. (2002). Invisible Punishment: An Instrument of Social Exclusion, in Invisible Punishment: The Collateral Consequences of Mass Imprisonment, Marc Mauer and Meda Chesney-Lind (eds.). New York: The New Press.

U.S. Department of Justice, Officer of Justice Programs, Bureau of Justice Statistics, *Prisoners in 2014,* by E. Ann Carson, (Washington, DC: Government Printing Office, September 2015).

Wacquant, L. (2000). The New Peculiar Institution, On the Prison as Surrogate Ghetto. Theoretical Criminology 4, (3).

West, H. (2010). Prisoners at Yearend 2009, Advance Counts. Washington, D.C.: Bureau of Justice Statistics.

Whyte, A. & Baker, J. (2000). Prison Labor on the Rise in U.S. Retrieved June, 25, 2010, from http://www.wsws.org/articles/2000/may2000/pris-m08. shtml, June 2010.

Wycliff, D. (2005). Book Review. The Prison-Industrial Complex of Invisible Punishment: The Collateral Consequences of Mass Imprisonment. Imprisoning America: The Social Effects of Mass Incarceration. Retrieved on August 6, 2010, from http://www.accessmylibrary.com/coms2/summary _0286-18936035_ITM.

Chapter 13

Politics, Policy and DMC Communities: The Impact of Community Political Disempowerment on DMC

Cherie Dawson-Edwards

Introduction

The criminal justice system provides a convenient vehicle for physically maintaining the old legally enforced color lines as African Americans are disproportionately policed, prosecuted, convicted, disenfranchised, and imprisoned (Brewer & Heitzeg, 2008, p. 633).

The right to vote is undeniably a key element to democratic governance. Many have noted its significance as the guarantor of all other rights afforded in a democracy. Some have argued that unequal distribution of political engagement based on one's group classification insinuates disinterest in the individual and his or her concerns (Brown-Dean, 2003; Dawson, 1994; Reuter, 1995; Sidanius, 1992; Ture & Hamilton, 1992). As such, most disenfranchised populations have gained the right to vote. This chapter reviews the existing literature on criminal disenfranchisement in the U.S. by specifically placing the topic in the context as a collateral consequence of disproportionate minority contact (DMC) and contributor of community political disempowerment. Specifically, the author will provide a framework for understanding the relationship between historical and modern political disenfranchisement, community instability and DMC in the adult and juvenile justice systems. Criminal disenfranchisement or felon disenfranchisement results in the rescinding of voting rights due to a felony conviction.

From a criminological perspective, the theoretical basis best used to adequately examine the impact of political disenfranchisement on DMC is the coercive mobility model presented by Rose and Clear (1998). This is one of the more valuable pieces of literature on the community level impact of mass incarceration which uses social disorganization theory to model that high incarceration rates lead to increasing crime rates (Rose & Clear, 1998). In this work, Rose and Clear (1998) expand on social disorganization theory and argue that it is necessary to include public control, such as law enforcement, as causes of crime, not just as responses to crime. Socially disorganized communities are characterized by their inability to develop a consensus regarding their values, norms, roles or hierarchical structure (Rose & Clear, 1998; Kornhauser, 1978; Shaw & McKay, 1942). Researchers have examined the reciprocity between crime and community structure and concluded that social disorganization contributes to crime and crime contributes to further disorganization (Rose & Clear, 1998; see Rose, 1995, Gottfredson & Taylor, 1988; Bursik & Grasmick, 1993). Furthermore, Rose and Clear (1998) suggest that high incarceration rates should be viewed as a contributing factor of community disorganization. This premise relies on evidence that shows that incarceration disturbs social systems by impairing sources of informal social controls (Clear, Rose, Waring & Scully, 2003).

As such, they developed a model based on the concept of "coercive mobility" (Rose & Clear, 1998, p. 34), which purports that the impact of incarceration is similar to voluntary mobility or middle class suburban migration (Wilson, 1987; Rose & Clear, 1998). Further, they argue that incarceration as coercive mobility impacts three of Shaw and McKay's (1942) original "disorganizing factors" (Rose & Clear, 1998, p. 450): socioeconomic composition, offender removal and reentry, and heterogeneity. In simpler terms, crime contributes to further disorganization through incarceration's continuous removal and reentry of community residents as a result of mass incarceration.

While it may seem rational to believe that removing criminals from the community will reduce crime and create a safer environment, this logic fails to acknowledge that by coercively removing criminals, public safety is jeopardized by the removal of human resources within the community. Crime could be only one hat that the offender wears. He or she might also wear the hat of a contributing family member, work a legitimate job, or contribute to neighborhood economics by purchasing items from local stores. Theoretically, a community that has impaired familial, economic and political systems will have more crime (Clear et al., 2003). For the purposes of this chapter, the breakdown of political systems is most pertinent. Rose and Clear (1998) contextualize this community disability in terms of the absence of collective action through such deficiencies such as the inability to organize and lack of political capacity.

The literature suggests that the theoretical underpinnings can be found in social disorganization theory rooted in the work of Shaw and McKay (1942). However, the examination of incarceration as a critical factor in the social disorganization of African-American communities dates as far back as the early works of W.E.B. Dubois. His work, *The Philadelphia Negro*, examined crime causation in the predominantly African-American Seventh Ward of Philadelphia in the late 1800s (DuBois, 1899/1973; Greene & Gabbidon, 2000). His examination included research on members of this community who were incarcerated and his inclusion of incarcerated and other ecological explanations has credited him as one of the first to use social disorganization as an approach to explaining crime in the African-American community.

This chapter draws on both Rose and Clear's coercive mobility hypothesis and DuBois' work that focused the uniqueness of African-American communities. While the coercive mobility hypothesis is useful for understanding the impact of concentrated incarceration, it seems to fall short in regards to including the role of institutional racism. As such, to better place this chapter's topic into context, it is necessary to begin with a historical review of how racism has shaped the way in which African-Americans interact with the criminal justice system.

Political Disempowerment and DMC: The History

In post-Civil War America, southern states strategically crafted their laws to include minor violations that would serve to facilitate disenfranchising African-Americans. In the other parts of the country, the laws were not so strategic. In fact, they "lacked socially distinct targets and generally were passed in a matter-of-fact fashion" (Keyssar, 2000, p. 162). The early laws varied by state, which is still reflected in current state criminal disenfranchisement laws. Though electoral fraud was included in every state's criminal disenfranchisement law, who was excluded, the length of exclusion, and the restoration process were diversely reflected in the individual state laws (Keyssar, 2000).

Convicted felons remain the only directly disenfranchised population across the nation upheld by constitutional law (Johnson-Parris, 2003). The history of the felon's severance from the democratic process dates beyond the conception of American society (Special Project, 1970; Thompson, 2002); however, the modern day interpretation and applicability of felon disenfranchisement laws is rooted in the post-Civil War America when the American electorate drastically changed due to the passage of the Reconstruction Amendments (13th, 14th, and 15th). After the ratification of the 13th Amendment, once only worth "three-fifths of all other persons," freed slaves became "five-fifths" of all other persons, as it relates to representation in Congress, which shifted apportionment and voting in many southern states (Chin, 2004). However, due to their restricted freedom, freed slaves could not hold public office or vote for those who would represent them (Chin, 2004; *Oregon v. Mitchell*, 1970).

Largely due to their inclusion of the "negro" as persons, the southern population boomed and southern states were able to secure national power (Chin, 2004). Subsequently, the Fifteenth Amendment was passed, which guaranteed suffrage independent of race. In an effort to preserve political power, it was critical for the African-American vote to be suppressed, while the southern states retained the right to count them for apportionment (Chin, 2004). To accomplish this, twenty years after the Fifteenth Amendment, creative felon disenfranchisement laws were written into many state constitutions (Simson, 2002). Though the laws had existed in many states since their inception, the re-emergence and re-wording of felon disenfranchisement laws in the 1890s cannot be attributed to irony. Public records for the constitutional conventions of Virginia (1901–02), South Carolina (1895), Mississippi (1890), and Alabama (1901) document that the purpose of the 19th century felon disenfranchisement laws in those states was to suppress the black vote (Kousser, 1984; Rose, 1906; Shapiro, 1993).

Another Post-Civil War practice can be seen as a corollary phenomenon to criminal disenfranchisement — the convict leasing system. Upon the abolishment of slavery, outside of the loss of political power, the South found itself in a rather perilous situation, not only politically, but economically as well. After years of essentially free labor, it found that supply virtually eliminated. With few exceptions, free labor ceased to exist. At the same time, the 'freed' laborers found themselves with no plantation in which they could live, work and eat. Therefore, many of them lived rather aimlessly in this immediate aftermath of emancipation. As such, some found themselves committing minor offenses, such as crop stealing or other forms of property crimes to survive. Politicians in the South took notice and began to capitalize on the freed slaves' directionless actions.

The southern legislators began to pass laws that would criminalize the perceived aimlessness of the freed slaves. Consequently, these were the same type of crimes of moral turpitude that also fed criminal disenfranchisement. For freed slaves, these criminal acts secured their admission into an unjust criminal system by which they were processed with no rights. This assembly line justice led to large numbers of black convicts who were often transported and leased to plantations-turned-prison-farms to work for free. The convict leasing system of the Reconstruction Era was born—a time in which it has been reported that convict leasing profits supplied 372% of state prison expenses (Mancini, 1978). While convict leasing existed prior to the emancipation of the slaves (see Shichor, 1995), the Reconstruction Era lease system was designed specifically to target the freed slave population and counteract the labor shortage issues in the south (Davis, 2003). For example, on May 11, 1868, Georgia's governor Thomas Rugor leased out 100 African-American inmates to work on the Georgia and Alabama railroad. Ten years later, the state of Georgia leased out a total of 1,239 convicts which 1,124 were African-American (Browne, 1995).

Over 100 years later, remnants of these antiquated laws still exist. The Supreme Court has upheld states' rights to criminal disenfranchisement (*Richardson v. Ramirez*, 1974) and interpreted its relation to the 14th Amendment's protection from discriminatory intent (*Hunter v. Underwood*, 1985). The modern version of the convict leasing system, the Prison Industrial Complex (PIC), is also alive and well with the return of prison labor, the toughening of drug laws and the rise of privatization as contributing factors. Angela Davis (2003, p. 95) puts this history in context when she noted:

> Vast amounts of black labor became increasingly available for use by private agents through the convict lease system and related systems such as debt peonage. This transition set the historical stage for the easy acceptance of disproportionately black prison populations today.... We are approaching the proportion of black prisoners to white, during the era of the southern convict lease and country chain gang systems. Whether this human raw material is used for purposes of labor or for the consumption of commodities provided by a rising number of corporations directly implicated in the prison industrial complex, it is clear that black bodies are considered dispensable within the "free world," but as a source of profit in the prison world (Brewer & Heitzeg, 2008).

While there is no concrete evidence that criminal disenfranchisement and convict leasing were part of a divine conspiracy, in conjunction with each other, one could surmise that both public policies cumulatively play a vital role in the history of the interrelatedness of the community disempowerment, instability and crime. In modern times, the U.S. has been incarcerating at an unprecedented rate. To put the disproportionate impact on African-American males in perspective, Boyd (2001) uses analogies to apartheid and U.S. Slavery. More specifically, it was reported that African-American men are currently incarcerated at a rate that is four times that of those in South Africa during apartheid (Miller & Garran, 2008). Even closer to home is the fact that the U.S. incarcerates quantities of black men that is eerily close to the numbers of black men enslaved at the peak of the U.S. slave era (Boyd, 2001; Miller & Garran, 2008).

Concentrated Community Incarceration and Political Disempowerment

Anti-racist literature places the relationship between concentrations of poverty, incarceration and political disempowerment under the broader category of institutional racism. According to Miller and Garran (2008), institutional racism is a phenomenon that "leads to exclusion from neighborhoods, jobs, schools, politics, health and mental health care . . ." (p. 32). They also suggest that institutional racism leads to a higher likelihood of contact with the criminal justice system. It is described as being widespread, persistent and deeply entrenched in the fabric of society. It includes areas governed by seemingly race neutral policies such as political racism, residential racism, educational racism and racism in the criminal justice system all of which play into the continued disorganization of certain communities. The following section will discuss the interrelationships of concentrated poverty, concentrated incarceration and concentrated political disempowerment on communities of color. The institutional racism theoretical framework is useful for guiding a discussion on these variables that contribute to community disempowerment and contextualizing how racism is "institutionally embedded" in the fabric of U.S. society (Miller & Garran, 2008, p. 63). The terms neighborhood and community are seemingly interchangeable but there is a need to distinguish the two for discussion centering on the interrelations of poverty, crime and political empowerment. Neighborhoods generally refer to geographic locations within a larger area (Clear, 2003). The term community is more about the residents of an area. This distinction becomes more imperative when looking at how certain communities developed and the cultures within those communities that have been sustained over time.

For the purpose of this chapter's analysis, the terms neighborhood and community will be used interchangeably. The focus will remain on urban high poverty neighborhoods (Jargowsky, 1997) with a predominately African-American impoverished population. At times referred to as "ghettos," these neighborhoods have traditionally been maintained by "legally sanctioned housing discrimination ... [such as] ... zoning, restrictive covenants, and overt violence ... " (Jargowsky, 1997, p. 12–13). Geographically concentrated poverty refers to "the interaction between a group's overall rate of poverty and its degree of segregation in society" (Massey & Denton, 1993, p. 118; Jargowsky, 1997, p. 140). Jargowsky and Bane (1991) found that areas with neighborhood poverty were comprised of predominately African-American residents and physically marked by "dilapidated housing, vacant units with broken or boarded up windows, abandoned and burned out cars and men hanging out on street corners"(p. 11).

Wilson (1987) found that residents of impoverished neighborhoods are "residentially isolated from the nonpoor, they are spatially and socially cut off from mainstream resources, opportunities and role models" (Jargowsky, 1997, p. 18). Decades later, Clear (2007) published his groundbreaking text that identified and explored the connection between the types of neighborhoods described by Wilson and the current incarceration boom. Subsequent research has extended this type of analysis and studied the relationship between impoverished communities, incarceration rates and voter disenfranchisement rates (see Roberts, 2004; Fagan, 2006). So how did this happen? How did these neighborhoods become socially and spatially isolated? As a continuation of the discussion of the Post-Civil War role in creating the racialized practices of felon disenfranchisement and convict leasing earlier in the chapter, an examination of politically disempowered communities must begin there as well. For predominately African-American impoverished communities, their development can be traced back to the Post-Civil War era. Unlike the external patterns of immigration that created many immigrant-specific neighborhoods, the internal migration patterns of African-Americans can be directly linked to former slaves and their offspring moving North in search of better opportunities.

In the immediate aftermath of the Civil War, freed slaves often lived in integrated communities (Wilson, 1973). The composition of mixed race neighborhoods began to change around 1890 as residential segregation forced many blacks to relocate through mechanisms such as "neighborhood improvement associations, economic boycotts ... acts of violence and ... restrictive covenants" (Spear, 1971, p. 159; Wilson, 1973, p. 104). The resulting neighborhoods are still largely comprised of African-American residents who maintain the majority at approximately 20 to 1 (Clear & Cadora, 2003). An individual's spatial location absolutely impacts his/her social location. The spatial location can be a determinant of the social opportunities afforded to an individual. As Clear and Cadora (2003) suggest, "place matters in life" (p. 9).

The question to be further examined here is: how do the causes of DMC and related phenomenon, concentrated poverty and incarceration, contribute to the political disempowerment of communities? Figure 1 indicates an over-lapping relationship between these issues with the semi-transparent circles revealing that they are all part of the same. The three innermost circles represent three areas that have been identified as underlying factors contributing to DMC (Hsia, Bridges & McHale, 2002). The next level reflects concentrated poverty and incarceration as neighborhood level factors that are characteristic in DMC communities. The outer circle shows concentrated disenfranchisement as extending beyond the first two levels because it impacts representation in the broader political arena in addition to the community political power and participation necessary to impact community level issues.

Figure 1.

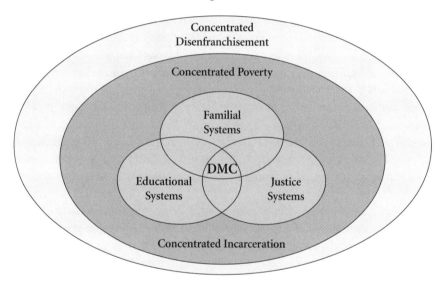

As mentioned previously, crime and community structure maintain a recip-rocal relationship. For years, researchers have examined the connection between crime and poverty in certain communities (see Lewis, 1965; Wilson, 1987; Jargowsky & Bane, 1991). In more recent times, this type of research has been extended to look at incarceration rates and disenfranchisement rates of impoverished communities (see Clear & Cadora, 2003; Fagan, 2006). At times, the research has been vague about the race or ethnicity of the residents in these communities (see Jargowsky, 1997); however, other researchers such as Massey and Denton (1993) clearly point out that concentrated poverty is "built into the experiences of urban blacks by racial segregation" (p. 118). Clearly, incarceration has detrimental effects on the prosperity of communities. Fasching-Varner, Mitchell, Martin and Harol (2014) reported that the formerly incarcerated achieve less upward mobility than those who have not experienced incarceration. More specifically, Pew Charitable Trust (2010) found that paternal incarceration impacts family income by 22% when compared to the year before the father was incarcerated.

In addition to a focus on the concentrated poverty in these communities, there is also the consideration of the broader concentrated disadvantage that even extends to health outcomes. Recent thought has been given to the other unique ways felon disenfranchisement impacts communities. Purtle (2013) presents a health equity perspective in which he asserts a "fundamental cause approach" to reducing disparities (p. 632). This perspective calls for combatting any discriminatory practices that have a collateral effect on the health of minority communities. He argues that felon disenfranchisement laws were rooted in the same post Civil War era as other discriminatory policies, such as housing discrimination and lending restrictions. Collectively, these practices are part of the larger issue of institutional racism that do not operate separately from the many other issues stressing the disenfranchised and their communities.

Within this type of distressed community structure, the residents are often perceived to be plagued with the inability to organize due to the breakdown in the heterogeneity of community values and norms. As a result, external interventions proposed may not adequately meet the needs of the community. Clear (2007) suggests that external interventions may take on a victim-approach strategy when the community may prefer a social problems approach and choose to combat the characteristics of disorganized communities such as poverty-related issues, ethnic conflict and outward mobility (Clear & Cadora, 2003).

Community instability is a characteristic of areas with high incarceration rates. The characteristics of these socially disorganized areas may conjure up images of crime ridden neighborhoods as seen depicted on television or in films. However, often missing from those perceptions is the community element—the people. This chapter acknowledges that socially disorganized areas and those who reside in them share similar concerns with wider society. They care about the well-being of their families, they want better schools and resources for their children, and they want to be treated equitably in society. While their daily lives may prohibit them from participating in local activities designed to invoke social change, there is no reason to believe that they do not desire such change. In fact, researchers such as Podelefsky and DuBow (1980) revealed collective action in many different types of neighborhoods.

Furthermore, Lynch and Sabol (2004) suggested that community solidarity is minimized by incarceration but collective efficacy — the effective use of informal social control — is improved.

Arguably, the key to combating the cyclical impact of community disempowerment on DMC is to involve the community in the intervention decision making process. Often policy makers are not in tune with or considerate of the perceptions of resident stakeholders in concentrated incarceration communities. This in turn contributes to community distrust towards outsiders and a feeling of alienation as it relates to larger society. At times, the necessities of such communities are in contrast with the norms of wider society. For instance, St. Jean (2006) found that "preexisting socio economic and other conditions [combined with] preexisting law enforcement factors — profiling, discrimination, different responses to crime committed by blacks and Hispanics as opposed to Whites" can lead to pessimism among community members that inhibits their interest in political participation (as cited in Clear, 2007, p. 112).

Suppressed political participation prevents community members from having influence over changes in public policy. Uggen and Manza (2004) reported that communities with higher incarceration rates tend to have lower voting rates. This is at least in part due to the diminished likelihood that individuals with a felony arrest will vote. Similarly, even when it is permitted, incarcerated individuals are 27 percent less likely to vote than those who are not incarcerated. The votes of incarcerated individuals would impact the communities in which they reside even if they are not currently located within them.

This self-imposed political suppression is aggravated by state sanctioned political oppression. For neighborhoods with fewer internal resources, a diminished political capacity may be a significant deficiency for increasing external resources (Bennett, 1995). Although this chapter focuses on the impact that felon voting and DMC have on communities, a brief review of research on individual felon voting perceptions can provide some insight into how they are politically affected by disenfranchisement. As stated by Roberts (2004), mass incarceration "translates the denial of individual felon's voting rights into the disenfranchisement of entire communities" (Clear, 2007, p. 114).

In his study of homeless, ex-felons, Cardinale (2004) found that disenfranchisement reportedly caused feelings of being "a fraction of a citizen" (p.7). He suggested that this information should be used to provide a framework for understanding "how disenfranchisement influences people's views of themselves and the legitimacy of politics in general" (p. 7). In communities of concentrated incarceration, research has also revealed that residents have a tendency to view law enforcement as unjust which results in a corrosive effect of views regarding the validity and trustworthiness of governmental authority in general (Tyler and Fagan, 2005; Clear, 2007). Detachment from the political process, specifically voting, appears to be linked to the whole voting process. In Kentucky, Wahler (2006) yielded similar results in a study of parolee perceptions of felon voting restrictions. The disenfranchised parolees revealed a desire for political participation and displayed frustration with political marginalization. One respondent stated:

> ... now I have kids and I want to do the right thing. Plus, I want to have a say in what happens around me. I don't like the President and the government now and I didn't get to vote to say what's happening.... If I don't vote, then I can't complain about it, I guess ... (Wahler, 2006, p. 13).

In a 2004 study, Uggen and Manza examined "political participation, partnerships, trust in government, and attitudes about other civil disabilities" (p. 12). In short, they wanted to address the ways in which felon disenfranchisement impacted inmate opinions about community inclusion. A citizenship argument was revealed in that felon disenfranchisement policies serve as a reminder that even though released into free society, the ex-offender will not regain full citizenship. One respondent stated:

> I have no right to vote on the school referendums that will affect my children. I have no right to vote on how my taxes is going to be spent or used, which I have to pay whether I'm a felon or not, you know? So basically I've lost all voice or control over my government.

The aforementioned quote is a remarkable illustration of the damaging impact of disenfranchisement on communities towards local government level decision making. The inability to have political influence on school-based decisions can be detrimental to the youth in these areas of concentrated disenfranchisement. Nicholson-Crotty and colleagues (2009) state "investigations of the existence of and contributors to disproportionate minority contact (DMC) have occurred parallel but largely disconnected bodies of scholarship" (p. 1004). Studies have found evidence that African-American youth are also overrepresented in school discipline (Wallace, Goodkind, Wallace & Bachman, 2008). For example, African-American students represent 32% of all suspensions while making up only 17% of public school enrollment nationwide (Raffaele Mendez & Knoff, 2003; Wallace, Goodkind, Wallace & Bachman, 2008).

Removing students from school via suspension or expulsion can be particularly damaging to their futures. An exclusion from an important institution, such as school, increases their visibility by other institutions like the justice system. Nicholson-Crotty et al (2009) suggest this might be an important community predictor for juvenile arrests, which has been a decision point at which disproportionality is greatest in some urban areas (see Dawson-Edwards, Tewksbury, Higgins and Rausch, 2014).

In addition, African-American youth are more likely to be suspended, expelled or arrested for committing the same infractions as their white counterparts (see The Civil Rights Project/Advancement Project, 2000; Raffaele Mendez & Knoff, 2003; Wald & Losen, 2003). In a 2008 study primarily focused on racial disparities in school discipline, Wallace et al. (2008) found that African-American youth have comparable rates of being sent to the office for disciplinary action; however, they have a greater likelihood than any other racial or ethnic group of being suspended or expelled.

According to the Office of Juvenile Justice Delinquency and Prevention's DMC Technical Assistance Manual, community characteristics appear to contribute to different rates of offending by minority youth. More specifically, low academic achievement or residing in socially disorganized communities place minority youth in a greater risk of justice system involvement. Research has even shown that students who reside in impoverished communities have an increased likelihood of being suspended or expelled (Skiba, Nardon and Peterson, 1997).

In a 2003 article, Skiba found a relationship between suspension and incarceration rates. More importantly, he found that racial disparities in school discipline decisions impacted the likelihood of incarceration. In many jurisdictions, school discipline can be the entry point into the justice system through a practice of dual punishment (Anderson, 2004).

> When school sanctioning is handed over to law enforcement in the first instance for the vast majority of minor school infractions, not only do the offender and the victim fail to learn from the incident, and not only is the consequence more likely to be crushing rather than illuminating, but the entire community fails to take hold of the problem as a school-community matter (Dohr, 2000, p. 164; Anderson, 2004, p. 1198).

In addition to suspension, research has connected placement in alternative schools as predictors of subsequent juvenile detention (Vanderhaar, Munoz and Petrosky, 2014). Once the gatekeepers (school officials and juvenile justice representatives) open the gates to the juvenile justice system, African-Americans are overrepresented at every decision point in the juvenile justice system. The nation's adult prisons are saturated with former youth who have been sucked into the school to prison pipeline. Research indicates alarming facts about the relationship between education and contact with the criminal and/or juvenile justice system. Wald and Losen (2003) reported that 75% of youth of serving prison sentences in adult prison did not have a 10th grade education; 70% of youth in the juvenile justice system have a learning disability; and 33% of youth in the juvenile justice system read below the 4th grade level.

According to Nicholson-Crotty, Birchmeier, and Valentine (2009), very little research has focused on the relationship between the school to prison pipeline and environmental variables (i.e., poverty or urbanization). In their study of school disciplinary decisions and their impact on DMC, Nicholson-Crotty et al (2009) found that income disparities by race are positively related to the relative rate index for African American referrals. They also found that for referrals to juvenile court, racial disproportionality was higher in urban areas.

Due to the school-to-prison pipeline, prison beds are guaranteed to be filled. Fasching-Varner and colleagues (2014) presented a different framework and encourage discourse centered on the "prison-to-school" pipeline, which asserts that incarceration is not merely a result of criminal activity and failing schools. Rather, they contend, the impact of the prison industrial complex and educational reform complex demonstrates that prisons demand a clientele and thus perpetuate policies designed that guarantee such clientele. While tough on crime rhetoric is becoming less politically popular, "Smart on Crime" initiatives do not appear to be focusing on the collateral consequences of conviction, such as felon disenfranchisement. Though states that are reducing the incarceration rates may eventually see less concentrated incarceration, in the immediate future these policies have no impact on concentrated disenfranchisement, especially in states with lifetime disenfranchisement policies. Without more bi-partisan attention communities will continue to be politically disempowered thus exacerbating DMC (see Dawson-Edwards, 2015) and the prison pipeline. Rose and Clear (1998) suggest that while the unintended consequences of incarceration may not seem to have a tremendous impact individually, "their combined effects may be devastating" (p. 457). The argument here is that the 'combined effects' are, in fact, devastating, especially to the African-American community in terms of the intentional and unintentional consequences on their political empowerment. While research has shown that incarceration is concentrated in certain areas and impacts categories of people demographically there still remains a dearth in the literature regarding its collateral damage in communities of color (Clear, Rose & Ryder, 2001). The concentration of incarceration is easily pinpointed through sentencing related statistics and sentencing disparities are empirically evident in both the adult and juvenile justice systems.

For adults, thirty-eight percent of incarcerated individuals are African-American (U.S. Census Bureau, 2007). According to The Sentencing Project (2010), racial and ethnic minorities make up over 60% of those imprisoned.

Furthermore, one in eight African-American males in their twenties is incarcerated (The Sentencing Project, 2010). Mauer and King (2007) reported that African-Americans make up 900,000 of the 2.2 million individuals behind bars. Across the country, incarceration ratios between African-Americans and whites vary tremendously with an average national ratio of 5.6. The King and Mauer (2007) report also showed that the highest black-to-white ratios of incarceration are found in states located in the Northeast or Midwest. In conjunction with incarceration ratios, research has shown a concentration of offender reentry patterns as well (Lynch & Sabol, 2001). In 1998, five states reportedly absorbed almost half of all released offenders (Lynch & Sabol, 2001).

Intrastate analysis reveals that the reentry concentration is found in certain counties and can even be extracted down to the neighborhood level. For example, research in Cuyahoga County, Ohio used census block groups to operationalize neighborhoods and communities near or in Cleveland. The research revealed that only three percent of the census blocks were the home community for 20% of the state prison population. In addition, the one day incarcerate rate was calculated and found an 8–15 percent rate for African-American males 18–29 years of age (Lynch & Sabol, 2001).

Statistics like these are easily disregarded by those who argue that the disparate impact would not be felt had the offender not committed the crime. However, the counterargument is such: the origins of these laws did not account for the numerous amounts of felonies possible in modern times. Offenses or activities that are now felonies were not considered so when felon disenfranchisement laws were created. For example, it has only been in the last twenty years that drug felonies such as "intent" and "conspiracy to distribute a controlled substance" have appeared. Other "get tough on crime" reforms, such as three-strikes-and-you're-out laws, make a third offense the eligible trigger for lifetime incarceration, which also has not been the historic punishment for most crimes.

Furthermore, research asserts that the dramatic increase in the U.S. correctional population, from 1.8 million in 1980 to 6.9 million in 2003 (King & Mauer, 2004), has had a significant collateral impact on the political engagement of African-Americans. This increase appears to have wider and arguably detrimental consequences for African-American men. Fellner and Mauer (1998) reported that 13% of African-American men in the U.S. are ineligible to vote due to felony convictions. As previously mentioned while, there are approximately 5.85 million Americans disenfranchised due to felony convictions (The Sentencing Project, 2015), 2.2 million African-Americans are barred from voting due to felony disenfranchisement (Uggen, Shannon and Manza, 2010). In addition, at some point in their life, three in 10 African-American men lose their right to vote due to a felony conviction (The Sentencing Project, 2008).

The statistics become more alarming when considering the state and local level impact. For instance, in Alabama and Florida, thirty-one percent of African-American men cannot vote due to felony convictions (Fellner & Mauer, 1998). Twenty-three percent of black Floridians are ineligible to vote due to felony convictions (The Sentencing Project, 2015). The League of Women Voters in Kentucky, in an October 2006 study reported an assessment of such dilution in the Commonwealth. First, they found that one of seventeen Kentuckians is disenfranchised due to a felony conviction. Second, Kentucky has the sixth highest disenfranchisement rate in the country. Third, 90% of disenfranchised Kentuckians are not imprisoned (League of Women Voters, 2006). Fourth, two-thirds of the Kentucky disenfranchised have completed their sentences. Finally, one in four African-Americans in Kentucky is disenfranchised due to felony convictions. This final statistic is triple the national rate for African-American felony disenfranchisement. More updated calculations find that twenty-two percent of black Kentucky adults cannot vote due to felony disenfranchisement (The Sentencing Project, 2015).

In *The Vanishing Black Electorate*, King and Mauer (2004) examined the state and local level impact of these laws, specifically focusing on areas with high levels of disenfranchised persons. Their findings illustrate the need for providing a voice for the voiceless. In the state of Georgia, one in eight black males is disenfranchised. For the city of Atlanta, one in seven black males cannot vote as a result of a felony conviction. This dilution is most prominent in zip codes that have high concentrations of convicted felons. In addition to the previously mentioned research, other data reflects an unfortunate trend of voter dilution as a result of felon voting prohibitions.

More importantly, black males are not affected in a vacuum. The collateral impact is felt in the political power of others in those communities (see Lynch & Sabol, 2001). Following this line of thinking, King and Mauer (2004) also looked at the effect disenfranchisement had on the diminished political strength and its "chilling effect on political engagement of certain neighborhoods" (p. 15). They reported that "given the concentration of felony disenfranchisement in primarily African-American communities, persons who have not been convicted of a felony are affected through the diminished strength of their political voice" (King & Mauer, 2004, p. 15).

King and Mauer (2004) note that political candidates focus on areas where they believe they have the potential for the most support. When a community's voting power is compromised by felon voting laws, then campaigning in that area is unlikely. The electoral campaign is often the point at which the candidate is open to talk with constituents, this disregard is disadvantageous for low income or minority populated communities because they are inhibited from communicating with potential lawmakers at the most influential time. King and Mauer (2004) assert that as the prison populations continue to increase, the demands of residents in communities of color will continue to be silenced due to felon disenfranchisement policies and subsequent community disempowerment. In her 2003 research, Brown-Dean captures this sentiment when she stated: "the cumulative impact of these statutes simultaneously dilutes the full development of African-American political equality and American democracy by reinforcing the politics of exclusion" (p. 15).

Conclusion

This chapter should not be construed as painting a bleak picture on the future of communities of color. Much can be done to mobilize and empower these disempowered and disorganized communities. The purpose here was to expose the invisible factors that exacerbate the cycle of despair. Communities with no political power are overlooked by political candidates. The campaign period is the time at which a political candidate hears the voices of constituents and makes promises in exchange for support. If candidates are not campaigning in communities because large numbers of members cannot vote, then the voice of the community is silenced. The communities discussed in this chapter cannot afford to be silenced. It is their silence that keeps them from progressing. With no voice in who is elected to represent them, they are left to be passively content with the manner in which children of color are treated by the school system, funneled into the juvenile justice system and caught in the cycles of exiles perpetuated by the adult criminal justice system.

> This disenfranchisement effect contributes to a vicious cycle within public policy development that further disadvantages low-income communities of color. The first means by which this occurs is through decisions on resource allocation. In citywide decisionmaking regarding spending for schools or social services, residents of certain neighborhoods will have considerably more political influence than others, solely because "one person, one vote" is distorted through the loss of voting rights (King & Mauer, 2004, p. 15).

Since it was public policy that provided the mechanisms for these disparities to exist, it seems likely that public policy will be the change needed to eradicate DMC. As it relates to political disempowerment of African-American communities, the Voting Rights Act of 1965 clearly outlaws voter dilution by race. The Act has increasingly become a popular mechanism by which to make claims, or at least arguments, against felony disenfranchisement. The Act was passed to circumvent strategies that were created to dilute or deny the minority vote. The act was particularly focused on southern states that purposefully eluded the Fifteenth Amendment through the use of literacy tests (Dugree-Pearson, 2002). It served to bolster the Fifteenth Amendment by barring any "voting qualification or prerequisite to voting, or standard, practice, or proce dure . . . by any state or political subdivision in a manner which results in a denial or abridgement of the right of a citizen of the United States to vote on account of race or color" (Hench, 1998, p. 744, 746).

The case, *Wesley v. Collins* (1986), concerned a Tennessee ex-felon who challenged the Tennessee Voting Rights Act by claiming it diluted the voting power of the non-criminal, minority community (Hench, 1998). The Sixth Circuit rejected the argument and held that although the totality of circumstances supported a claim of discrimination the "facts could not be tied to historical tradition and rationale for the disenfranchisement of felons" (Simson, 2002, p. 61). Since *Wesley*, there have been a number of felon voting rights cases that demonstrate the continued confusion the judiciary has in finding a consistent interpretation of the Voting Rights Act. As it stands, the very piece of legislation designed to protect against voter dilution has been deemed inapplicable due to the indirect disempowerment to minority communities. This is incomprehensible considering this entire chapter has outlined how the disempowerment of communities of color is a direct result of discriminatory practices of the past. Countless discriminatory actions and policies have compounded the problems of the "ghetto" to the extent that many interpret these ills as inherent in the fabric of these neighborhoods. These are not ills inherent to the people in high poverty-high incarceration-disproportionately disenfranchised communities. They are a result of a perfect storm of public policy coupled with institutional racism that continues to block a segment of citizens out of democracy.

As a form of political racism, felon disenfranchisement is a practice that continues the legacy of barring certain categories citizens from tapping into the power of government and politics. Political racism is apparent in the results of elections, the power brokers behind the scenes and political appointments (Miller & Garran, 2008). While there is evidence that felon voting laws have impacted the number of eligible voters enough to change outcomes of state and federal elections, the direct impact it has on communities needs to be further examined. Since public policy and courts are not likely to change these laws, the daily lives of residents in these politically suppressed communities are not likely to change until more evidence of dilution is presented and community empowerment is demanded.

References

Advancement Project, (2005). *Education on Lockdown: The Schoolhouse to Jail-house Track.* Available online at: http://www.advancementproject.org/sites/default/files/publications/FINALEOLrep.pdf.

Anderson, C.L. (2004). Double jeopardy: The modern dilemma for juvenile justice. *University of Pennsylvania Law Review,* 152, 1181.

Baker v. Pataki, 85 F. 3d 919 (2nd Cir. 1996).

Behrens, A. (2004). Voting—not quite a fundamental right? A look at the legal and legislative challenges to felon disenfranchisement law. *Minnesota Law Review* 89, 231.

Behrens, A., Uggen, C. & Manza, J. (2003). Ballot manipulation and the "menace of negro domination": Racial threat and felon disenfranchisement in the United States, 1850–2002. *American Journal of Sociology,* 109 (3), 559–605.

Bennett, S.F. (1995). Community organizations and crime. *Annals of the American Academy of Political and Social Science,* 539, 72–84.

Bonczar, T.P. (2003). Prevalence of Imprisonment in the U.S. Population, 1974–2001. Washington, DC: Bureau of Justice Statistics.

Boyd, G. (2001). The drug war is the new Jim Crow. New York: American Civil Liberties Union.

Brewer, R.M. & Heitzeg, N.A. (2008). The racialization of crime and punishment criminal justice, color-blind racism, and the political economy of the Prison Industrial Complex. *American Behavioral Scientist,* 51 (5), 625–644.

Brown-Dean, K. (2003). *One lens, multiple views: Felon disenfranchisement laws and American political inequality.* (Doctoral dissertation, The Ohio State University, 2003). *Dissertation Abstracts International,* 65, 675.

Browne, J. (nd). The labor of doing time. Available at: http://www.angelfire.com/sc2/mplu/time.html.

Bursik, Jr., R. J., and Grasmick, H.G. (1993). *Neighborhoods and Crime: The Dimensions of Effective Community Control.* New York: Lexington Books.

Cardinale, M. (2004). *Triple Decker Disenfranchisement: First Person Accounts of Losing the Right to Vote Among Poor, Homeless Americans with a Felony Conviction.* The Sentencing Project. Available online at: www.sentencingproject.org.

Chin, G.J. (2004). Reconstruction, felon disenfranchisement, and the right to vote: Did the Fifteenth Amendment repeal Section 2 of the Fourteenth Amendment? *Georgetown Law Journal,* 92, 259.

City of Mobile v. Bolden, 446 U.S. 55, (1980).

Clear, T.R. (2007). *Imprisoning Communities: How Mass Incarceration Makes Disadvantaged Neighborhoods Worse.* Oxford University Press: New York, NY.

Clear, T.R. & Cadora, E. (2003). *Community Justice*. Wadsworth: Belmont, CA.

Clear, T.R., Rose, D. & Ryder, J.A. (2001). Incarceration and the community: The problem of removing and returning offenders. *Crime & Delinquency*, 47(3), 335–351.

Clear, T.R., Rose, D.R., Waring, E. & Scully, K. (2003). Coercive mobility and crime: A preliminary examination of concentrated incarceration and social disorganization. *Justice Quarterly*, 20(1), 33–64.

Coyle, M. (2003). State-based advocacy on felony disenfranchisement. Available online at: http://www.sentencingproject.org/pdfs/5083.pdf.

Davis, A. (2003). *Are prisons obsolete?* New York: Seven Stories Press.

Dawson, M. (1994). *Behind the Mule: Race and class in African American politics*. Princeton, NJ: Princeton University Press.

Dawson-Edwards, C., Tewksbury, R., Higgins, G,E. & Rausch, C. (2014). Kentucky DMC Assessment Report.

Dawson-Edwards, C. (2015). Disrupting Democracy: Felony disenfranchisement laws in the Smart on Crime Era. Uprooting Criminology. Available online at: http://uprootingcriminology.org/blogs/disrupting-democracy -felony-disenfranchisement-laws-smart-crime-era/

Dohr, B. (2000). Look out, kid, It's something you did: The criminalization of children. In *The Public Assault on America's Children: Poverty, Violence, and Juvenile Injustice*. Ed. Valerie Polakow.

Dubois, W.E.B. (1899/1973). *The Philadelphia Negro: A Social Study*. Millwood, New York: Kraus-Thomson Organization Limited.

Dubois, W.E.B. (1901). The spawn of slavery. *The Missionary Review of the World, 14*, 737–745.

Dubois, W.E.B. (1935). *Black Reconstruction in America*. New York: Hartcourt, Brace & Company.

Dugree-Pearson, T. (2002). Disenfranchisement — A race neutral punishment for felony offenders or way to diminish the minority vote? *Hamline Journal of Public Law & Policy, 23*, 359.

Fagan, J. (2006). *Incarceration and Voting*. Unpublished memorandum to the Project on Concentrated Incarceration of the Open Institute.

Fasching-Varner, K.J., Mitchell, R.W. & Martin, L.L. (2014). Beyond school to prison pipeline and toward an educational and penal realism. *Equity and Excellence in Education*, 47(4), 410–429.

Fellner, J. & Mauer, M. (1998). Losing the vote: The impact of felony disenfranchisement laws in the United States. Human Rights Watch & The Sentencing Commission. Available at: http://www.hrw.org/reports98/vote.

Fuentes, (2003). Discipline and punish. The Nation.

Glanton, D. (2004, July 28). Restoring felons' voting rights a heated election-year issue in Fla., *Chicago Tribune*. Retrieved on October, 29, 2004 at www.kentucky.com.

Gottfredson, S.D. &. Taylor, R. B. (1988). Community contexts and criminal offenders. In Tim Hope and Margaret Shaw (Eds.), *Communities and Crime Reduction*. London: Her Majesty's Stationery Office.

Greene, H.T. & Gabbidon, S.L. (2000). *African American Criminological Thought*. Albany, NY: State University of New York Press.

Hench, V.E. (1998). The death of voting rights: The legal disenfranchisement of minority voters. *Case Western Reserve*, 48, 777.

Hsia, H.M., Bridges, G.S. & McHale, R. (2004). *Disproportionate Minority Confinement: 2002 Update*. Office of Juvenile Justice and Delinquency. Available online at: http://www.ncjrs.gov/pdffiles1/ojjdp/201240.pdf.

Hunter v. Underwood, 471 U.S. 222 (1985).

Jargowsky, P.A. (1997). *Poverty and Place: Ghettos, Barrios, and the American City*. Sage: New York, NY.

Jargowsky, P.A. & Bane, M.J. (1991). Ghetto Poverty: Basic Questions. In C. Jenks & P.E. Peterson (Eds.). *The Urban Underclass*. Washington: The Brookings Institute.

Johnson-Parris, A.S. (2003). Felon disenfranchisement: The unconscionable social contract breached. *Virginia Law Review, 89*, 109.

Kempf-Leonard, K. (2007). Minority youths and juvenile justice: Disproportionate minority contact after 20 years of reform efforts. *Youth Violence and Juvenile Justice*, 5(1), 71–87.

Keyssar, A. (2000). *The Right to Vote: The Contested History of Democracy in the United States*. New York: Basic Books.

King, R.S. & Mauer, M. (2004). The Vanishing Black Electorate: Felony Disenfranchisement in Atlanta, Georgia. The Sentencing Project. Available [online] at: www.sentencingproject.org.

Kornhauser, R.R. (1978). *Social Sources of Delinquency: An Appraisal of Analytic Models*. Chicago: University of Chicago Press.

Kousser, J.M. (1984). The undermining of the First Reconstruction lessons for the Second. *Minority Dilution, 27*, 34.

League of Women Voters. (2006). Felony Disenfranchisement in the Commonwealth of Kentucky: A Report of the League of Women Voters of Kentucky. The Sentencing Project.

Lynch, J.P. & Sabol, W.J. (2001). Prisoner Reentry in Perspective. The Urban Institute. Available online at: www.urban.org/uploadedPDF/410213_reentry.pdf.

Mancini, M.J. (1978). Race, economics, and the abandonment of convict leasing. *The Journal of Negro History*, Vol. 63, No. 4 (Oct., 1978), pp. 339–352.

Manza, J., Brooks, C. & Uggen, C. (2004). Public attitudes toward felon disenfranchisement in the United States. *Public Opinion Quarterly*, 68 (2): 275–286.

Manza, J. & Uggen, C. (2002). Democratic contradiction? The political consequences of felon disenfranchisement. *American Sociological Review 67*, 777–803.

Manza, J. & Uggen, C. (2006). *Locked Out: Felon Disenfranchisement and American Democracy*. Oxford University Press: New York, NY.

Massey, D.S. & Denton, N.A. (1993). The spatial concentration of affluence and poverty during the 1970s. *Urban Affairs Quarterly*, 29, 299–315.

Mauer, M. & King, R. (2007). *A 25-year Quagmire: The War on Drugs and its Impact on Society*. The Sentencing Project. Available online at: http://www.sentencingproject.org/doc/publications/dp_25yearquagmire.pdf.

Miller, J. & Garran, A. (2008). *Racisim in the United States: Implications for the Helping Professions*. Brooks/Cole: Belmont, CA.

Muntaqim v. Coombe, 366 F. 3d. 102 (2nd Cir. 2004).

NAACP Legal Defense Fund. Dismantling the School to Prison Pipeline. Available online at: http://www.naacpldf.org/content/pdf/pipeline/Dismantling_the_School_to_Prison_Pipeline.pdf.

National Council on Crime and Delinquency. (2007). *And Justice for Some: Differential Treatment of Youth of Color in the Justice System*. Oakland: NCCD.

Nicholson-Crotty, S., Birchmeier, Z. & Valentine, D. (2009). Exploring the impact of school discipline on racial disproportionality in the juvenile justice system. *Social Science Quarterly*, 90(4), 1003–1018.

Office of Juvenile Justice Delinquency Prevention (2009). DMC Technical Assistance Manual. Available online at: http://www.ojjdp.gov/compliance/dmc_ta_manual.pdf

Oregon v. Mitchell, 400 U.S. 112 (1970).

Podolefsky, A. & DuBow, F. (1980). *Strategies for Community Crime Prevention: Collective Responses to Crime in Urban America*. Reactions to Crime Project, Center for Urban Affairs. Evanston, IL: Northwestern University Press.

Price, M. (2002). Addressing ex-felon disenfranchisement: legislation vs. litigation. *Journal of Law and Policy*, 11, 369.

Raffaele Mendez, L.M. & Knoff, H.M. (2003). Who gets suspended from school and why: A demographic analysis of schools and disciplinary infractions in a large school district. *Education and Treatment of Children*, 26, 30–51.

Reuter, Theodore. 1995. "The New Black Conservatives." In T.J. Reuter (Ed.), *The Politics of Race: African Americans and the Political System*. New York: M.E. Sharpe.

Richardson v. Ramirez, 418 U.S. 24 (1974).

Roberts, D. (2004). The social and moral cost of mass incarceration in African American communities. *Stanford Law Review, 56*(5), 1271–1305.

Rose, D.R. (1995). Fighting back against crime and disorder: An examination of Neighborhood based organizations and social disorganization theory. Unpublished dissertation, Department of Sociology, Duke University, Durham, N.C.

Rose, J.C. (1906). Negro suffrage: The constitutional point of view. *American Political Science Review, 1* (17), 25–27.

Rose, D.R. & Clear, T.R. (1998). Incarceration, social capital, and crime: Implications for Social Disorganization Theory. Criminology, 36(3), 441–480.

Shapiro, A.L. (1993). Challenging criminal disenfranchisement under the Voting Rights Act: A new strategy. *Yale Law Journal, 103*, 537.

Shaw, C. R. & McKay, H.D. (1942). *Juvenile Delinquency and Urban Areas*. Chicago: University of Chicago Press.

Shichor, D. (1995). *Punishment for Profit Private Prisons/Public Concerns*. Thousand Oaks, CA: Sage Publications.

Sidanius, James. 1993. "The Inevitability of Oppression and the Dynamics of Social Dominance." In P.M. Sniderman, P.E. Tetlock & E.G. Carmines (Eds.), *Prejudice, Politics, and the American Dilemma*. Stanford: Stanford University Press.

Simson, E. (2002). Justice denied: How felony disenfranchisement laws undermine American democracy. Americans For Democratic Action Education Fund. Available online at: www.adaction.org.

Skiba, R.J., Nardon, R.S., & Peterson, R.L. (2002). The color of discipline: Sources of racial and gender disproportionality in school punishment. *The Urban Review*, 34(4), 317–342.

Skiba, R., Simmons, A., Staudinger, L., Rausch, M., Dow, G. & Feggins, R. (2003). *Consistent removal: Contributions of school discipline to the school-prison pipeline*. Paper presented at the School to Prison Pipeline Conference, Harvard University, Cambridge, MA.

Spear, A. (1971). The origins of the urban ghetto, 1870–1915. In N.I. Huggins, M. Kilson & D.M. Fox (Eds.). *Key Issues in the Afro-American Experience*. New York: Harcourt Brace Jovanovich, Inc.

Special Project. (1970). Collateral Consequences of a Criminal Conviction, *Vanderbilt Law Review, 23*, p. 929.

Stahl, A., Finnegan, T. & Kang, W. (2005). *Easy access to juvenile court statistics: 1985–2002.* Retrieved from http://ojjdp.ncjrs.org/ojstatbb/ezajcs/.

Stinchcomb, Bazemore, Reistenberg, (2006). Beyond zero tolerance: Restoring justice in secondary schools. *Youth Violence and Juvenile Justice,* 4, 123–147.

The Sentencing Project. (2008). Felony Disenfranchisement Laws in the United States. Available online at: http://sentencingproject.org/Admin/Docu ments/publications/fd_bs_fdlawsinus.pdf.

The Sentencing Project. (2010). Racial Disparity Page. Available online at: http://www.sentencingproject.org/template/page.cfm?id=122.

The Sentencing Project. (2015). Policy Brief: Felony Disenfranchisement.http://sentencingproject.org/doc/publications/fd_Felony%20Disenfranchise ment%20Primer.pdf.

Thompson, M.E. (2002). Don't do the crime if you ever intend to vote again: Challenging disenfranchisement of ex-felons as cruel and unusual punishment. *Seton Hall Law Review, 33,* 167.

Ture, K. & Hamilton, C. [1967]1992. *Black Power: The Politics of Liberation in America.* New York: Random House.

Tyler, T.R. & Fagan, J. (2005). *Legitimacy and Cooperation: Why Do People Help the Police Fight Crime in Their Communities?* Columbia Public Law Research Paper No. 06-99. Available at SSRN: http://ssrn.com/abstract=887737.

Vanderhaar, J., Munoz, M. & Petrosko, J. (2014) "Reconsidering the Alternatives: The Relationship Between Suspension, Disciplinary Alternative School Placement, Subsequent Juvenile Detention, and the Salience of Race," *Journal of Applied Research on Children: Informing Policy for Children at Risk.* 5(2), Available at: http://digitalcommons.library.tmc.edu/childre natrisk/vol5/iss2/14

Wahler, E. (2006). Losing the right to vote: Perceptions of permanent disenfranchisement and the civil rights restoration application process in the state of Kentucky. The Sentencing Project. Available [online] at: http://www.sentencingproject.org/pdfs/ky-losingtherighttovote.pdf.

Wald J. & Losen D.J. (2003). Defining and redirecting a school-to-prison pipeline. *New Directions for Youth Development,* 99, 9–15.

Wallace, J.M., Goodkind, S., Wallace, C.M. & Bachman, A.G. (2008). Racial, ethnic, and gender differences in school discipline among U.S. high school students. *Negro Education Review,* 59(1–2), 47–62.

Wesley v. Collins, 791 F.2d 1255, 1262 (6th Cir. 1986).

Wilson, W.J. (1973). *Power, Racism, and Privilege: Race Relations in Theoretical and Sociopolitical Perspectives.* New York: Free Press.

Wilson, W.J. (1987). *The Truly Disadvantaged.* Chicago: University of Chicago.

Uggen, C. & Manza, J. (2004). Lost Voices: The Civic and Political Views of Disenfranchised Felons. P. 165–204. In D.M. Dattilo, D. Weiman & Western, B. (Eds.), *Imprisoning America: The Social Effects of Mass Incarceration*. New York: Russell Sage Foundation.

Uggen, C. & Manza, J. (2004). Punishment and democracy: Disenfranchisement of nonincarcerated felons in the United States. Symposium: *U.S. Elections*, 2 (30).

Uggen, C., Shannon, S. & Manza, J. (2010). State-level estimates of felon disenfranchisement in the United States, 2010. Washington, D.C.: The Sentencing Project. Retrieved from http://www.sentencingproject.org/doc/publications/fd_State_Level_Estimates_of_Felon_Disen_2010.pdf

U.S. Census Bureau. (2007). 2006 American Community Survey. Available online at: http://www.census.gove/acs/www/index.html.

Chapter 14

Tackling the DMC Mandate: Researchers and Universities as Local Resources

Nicolle Parsons-Pollard

This chapter was an outgrowth of many conversations with local agency heads, judges, court service unit employees, and other practitioners in the field of criminal and juvenile justice systems that have heard of disproportionate minority contact (DMC) and thought their jurisdiction might have a problem but had no idea how the DMC mandate impacted them or what, if anything, to do about it.

From 2007 to 2013 Virginia State University has hosted a conference along with the Virginia Department of Criminal Justice Services (DCJS) and the Virginia Department of Corrections on disproportionate minority contact in the criminal and juvenile justice systems. The initial conference was funded by an internal grant at the university and provided the funds necessary to secure a location, materials and a guest speaker, William Feyerherm, who was one of the parties responsible for devising the method used to measure disproportionality. While the conference topics have ranged from policing and race to the impact of race and ethnicity on social service issues, there have been few *real* discussions about how the requirements of the Juvenile Justice and Delinquency Prevention (JJDP) Act of 1974, as amended, are applicable. Likewise, the Office of Juvenile Justice and Delinquency Prevention (OJJDP) has several documents available on its website from literature reviews to projects on risk assessment and just recently added a practical manual entitled *Reducing Disproportionate Minority Contact: Preparation at the Local Level.* This latest document and another funded by OJJDP, *Seven Steps to Develop and Evaluate Strategies to Reduce Disproportionate Minority Contact (DMC),* coupled with the *DMC Technical Assistance Manual 4th Edition,* get closest to what localities can actually "do" about reducing disproportionate minority contact in their area. But while these documents exist, discussions about their utility are often very different when I talk to practitioners. Unlike academicians and researchers, I have found that some practitioners are mired down in the real down and dirty details of the system and the day-to-day operations and have little time to pontificate about how to best incorporate some of the existing research. This chapter will hopefully shed some light on how practitioners can partner with researchers to get to the meat of the DMC mandate and answer some of the questions necessary to cope with overrepresentation.

The DMC Mandate

Disproportionate minority contact (DMC) means that a disparate number of minorities come into contact with the criminal and juvenile justice systems in relationship to their representation in the general population. Since 1988 Congress has attempted to respond to DMC through the Juvenile Justice and Delinquency Prevention (JJDP) Act. The Act has been revised several times and each time the emphasis on DMC issues was strengthened (Kakar, 2006). In the past, DMC focused strictly on "confinement" in secure and correctional facilities and adult jails and lockups, but after much observation it was determined that disproportionality existed across all decision points therefore DMC was changed to focus on "contact" throughout the system. In 1992, the reauthorization of the JJDP Act included disproportionate minority confinement as a core requirement for states receiving Title II Formula Grant funding and in 2002 the emphasis was changed to "disproportionate minority contact" (Nellis, 2005).

OJJDP mandates that States address the issue of DMC in phases, which include: identification, assessment, intervention, and evaluation and monitoring (U.S. Department of Justice, 2000). Phase one of the mandate entails descriptive data collection to determine if DMC exists and the extent of the problem in which of the decision points (arrest, referral, diversion, detention, petition/charges filed, delinquent findings, probation, confinement in secure correctional facilities, and transfer to adult court). The second phase attempts to explain why minority overrepresentation exists and what factors are contributing to it. Because each phase builds on the next, if a locality has difficulty in gathering comprehensive data in phase one it will undoubtedly impact phase two. Phases three and four deal directly with the interventions and performance measures. Phase three focuses on developing interventions or programs to reduce overrepresentation and phase four requires evaluation of implemented interventions. Lastly, phase five addresses the ongoing monitoring of trends to determine whether DMC has improved, worsened or remained steady.

While decades have passed since the initial DMC mandate was approved, its effectiveness has received some criticism (Leiber, 2002; Nellis & Richardson, 2010). For example, black youth comprised 17% of the population aged 10–17 yet they represented 52% of arrests for violent crimes in 2012 (Puzzanchera, 2012). Since the first edition of this book the violent arrest rate for black youth rose 1 percent from 51% (Puzzanchera, 2007). And according to Pope and Feyerherm (1995) a "race effect" can be found at various decision points and may have direct or indirect impacts and amass as juveniles move deeper into the system.

Researchers and Universities as Local Partners

When reviewing the DMC mandate it becomes apparent that universities hold a vast amount of resources that can be helpful in reducing overrepresentation. However, one of the greatest problems organizations can have is deciding with whom to develop partnerships. Soler and Garry (2009) suggest that organizations establish steering committees and work with a variety of stakeholders. While this is of the utmost importance, committee members and stakeholders generally won't possess the levels of expertise or time to assist agencies in the research process. From the perspective of this chapter, one logical partner would be universities and their faculty. As faculty, most are obligated to do research, service (including community service), and teach. While this is evident to those in academia, it is not so obvious to others. I often hear from my practitioner friends that they didn't realize faculty had to do anything other than teach for the most part and even if they knew that publishing was a part of those obligations practitioners aren't always sure where that fits into the grand scheme of things for them.

Specifically, when analyzing the five phases of the mandate, it requires that localities collaborate with outside agencies to successfully complete each phase. For example, whether it is data collection for the identification phase, assessment, assistance with implementation or evaluation, most universities have faculty that are not only willing but also extremely capable. There is rarely a project too big or too small with which some faculty won't want to be involved. And while the motive may be self-serving on both parts, what could be better than a partnership with people who are vested in a positive outcome for their community?

Other Resources for Partnership

There are others who work closely with the issue of DMC and they are often looking for ways to merge their interests with other agencies and organizations as well. For example, the W. Haywood Burns Institute is a nonprofit organization that works with more than forty jurisdictions in the United States to reduce DMC. The Burns Institute utilizes data and consensus building to help stakeholders develop community based alternatives to detention for youth (www.burnsinstitute.org).

The Annie E. Casey Foundation is a charitable organization, which was founded to "foster public policies, human-service reforms, and community supports that more effectively meet the needs of today's vulnerable children and families" (www.aecf.org). One of the Casey Foundation's missions is to reduce the number of youth in juvenile detention through their Juvenile Detention Alternatives Initiative (JDAI). JDAI has been implemented in 100 jurisdictions and supplies participants with grant funding, training, planning, and technical support (www.aecf.org). The John D. and Catherine T. MacArthur Foundation also has a DMC focus through the Models for Change initiative, which supports selected states to reform the juvenile justice system while holding youthful offenders accountable for their actions (www.modelsforchange.net).

In contrast to the aforementioned organizations that work with juveniles, the Sentencing Project focuses on adult disparity. The Sentencing Project was originally founded to provide defense attorneys advocacy training with the intention of reducing incarceration rates (www.sentencingproject.org). Since that time it has also become a leader in research and promotion of disparate treatment, sentencing policy, collateral consequences of incarceration and felony disenfranchisement. Lastly, agencies should remember to look toward federal agencies like the Office of Juvenile Justice and Delinquency Prevention (OJJDP). OJJDP has led the charge against DMC and has supported the reauthorization of the JJDP Act and works closely with states to fulfill the requirements. While all of the previously mentioned resources are important to ameliorating DMC, the most important resource for any jurisdiction will be the local resources that will be available once the hard work of addressing the mandate has started and any ongoing monitoring afterwards.

You Have a Partnership, Now What?

To tackle any issue one must first know if there is a problem and if so to what extent. Most agencies, whether they believe they have a DMC problem or not, are basing their assertions on anecdotal information. Partnering with some of the entities previously mentioned as well as university researchers can provide agencies with the information and manpower to find out whether DMC really exists, where, and how to deal with it.

Do We Have an Issue with DMC?

The first phase is identification. According to the OJJDP *DMC Technical Assistance Manual* (2009) this stage involves describing the extent of overrepresentation and where the overrepresentation takes place in the system, and provides an ongoing measurement of DMC. Disproportionate minority contact is measured utilizing the relative rate index (RRI). The RRI is a calculation used to compare juvenile justice contact by different racial and ethnic groups. The Office of Juvenile Justice and Delinquency Prevention defines minorities as American Indian and Alaska Native, Asian, Black or African American, Hispanic or Latino, and Native Hawaiian or other Pacific Islanders (www.ojjdp.ncjrs.gov). For each group the RRI can be determined by dividing one group's rate at any given decision point (intake, arrest, court referral, waiver, etc.) by another group's rate. For example, in 2013, the national RRI for juvenile arrests for blacks in comparison to whites was 2.3, which represents an increase from the 2005 data initially used in the first edition of this text (www.ojjdp.ncjrs.gov). This indicates that blacks were arrested at more than twice the rate of whites.

The process of gathering the appropriate data for the identification phase is vitally important not only because it impacts the development of the other phases but because studies have shown that overrepresentation is rarely reflected in a "single decision" or in "the presence or absences of a single attribute in a juvenile justice system" (Devine, Coolbaugh & Jenkins, 1998, p. 4).

Utilizing researchers from universities at this phase will provide a few advantages: 1) data collection can be done right the first time; 2) researchers have the ability to apply greater statistical analysis to the data; and 3) researchers can provide a road map for the other phases.

Collecting the data correctly the first time is crucial. Data collection can be a daunting task simply because many states don't have systems that share information with one another. So police data, court data, and child welfare data may all have information on the same juvenile but they in no way connect to one another. According to Bilchik (2010), one of the five key elements to achieving racial and ethnic equity is to increase transparency. He asserts that increased transparency will allow data collection across agency boundaries. Researchers can provide some assistance in understanding how the systems are interrelated and how best to get the appropriate data and more importantly what to do when you can't.

Researchers also have the ability to apply greater statistical analysis to the data. For example, it is suggested that juvenile justice data should be utilized as baseline data but the collection of qualitative data may also prove useful. Collecting information from juveniles in the system and practitioners who work with them can also shed light on the quantitative baseline data (Nellis, 2005). In addition to qualitative analysis, it may be necessary to utilize multivariate analysis. This type of analysis allows for observing more than one variable at a time (or in this case, factors impacting DMC) and holds other factors constant to determine the influence. This type of analysis is also very helpful in the other phases of the DMC mandate.

Lastly, researchers can help to provide guidance on the project for the future. Since the identification phase is the first phase, researchers will be able to advise agencies about future phases based on the data collected. Given that the data collected in the identification stage impacts the rest of the processes, it is vital that agencies know what lies ahead.

You Have a DMC Issue, Now What?

Disproportionate minority contact is a very touchy issue because it deals with race and ethnicity and once you say it is a problem no one wants to be the cause for that problem. First and foremost, agencies should use their researchers to their advantage. Let the researchers do the dirty work of reporting where in the system DMC exists and introduce what the literature supports to reduce it. Allowing the researchers to take over this part of the discussion takes away any hard feelings between parties that will have to work together after this phase of the project has been completed.

Often once a jurisdiction finds they have a DMC problem they skip to the intervention phase and start new programs or decide to continue doing what they have always done but "*tweak*" it to focus on DMC. Rarely do these approaches have any long lasting impact. As noted in chapter 2, this has been identified as one of the reasons why most jurisdictions don't see a reduction in DMC. The fact of the matter is practitioners think very differently about funding than researchers think of it. While well meaning, practitioners generally want to take funding and dive right into creating programs to help people. After all, they are generally in what we refer to as "helping professions" and from their perspective getting funding as closely aligned with those who are having the challenges is the best possible solution. However, when working with researchers they can help agencies and practitioners understand the benefits of assessment prior to the implementation of a program that seems promising.

Assessment

The assessment stage is probably the most important stage and yet the most difficult. As previously mentioned the success of this stage is largely dependent on comprehensiveness of the identification stage. The assessment stage is where a jurisdiction looks at the decision points (arrest, referral, diversion, detention, petition/charges filed, delinquent findings, probation, confinement in secure correctional facilities, and transfer to adult court) to determine what is contributing to DMC.

This portion of the DMC work requires a great deal of cooperation with other stakeholders (see later discussion) because the data necessary for assessment is largely dispersed throughout the juvenile system and access to it will be necessary. The *DMC Technical Assistance Manual* provides great detail about this stage and how localities can move through the recommended multistage process.

The stages include generating possible explanations for DMC, identifying types of data and patterns, obtaining data, and analyzing the data to identify mechanisms that contribute to DMC (OJJDP DMC Technical Assistance Manual, 2009). Utilizing researchers in this stage is probably the best way to generate valid results. Beginning with generating possible explanations, researchers can be helpful in assisting jurisdictions with teasing through the existing literature and research on contributing mechanisms for DMC such as differential offending, which asserts that certain racial groups are involved in criminal activity at varying rates. This is bound to be one of the explanations that will be a topic of conversation. This is also one of the ways in which stakeholders take the emphasis off of themselves and the "system" as a way to explain disparity. If done properly, this step will provide some focus for the next phases and the information gathered here is also largely linked to the identification stage.

Once the jurisdiction has focused on some possible explanations, this information should be utilized to determine what data would be needed and how best to obtain such data. Once there has been a decision about what data are necessary there may be a decision to also collect additional data and the methods that should be used such as whether to include the use of supplementary qualitative data. Researchers will have the expertise to understand this process and help jurisdictions so that they don't get stalled at this step. It is often at this stage when the inadequacies of data warehousing and data sharing among agencies become evident. According to Hsia, Bridges, and McHale (2004) one of the challenges to DMC efforts has proven to be "incomplete or inconsistent data systems." This is why it is vitally important to include the necessary stakeholders and create the kind of "buy in" necessary so that transparency is achieved.

OJJDP's *DMC Technical Assistance Manual* provides a table of possible mechanisms along with a description of the types of data a jurisdiction might need to collect and the pattern that would be expected if the mechanism were present. While the detail of information provided is helpful, it is likely that additional assistance from researchers will be needed to make it applicable and certainly to progress to the next stage, which is analyzing the data collected.

When analyzing the data there are a variety of procedures that can be appropriate depending on the confidence the jurisdiction wants to place on the findings. For example, cross-tabulations are helpful in comparing two variables and easy to do but they provide less confidence in the results than higher levels of statistics such as multivariate analyses (Technical Assistance Manual chapter 2). A jurisdiction that has someone on staff with the proficiency and time available to implement higher level statistics for a project of this magnitude is rare.

Intervention

The intervention stage utilizes all of the previous stages to determine where best to focus precious time and resources to reduce overrepresentation. Jurisdictions should communicate the findings to political leaders and other stakeholders so that they can build consensus on what to do. Most interventions include either direct services, training and technical assistance or systems change (Technical Assistance Manual chapter 4). While what is best for each jurisdiction will vary, OJJDP suggest using multimodal approaches. As stated previously, disparity is often present in more than one decision point; therefore, an approach that utilizes a variety of strategies at varying points will in most cases work better than a single approach.

Researchers can be vital at this stage because they can provide guidance in selecting the proper interventions utilizing evidenced based programs, providing proper training for professionals or guiding agencies through necessary systems change. For example, there is a plethora of research on effective programming that is likely to reduce recidivism. Since the late 1970s when Martinson declared that "nothing works," researchers have discovered that some

things do work and they include common characteristics such as risk, criminogenic needs, responsivity, and fidelity (Latessa, 2004; Andrews, Zinger, Hoge,
Bonta, Gendreau, and Cullen, 1990; McGuire and Priestley, 1995). Knowing
how to apply this type of information and utilize OJJDP's list of model programs and best practices is essential to this stage. As noted by OJJDP, "identifying high-quality programs that can address specific DMC factors in a given
community has been one the most difficult obstacles to developing effective
DMC initiatives" (OJJDP DMC Technical Assistance Manual chapter 4, pg. 4).

As previously mentioned, practitioners are generally well poised for developing interventions based on their dealings with clients on a daily basis; however, utilizing researchers to help in synthesizing the data from the assessment
process can help in creating more effective interventions. One such issue is that
the programs generally developed at this stage focus on reducing the involvement in the juvenile justice system for *all* youth while providing little focus on
reductions in DMC. While it can be difficult to explain to an advisory group
or community leaders that what is good for all is not necessarily good for minority youth, the fact of the matter is that most "greater good" types of interventions miss the mark on reducing the probability of minority youth involvement
in the juvenile and criminal justice systems. Researchers can be an ally in these
talks as they can be better equipped to explain what the research has shown
over the years and why more targeted approaches will yield better results.

Evaluation and Monitoring

The goal-setting component is a step that is often not achieved by jurisdictions. Localities will normally decide on an intervention without focusing on
how they will know it was or was not successful. Most researchers will stress
the importance that all interventions should be evaluated and the best way to
plan for a future evaluation is to determine how you will measure success before
you get started. All goals should be connected to the activities the group decides
to undertake and they should be measurable.

The purpose of the evaluation stage is to determine if the intervention(s)
implemented was effective, to what degree, and to assess the impact of other
factors on the outcomes. While many jurisdictions may be familiar with performance measures because they have been required to report this information to a government entity or others, they are not normally well versed on how
to use some of the performance measures to evaluate the intervention. According to OJJDP, "evaluation entails significantly more extensive analysis, requires
more resources, and deals with more complex issues of causality" (chapter 5,

p. 1). The DMC Technical Assistance Manual also provides a comparison chart that details the differences in evaluation and performance measurement. Also important to note, this phase of the mandate does not end. Not only should periodic evaluations take place but ongoing monitoring, phase five, and data collection are a must to being successful.

Likewise, hiring a professional evaluator will provide the specialized knowledge necessary to create and implement the appropriate evaluation design, enhance the objectivity needed for what can be the touchy topic of race, lend credibility to the findings, and provide a perspective that is very different from practitioners in the field (Justice Research and Statistics Association's Juvenile Justice Evaluation Center, 2001). With that said, when selecting a researcher to evaluate DMC initiatives it is important that the person also have some experience in race issues in the criminal justice system.

Evaluation can be costly. If an agency would like to defray the costs of the evaluation one of the things to do is work with researchers/evaluators who are willing to assist in finding grant funding. While this may take longer, if the evaluator is involved in the DMC process from the beginning this can be done as the group moves through the stages. As stated previously, these types of collaborations are beneficial for everyone. Researchers need to publish, they are often rewarded professionally for soliciting grants, and they love having access to data so marrying their interests with a local agency seems to make perfect sense.

Other Important Considerations

In addition to building partnerships with researchers at universities, there are other steps that are vital to making this work. The main focus of this chapter was to highlight why and how researchers can be helpful but it would be remiss not to mention the following very important aspects as well: 1) stakeholders, 2) priorities, 3) political will, 4) local outreach, and 5) setting goals.

Identifying Stakeholders

Identifying stakeholders is essential to DMC reduction. The complexities of the criminal and juvenile justice systems require that the stakeholders agree on the priorities set forth in the beginning. Deciding who should be involved is often difficult but this is why narrowing the focus of your DMC reduction efforts is so important. Stakeholders can be people inside the system and outside of it as well. It can include and should include political supporters to press your agenda (see political will).

Priorities

Depending on the information gathered from the initial data collection to the locality's RRI, priorities will differ from jurisdictions to jurisdiction. Localities often examine what others are doing and decide to see if it will work in their area. While this can garner important information, it is imperative that when dealing with DMC, agencies focus on their locality because it may differ in a variety of ways such as minority population, community culture, policing priorities, political agenda, and funding streams.

Whatever the case, agencies must decide what their priority is and narrow their focus in a way that success is possible. While this might seem like lowering expectations, it is about ensuring that stakeholders, community leaders, and political officials can see how your efforts have made an impact even if that impact is small. Small successes will ensure that your agency is given the permission to continue its efforts in the long run.

Researchers can be vital to this step because after they have assisted with data collection, setting the priorities should be based on the initial findings. Researchers can help by keeping the project focus narrow and task driven. As discussed in chapter 2, not following the strategic plan and not having clear and measurable goals and objectives can be the downfall of any DMC effort. Researchers who lead these projects can not only keep participants on task but they can also guide discussions that can stray away from DMC to larger issues of intuitional racism that do not focus on reducing disparate impacts in the juvenile and criminal justice systems.

Political Will

Depending on the political climate and crime in your area, garnering political capital can be difficult. As one might imagine, no one wants to be perceived as soft on crime, which is not what DMC is about. Working with researchers to utilize the data will be paramount to this process. While politicians deal with perception, the reality of the data can also be sobering. If agencies are prepared to show that they are working with experts in the field and present the literature that supports changes to policy or processes acquiring political support will be easier. However, the best leverage when working with politicians is ensuring them that this is in the best interest of their constituents and it is exactly what they would desire. This can be achieved through a variety of means but utilizing your stakeholders will be beneficial at this end. Having the proper support in the community through non-profit agencies, other governmental entities, and businesses can help to influence the type of political support necessary.

Local Outreach

When agencies put together a list of stakeholders they often stick to those inside of the justice system. It is important that the stakeholders include those external to the system as well. Outside stakeholders not only have a perspective that is very different but they also have a different type of contact with the greater population. Their thoughts and opinions can provide vast insight into how communities will react and how they can be approached to support DMC reduction efforts.

The Departments of Criminal Justice Services, Corrections, the City of Petersburg and Virginia State University

At the beginning of this chapter I mentioned a conference on DMC hosted by Virginia State University (VSU) in collaboration with the Department of Criminal Justice Services (DCJS), and the Department of Corrections (DOC). In April 2013 VSU hosted this conference for the last time. After seven years, the audience broadened, the topics grew more interesting, and the discussion of disparity increased to a new level. For example, as a result of the DMC conference one locality that didn't think they had a DMC issue because the population is largely African American, created a DMC workgroup and is working closely with the state DMC coordinator on a comprehensive plan.

Also as a result of the DMC conference the Department of Corrections decided to co-sponsor the conference in its third year. Whereas they understood that much of the focus is related to the juvenile justice system, they also understood the importance of the issue overall and the impact it has on families and future offending. The adult side of corrections also has a responsibility when it comes to other mandates of the JJDP Act of 1974, as amended, such as deinstitutionalization of status offender, sight and sound separation, and removal from adult jails and lockups. The ability to bring these agencies together to discuss the importance of disparity in the system was no easy feat but it definitely positions them closer in regards to information sharing and transparency.

Another consequence of the DMC conference was a grant funding opportunity with the City of Petersburg. An agency head in the juvenile justice system had been a guest speaker and attendee of the DMC conference for three years so when she saw the grant solicitation she decided to contact the university to see if anyone was interested. In this case, the connection was obvious because the university already had DMC on its agenda but this is also worth exploring even if the university doesn't already have a connection to the issue. The grant focused on reducing DMC through the use of a peer-mentoring program, which is one of the OJJDP model programs. The mentoring program allows VSU students to act as mentors with court involved youth. The program was funded for four years and is currently being solely implemented by the local court service unit office.

While there has been a discussion of how working with universities can be a "win-win" for the researcher and locality, it is also a great benefit for students attending the university. Students are provided some firsthand experiences that might not otherwise be available — working with juveniles and working with agencies they one day hope to be employed with. How this collaboration is designed is up to the university but VSU has found that utilizing service learning courses to provide mentors has been the best route. Service learning is a teaching and learning approach that allows students to "get involved with their communities in a tangible way by integrating service projects with classroom learning" (www.learnandserve.gov). The college students that mentor in the program get just as much from their service experience as those being mentored. Despite the fact that all jurisdictions are different, this type of collaboration between universities and local agencies is a viable example of how universities can act as resources for reducing overrepresentation.

One caveat I have for agencies when working with universities is to ensure that you are not wedded to one person at the university or to one university for that matter. If possible, work with a variety of faculty members across the campus. For example, DMC is not just a criminal justice matter it is a sociological matter, a psychological issue, an educational and financial access challenge, and a social service concern. Based on this alone, an agency could work with faculty from sociology, psychology, education, business, and social sork disciplines. And if your jurisdiction is fortunate enough to have more than one university in the area, you can choose to work with each of them based on their areas of expertise, mission and focus. Utilizing a broad range of faculty and exercising the right to work with a variety of institutions will ensure that agencies have allies that stretch a broad geographic range, which can only aid in collaboration and exposure for reducing DMC.

Conclusion

As mentioned, this chapter is a result of experiences and conversations with practitioners in a particular locality. While this information is no panacea for disproportionality and racial and ethnic disparities in the juvenile and criminal justice systems, it is a starting point. These partnerships can result in "win win" situations for both the locality and the university researchers.

The DMC mandate requires that jurisdictions not only partner with other agencies that share information and work in coordination with youth in the community but it also requires that the data shared are analyzed. As this chapter expresses, the manner in which data are collected and later analyzed can have a tremendous impact on the results. Utilizing universities and their faculty as local resources helps to move the DMC agenda, allows opportunities for stronger community partnerships, and helps to shed light on the issue of overrepresentation from an empirical perspective. As demonstrated, the DMC mandate as dictated by the JJDP Act of 1974, as amended, is not a simple process. Experienced, well-qualified researchers can be just the expertise needed to help agencies fulfill their obligations to the Act and the youth they serve.

References

Andrews, D. A., Zinger, I., Hoge, R., Bonta, J., Gendreau, P. & Cullen, F. (1990). Does Correctional Treatment Work? A Clinically-Relevant and Psychologically-Informed Meta-Analysis. *Criminology*, 28, 369–404.

Bilchik, S. (2010). Working together across systems to achieve racial and ethnic equity. Presentation May 24, 2010 at conference Addressing Racial and Ethnic Disparity and Disproportionality in Juvenile Justice and Child Welfare in Virginia.

Devine, P., Coolbaugh, K. & Jenkins, S. 1998. *Disproportionate Minority Confinement: Lessons Learned From Five States.* Bulletin. Washington, DC: U.S. Department of Justice, Office of Justice Programs, Office of Juvenile Justice and Delinquency Prevention.

Feyerherm, W. H., Snyder, H. & Villarruel, F. (2009). Identification and Monitoring. Disproportionate Minority Contact Technical Assistance Manual.

4th ed. Washington, DC: U.S. Dept of Justice. Office of Juvenile Justice and Delinquency Prevention.

Gies, S., Cohen, M. & Villarruel, F. (2009). Intervention. Disproportionate Minority Contact Technical Assistance Manual. 4th ed. Washington, DC: U.S. Dept of Justice. Office of Juvenile Justice and Delinquency Prevention.

Hsia, H., Bridges, G., and McHale, R. (2004). Disproportionate Confinement? 2002 Update. Summary. Washington, DC: U.S. Department of Justice, Office of Justice Programs, Office of Juvenile Justice and Delinquency Prevention.

Juvenile Justice Evaluation Center. (2001). Hiring and working with an evaluator. Washington, DC: Author.

Latessa, E. J. (2004). "From theory to practice: What works in reducing recidivism?" In State of Crime and Justice in Ohio: Corrections. Candace Peters. Columbus, Ohio: Ohio Office of Criminal Justice Services, pp. 170–171.

Learn and Service America http://www.learnandserve.gov/.

Leiber, M., Richetelli, D. & Feyerherm, W. (2009). Assessment. Disproportionate Minority Contact Technical Assistance Manual. 4th ed. Washington, DC: U.S. Dept of Justice. Office of Juvenile Justice and Delinquency Prevention.

Leiber, M. (2002). Disproportionate Minority Confinement (DMC) of Youth: An Analysis of State and Federal Efforts to Address the Issue. Crime & Delinquency, (48) 1, 3–45.

McGuire J., Priestley, P. (1995). Reviewing 'What Works': Past, Present and Future. In McGuire, J. (Ed.) What Works: Reducing Reoffending—Guide lines from Research and Practice (pp. 3–34). Chichester: John Wiley & Sons.

Pope, C.E. & Feyerherm, W. (1995). Minorities in the juvenile justice system. Washington D.C.: U.S. Department of Justice, Office of Justice Programs, Office of Juvenile Justice and Delinquency Prevention.

Puzzanchera, C. (2009). Juvenile arrests 2007. Washington, DC: Office of Juvenile Justice and Delinquency Prevention.

Puzzanchera, C. (2014). Juvenile arrests 2012. Washington, DC: Office of Juvenile Justice and Delinquency Prevention.

Nellis, A., Richardson, B. (2010). Getting Beyond Failure: Promising Approaches for Reducing DMC. Youth Violence and Juvenile Justice. doi: 10.177/1541 204009361180.

Nellis, A. & Cohen, M. (2009). Evaluation. Disproportionate Minority Contact Technical Assistance Manual. 4th ed. Washington, DC: U.S. Dept of Justice. Office of Juvenile Justice and Delinquency Prevention.

Nellis, A. (2005). Seven steps to develop and evaluate strategies to reduce disproportionate minority contact (DMC). Washington, DC: Justice Research and Statistics Association.

Office of Juvenile Justice and Delinquency Prevention. (2000). Disproportionate minority contact technical assistance manual (4th ed.). Washington,
DC.

Soler, M. & Garry, L.M. (2009). Preparation at the Local Level. Disproportionate Minority Contact Technical Assistance Manual. 4th ed. Washington, DC: U.S. Dept of Justice. Office of Juvenile Justice and Delinquency
Prevention.

U.S. Department of Justice. (2000). *Disproportionate minority confinement technical assistance manual*. Washington, DC: Office of Juvenile Justice and
Delinquency Prevention.

Contributor Biographical Information

Mary Poulin Carlton is a Social Science Analyst at the Court Services and Offender Supervision Agency in Washington, DC. She was previously a a Senior Research Associate at the Justice Research and Statistics Association (JRSA) in Washington, DC. where she managed a variety of research and evaluation projects funded by the Department of Justice and other organizations. While there she worked on an Office of Juvenile Justice and Delinquency Prevention (OJJDP)-funded project that involved evaluating disproportionate minority contact initiatives. Dr. Carlton has 20 years of experience in the evaluation of justice programs and has provided evaluation-related training and technical assistance to criminal and juvenile justice system practitioners for several years. She received her Ph.D. in criminal justice from Temple University.

Andrea R. Coleman is the Disproportionate Minority Contact Coordinator with the Office of Juvenile Justice and Delinquency Prevention. In this capacity Ms. Coleman is charged with ensuring participating states and territories address juvenile delinquency prevention and system improvement efforts designed to reduce the disproportionate number of minority groups who come into contact with the juvenile justice system, and also serves as co-chair of the Coordinating Council on Juvenile Justice's Racial and Ethnic Disparities Team. She has over fifteen years of experience working with at risk and delinquent youth in various settings and capacities, including managing federal and state grant initiatives in her capacity as the Disproportionate Minority Contact Coordinator for Kentucky, local initiatives as the first Coordinator of the Lexington-Fayette County, Kentucky Juvenile Delinquency Prevention Council, and as a Title V Coordinator.

Ms. Coleman has a Master of Science in Criminal Justice from the University of Cincinnati and a Bachelor of Arts in Political Science from Berea College. She received the 2009 *Assistant Attorney General's Award* in recognition of her outstanding contributions to the mission and goals of the U.S. Department of Justice's Office of Justice Programs. Ms. Coleman's current publications include *The Role of DMC Coordinators* in the DMC *Technical Assistance Manual 4th Edition*, co-author of the OJJDP's Disproportionate Minority Contact Fact Sheet, the upcoming Bulletin *Disproportionate Minority Contact: American Indian and Alaska Native Youth*, and a textbook chapter on the historical and contemporary perspective of DMC.

Amy Cook is an assistant professor at Virginia Commonwealth University in the Criminal Justice Department. She earned her Ph.D. in Public Policy and Administration from Virginia Commonwealth University and her Master's in Liberal Arts from University of Richmond. Her areas of research interests are juvenile justice, intimate partner violence, and policing. Prior to academia, Amy worked for the Virginia Department of Juvenile Justice.

Cherie Dawson-Edwards is an Associate Professor in the Department of Criminal Justice at the University of Louisville. Dr. Edwards has a Ph.D. in Public Policy and Administration from Virginia Commonwealth University. In addition, she holds Bachelor's degrees in Sociology and Journalism from Western Kentucky University and a M.S. in Justice Administration from the University of Louisville. She has taught a variety of criminal justice courses, but her research and teaching interests center on the intersection of public policy and criminal justice with a specific focus on corrections and juvenile justice. In addition to a career in teaching, Dr. Edwards has held positions in probation and victim services. She is a National Board Member for the American Civil Liberties Union (ACLU). She also serves on the statewide Subcommittee for Equity and Justice for All Youth (SEJAY) — the statewide Disproportionate Minority Contact (DMC) committee. Her most recent publications can be found in the *International Criminal Justice Review* and *Criminal Justice Studies*.

William Feyerherm is a Professor of Criminology and Criminal Justice at Portland State University, where he was the Vice Provost for Research and Dean of Graduate Studies for the past 14 years. Dr. Feyerherm has published on topics such as race and its impact on processing in the justice system. He currently serves as a member of the Oregon Juvenile Justice Advisory Commission (SAG), the Multnomah County Juvenile Justice Advisory Council and the Multnomah County Local Public Safety Coordinating Council. He served for six years as a member of the Oregon Law Enforcement Contacts Policy Commission (examining racial profiling) and is a consultant to the Office of Juvenile Justice and Delinquency Prevention on disproportionate minority contact issues, including the development and interpretation of the Relative Rate Index measure for Disproportionate Minority Contact. In 2002, Dr. Feyerherm received the W. E. B. DuBois Award from the Western Society of Criminology for his contributions to racial and ethnic issues in criminology.

Myra Fields completed her two Bachelor of Science degrees in Psychology and Criminal Justice from Radford University in 2007. While completing her degrees she worked as a crisis intervention specialist for the local community service board, which focused on the mental health and substance abuse population. After graduation she continued her education at Virginia Commonwealth University where in 2009 she completed the Masters of Science program in Criminal Justice with a concentration in Justice studies. Her research interests are in the juvenile justice system where she is currently employed as a rehabilitation counselor.

Marian S. Harris is a Professor at the University of Washington Tacoma, Social Work and Criminal Justice Program and Adjunct Professor, University of Washington, School of Social Work, Seattle. She is an Adjunct Professor and Research Advisor, Smith College School for Social Work, Northampton, MA. Dr. Harris is a former Faculty Associate at the Chapin Hall Center for Children, University of Chicago and a former consultant for the U.S. Children's Bureau and Casey Family Programs, Seattle. She is a former Co-Chair of the Washington State Racial Disproportionality Advisory Committee and the former Chair of the Research Sub-Committee. Her research and publications are primarily focused on issues of children and families in the child welfare system including racial disproportionality, substance abuse problem severity, adult attachment typology in high risk mothers, parental stress, outcomes of youth who have exited the system, race and family structure, and kinship care. Her most recent book is *Racial Disproportionality in Child Welfare* (2014, New York: Columbia University Press). Dr. Harris is a member of numerous professional organizations and serves on the editorial boards for several social work journals. She received the 2016 Educator of the Year Award from the Washington State Chapter of the National Association of Social Workers and the Day Garrett Award in 2015 from the Smith College School for Social Work.

Janice A. Iwama is a Ph.D. Candidate at the School of Criminology and Criminal Justice at Northeastern University. She is a recipient of the 2014 American Society of Criminology Ruth Peterson Fellowship and the Division on People of Color & Crime Outstanding Student Award. Her research interests involve the impact of communities on crime, disproportionate minority contact, prevalence of hate crimes, racial and ethnic issues, and the victimization of immigrants. As the project manager at the Institute on Race and Justice at Northeastern University, she recently worked on a National Institute of Justice-funded study examining national trends in hate crimes against immigrants and Hispanic-Americans and is presently working on a study examining police activity in Seattle, WA, with the Department of Justice.

Shanieka S. Jones is the Crime Prevention and Clery Compliance Specialist at California State University, Monterey Bay where she is the liaison for the University Police community outreach and education initiatives and manages the institution's Clery Act compliance program. Shanieka earned her Bachelor and Master of Science degrees from Virginia State University in 2007 and 2012, respectively; and currently attends Walden University. Her program of study is Public Policy and Administration, and her current research interests include policy analysis of and noncompliance in the Jeanne Clery Disclosure of Campus Security Policy and Campus Crime Statistics Act and its regulatory legislation.

Michael Leiber is a Professor and Chair of the Department of Criminology at the University of South Florida. He earned his Ph.D. in Criminal Justice from the University of Albany- State University of New York. His main research interests and publications lie in juvenile delinquency, juvenile justice and race/ethnicity. Currently, he is the editor of the *Journal of Crime & Justice,* a journal of the Midwest Criminal Justice Association.

Bryan Lagae is a doctoral student in the Department of Sociology at the University of Miami. His doctoral dissertation focuses on the cumulative effects of racial disadvantage across the early-career years in the American labor market.

Michael J. Lynch is a Professor in the Department of Criminology, and Associated Faculty in the School of Global Sustainability, University of South Florida. In addition to racial biases in criminal justice processes, his research examines environmental justice, environmental and corporate crime, and radical criminology. His research has appeared in journals representing several different disciplines.

Shana Mell is a doctoral student in Public Policy and Administration at Virginia Commonwealth University. Her interests include procedural justice and police legitimacy. Mell is a policy analyst at the VCU Police Department.

Ojmarrh Mitchell is an Assistant Professor in the Department of Criminology at the University of South Florida. Professor Mitchell earned his Ph.D. in Criminal Justice and Criminology from the University of Maryland with a doctoral minor in Measurement, Statistics, and Evaluation. His research interests include drugs and crime, corrections and sentencing, race and crime, and meta-analysis.

Ashley Nellis has an academic and professional background in analyzing criminal justice policies and practice, and has extensive experience in analyzing racial and ethnic disparities in the justice system. She regularly delivers testimony, writes articles and reports, and conducts research in the areas of juvenile and criminal justice. Her work is particularly concerned with elevating awareness about the growing number of individuals serving lengthy sentences in prison such as life sentences and sentences of life without parole (LWOP).

Nellis is the author of *A Return to Justice: Rethinking our Approach to Juveniles in the System*, which chronicles America's historical treatment of youth in the justice system and discusses the work that remains in order to reorient the juvenile justice practices toward the original vision. She received her Ph.D. in Justice, Law and Society from American University's School of Public Affairs.

Nadia T. Nelson is currently a Ph.D. student in the Criminal Justice Department at the University of Louisville. Nadia received her M.S. from the University of Central Florida (Orlando, FL) and her B.A. from Temple University (Philadelphia, PA). Her research includes studies focusing on corrections policy, prison reform, offender rehabilitation, and race and gender issues. Further areas of interest include civil liability (corrections and law enforcement), international crimes, and criminological theory. Courses taught include Introduction to Corrections, Prisons and Jails in the U.S., and Legal Issues in Corrections. Her current research projects include an examination into the prevalence of substance abuse amongst incarcerated offenders and a study regarding the presupposition of high crime rates amongst predominantly immigrant neighborhoods.

Katie Nuss teaches sophomore English at Fern Creek High School in Louisville, Kentucky, and is currently a Ph.D. student studying discipline equity and the school-to-prison pipeline issues at the University of Louisville. Previously, she studied Arts and Letters at the University of Notre Dame, and earned her Master's degrees in Secondary Education and Educational Psychology from Ball State University.

Stan Orchowsky is Research Director for the Justice Research and Statistics Association, where he oversees a variety of national research and evaluation projects related to criminal and juvenile justice. Prior to joining JRSA in 1995, Dr. Orchowsky served as Evaluation Section Chief for the Virginia Department of Criminal Justice Services, and as a Research Associate for the Virginia Department of Corrections. Dr. Orchowsky received his B.A. in Social Psychology from Florida Atlantic University and earned his M.S. and Ph.D. degrees in psychology from Virginia Commonwealth University.

Nicolle Parsons-Pollard is the Vice Provost for Academic and Faculty Affairs and a Professor in the Criminal Justice Program at Monmouth University. She is a graduate of Virginia Commonwealth University (VCU) and has a Ph.D. in Public Policy and Administration. Currently, her research includes juvenile delinquency, truancy, disproportionate minority contact (DMC), and program evaluation.

Jennifer H. Peck is an Assistant Professor in the Department of Criminal Justice at the University of Central Florida. She received her Ph.D. in Criminology from the University of South Florida. Her research interests include the role of race/ethnicity in juvenile justice processing, the treatment of disadvantaged groups in the juvenile justice system, and the causes and correlates of delinquent behavior.

William V. Pelfrey, Jr., is an Associate Professor at Virginia Commonwealth University in the Criminal Justice Department and the Homeland Security/Emergency Preparedness Department, which he chairs. He earned his Ph.D. in Criminal Justice from Temple University and his Master's in Clinical Psychology from Radford University. He has published scholarly articles in the areas of policing, homeland security, the psychology of the offender, and cyberbullying. His articles have appeared in a variety of criminology, criminal justice, homeland security, and interdisciplinary journals.

Alex R. Piquero is Ashbel Smith Professor of Criminology and Associate Dean for Graduate Programs in the School of Economic, Political and Policy Sciences at the University of Texas at Dallas. His research interests include criminal careers, criminological theory, and quantitative research methods. He has received several research, teaching, and service awards and is Fellow of both the American Society of Criminology and the Academy of Criminal Justice Sciences. In 2014, he received The University of Texas System Regents' Outstanding Teaching Award.

John David Reitzel specializes in research at the intersection of race/ethnicity, serious crime, and criminal justice, focusing on the structural aspects of disparities in arrests and sentencing outcomes, public perceptions of policing, evidence based policing models, and crime trends. His published research has appeared in various academic journals.

Isis N. Walton is an Associate Professor of Criminal Justice at Virginia State University. Currently her research interests include juvenile justice issues, minority disenfranchisement and racial disparities, as well as collegiate victimization and alcohol use.

George Wilson is Professor of Sociology at the University of Miami. He has published over 80 articles and book chapters on his research interests, which encompass the institutional production of racial/ethnic inequality in the American workplace as well as the incidence, causes and consequences of racial worldviews about the American stratification system.

Index